THE MILITARY ESTABLISHMENT

THE MILITARY

A TWENTIETH CENTURY FUND STUDY

ESTABLISHMENT

Its Impacts on American Society

By Adam Yarmolinsky

HARPER & ROW, PUBLISHERS

1817

NEW YORK, EVANSTON, AND LONDON

LIBRARY OF CONGRESS CATALOG CARD NUMBER: 73-127839

For the generation that will succeed
in beating its swords into plowshares

The Twentieth Century Fund is a research foundation which undertakes timely, critical, and analytical studies of major economic, political, and social institutions and issues. Nonprofit and nonpartisan, the Fund was founded in 1919 and endowed by Edward A Filene.

Contents

Tables and Charts

Charts

Foreword

Well over three years ago, before the tragedy—and agony—of Vietnam was fully comprehended and before the military came under critical attack on the campuses and in Congress, the Trustees of the Twentieth Century Fund expressed interest in undertaking a broad study of the military establishment and its impacts on American society. They were concerned not only with the power of the so-called military-industrial complex as such but also with the influence and reach of the Pentagon in nonmilitary areas, and they sought an objective and comprehensive assessment of the many ways, some overt and some covert, in which the military affected our national life. In suggesting such a study there was no hostility implied toward the military. Rather, the Trustees were genuinely interested in trying to trace and to measure the phenomenal growth of the military in the post-World War II era so that its role could be better understood and evaluated.

The very size and scope of the military establishment, which has become the world's biggest institution, indicated that the task of research would be a formidable one. For the military, quite clearly, is more than just a gigantic spending machine. It provides more work for more people than any other institution and serves as an educator on a massive scale. It also clothes, houses, and feeds them, and propagandizes in gargantuan fashion. And, in the postwar era, it has had an enormous influence on foreign policy, on race relations, on technology and management, on ideology and on the intellectual and scientific communities. Obviously, to produce a study that would encompass all of these elements, some of them extremely difficult to define and determine, required extraordinary breadth of mind and experience as well as a sense of commitment to the task.

The Fund was most fortunate to obtain the services of Adam Yarmolinsky as research director for the study because he possesses all the essential qualities needed. As former Deputy Assistant Secretary of Defense for International Security Affairs, he had firsthand contact, experience, and knowledge of the military establishment. And as a lawyer, editor, and educator, he has a grasp of the complex and intricate relationships that the military has established across the nation and, indeed, around the world. From the outset, however, Mr. Yarmolinsky recognized the need to gather information and opinion from other authorities simply because the reach of the military was so extensive that no one man had the expertise to deal with all of its ramifications. He succeeded in assembling a group of brilliant and diverse experts from different disciplines who, as he acknowledges, made a significant contribution to his own analysis and conception of the military establishment, and the Fund is indebted to them, too.

Mr. Yarmolinsky and his team of contributors had complete independence in carrying out the study for the Fund. Our concern, as always, was that the research director not merely examine his subject but, if changes were required, propose reforms. For it is the Fund's view that all of our major institutions must be responsive and responsible to the changing needs of our society.

Mr. Yarmolinsky's study must be viewed in its institutional setting. Perhaps his most important finding is that the military establishment since World War II has pervaded every nook and cranny of our national life almost without our knowing it. He also finds, however, that it has not attained its present size and power without being "civilianized," at least in part, in return. A related finding is that the military establishment's huge growth can be traced to the complacent attitude of civilian institutions, so that greater responsiveness by the military institution and increased control over it depend on more effective pressure from civilian bodies.

The study cannot be considered an antimilitary document, nor was it intended as such. In fact, Mr. Yarmolinsky cites many accomplishments of the military establishment, especially in the fields of education and race relations. The even-handed appraisal that Mr. Yarmolinsky provides is precisely what is needed for understanding the military and determining how best to direct it toward democratically determined national goals.

It is probable that Mr. Yarmolinsky's findings as well as his recommendations will provoke debate. But it is our belief that this debate will be much more informed because of his careful and comprehensive study. Indeed, it may well be indispensable for all citizens concerned with the role of the military establishment in a civilian and democratic society.

—M. J. ROSSANT, Director
May 1970   *The Twentieth Century Fund*

Preface

A purportedly analytical work about the United States military establishment, appearing in so dark a time, labors under a considerable handicap. Why take the trouble to understand what is so easy to condemn? Even the effort of understanding could be taken as an expression of sympathy with military operations in which the establishment is engaged—operations unwisely begun (as this author concluded only well after the fact) and now recognized as politically self-destructive and morally repugnant to vast and increasing numbers of Americans. Against this backdrop it is impossible to write without emotion, but it is impermissible to allow emotion to cloud analysis.

If one believes that a military establishment, and a substantial one, is unavoidable and indeed necessary for the foreseeable future, then one must face up to the question of how that establishment is to be shaped and controlled, especially when its potential for cataclysm has never been greater. In fact, a much smaller military establishment than the present one would still be very substantial, and we cannot expect this or any other major institution in our society to control itself. If it is to be controlled intelligently, and not by fits and starts, its capabilities and its limitations must be understood by people *outside* the institution. This book is an attempt to contribute to that understanding, and to suggest ways in which outside controls can be strengthened.

It is literally the work of many hands. It was originally conceived as a series of essays covering the principal areas of social impact of the military establishment, to be supplemented by a pamphlet series on more specialized topics within the general scope of the project. When the present plan of the book was adopted, these materials were drawn on as basic resources, and large portions of them were incorporated into the text. Although the original contributors are therefore in no sense responsible for the fate of their literary offspring, their parenthood is gratefully acknowledged, as well as their avuncular advice and counsel throughout the course of the project. In the measure of their effort, they are in a very real sense co-authors.

The principal contributors and their respective areas of concern are as follows:

Economic impact: Burton H. Klein, Robert Perry, and Murray L. Weidenbaum

Social impact: Morris Janowitz

Foreign policy impact: Ernest R. May

Impact on the media and the political process: Philip Geyelin, Robert Manning, and James Phillips

Impact on the scientific and educational community: Harvey Brooks

Impact on race relations: Donald Canty, James Bailey, and Lee Nichols

Political attitudes of the military: Gene M. Lyons

Military justice: Edward Sherman

Military decision-making techniques: John Steinbruner and David S. Mundel

Role of the military in civil disturbances: Jack Rosenthal

Role of retired military personnel: Albert D. Biderman

The military educational system: Laurence I. Radway

The civil functions of the Corps of Engineers: William B. Lord and Richard L. Hilliker

The Selective Service System: Alfred B. Fitt

Other essential material was contributed by Graham Allison, John Ferren, William R. Harris, Glenn S. Koppel, Lester W. Roane, and Richard Smoke.

Colleagues and friends who gave generously of their experience and advice include Daniel Bell, William Capron, Ira Glasser, William Kaufmann, Hans Linde, Richard Neustadt, Henry Rowen and Frank Waldrop. Maury Feld, Richard Smoke, John Woodman, and Peter Coogan, as research assistants, and Helen McFadden and Jean Baptiste, as secretaries, worked diligently and contributed essential services. My editor, Jeannette Hopkins, brought order out of organizational chaos.

Penultimately, I am most grateful to the Trustees of the Twentieth Century Fund and to its Director, M. J. Rossant, for conceiving the idea of this study and providing the support, both financial and intellectual, to carry it through.

And finally, my gratitude is quite inexpressible to my wife and children, who put it all in context.

ADAM YARMOLINSKY

Cambridge, Massachusetts
June 1970

I

THE RISE OF THE U.S.

MILITARY ESTABLISHMENT

1

Introduction: The Significant Themes

This book does not concern itself with the nature of the military establishment generally, nor, except incidentally, with its history. Rather, it is concerned with the impacts of this massive, powerful, and pervasive organization on American society, and with the extent to which and the ways in which the society is affected and shaped by military purposes.

In examining the impacts of the military establishment on our society, the factors that are common to large public establishments must be distinguished from the factors that are peculiar to the military establishment. These factors work together to produce a total impact, but they must be separated in analysis if their impact is to be understood. Since military activity is not distinguishable from much nonmilitary activity by a significantly higher degree of large-scale functional organization—as it often is in less developed societies—and since a progressively smaller proportion of military activity can be described as combat (even for those engaged in so-called "combat functions"), its distinctiveness depends more on the purpose than on the structure of its power.

Albert Biderman has defined the military as a "specialized institution for guarding and securing ultimate and sacred values of the society."[1] His definition distinguishes the military establishment from almost all other institutions in American society. Business supplies man's material needs; civil government attempts to provide for his peaceful enjoyment of them. Education is essentially secular; the law and the courts are primarily occupied with taking from A to give to B; and, in a predominantly Protestant society, the ministry does not assume ultimate responsibility for sacred values. Only the

1. Albert D. Biderman, "What Is Military?", in *The Draft: A Handbook of Facts and Alternatives,* Sol Tax, ed. (Chicago: University of Chicago Press, 1967).

3

military is kept apart from everyday problems, its function only to be invoked in times of crisis. Its claim on resources and its over-all impact are correspondingly strengthened.

But Biderman's definition consciously avoids the fact that the guarding and securing are to be accomplished by inflicting or threatening to inflict death and destruction. He does this because he is seeking a more civilian rationale for military institutions, an institutional counterpart to William James's moral equivalent of war. Yet the martial purpose of the military establishment is still paramount, although the deterrent/preventive role may gradually replace it.

In comparing military and civilian institutions, the obvious transformation effected by a wartime situation should not be overlooked; but since the line between war and peace has become more and more obscure, just as has the distinction between the civilian and the military, this transformation, too, is somewhat eroded. Modern wars are all conducted in the shadow of the nuclear threat, so that all conflict is, to a greater or lesser extent, limited conflict, for fear of precipitating a general nuclear war. In May 1970 the United States had more than 350,000 men serving overseas (apart from the 420,000 in Vietnam) in peacetime situations but exposed in varying degrees to the possibility of hostile military action. Unless a radical change occurs in American foreign policy, this number is likely to remain substantial in the foreseeable future. Even in the Southeast Asian situation, the administration has gone to great lengths to avoid expressions of total commitment by a declaration of war, or a general mobilization of reserves (although many charge that the reason is unwillingness to face the public and congressional test involved in such commitments).

The impact of the Vietnam casualty figures, or anything like them, is drastically different in kind from the impact of continuing overseas service of the 50,000 men in Korea, or the 300,000 men in Europe. When sons and husbands are selected by lot, not only to undergo boredom and discomfort for two years, but also to run the risk of death or injury, the effects are grave. It can be argued that the Vietnam casualty figures were mainly responsible for causing a President of the United States to forgo the certainty of nomination for a second term. The military establishment may look similar in peacetime (or quasi-peacetime) and in wartime (or quasi-wartime), but its impact on individual lives is significantly different, and that difference makes itself felt in the life of the nation.

We are concerned in this volume not primarily with the military establishment itself, but rather with its impact on the outside world. One way to describe the establishment is to mark out the orbit of its influence. In this sense, the balance of the book is devoted to a description of the establishment as it is reflected in the mirror of the outside world. But before examining its impact on specific areas of American society, we need to look at the terms in which that impact can be measured.

There are at least four different and overlapping ways to describe the impacts of the military:

As it affects the lives of individuals;

As it affects the style and temper of society;

As it affects the range of alternatives open to political decision-makers; and

As it affects the decision-making process itself.

The most immediate and obvious impact of the military establishment is on the individuals who are selected, or who select themselves, for military service. The fact of selection, and the military experience itself, can have a decisive impact on postservice career plans, and on social mobility. For the career military man, life in the service affects him in profound and relatively predictable ways. But his numbers are very small, even within the establishment.

The effects on the temper of society are a good deal more pervasive. Few communities within the United States are without daily reminders of military activity. The military is a staple of radio and television newscasts and newspaper front pages.

In the long run, such encounters must lead Americans to take the ubiquitous military presence more nearly for granted. Whether this kind of acceptance makes American society more "militaristic" is one of the questions this book explores. If military activity accelerates, the pervasiveness of the military impact will grow. Most wars unite the nation, but some, like the war in Vietnam, or the Mexican War, or the War of 1812, or, to some extent, the Spanish-American War, divide it. The power of the military establishment applied for purposes that the public does not endorse tends to produce its own antidote.

Similarly, the ready availability of military power would seem to broaden the range of alternatives available to decision-makers—what is not achievable by persuasion may be achievable by force—but the existence of a potential for the use of force, where that potential may not have existed before, creates its own imperatives. Military intervention, without the use of nuclear weapons, was not a live option for the United States during the siege of Dienbienphu. But if the option had existed, the hands of the decision-makers in Washington might have been forced. The awareness that superior power is available may even diminish in subtle and subliminal ways the energies with which decision-makers pursue ingenious alternatives to the use of force.

Throughout the discussion that follows, a number of major themes emerge, cutting across the substantive and procedural areas discussed. Some of these themes may be worth noting at the outset:

—The size and pervasiveness of the military establishment;

—The absence of a countervailing institutional power, including the

Executive and the Congress, sufficient to offset the postwar power of the military-industrial establishment; and the beginning of counter-response;

—The coincidence of self-interest, in regard to military expansion, between Congress and the military-industrial establishment;

—The convergence of military and civilian styles, leading to increased "civilianization" of the military and increased militarization of the civilian sector;

—The public indecisiveness about national priorities, reinforced by ambivalence toward the military;

—The assertion of prior military claim for scarce economic and social resources in contrast with the lower priority given to urgent domestic problems;

—The effect of the ready availability of military force on attitudes and decisions about the place of the United States in the world, and on the choice of alternative foreign policy instruments;

—The willingness to accept military priorities and military authority out of fear of a potential enemy or enemies;

—The appeal of counterinsurgency below the threshold of nuclear deterrence;

—The military impact on the intervenor role of paramilitary groups in revolution and counterrevolution;

—The erosion of earlier restraints on the use of federal military force in suppressing or containing domestic social unrest, with a rising civilian reliance on military and paramilitary techniques;

—The techniques of self-perpetuation of the military establishment through an extensive public relations and public education network, through classification of information, and through the system of military education;

—The escalation of costs and the elaboration of technology in military implementation of research;

—The role of weapons development and acquisition in escalation of arms purchases;

—The dependence of the defense industry on military decisions; its attempts at diversification; the weakness of quality and price control;

—The independence of defense spending from the business cycle; the effects on private spending; the inadequate control of public monopoly;

—The development of systems analysis and "war gaming" in military decision-making, and the spillover into problem-solving in domestic affairs;

—The dependence of scientific research on military expenditures, and its

TABLE 2.1 Department of Defense Expenditures, Fiscal Years 1961–70

Fiscal Year	Actual Expenditures			In Constant 1958 $[1]			As % of GNP		
	For Vietnam	All other	Total	For Vietnam	All other	Total	For Vietnam	All others	Total
1961	—	$44,676,000,000	$44,676,000,000	—	$42,419,000,000	$42,419,000,000	—	8.8%	8.8%
1962	—	48,205,000,000	48,205,000,000	—	45,900,000,000	45,900,000,000	—	8.9%	8.9%
1963	—	49,973,000,000	49,973,000,000	—	46,050,000,000	46,050,000,000	—	8.7%	8.7%
1964	—	51,245,000,000	51,245,000,000	—	46,595,000,000	46,595,000,000	—	8.4%	8.4%
1965	$ 103,000,000	47,298,000,000	47,401,000,000	$ 91,000,000	41,562,000,000	41,653,000,000	*	7.2%	7.3%
1966	5,812,000,000	49,565,000,000	55,377,000,000	4,961,000,000	42,309,000,000	42,270,000,000	.8%	6.9%	7.7%
1967	20,133,000,000	48,198,000,000	68,331,000,000	16,789,000,000	40,192,000,000	56,981,000,000	2.6%	6.2%	8.7%
1968	26,547,000,000	50,826,000,000	77,373,000,000	19,879,000,000	40,266,000,000	60,145,000,000	2.9%	6.2%	9.1%
1969[2]	28,800,000,000	49,600,000,000	78,400,000,000	22,500,000,000	38,700,000,000	61,200,000,000	3.0%	5.3%	8.3%
1970[2]	24,900,000,000	53,000,000,000	77,900,000,000	18,700,000,000	39,700,000,000	58,400,000,000	2.6%	5.5%	8.1%

1 Actual $ figures deflated by Dept. of Commerce deflator for federal purchase of goods and services.

* Less than .1%

2 Figures for 1969 and 1970 are presented to the nearest hundred-million only.

Note: Excludes DOD civil functions such as rivers and harbors work of the Corps of Engineers.

Source: Budget of the United States Government, Fiscal Year 1969; Survey of Current Business, August 1968; Releases of the U.S. Dept. of Defenses. See also Testimony of Robert C. Moot in The Military Budget and National Economic Priorities, Hearings before the Subcommittee on Economy in Government of the Joint Economic Committee, 91 Cong. 1 Sess. (1969), Part 1, p. 320. Mr. Moot, Assistant Secretary of Defense (Comptroller), argues in support of the official figures for Vietnam expenditures given here. These figures are challenged as substantial overestimates in Chapter 2, "Defense" in Charles Schultze, Setting National Priorities: The 1971 Budget (The Brookings Institution, 1970). For a more extended discussion of these and related issues, see Parts 1 and 2 of the referenced Hearings.

TABLE 2.2 National Security Expenditures, Fiscal Years 1961–70

Fiscal Year	Department of Defense	Atomic Energy Commission[1]	Veterans Administration	Selective Service System	Total
1961	$44,676,000,000	$1,356,000,000	$5,376,000,000	$33,000,000	$51,441,000,000
1962	48,205,000,000	1,403,000,000	5,378,000,000	35,000,000	55,021,000,000
1963	49,973,000,000	1,379,000,000	5,666,000,000	35,000,000	57,053,000,000
1964	51,245,000,000	1,382,000,000	5,552,000,000	41,000,000	58,220,000,000
1965	47,401,000,000	1,312,000,000	5,634,000,000	43,000,000	54,390,000,000
1966	55,377,000,000	1,202,000,000	5,707,000,000	54,000,000	62,340,000,000
1967	68,331,000,000	1,132,000,000	6,366,000,000	58,000,000	75,887,000,000
1968	78,840,000,000	1,232,000,000	6,858,000,000	61,000,000	86,991,000,000
1969	77,877,000,000	1,225,000,000	7,263,000,000	65,000,000	86,430,000,000
1970[2]	76,504,000,000	1,230,000,000	8,196,000,000	74,000,000	86,004,000,000

[1] National security related portion assumed to = ½ of total
[2] Figures for 1970 are estimates. The total for 1971 is estimated at about $81,000,000,000.
Note: In addition to the above figures, several federal subsidy programs are justified wholly or partially on military grounds. Examples include the maritime subsidy, the minerals stockpile, the federal Interstate Highway Program of 1956, the National Defense Education Act, the federal Program for Support of Airport Construction, and oil depletion allowance. Some portions of foreign economic aid and the space program are justified partially on national security grounds.
Source: Federal Budget documents; U.S. Department of Defense releases.

To the extent that the sources of funding for the military establishment extend beyond the Department of Defense, they are included in Table 2.2. We have assumed that half of the Atomic Energy Commission's activities are for military purposes.[2] The cost of medical care, disability payments, and low-cost insurance for veterans of past wars, provided by the Veterans Administration, are listed as national security expenses, although it can be argued that many VA services are a substitute for welfare payments by other public authorities.

The Supporting Assistance program of the Agency for International Development is designed to improve the military and police forces of countries whose stability is deemed vital to American security, but the money comes from the State Department rather than the Defense Department, and is not included in Table 2.2.

The Kennedy and Johnson administrations went to considerable lengths to distinguish between the military space program of the Department of Defense and the program of the National Aeronautics and Space Administration, but many major industrial entities that do business with NASA also depend on the Defense Department as their only other important customer in the aerospace industry. And since NASA pays its share of fixed costs, as well as helping to balance out the peaks and valleys in defense production, there is some justification for including some portion of the NASA budget as part of defense costs. Because of the uncertainty of the calculation, however, it is excluded.[3] Similarly, there is no item for the Central Intelligence Agency, because its over-all budget and the proportion devoted to clearly military purposes are both secret.

Of the total expenditures by the military establishment, 60 per cent goes for the purchase of plant, equipment, and supplies, as distinguished from compensation for military and civilian personnel. And of this percentage, about 60 per cent goes for material for which there is no significant commercial market: it consists exclusively of guns rather than butter. A tabulation for the fiscal years 1961-70 appears in Table 2.3, showing that the military establishment is clearly the largest single customer in the United States and, by a wide margin, the largest single purchaser of goods for which there is no other market. For these unique goods, it represents in a sense a uniquely protected market, where continuing relationships are particularly important, since the unsuccessful seller cannot seek out other buyers.

The people who work in the military establishment themselves constitute a market for food, clothing and shelter, for automobiles and television sets and, later, for retirement cottages. As a group, their needs may be indis-

2. The extent to which large expenditures for research and development also have civilian applications will be discussed in Chapters 18 and 19.
3. Elsewhere in this book, however, the aerospace industry is necessarily treated as a single entity, serving both military and civilian space programs.

TABLE 2.3 Department of Defense Expenditures, by Category, Fiscal Years 1961–70

Fiscal Year	Military-oriented[1]	Capital Outlays and Supplies		Pay and allowances	Total
		Common to military and civilian use[2]	Sub-total		
1961	$19,200,000,000	$ 8,900,000,000	$28,100,000,000	$16,600,000,000	$44,700,000,000
1962	20,900,000,000	9,500,000,000	30,400,000,000	17,800,000,000	48,200,000,000
1963	23,000,000,000	9,000,000,000	32,000,000,000	18,000,000,000	50,000,000,000
1964	22,400,000,000	9,700,000,000	32,100,000,000	19,100,000,000	51,200,000,000
1965	18,100,000,000	9,600,000,000	27,700,000,000	19,700,000,000	47,400,000,000
1966	20,600,000,000	12,700,000,000	33,300,000,000	22,100,000,000	55,400,000,000
1967	26,200,000,000	16,400,000,000	42,600,000,000	25,700,000,000	68,300,000,000
1968	31,000,000,000	25,000,000,000	56,000,000,000	22,000,000,000	78,000,000,000
1969	31,500,000,000	25,000,000,000	56,500,000,000	21,400,000,000	77,900,000,000
1970[3]	28,800,000,000	25,400,000,000	54,200,000,000	22,300,000,000	76,500,000,000

[1] Consists of procurement and RDT & E expenditures for weapons systems and related hard goods.
[2] Consists of all other purchases, including construction, services, and soft goods.
[3] Figures for 1970 are estimates. The estimate for the fiscal 1971 total is $71,200,000,000.
Source: U.S. Department of Defense.

tinguishable from those of the rest of the population, but in particular communities, and in some larger areas—southern California, tidewater Virginia—they dominate the economic landscape because of their sheer mass, a dominance that is most vividly apparent when a military base is abandoned or a big defense plant loses contracts. The comparative importance of the military establishment in each state is shown in Chart 2.1, which provides the percentage of total employment that is defense-generated. The kinds of organizations that figure in the list of defense contractors range from General Electric and General Motors to small machine shops. They are all parts of the military establishment.

For most of the people to whom defense dollars are paid, those dollars are their primary connection with the military establishment. But for some of the most important members of the establishment—civilian political appointees, key senior officers—the cash nexus is their least significant connection with it (as is the case with draftees as well). And some of the people who receive significant amounts of defense dollars—stockholders in businesses with mixed defense and commercial markets, academic administrators whose budgets include substantial defense contracts—may not think of themselves as part of the military establishment at all.

The major population elements in the military establishment are military personnel, direct-hire civilians, and employees of defense contractors. There is a fourth large category of persons primarily dependent on members of the first three groups: wives and dependent children; tradesmen, from the military tailor to the lunchroom proprietor around the corner from the defense plant, whose customers are members of the military establishment; the professional men—lawyers and accountants, bankers and brokers, public relations counselors and trade journalists—who serve defense contractors; the retired military men for whom the establishment provides a second income, and often the basis for their postmilitary retirement occupation;[4] and others various degrees removed.

A former Pentagon reporter for the *New York Times,* Jack Raymond, noted that the reach of the military budget is larger than generally imagined. As he observed, "It provides, for example, $6,000 for flowers for American battle monuments. Flower growers, too, can be a part of the military-industrial complex." And so can the many other peripheral groups that contribute, whether overtly or covertly, to the furthering of the military-industrial image in the public consciousness.[5]

How far should such a list extend? Should it include the labor leaders

4. By 1980, expenditures for retirement pay are projected to be roughly one-fifth of the total budget for military personnel, and by 2020, almost 30 per cent.

5. Jack Raymond, "The Growing Threat of Our Military-Industrial Complex," *Harvard Business Review,* Vol. 46, #3 (May-June 1968), p. 53.

Chart 1.1 Geographic Importance of Defense Activity, 1963

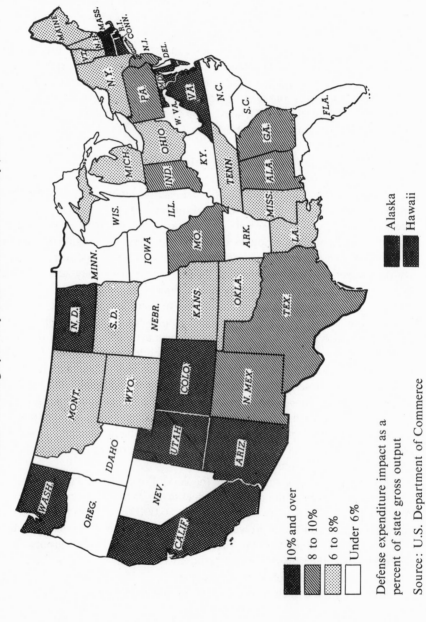

10% and over

8 to 10%

6 to 8%

Under 6%

Alaska

Hawaii

Defense expenditure impact as a
percent of state gross output

Source: U.S. Department of Commerce

of defense plant unions? The editors and publishers of newspapers in communities with substantial defense plants or military bases? The ministers of the principal churches in such communities? The members and staffs of the Armed Services Committees and military appropriations subcommittees of the House and Senate? The Congressmen from districts with substantial defense business? The president of a university seeking to retain (or to attract) faculty whose research interests are dependent (to a greater or lesser extent) on defense research assistance? While it seems possible to define and measure the population of the military establishment, the fact is that the list of persons ultimately connected with the military is almost infinitely extensible.

Nevertheless, several conclusions about the population of the military establishment appear from Tables 2.4 and 2.5. About 40 per cent of the

TABLE 2.4 Defense-Generated Employment, Fiscal Years 1965–67

Category	1965	1967
Armed Services	2,716,000	3,350,000
Civilian employees of the federal government	919,000	1,088,000
Employees of state and local governments	13,000	19,000
Employees of defense contractors, subcontractors, and their suppliers	2,101,000	2,972,000
Total:	5,749,000	7,429,000
Occupational group of civilian employees included above:		
Professional workers	495,000	635,000
Managers, officials, and proprietors	255,000	333,000
Salesworkers	66,000	95,000
Clerical and kindred workers	567,000	745,000
Craftsmen, foremen, and kindred workers	615,000	860,000
Operatives (semi-skilled)	710,000	990,000
Service workers	135,000	165,000
Laborers and farm workers	190,000	255,000
Total:	3,033,000	4,078,000

Source: *Monthly Labor Review*, September 1967, pp. 10, 18.

people are not directly employed by the government; most who are so employed are probably not career employees, at least among the rank and file of military personnel. (The line between career and noncareer is harder to draw among civilian employees since the civilian retirement system does not create the inducements to career commitment after the first few years of service that the military retirement system does.)

The military establishment as an organization is usually visualized as a monolith, but in reality it is more like a modern structure of prestressed concrete, held together by the tensions between opposing forces. From 1947 until 1961, the Department of Defense was a loose confederation of inde-

TABLE 2.5 Department of Defense Employment, by Category, 1961–68, as of June 30 of each year

Military Manpower[1]

Year	Career Officers	Non-Career Officers[2]	Sub-Total, Officers	Career Enlisted Men	Non-Career Enlisted Men[3]	Sub-Total, Enlisted Men	Total Military Manpower
1961	246,000	69,000	315,000[5]	1,030,000	1,129,000	2,159,000	2,473,000
1962	271,000	72,000	343,000	1,047,000	1,406,000	2,452,000	2,796,000
1963	257,000	77,000	334,000	1,014,000	1,341,000	2,355,000	2,689,000
1964	255,000	83,000	338,000	993,000	1,345,000	2,338,000	2,676,000
1965	251,000	88,000	339,000	998,000	1,307,000	2,305,000	2,644,000
1966	257,000	92,000	349,000	996,000	1,736,000	2,733,000	3,082,000
1967	264,000	120,000	384,000	996,000[6]	1,985,000[6]	2,981,000	3,365,000
1968[6]	278,000	118,000	396,000	996,000	2,020,000	3,016,000	3,412,000

Civilian and Total Manpower

Year	GS-1 through GS-7	GS-8 through GS-18[4]	Subtotal, Classified Employees	Wage Board Employees	Total Civilian Manpower	Total Department of Defense Manpower
1961	316,000	178,000	506,000	536,000	1,042,000	3,515,000
1962	326,000	191,000	525,000	544,000	1,070,000	3,866,000
1963	313,000	203,000	528,000	522,000	1,050,000	3,739,000
1964	308,000	217,000	536,000	494,000	1,030,000	3,706,000
1965	305,000	226,000	547,000	487,000	1,034,000	3,678,000
1966	341,000	237,000	594,000	544,000	1,138,000	4,220,000
1967	374,000	249,000	654,000	648,000	1,303,000	4,668,000
1968	NA	NA	675,000	642,000	1,317,000	4,729,000

[1] Excludes officer candidates such as academy cadets and midshipmen, aviation cadets, etc.
[2] Less than four years of service.
[3] Four years or less of service, except Army (three years or less).
[4] Includes P.L. 313 and other salaried employees. GS-1 through GS-7 are primarily clerical and secretarial positions. GS-8 through GS-18 are primarily managerial and professional positions. P.L. 313 covers high-level scientific and technical positions.
[5] Approximated from sample and inventory data.
[6] Estimated.
NA = Not available

Note: Details may not add to totals due to rounding.
Source: U.S. Department of Defense.

pendent fiefdoms, uneasily presided over by the Secretary of Defense. The Army, the Navy, the Marine Corps, and the Air Force controlled their own budgets and determined their own force structures, with a minimum of coordination among them, although the President and the Secretary of Defense did determine totals. Discussion had taken place on how the Department of Defense should be organized as a department, to deal with the problem of strategic nuclear war, or with the development of new weapons systems, but the controversies that engaged their protagonists most intensely were those that turned on the quasi-theological question of roles and missions. Were missiles a new form of artillery, and therefore within the proper domain of the Army, or a new kind of airplane and, therefore, the preserve of the Air Force? Could the Army properly use close support aircraft painted Army color and flown by pilots in Army uniforms, or should these planes be painted Air Force color and flown by pilots in Air Force uniforms? How far should the Marines carry amphibious warfare beyond the beachhead?

At its inception, the new Defense Department was still adjusting to the shrinkage of Army manpower from a World War II high of 8,226,373 men in 1945 to a low of 591,487 in 1950, just before the Korean War. The most violent controversies arose over scarce congressional appropriations, as in the 1949 fight between the carrier admirals and the Air Force proponents of strategic bombing, when the fight was carried into the press and rival columnists were enlisted by the opposing sides.

These controversies extended to intraservice rivalry as well. Within the Army, the "technical services"[6] had for decades successfully resisted efforts to streamline and integrate their operations. In the Navy, the old-line bureaus presented the same problem. Even the newest service, the Air Force, suffered from the efforts, often successful, of the Strategic Air Command (SAC) to dominate the entire organization.

Some small beginnings to resolve these conflicts into a unitary, orderly process had been made in the 1949, 1953, and 1958 amendments to the National Security Act, which established the legal basis for a single Department of Defense, and Secretary of Defense Thomas S. Gates had taken a firmer hand than his predecessors in reducing rivalries. But during 1961 and 1962, under Secretary Robert S. McNamara, essential new machinery was created, particularly the "five-year program and force structure," to begin to resolve the conflicts in more orderly fashion. The Systems Analysis shop was created within the Office of the Secretary of Defense to give the Secretary the analytical tools to evaluate proposals from the individual services (see Chapter 23) and the services themselves were re-

6. Adjutant General, Army Medical Service, Chemical Warfare, Finance, Military Police, Ordnance, Quartermaster, Transportation. (The Signal Corps is considered partly combat and partly service.)

organized, substantially overhauling the Army technical service and Navy bureau structures.

What has emerged is still by no means monolithic. As Chart 2.2 makes clear, the line of operational command of forces in the field goes from the President and the Secretary of Defense through the Joint Chiefs of Staff to the commanders in chief of the eight field commands.[7] The military departments—Army, Navy, Air Force—train and supply the men, and develop and procure the equipment for the operating commands, but there are no units under the direct operational authority of any military department. While this is an accurate description of existing arrangements, it is not the whole truth. If Chart 2.2 was shown to field-grade officers—colonels and majors—now on active duty, many of them would deny that it represented the formal command arrangements, and would insist that the mili-

Chart 2.2: Command Relationships for U.S. Forces

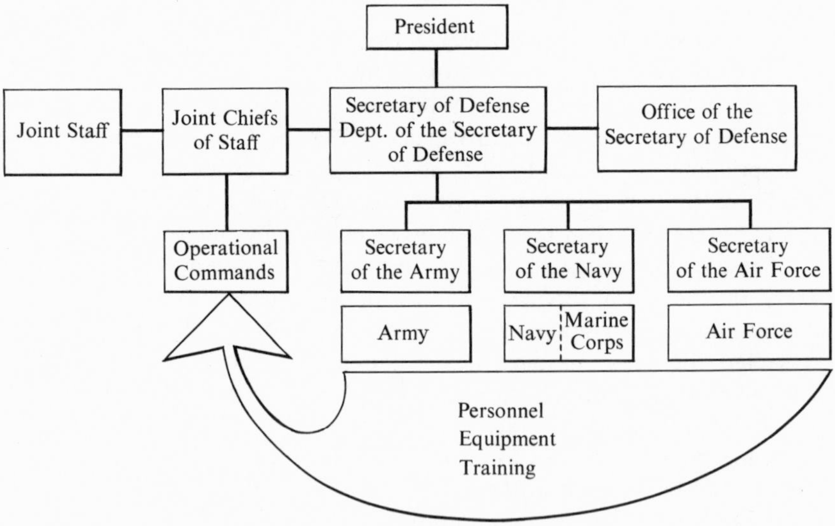

tary services do control their own troops in the field. For these officers, the Department of Defense is not an overarching organization of which their service is a part. When they speak colloquially of the department, or "DOD," they do not customarily include their own organizations, but only the Secretary of Defense and his staff (technically the Office of the Secretary

7. These are currently the Alaskan, Atlantic, Continental Air Defense, European, Pacific, Southern, Strategic Air, and Strike commands. The last is an emergency fire-fighting force around the world. As an indication of how rapidly bureaucracies become stratified, the United States command in Vietnam, by far the largest of the commands, does not report directly to the Joint Chiefs, but through the commander in chief of the Pacific Command.

of Defense, or OSD), a separate and alien entity with which their organization is forced occasionally to deal, rather like a foreign power.

Their belief about the lines of command is partly true. The people who do the work for the Joint Chiefs are the 400 officers of the Joint Staff—with several appendages which swell their numbers to perhaps twice that figure. These officers prepare the memoranda on proposed policy issues, take them through the various stages of evolution—first the blue, then the buff, then the green, then the purple (if the Joint Chiefs disagree), and finally the white memorandum, which goes to the Secretary. But the Joint Staff doesn't do the real work. That is done by the staffs in each military department, who prepare the service position on every issue, and these positions are then negotiated out, if possible, within the Joint Staff. The primary role of each member of the Joint Chiefs, except the chairman, is to serve as chief of his own service, and he is briefed for the weekly Chiefs' session not by the Joint Staff, but by his own service staff.

This arrangement is what the Congress had in mind when it amended the military unification legislation in 1958 to include a specific prohibition against the creation of a single general staff, and the numerical restrictions on the size of the Joint Staff are intended to carry out this explicit policy. Congress feared the power of a fully militarized Department of Defense, and sought to perpetuate interservice competition, or, as it has been put more cynically, a situation in which one service could be played off against the others. This competition may be an important tool in preserving civilian control.

In this process, the services provide a powerful assist. In 1961, for example, the Secretary of Defense transferred the strategic intelligence staffs out of the military departments, to form the Defense Intelligence Agency, reporting to the Secretary of Defense through the Joint Chiefs. This was done in part on the ground that strategic intelligence was a function of the operating commands and should be placed in operations, rather than with training and supply. When the intelligence staffs were transferred out of the military departments, the departments began to build up their staffs in areas called, euphemistically, "foreign technology," so that they were able to compete, to some extent at least, with the new interservice agency.

By the same token, the legislative liaison staffs of the individual services vastly outnumbered the legislative liaison staff of the Secretary of Defense— and his efforts to reduce their numbers have thus far been unavailing. Tampering with these staffs means intervening directly in long-established relationships with key legislators and congressional committees; in an organization the size of a military department, the organization can compensate internally for externally imposed reductions. Service links with the Congress, and particularly with the Armed Services Committees and their senior members and staff, are closer than the links between the Secretary of Defense and his staff and the Congress and congressional staff. The controversy over these relationships resulted in the disbanding in 1965 of the Capitol Hill active Reserve units, including the famous 999th Air Force Reserve Squadron commanded by Major General Barry M. Goldwater, USAF, which permitted eighty-three Congressmen and Senators to spend short periods of active duty in such prime military observation posts as London and Paris. But the 999th was only a surface manifestation of a more deep-seated and persistent phenomenon.

In the field, the joint operational commands exercise more authority in form than they do in fact over their separate service components. Until recently, the principal staff officers of the service components of a joint command—for example, the Assistant Chief of Staff for Operations, U.S. Army, Pacific—would outrank their opposite numbers for the entire joint command itself. Even in Vietnam, the complaint has frequently been made, and not infrequently well documented, that service interests have not been subordinated to common concerns. While civilians have been agonizingly conscious of the Vietnam war's needs and demands dominating the political landscape, military observers complain bitterly that the Pentagon practices business as usual—that the military departments do not give the war priority over the internal needs of the military organization; that command rotation policies, for example, were designed to give everyone a turn, rather than to achieve the most efficient level of operations, and that departmental research and development programs have not been sufficiently oriented to the needs of the war.

Beyond the Department of Defense itself, the organizational picture is even less monolithic. The Atomic Energy Commission, for example, determines with the advice of the Defense Department the amount of weapons-grade nuclear material to be produced, subject only to White House review. The serpentine wall between the military and civilian space programs has been difficult to trace, and is likely to shift significantly depending on the perspective from which it is viewed. The management of clandestine and covert operations of a military or quasi-military nature has reportedly been a bone of contention between the CIA and the Department of Defense for some time. And defense contractors involved in the development of new weapons systems not frequently find that they must choose between the service staff position and the position of the Secretary of Defense's own staff—and they choose at their peril.

In the TFX (tactical fighter, experimental) competition, for example, the essential difference between the Boeing and the General Dynamics proposals was that General Dynamics bet that the Secretary of Defense meant what he said about producing a common Air Force-Navy airplane, and Boeing bet that the services would persuade the Secretary to forget it. Boeing lost. In the same vein, a major international incident was precipitated when the Royal Air Force, listening only to its opposite numbers in the U.S. Air Force, and ignoring the analysts in the Office of the Secretary of Defense, as well as those on the President's Science Advisory Committee, assured their superiors that America's Skybolt missile program, on which Britain hoped to build an essential element of its strategic air power, would not be abandoned.

Each of the services has its own link with its major industrial suppliers through a kind of alumni association—the Association of the United States Army, the Navy League, the Marine Corps League, and the Air Force Association. These associations relate retired military personnel to the more active elements in the Reserves, with financial support from major defense contractors. Each association, not surprisingly, takes a generally expansionist view of its alma mater. But this view may bring it into conflict with the other associations, or even with the civilian hierarchy of the military department, as in 1963, when the Air Force Association opposed the administration's policy of nuclear restraint, and Secretary of the Air Force Eugene Zuckert refused to attend the Association's reception in his honor.[8]

The military establishment, then, is no simple pyramid of power. But its base is more than broad enough to accommodate a good deal of internal bureaucratic conflict without diminishing significantly its over-all impact on American society.

8. These associations, and other related entities, are discussed more fully in Chapter 13.

II

THE WEAKNESS OF

COUNTERVAILING POWER

3

The Military Influence
Within the Executive Branch

In the oval office of the President of the United States a little less than two weeks after his inauguration, President Richard M. Nixon was apologizing for the barrenness of the office; his books and other personal belongings were still in New York. But the office was not devoid of panoply. He pointed to the flags of the four services off to one side of his desk. "They" had sent them over that very day, when they discovered that Lyndon Johnson had removed his service flags. There were no emblems or banners from any other branch or department of government, nothing to represent the Foreign Service or the judicial branch or the Congress—but there were the emblems of the military, richly symbolic of the relationship of the President to the armed services. It is a role all too often forgotten when one mentions the power of the military establishment, for the military is at no time more powerful than the President of the United States—the Commander in Chief of the Armed Forces—is prepared to allow it to be.

There have been other societies in which the military establishment played a more influential, if not a completely dominant role, from ancient Sparta to some parts of present-day Latin America. Communist China spends a larger percentage of a much smaller gross national product on its military budget. But the United States and the Soviet Union are the only industrialized societies in which the military establishment is the largest single feature in the economic and political landscape.

It has not always been thus. The growth of military influence within the executive branch has been gradual, advancing in periods of war and military crisis until it came to dominate by its own accumulated mass. Historically the tradition of the American military has been an apolitical

25

one. Early in this country, a professional soldier recalled how the military ". . . lived apart in their tiny secluded garrisons much after the manner of military monks and . . . rarely came into contact with the mass of our citizens."[1] The military was only indirectly influential in executive decision-making—in matters of defense as well as foreign policy—up to World War I, and even then its influence was largely apolitical.

President Theodore Roosevelt and President William Howard Taft felt free to contact senior officers without bothering their service secretaries, but their communications were scarcely on matters of high policy. A typical letter from Roosevelt to an Army Chief of Staff ran: "Ought we not sometimes to practice our cavalry in charging? If so, would it not be practicable to arrange a row of dummies so that at the culminating moment of the charge the cavalry could actually ride home and hit the dummies? . . . I wish you would see if this dummy idea could not be worked up."[2]

In Woodrow Wilson's time, more memoranda from the service staffs went to the White House as problems of the period—trouble with Japan, civil war in Mexico, and war in Europe—seemed to call more urgently for military commentary than had most issues of the McKinley-Roosevelt-Taft era. But President Wilson resisted recommendations from the General Board and Joint Board when they suggested transferring the fleet to the Pacific during a crisis with Japan. He decided not to do so, and when the Joint Board asked him to reconsider, he replied: "When a policy has been settled by the Administration and when it is communicated to the Joint Board, they have no right to be trying to force a different course." To his Navy Secretary he said, "I wish you would say to them that if this should occur again, there will be no General or Joint Boards. They will be abolished." For a time, Wilson forbade the Joint Board even to meet.[3] And, although he gave great discretion to his military commanders in World War I, Wilson kept in his own hand all matters which he regarded as political, particularly preparations for peace negotiations.[4]

In 1920 and 1921, the military made further efforts to acquire a voice

1. Quoted in Pendleton Herring, *The Impact of War: Our American Democracy Under Arms* (New York: Farrar and Rinehart, 1941), p. 48. See also Samuel P. Huntington, *The Soldier and the State* (Cambridge: Harvard University Press, Belknap Press, 1957), for a thorough review of the traditional role of the military.

2. Elting E. Morison, ed., *The Letters of Theodore Roosevelt, The Square Deal, 1901–1904*, Vols. III-IV, (Cambridge; Harvard University Press, 1951), III, p. 546.

3. Arthur S. Link, *Wilson: The New Freedom*, Vol. II (Princeton: Princeton University Press, 1956), pp. 298-299. The General Board at that time was the highest-level planning agency in the Navy. The Joint Board was the combined Navy General Board and its Army equivalent.

4. Ernest R. May, "Wilson," in *The Ultimate Decision: The President as Commander in Chief*, Ernest R. May, ed. (New York; George Braziller, 1960), pp. 111-131; David F. Trask, *The United States in the Supreme War Council: American War Aims and Inter-Allied Strategy, 1917–1918* (Middletown, Conn.: Wesleyan University Press, 1961), *passim*.

in policy. Neither President Warren G. Harding nor his Secretary of State, Charles Evans Hughes, paid heed to strong objections from military professionals to the Washington treaty decisions which limited military expansion. Nor did the military regain power in the thirties. In the crisis of 1931 following Japan's seizure of Manchuria, President Herbert Hoover took charge himself. He consulted with the service heads only once, and then not about what he ought to do but merely about what they could do if necessary.[5]

Civilians in the military establishment had access to and influence on the White House, however, during the years just before World War II. Theodore Roosevelt, Taft, Wilson, the Republican Presidents of the 1920's, and Franklin D. Roosevelt, all made use of service secretaries or assistant secretaries in discussions on policy. By and large, these civilians acted as little more than conduits for advice prepared by professional officers. Through such civilian liaison, therefore, the military possessed a continuous—if limited—voice in presidential decision-making despite the lack of overt power.

With the approach of World War II, the relationship between the military and the Executive changed significantly. Successive crises—war between Italy and Ethiopia, Hitler's remilitarization of the Rhineland, civil war in Spain, and a Japanese drive to conquer China—drew Roosevelt's attention away from domestic affairs. He turned for advice to generals and admirals as well as to diplomats. He decreed that the Chiefs of Staff have direct access to him, without going through the civilian secretaries. During difficult periods after 1940, when he pondered the destroyer deal, Lend-Lease, Atlantic convoys and submarine patrols, aid to Russia, and economic sanctions against Japan, he frequently sought military advice and, after Pearl Harbor, he leaned even more heavily on the military.[6]

Prior to World War II Chiefs of Staff saw Presidents occasionally, but had no higher standing as presidential advisers than senior civil servants in, say, the Interior and Labor departments. Certainly, on foreign policy issues, they did not have status comparable to that of Assistant Secretaries of State or ambassadors. With World War II, their position changed dramatically.

5. Michael D. Reagan, "The Far Eastern Crisis of 1931–1932: Stimson, Hoover and the Armed Services," in *American Civil-Military Decisions: A Book of Case Studies,* Harold Stein, ed., (Birmingham, Ala.: University of Alabama Press, 1963), pp. 27-42.

6. Reagan, "The Helium Controversy," in Stern, pp. 43-59; Ray S. Cline, *Washington Command Post: The Operations Division* (Washington, D.C.: Office of the Chief of Military History, Department of the Army, 1951), pp. 1-74; Maurice Matloff and Edwin M. Snell, *Strategic Planning for Coalition Warfare, 1941–1942* (Washington, D.C.: Office of the Chief of Military History, Department of the Army, 1953), pp. 1-96; Forrest C. Pogue, *George C. Marshall: Ordeal and Hope, 1939–1943,* Vol. II, (New York: Viking, 1963), *passim.*

In terms of entree to the White House and influence on a broad range of presidential decisions, members of the Joint Chiefs outranked cabinet secretaries. Roosevelt sought advice from the Joint Chiefs on a range of issues that he and his predecessors would have regarded, before 1938, as primarily State Department business. The President gave the Chiefs decisive responsibility, for example, for devising surrender terms and occupation plans, even involving them in arrangements for a postwar United Nations Organization.[7]

Although the military had previously sought a role in policy-making, they showed some reluctance to assume as much responsibility as Roosevelt thrust upon them. The Joint Chiefs and their staff committees dutifully prepared plans dealing with political as well as military contingencies. They attempted to forecast postwar trends and to analyze such subjects as future relations with the Soviet Union. But, by and large, the officers involved did not relish working on intangible problems with little relation to the war in progress. They always took care to write that their judgments reflected a strictly military viewpoint. As far as possible, they tried to shift responsibility to the State Department. After 1945, this reluctance ceased.

Truman, for his part, viewed the military with some mistrust. Roosevelt's first military contacts had been with admirals and Social Register naval officers whom he had first met as Assistant Secretary of the Navy, but Truman recalled his experience as a National Guard officer in World War I when he ran afoul of Regular Army red tape. Later, as chairman of a Senate committee scrutinizing the military conduct of World War II, Truman saw abundant evidence of the services' expensive inefficiency. He did not instinctively think of the military as a source of wisdom on issues of high national policy.

As in the years immediately after World War I, the professional military after World War II again sought a recognized place in the policy advisory process. This time they succeeded. For, like FDR, Truman found himself facing situations in which he felt need for military counsel; for example, the Soviet Union's failure to evacuate Iranian Azerbaijan and the withdrawal of British support from Turkey and Greece.[8] As he felt compelled to consult the military, he acquired more and more confidence in them. In contrast to wordy, vague, and inconclusive memoranda so often sent from State, papers from the Pentagon on foreign policy issues appeared to him terse, thorough, reliable, and clearly focused on requirements for action. In 1947 Truman agreed that, at least in form, the military establishment should have an

7. Cline, *Washington Command Post*, pp. 312-332; Paul Y. Hammond, "Directives for the Occupation of Germany: The Washington Controversy," in Stein, *American Civil-Military Decisions*, pp. 311-464; Harley F. Notter, *Postwar Foreign Policy Preparation, 1939-1945* (Washington, D.C.: Department of State, 1949), pp. 248-249.

8. Harry S. Truman, *Memoirs: Years of Trial and Hope*, Vol. II (New York: Doubleday, 1958), pp. 93-107; Joseph M. Jones, *The Fifteen Weeks: February 21– June 5, 1947* (New York: Viking, 1955).

institutionalized role in advising him on foreign policy. He sponsored a National Security Act which, in addition to making the Air Force a separate service and providing for a Secretary of Defense, set up a statutory National Security Council designed as an inner cabinet to deal with issues of foreign and defense policy—"Mr. Truman's Politburo," as John Fischer called it.[9]

The same act was amended in 1949 to guarantee in law the practice, previously carried on *de facto,* of "legislative insubordination" by the Joint Chiefs. The act provides that "no provision of this Act shall be so construed as to prevent a Secretary of a military department or a member of the Joint Chiefs of Staff from presenting to the Congress, on his own initiative, after first so informing the Secretary of Defense, any recommendations relating to the Department of Defense that he may deem proper."[10]

Nevertheless, President Truman did not revert to Roosevelt's practice of depending on the military as primary policy advisers. After a period of collaboration between the State Department and the Pentagon under George C. Marshall, Truman exhibited some concern about the policy role of the military and encouraged a full-scale review of American commitments and the forces required to sustain them.[11] But with the outbreak of the Korean War, he was obliged to bring military men back into the inner circle of policy-making. General Omar N. Bradley, as chairman of the Joint Chiefs of Staff, began to function much as had Admiral William D. Leahy during World War II, briefing the President almost daily. Truman met occasionally with some or all of the service chiefs to discuss not only military plans and weapons requirements but also such issues as how, by diplomacy, to keep the Chinese out of the war and how to persuade Europeans that the United States government still gave their continent first priority.[12] Even during the hottest phases of the Korean War, however, he never went as far as Franklin Roosevelt in relying on the uniformed military for policy advice. Military professionals functioned as presidential advisers, but for the most part at a secondary level.

Because of his own five-star rank and his personal popularity, President Eisenhower had less need than Truman for clear support from the military.

9. Truman, *Years of Trial and Hope,* pp. 164-165; Walter Millis and Eugene S. Duffield, eds., *The Forrestal Diaries* (New York: Viking, 1951), pp. 62-63; Public Law 252, 80th Congress, July 27, 1947, 61 Stat. 495 (the National Security Act of 1947); Paul Y. Hammond, *Organizing for Defense: The American Military Establishment in the Twentieth Century* (Princeton: Princeton University Press, 1961), pp. 186-232; "Mr. Truman's Politburo" is a chapter title in John Fischer, *Master Plan U.S.A.: An Informal Report on America's Foreign Policy and the Men Who Make It* (New York: Harper & Brothers, 1951).

10. National Security Act of 1947, as Amended, Sec. 202(c)8.

11. Warner R. Schilling, "The H-Bomb Decision: How to Decide Without Actually Choosing," *Political Science Quarterly,* March 1961.

12. Truman, *Years of Trial and Hope,* pp. 333-335, 378-380, 382-386, 418-419. See also Richard E. Neustadt, *Presidential Power* (New York: Wiley, 1960), Chapter 5.

If anything, his military background made him less responsive to the services. He felt qualified to judge as well as to discount advice. Recognizing that political opponents might charge him with allowing the military excessive influence, he took pains to keep his former colleagues at arm's length. He accepted and put into effect early in his administration a task force report which had the apparent effect of giving the civilian Secretary of Defense larger powers.[13] In practice, Eisenhower depended on the Joint Chiefs less than had Truman. During the 1954 crisis over Indochina, for example, he considered ordering air strikes in support of the French even though the service chiefs had advised against such action.[14] In subsequent crises over the Chinese offshore islands, Suez, Hungary, and renewed Soviet threats to Berlin, he showed similar independence. But at the same time, Eisenhower used one military man in the kind of top-level advisory role that Truman had reserved for his civilian secretaries. From 1953 to 1957, Admiral Arthur W. Radford, the JCS chairman, occupied a place in Eisenhower's foreign policy councils second only to that of Secretary of State John Foster Dulles. His period as chairman and Marshall's as Army Chief of Staff probably mark the two points at which professional military men have had the biggest voice in presidential decisions.

Kennedy assumed the presidency after having read such books as those of General Matthew Ridgway, *Soldier,* and General Maxwell Taylor, *The Uncertain Trumpet,* James M. Gavin's *War and Peace in the Space Age,* and reports by various analysts charging that the Eisenhower administration had sacrificed to the sacred cow of a balanced budget the military wherewithal for a forceful, flexible, and effective diplomacy. Kennedy intended to give generals and admirals freer access to the oval office. His first dealings with the Chiefs of Staff, however, came with the Bay of Pigs. The next was with Laos. In the first case, the President felt that he had been deceived—the Chiefs had not made plain the probability that the landing would fail unless given overt American military support. On Laos, Kennedy asked the hard questions he had neglected to ask about the Cuban operation.[15] He emerged from both experiences mistrusting not only the judgment of the Chiefs but also their competence.

For self-protection, Kennedy called Maxwell Taylor out of retirement to serve on the White House staff and, in 1962, appointed him chairman

13. Dwight D. Eisenhower, *The White House Years: Mandate for Change, 1953–1956,* (New York: Doubleday, Vol. I, 1963), pp. 88-89; Hammond, *Organizing for Defense,* pp. 288-298.

14. Eisenhower, *Mandate for Change,* p. 354; see also Melvin Gurtov, *The First Vietnam Crisis: Chinese Communist Strategy and United States Involvement, 1953–1954* (New York: Columbia University Press, 1967).

15. Arthur M. Schlesinger, Jr., *A Thousand Days: John F. Kennedy in the White House* (Boston: Houghton Mifflin, 1965), pp. 233-266, 337-338; Theodore C. Sorensen, *Kennedy* (New York: Harper & Row, 1965), pp. 326-346, 726-729.

of the Joint Chiefs of Staff. Even so, he never gave Taylor a status comparable to Radford's under Eisenhower. The President's relations with other professional military men remained at best cool, distant, and wary. For practical purposes, Kennedy received military advice only as it filtered to him through his civilian Secretary of Defense. In his brief thousand days, he never faced a test comparable to Truman's in 1951.[16] He did, however, ask the military establishment for help in some close battles on Capitol Hill. He judged it indispensable for Senate ratification of the limited test-ban treaty that the Joint Chiefs certify the treaty as not contrary to American interests; he devoted almost as much effort to negotiations with the Chiefs as to negotiations with Moscow.[17]

During the presidency of his successor, the pattern of caution and wariness was at first preserved. As a long-time member of the Armed Services Committee, Lyndon Johnson brought to the presidency attitudes somewhat similar to Truman's. "The generals," he once said, "know only two words—spend and bomb."[18] On Vietnam and the Dominican Republic, Johnson treated the professional military as agents of doubtful reliability. He decided on a bombing campaign against North Vietnam, and would not let the Chiefs add any bombing targets without his personal approval. During the Dominican · occupation, he sent a succession of high-level civilian officials to check on and oversee the operations of the forces landed there. To be sure, Johnson could not be characterized as trustful in his relations with *any* group; still, he showed somewhat greater suspiciousness of the military than most groups.[19]

Nevertheless, in a pattern by now familiar, war forced an alliance between the Executive and the military. As the war in Vietnam wore on and came under more and more criticism at home, Johnson developed a closer relationship with the professional military. By 1968, the crucial choice before him, one that affected almost all international and domestic problems, was whether to step down or to step up the scale of air operations in Vietnam. The Joint Chiefs and the American commander in Vietnam inevitably formed part of the circle from which he sought advice.

Johnson, like Truman at the time of Korea, attempted to counter waning popularity by demonstrating that his policies commanded support from the military establishment. For a time he kept McNamara so much in the foreground that reporters spoke of the war as "McNamara's war." When

16. Even during the Cuban missile crisis, the President did not face any overt challenge from the military, and disagreement over courses of action did not break along civilian-military lines.

17. Schlesinger, *A Thousand Days*, pp. 911-913.

18. Rowland Evans and Robert Novak, *Lyndon B. Johnson: The Exercise of Power* (New York: New American Library, 1966), p. 539.

19. *Ibid.*, pp. 510-574; Philip L. Geyelin, *Lyndon B. Johnson and the World* (New York: Praeger, 1966), pp. 31-32, 181-223, 236-258.

this tactic failed, the President turned more to the professionals. In the winter of 1967-68 he summoned the field commander, General William C. Westmoreland, to address a joint session of Congress. Johnson emphasized that his own actions accorded with advice from Westmoreland and the Joint Chiefs, although there is some reason to suppose that he used the military more as advocates in defense of his position than as counselors on his choice of options.

The Nixon administration appears to be establishing a pattern of civil-military relations which reverses that of the Kennedy and Johnson years. While Secretaries McNamara and Clark M. Clifford kept the uniformed military on a comparatively tight rein and permitted civilian Defense staffs to proliferate, Secretary Melvin R. Laird seems to be granting the military more autonomy and reducing the role of civilian staffers. Simultaneously, Henry A. Kissinger's highly structured National Security Council staff, and the new Defense Policy Review Committee, suggest that President Richard M. Nixon may be substituting rigorous civilian institutional procedures for the rigorous civilian systems analysis of his predecessors, as his means of assuring civilian control.[20]

As the military establishment has grown, the relative strength of the State Department and the Pentagon has shifted. Defense is now usually dominant. The most obvious and perhaps the most important difference between the Department of Defense and the Department of State is one of size. Expenditure for defense is now running at a rate some twenty times the rate for all other international activities, including foreign aid and the U.S. Information Agency (if Vietnam expenditures are excluded the ratio might be down to fifteen to one, although a large part of foreign aid expenditures also go to Vietnam). Even in terms of physical plant, the new State Department building in Foggy Bottom does not begin to compete in size with the Pentagon itself, quite apart from the Little Pentagon in the redevelopment area on the Washington side of the Potomac.

The size of the military establishment not only provides economies of scale, but also makes resources available at the top, in manpower, in expertise, and in the variety of services that can make the difference between crisply executed operations and constantly cramped and curtailed operations. It may not be true that overseas commercial telephone conversations between State Department officials and embassies abroad have been cut off in mid-ocean because appropriations were exhausted; but it is true that only the Defense Department (and through it, the White House) has effective immediate voice communications throughout the world. United

20. Detailed information on these new patterns of Defense organization within the Nixon administration may be found on pp. 8-9, 13-20, 32-33, and 74-86 of Secretary Laird's *Posture Statement* for fiscal year 1971, and in President Nixon's *State of the World* address of February 1970.

States ambassadors abroad have to ask for rides in their military attachés' aircraft, and State Department officials at home have to ask for rides in their Pentagon colleagues' official automobiles.

Not only is the Defense Department much bigger, but it is much more pervasive. The State Department has embassies and consulates girdling the globe, and in most of those posts foreign service officers are matched by members of United States military missions.

As of June 30, 1969, there was a total of 8,264 representatives of the Defense Department, compared with only 5,166 representatives of State at these overseas missions.[21] At least one ambassador to a Latin American country asked that the military mission in his country be reduced substantially, but his request was never acted on.

The military presence extends also into the heartland of the United States. Where the State Department has established only a few toe- and fingerholds in the local councils on foreign relations in the largest urban centers, military establishments and defense plants mark the length and breadth of the country. Thus the influence of the Defense Department, as measured by its presence and its spending power, is diffused throughout the United States, somewhat unevenly, but very widely; while the much more limited potential influence of the State Department and its ancillary agencies is limited to the nearly voteless District of Columbia and to voteless constituencies overseas.

The Defense Department's extensive domestic involvement gives it an advantage apart from the relative strengths of constituencies—it sensitizes the department to domestic political realities. It is spending taxpayers' dollars. It is drafting the sons of citizens and voters. It is making decisions that affect the economic climate of American communities and the economic welfare of American companies. By contrast, the State Department is generally observing and reporting on a bewildering jumble of activities beyond the reach of the sovereign power of the United States. At least until recently, Defense has had a good deal less difficulty gaining congressional approval for its enormous budget than State has had with its small one. But the Pentagon's budgetary victories were as much a measure of its involvement in domestic politics as the State Department's budgetary defeats are a measure of its estrangement from domestic politics. Pentagon policy-makers are much less likely than State Department planners to ignore the primacy of American domestic politics in making calculations about the political behavior of their own government. It may seem paradoxical yet be a reflection of its strength that by far the stronger of the two departments should be more responsive to domestic political pressures.

The fact that the Defense Department is primarily responsible for the

21. *Hearings on H.R. 12964,* Committee on Appropriations, U.S. Senate, 91st Congress, 1st Session, p. 950.

management of its huge resources gives it still another advantage over the State Department. The Secretary of State, under at least three Presidents, has seen it as his primary responsibility to advise the President, rather than to direct the affairs of his department. The under secretaries and the assistant secretaries see their primary role as furnishing policy advice to the Secretary, rather than carrying out the policies he and the President establish. The bureau chiefs, the section chiefs, and the branch chiefs in turn see themselves primarily as policy advisers, looking up toward their superiors rather than down toward the management of their own departments. Whatever criticisms can be made of Defense management—and current evidence indicates they can be made with considerable effectiveness—it must be recognized that Defense Department officials, military and civilian, regard the management of the defense establishment as their primary and ultimate responsibility. They do not suffer from the disease of heliotropism which seriously afflicts the Department of State. The Defense Department's orientation toward the management of men and machines in turn puts an emphasis on speed and efficiency in Defense operations which State fails to match, even making allowances for the relative strengths in resources available to management. Somehow the responsible officials in Defense have tended in recent years to learn about a new crisis before the State Department officials got the word. The State Department memorandum reaches the White House a day or two after the Defense Department memorandum, and the staff work in the State memorandum is frequently not as crisply or as effectively done. A former White House staff officer noted that when he called for briefing papers on short notice from State for a presidential overseas trip, his first deadline passed without any response. He then turned to the office of International Security Affairs at Defense, which responded with a complete, concise, and thoroughly indexed briefing book. State finally crashed through with several cardboard cartons of unsorted cables on the countries listed in the President's itinerary. These are clearly differences that do not go to the merits or to the wisdom of the recommendations emanating from the two departments. They do go to the likelihood that the earlier and better buttressed recommendations will be acted on, and acted on favorably.

One of the consequences of the military-civilian competition in the area of weapons development was first the creation of a (primarily civilian) office of Systems Analysis within the Office of the Secretary of Defense, and then the creation of matching capabilities by the Joint Chiefs. Similarly, in the foreign policy area, the office of International Security Affairs developed almost as a miniature State Department, and this development was followed by parallel functions in the Plans and Policy Directorate of the Joint Staff, complete with its own regional desks, like the regional desks in the Secretary's office and the regional bureaus in the

Department of State. Here, as elsewhere, imitation proved to be the sincerest form of flattery.

Military considerations and military logic have dominated United States foreign policy in part because the American people, in the period after World War II, came to repose special trust in the judgment of professional military men and also because this trust arose out of fear of a cold war antagonist.

That this assertion had some basis in reality is demonstrated, paradoxically, by an episode often cited as proving the vitality of the principle of civilian supremacy—the MacArthur crisis of 1951.[22] Dissenting publicly against rulings by the President, General Douglas MacArthur had called for enlarging the Korean War and backing a Chinese Nationalist campaign against the mainland Communists. After repeated instances of insubordination, Truman relieved the general of his command. There followed an outcry in the press and on Capitol Hill, a hero's welcome for MacArthur in Los Angeles and New York, and a two-month hearing conducted jointly by the Foreign Relations and Armed Services Committees of the Senate. Since this hearing ended with all members of both committees agreeing that the President had not exceeded his constitutional powers, the result was hailed at the time, and has been hailed since, as a reaffirmation that the elected civilian representative of the people retains ultimate control over policy and strategy.

Yet, if one looks more closely, another conclusion might be drawn. The President's party held majorities in both houses of Congress. Of the twenty-eight Senators on the two committees that conducted the hearings, only eight sided openly with MacArthur on the question of how the war should be fought. One would suppose that an outcome favorable to the President might have been predictable from the beginning. Evidently, however, administration supporters on the two committees felt an intensive investigation was necessary. During the hearings they interrogated fourteen witnesses, including the Secretary of Defense, four members of the JCS, and five additional generals or admirals. The friends of the administration pressed each representative of the military establishment to say that the President had had their advice on the relevant issues of strategy and policy before he overruled a recommendation from MacArthur.[23]

It cannot be proved, of course, that the outcome of the hearings would have been different if this parade of military witnesses had not appeared in

22. The most carefully researched account is by John W. Spanier, *The Truman-MacArthur Controversy and the Korean War* (Cambridge: Harvard University Press, 1959); the liveliest is Richard Rovere and Arthur M. Schlesinger, Jr., *The General and the President* (New York: Farrar, Straus, 1951).

23. *Hearings, Military Situation in the Far East,* Congress, Senate, Armed Services and Foreign Relations Committees, 82nd Congress, 1st Session, *passim.*

support of the President. On the other hand, it is not hard to surmise that the verdict in the two committees, in Congress, and in the country might have been much closer, or indeed have gone against Truman, had Secretary of Defense Marshall, Chairman Bradley, and the other Chiefs sided instead with MacArthur. Of course, it can be said that the issues of 1951 were partly military issues. It can also be argued that Marshall, the Chiefs, and Eisenhower believed they owed loyalty to President Truman, regardless of whether he had accepted their recommendations. When pressed as to whether he would himself speak out publicly if he believed presidential decisions to be militarily wrong, Bradley replied, "No, sir. . . . I have been brought up a little differently."[24] Nevertheless, the conclusion is almost inescapable that Harry Truman had to have demonstrable support from the military establishment. It was a political necessity. It may have been a prerequisite of his survival as President.

In part, hero worship, carrying over from World War II, explained the extraordinary public confidence enjoyed by the military. The popularity that attached after the Revolutionary War and the Civil War to George Washington, Ulysses Grant, and other generals attached after World War II to Marshall, MacArthur, Eisenhower, Bradley, and a few others. In part, the preoccupying issues of the period accounted for public attitudes, for the citizenry would, under the circumstances, have looked to military men for some counsel. Also the unusual position occupied by the military was due to the weakness of the competition. A long-term secular trend had diminished the stature of the clergy; the Depression had shaken people's faith in businessmen, Roosevelt's duel with the "nine old men" and controversies aroused by the Earl Warren Court cut into the prestige of the judiciary and, by extension, the legal profession. Of national political leaders after FDR, only Eisenhower commanded blind trust among large numbers of citizens. (The Kennedy magic developed largely after his assassination, not before.) And Eisenhower came from the military.

In retrospect, the militarization of American foreign policy appears almost inevitable. The wartime atmosphere soon resumed after World War II. The Soviet Union from 1945 onward seemed to many observers aggressively expansionistic and implacably hostile. Awareness of advances in weaponry and delivery systems made Americans newly apprehensive about their own safety. It is hard to conceive, under the circumstances, how reasonable men in the executive branch could have developed or espoused any policies other than those emphasizing military security, enemy capabilities, and readiness for worst contingencies. In any event, they did not, despite periods of vacillation and sporadic attempts at applying civilian checks and balances.

The large role played by the military establishment in framing and

24. *Ibid.*, Part I, p. 753.

executing foreign policies was merely one by-product of the forces that produced the policies themselves. Civilians like Dean Acheson, Dulles, and Dean Rusk did not speak lines written for them by the Joint Chiefs or by Secretaries of Defense. They spoke their convictions in the language most likely to persuade Congress and the public. They framed their proposals in such a way as to justify open support by military men. It is fair to say that if American foreign policy became partially militarized, the blame should not be laid primarily on the military establishment but on Presidents, civilian policy-makers, the Congress, and the American people—and on the situation in which they found themselves.

Whether the military is preserving its dominant role under the Nixon administration—at a time of tightening controls and declining military popularity, yet with a continuing and expanding war—remains to be seen.

4

The Military-Congressional Interdependence

If the first line of defense against military encroachment on matters of public policy is the Executive, the second is the Congress. Yet here, too, countervailing power has been inconsistently and infrequently applied.

The rationale of many Congressmen to support a passive or an acquiescent role was put bluntly in 1963, at the height of a public controversy over the performance of Secretary of Defense Robert McNamara, by Republican Congressman Leslie C. Arends of Illinois:

Is our military defense strategy, our defense plans, and our future defense posture to be entrusted to civilian theorists, with no military training or experience, or is our defense strategy, plans, and posture to be entrusted to the experienced military judgment of our Joint Chiefs of Staff?[1]

In part, the problem of inadequate checks and balances derives not merely from abdication of congressional responsibility but, in part, from the fact that the interests of the military are a matter of self-interest for Congressmen. Senator Philip A. Hart of Michigan has described the temptation as follows:

A military man is disciplined to overestimate enemy capacity and underestimate his own. He puts an imaginative mind to work trying to anticipate every possible enemy tactic, every potential ruse, every combination of weapons. Then it is his job to protect against them, to close every defense chink. If we give him that assignment, we have no right to be surprised if he tends to spend heavily. He is simply doing his job. But it is a job that needs supervision, and here, after World War II, Congress failed. Congress was

1. *Congressional Record,* May 7, 1963, 88th Congress, 1st Session, Vol. 109, Part 6, p. 7885.

uncritical. It reflected the nation's sense of threat and a victorious people's confidence in their military.

In time a new element crept in. . . . As procurement moved steadily upward, every member of Congress began to develop constituencies that were in some degree dependent on defense jobs and contracts. . . . It is not politically hard for me to vote against, say, a new aircraft carrier. But if the shipyard were in my state and five thousand people were waiting for the work, I would be examining very closely, and perhaps less critically, all those reasons why the carrier might be essential to national security.[2]

The evidence of the political and economic forces of interdependence generated by military procurement is pervasive—in the daily ritual which allows individual Senators and Congressmen to announce new defense contracts with companies in their states or districts; in corporate advertising campaigns which take as their theme the contribution of company X to national security as a prime contractor for a weapons system; in running controversies over cost overruns and contract awards; in support by particular Congressmen for particular military projects or weapons systems; in the favors given members of Congress by the Pentagon in the form of free plane rides to home districts or to the far corners of the world; and in the kid-glove treatment accorded military officers, at least until recently, during their appearances before congressional committees in support of their appropriation requests.

Certainly the military-industrial-congressional complex is not a conspiracy. But there are coincidences of interest among the military project officer who is looking for a star, the civilian who sees an opening for a new branch chief, the defense contractor who is running out of work, the union business agents who can see layoffs coming, and the Congressman who is concerned about campaign contributions from business and labor as well as about the prosperity of his district. Each of these constellations of interests wants to expand the defense establishment in its own direction. Members of Congress are not bashful about their appetite for defense dollars and defense activity. Writing in the Louisville Courier-Journal (May 22-25, 1963), Richard Harwood reports the description by James Wright, Congressman from Fort Worth, of his efforts to secure the $6 billion TFX fighter contract for the General Dynamics plant at Fort Worth.

" 'Let me be completely frank,' " Harwood quotes Wright as saying.

"During the course of last year, I talked about this subject with everybody whom I could get to listen. Believing that good and adequate reasons existed for giving every fair and just consideration to the General Dynamics submission, I made it my business to try to persuade people to this point of view. I am not ashamed of that. I considered it my duty. There is nothing sinister

2. Philip A. Hart, "Militarism in America," *The Center Magazine,* Vol. III, No. 1 (January 1970).

about it. I made no secret of the fact. I talked to both military and civilian officials. I tried to be as persuasive as I knew how to be."

That Wright's efforts had no effect on the contract award decision does not reduce their impact on Wright's own attitudes toward the military budget. In the same article Harwood goes on to report that Congressman John Brademas of South Bend, Indiana, "spends many hours promoting defense contracts for Studebaker and Bendix Corporation and frankly contends 'anyone who didn't do it wouldn't be here very long.' " Harwood continues:

In a Senate debate on an Air Force appropriation bill, Maryland Senator J. Glenn Beall begged his colleagues to add money for the purchase of transport planes from Fairchild Aircraft Company in Hagerstown, Maryland. "All we ask for Fairchild is $11,000,000," said Beall. On another occasion, West Virginia Representative Ken Hechler complained to the House: "I am firmly against the kind of logrolling which would subject our defense program to narrowly sectional or selfish pulling and hauling. But I am getting pretty hot under the collar about the way my state . . . is short-changed in Army, Navy, and Air Force installations. . . . I am going to stand up on my hind legs and roar until West Virginia gets the fair treatment she deserves."

And, in 1968, Senator Russell B. Long of Louisiana proudly accepted credit for applying the pressure that, he claimed, persuaded President Johnson to name Fort Polk, Louisiana, a permanent military installation, thus making the base eligible for a share of the more than $1 billion appropriated each year in military construction funds. The *Congressional Quarterly* of November, 1, 1968, quoted a Long assistant as saying that "the decision really was a rather direct result of pressure from us and the rest of the state's delegation. . . . This was one of those things that Russell Long could go to LBJ and ask for in the closing days of his administration. . . . LBJ knows what the base means to the state. . . ."

The military establishment is also responsible for a congressional bonanza to at least half of the nation's school districts. "Impacted Aid," as it is called, currently provides more than $500 million for more than 4,500 districts with a high proportion of military-connected families in residence. The congressional intent is for the federal government to bear its share of the costs of both construction and operation of public schools in qualifying areas. The origins of the program lie in federal support for on-post schools, with occasional aid to civilian school districts for what amounted to tuition payments. The 1940 Lanham Act, which provided substantial compensation for the World War II mobilization impact, was extended year by year until, in 1950, the current "Impacted Aid" program was born. This program marked the end of the Department of Defense's formal involvement with public school aid; all funds and responsibility for administration were placed with the Office of Education. But, because few nonmilitary government activities place a sufficient burden on the local schools to quality (the threshold is about 3 per cent of the total school population), Impacted Aid remains closely identified with defense activities.

Impacted Aid began with roughly $105 million distributed to just over 1,100 school districts. The money came with virtually no strings attached, and the program proved to be quite popular. Unlike other federal assistance programs, Impacted Aid may be used wholly at the discretion of the local officials and administrators. About half the total public school population attends these schools, which, incidentally, are located in nine out of ten congressional districts. It is clear, then, that Impacted Aid has a very wide base of support.

All attempts to eliminate or sharply curtail it have been unsuccessful, despite arguments that many of the impacted areas don't "need" the aid or, at any rate, need it far less than other districts, particularly urban areas, whose resources are more limited. Four Presidents (Eisenhower, Kennedy, Johnson, and Nixon) have made public attempts to reduce the Impacted Aid program, but in vain.

Candor on the issue of defense contracts is not restricted to Congressmen; candidates for the presidency are also quite open about it. Richard Nixon, campaigning in 1960, told a crowd at Fort Worth, Texas: "I can assure you that we are going to remember the state of Texas on defense contracts and certainly Texas is going to get its fair share—you can be sure of that—under my administration."[3] The candidate for President on the Democratic ticket, John F. Kennedy, told a crowd at the Bell Aircraft plant at Niagara Falls that year: "I think defense contracts should be fairly distributed across the nation. . . . I think we can use defense contracts to strengthen the economy as well as strengthen the country. In any case if we are successful [in the election], we will try to distribute defense contracts fairly so that it protects the United States and protects the economy."[4]

Under the circumstances, lobbying by the military within Congress would seem to be wasteful. Still, a great deal of it is done. The Pentagon takes a "carrot and stick" approach to Congress. The biggest contract awards have tended over the years to go to districts of key members of the military committees, who in turn usually vote for the Pentagon's program. One former White House assistant said a special technique was employed by the services whenever the White House or the Secretary of Defense

3. Speech at Burk Burnett Park, Nov. 4, 1960. See p. 999 of *The Speeches of Vice President Richard M. Nixon, Presidential Campaign of 1960*, Committee on Commerce. U.S. Senate, Subcommittee of the Subcommittee on Communications (Washington, D.C.: Government Printing Office).
4. Speech, Sept. 28, 1960. See p. 384 of *The Speeches of Senator John F. Kennedy, Presidental Campaign of 1960, op. cit.*

vetoed one of the services' favorite projects or wanted it to buy something it did not want. "In this case," he said, "the service lines up a friendly Congressman to plant questions when the chief of staff of that service or another high-ranking officer appears on the Hill. The Congressman will ask the officer his 'professional' opinion of the weapons system, as opposed to the official Defense Department line." Then, he said, after the officer rendered his opinion, "the friendly faction on the committee has a field day criticizing the Secretary of Defense for not doing something the service chief thinks is in the national interest."

On at least two occasions, the services severely undercut Defense Secretary McNamara over key weapons decisions. The first came in 1966 when the Joint Chiefs made known to the House Armed Services Committee that McNamara had overruled their unanimous decision to move toward procurement of an advanced manned bomber. Congress responded by approving $11.8 million not requested (nor later spent) by McNamara. In 1968 the FB-111 (TFX) fighter bomber aircraft—a project favored by McNamara but strongly opposed by the Navy—was killed after the Senate Armed Services Committee asked and received the Navy Air Staff's "professional" advice on the project.

One high Nixon administration official with experience in lobbying for the Pentagon said that most defense lobbying was done as a joint Pentagon-industry venture after the Pentagon had approved a weapons system and wanted to sell it to Congress. He said the Pentagon had Congress organized like a "Marine Corps landing," with generals, admirals, and top civilians "always ready to run up to the Hill whenever a problem develops."[5] The visible part of the Pentagon's lobby force is its "legislative liaison" office, which in 1967 was appropriated a total of $3,810,458—more than ten times the $277,524 in lobby expenses reported by the United Federation of Postal Clerks, the biggest spender that year among private groups required to report their spending under the federal Regulation of Lobbying Act.

Although the government lobbyists "crawl unabashedly" all over the Hill, defense contractors are "far more discreet." "Some Congressmen look askance," the Nixon administration official said, "when a company that's 95 per cent owned by the government asks them to support a project because it will increase business for them." Consequently, he said, the contractors' tactics were to "tiptoe up to the Hill in the middle of the night in tennis shoes and always cover up their tracks." But the members with important defense plants in their districts seldom had to be lobbied because "they vote the way the bread is buttered."[6]

Army engineers hold strategic ground in the battle of divergent interests. For the Congressman who must demonstrate his ability to serve his con-

5. Private confidential communication with James Phillips.
6. *Ibid.*

stituency in direct and visible ways, few ways are as visible and as direct as the public works projects of the Army Corps of Engineers. Each project is considered separately by the Congress, so that it need not be and is not viewed as a part of a larger program. The power to dispense or deny such politically valuable assets as dams and navigation systems is a substantial one and it can be used to advantage by the politician or bureaucrat who holds it to persuade others to support his efforts in other areas. Thus, a President may include in his budget request funds for a dam in Illinois in order to obtain the support of a powerful Illinois Senator in the area of civil rights or some other national program of major importance. Or a House Public Works Appropriations Subcommittee Chairman may add funds for a new waterway in Alabama to buy support for his own favored project in Ohio. Or a senior civil servant in a water agency may argue for the inclusion of a project in Louisiana to maintain the good will and the sympathetic consideration of the powerful chairman of the Senate Appropriations Committee. Or a top Budget Bureau official may approve a waterway in Texas because a Congressman from the local district is a supporter of the President's programs and faces tough opposition in a coming election.

Little matter that the Texas waterway would cost $2 billion to do a job that existing railroads could do at far less cost but with the railroad bill paid by Texas shippers rather than, as in the case of the waterway, by the taxpayers of all fifty states. Little matter that the Illinois dam provides municipal water supply, at little cost to Illinois interests, which could be provided much less expensively from ground water—but at the expense of the consuming Illinois communities. Little matter that the Alabama, Louisiana, and Ohio waterways are immensely costly projects which would create little new wealth but instead would divert economic growth from forty-seven states, which pay most of the bill, to the three states which benefit directly.

The Corps itself, and a few congressional committees, hold greater power to influence the civil works program than does the President. The civil works program has often been called a congressional program, for higher echelons within the executive branch exercise relatively weak control, vis-à-vis the Congress, compared with most military programs. In fact, the Secretary of Defense has delegated program decisions almost entirely to the Secretary of the Army, who in turn has vested this responsibility in his General Counsel (who has the additional title of Special Assistant for Civil Functions). The Congress jealously guards its control over civil works, and strenuously opposes changes, such as the presidential item veto or stronger Water Resources Council coordination, which could transfer some of that control to the executive branch. In the past the ability to provide politically valued projects in specific congressional districts has given the Army a valuable means of enlisting congressional support for other

Army programs, but this political value has diminished in recent years as the size and economic impact of other military programs has outpaced the civil works program.

The Army added the civil works function to its other responsibilities many years ago because it alone could muster the needed engineering capability. The rationale most often offered for keeping the function there is that a military organization can respond more immediately to floods and other civil emergencies and that a continuing peacetime civil works program maintains a military engineering capability for use in times of military need. Neither of these arguments will stand close scrutiny. However, the immense political conflict necessary to transfer the civil works program to a civilian agency within, say, the Department of the Interior, might produce scarcely noticeable dividends in terms of program change and increased efficiency. In fact, it can be argued that interagency competition is a salutary force for the most part and that internalizing conflicts within a single executive department might serve chiefly to take important conflicts out of the public view and increase covert decision-making.

Although there have been and are close links between the military and politicians, the professional military seldom enter directly into political life. Despite the fact that the managerial leadership and symbolic skills of a successful military career tend increasingly to converge, as compared with the characteristic "old" military, toward the requirements of elected office, the opposition of the political professional to outsiders, the self-imposed inhibitions of the military career officer, and the electorate's ambivalence toward the regulars reinforce the pattern of individual nonparticipation. Nor do many officers, retiring as relatively young men, choose politics as their second career.[7]

Although several individual ex-military men have attained political prominence in recent years, retirees as a group have not constituted an important collective political force. The military ethic of political neutrality has to a considerable extent carried over to retirement. Organized political activity among them has been limited to matters of direct material concern, such as retired pay legislation, although the retired military do have a potential influence nationally and, more particularly, in a number of local areas, including the national capital.

7. In recent years only two retired regular officers have served in Congress: Colonel Frank Kowalski, Jr., a 1930 West Point graduate, who retired in 1958 and served as Congressman at Large from Connecticut in the 86th and 87th Congresses, and who made a campaign issue of his opposition to military perquisites; and Navy Captain William R. Anderson, who took a nuclear submarine under the Polar ice cap, currently serving in the Congress from the Sixth District of Tennessee. Morris Janowitz, *The Professional Soldier* (Glencoe, Ill.: The Free Press, 1960), pp. 388-392.

Former military leaders are, like General Lucius D. Clay, more apt to be in the public eye in either national elder-statesman roles, or in roles removed from the mainstream of political life, as exemplified by the deviant, ideological politics of General Edwin A. Walker or Captain John G. Crommelin or General Curtis LeMay. There is doubtless considerable homogeneity of political outlook among the majority of retirees. The mobilization of the retired military for political activity of a rightist character is conceivable under conditions in which personally experienced disadvantage is seen as of a piece with fundamental political decadence in national affairs. There are incipient themes of this character in the media directed to retirees.

But to have served one's military term as a citizen soldier—especially to be a war veteran—is a powerful asset for candidacy for elective office. It is more than that; military service is viewed as a certification of national loyalty, a kind of testing ground of national commitments. There is little evidence that the elected officials' military experience serves to enhance their capacity to pass judgment on military matters, since it often produces a highly personalized perspective, fraught with personal frustration. Nor, as research by John N. Colas demonstrates, does military service produce markedly different political attitudes among national legislators in matters of foreign and military policy.[8] It does serve as a catalyst for political ambition for men whose military experience has brought them closer to identification with the national and international community. Military experience serves many as a substitute for an education in American history. Veteran status operates to give the armed forces the feeling that its needs and requirements will be sympathetically assessed by the legislators; each of the armed forces looks to a group of national legislators who have served in their ranks as their special spokesmen.

Colas's study of the 88th United States Congress reported that two-thirds of the legislators were veterans, and that the concentration was the same in both houses. For the population as a whole, the concentration of veterans is roughly one out of eight, so that veterans are highly overrepresented in the national legislature; in fact, there is no other social characteristic (except being a male) so overrepresented. And since the age distribution of the Senators and Congressmen is much older than that of the veteran population, the veteran concentration for comparable age groups is even greater. Their concentration in Congress is likely to increase in the immediate years ahead, a reflection of the numbers of veterans in the age categories from which congressional membership will increasingly begin to draw.

Colas divides the group into *veterans*—those who have spent some

8. Unpublished manuscript.

portion of their prelegislative careers on active military duty—and *warrior-legislators*—those who have a more intensive relationship with the military, currently either members of the National Guard or the Reserves. He found that of the 66 per cent with military experience, 45 per cent (245) were veterans while 21 per cent (108) were warrior-legislators. Officer status was the typical level of achievement. Among the warrior-legislators, the highest military rank was general grade, 5 per cent; field grade, 80 per cent; company grade, 14 per cent; and enlisted reserve, 1 per cent. The veterans and warrior groups were more Protestant and rural than otherwise, paralleling the recruitment patterns of the military profession and reflecting a "conservative" sociopolitical background. There was a high percentage of Southerners among the Democratic warrior-legislator group, and among the Navy affiliated warrior-legislators Republicans predominated.[9]

There is no reason to believe that prior military status—either as a veteran or in the National Guard or Reserves—gives a political candidate a decisive edge over a nonveteran in winning elections. The available information is mixed, indicating no consistent advantage at best.[10] Nor is there any reason to believe that the political orientation of legislators with or without military experience is decisively different because of this variable. Colas found, for example, that support for the conservative coalition in Congress in 1963-64, within the blocs of Northern Democrats, Southern Democrats, or Republicans, was not related to prior military experience. When it came to support of military-related legislation, the added support given by the warrior-legislators was limited indeed. Critical support was forthcoming not, on the whole, for military establishment legislation in general, but for particular service programs from subgroups of warrior-legislators who had developed close ties with their own service.[11]

The social structure of the United States reflects the consequences of the military experience which national legislators have accumulated. Military service in the armed forces, the National Guard, and the Reserves, buttressed by a network of voluntary associations, creates the social matrix within which national support for the military establishment and its operations are generated. In turn, the political elite of the United States is legitimated by its veteran status. Given the vast size of the military establishment and its crucial role, it is abundantly clear that the linkages between the military and the elected political leadership could not be limited to a few top level points of contact specified by constitutional and formal regulations.

The social structure prevents the direct intervention of career officers into the political arena; but the military serves to certify citizen soldiers as

9. *Ibid.*
10. *Ibid.*
11. *Ibid.*

veterans and therefore as appropriate material for public office. Such a matrix has supplied a significant channel for representing the personnel interests of the military, and, to a lesser extent, a vehicle for transmitting national political objectives to the military.

Intervention by elements of the military establishment in political-level decisions is more likely to be indirect and interstitial than direct and primary. The business of fixing the size and shape of the annual budget request to the Congress, and shepherding it through the authorization and appropriations processes, provides one context for such intervention.

The role of the Congress in the budgetary process for the military establishment is limited primarily by the complexity of the process itself, as well as by the fear of being charged with neglect of the nation's defenses, and by the concern of individual Congressmen and Senators with the welfare of their states and districts. The Congress is not well served by its staff apparatus for digesting and explaining the military budget. The General Accounting Office, the congressional watchdog of the treasury, is preoccupied with playing cops and robbers, exploring and exploiting individual and often atypical instances of mismanagement within the military establishment, and reporting them with considerable fanfare, several years after the event, and sometimes even after corrective measures have been taken within the executive branch. The energies and resources of the GAO might be focused more profitably on broad-scale management reviews.

The Defense budget proposals originate in the military departments, although they are constrained to some extent by the figures in the five-year projections kept up from year to year by the Secretary of Defense's own staff, and changed only with his approval. These proposals are reviewed and modified by the secretaries of the military departments, in consultation with their military chiefs of staff, and submitted to the Secretary of Defense, who also reviews and modifies them, with advice from the service secretaries and military chiefs, and with the help of his own staff, which has been in fairly constant communication with the service staffs all the way through the process, as has the staff of the Bureau of the Budget. The Secretary in turn submits the proposed budget to the President, with whom he has had, of course, periodic consultations on the subject throughout the budgetary process. Before the budget is put in final form, the President will also consult directly with the Joint Chiefs on the major issues involved, as well as with his own White House staff advisers.

In order to give the President, for his part, a sounder basis of factual information and analyses on which to make his budgetary decisions, it has seemed particularly important to strengthen the position of the Bureau of the Budget vis-à-vis the Department of Defense. Throughout the Kennedy and Johnson administrations, the Director of the Budget Bureau was not interposed between the Defense Department and the White House in the same manner as that applied to all other operating agencies. The Budget Director had the power to challenge the Secretary of Defense's rulings before the President, but the burden of proof was upon the Budget Bureau. Throughout the rest of the government, it is the heads of the operating agencies who must appeal the Budget Director's decisions, and bear the burden of the proof. It was this exceptional location of the burden of the proof, rather than the number of budgetary analysts available as such, which resulted in the comparative impotence of the Budget Bureau during the 1960's on national security matters. Shortly after his inauguration, however, President Nixon announced that the Budget Bureau would assume for the Defense budget the same decision-making role it possesses elsewhere, placing the burden of appeal upon the Defense Department Secretary. It remains to be seen whether this alteration will succeed in giving the Budget Bureau operational control over the Defense budget, or whether that budget's size, and its many defenders, will in practice defeat this control.

The Budget Bureau and the Council of Economic Advisers could also perform a more extensive staff role for the President in attempting to assess the broad consequences of adopting different levels of military spending, both on nonmilitary budgets (at all levels of government) and on the entire national economy. The division of national resources between guns and butter is peculiarly a question for presidential decision, but the data base for decision can be improved by providing additional analytical material covering government-wide information. The extension throughout the executive branch of programming-planning-budgeting techniques (PPB) developed in the Department of Defense, under the guidance of the Budget Bureau (and discussed more fully in Chapter 23), and into state and local governments, makes these comparative studies less difficult to accomplish.

There are ample opportunities for interested parties to participate in the initiation of new budget items. A manufacturer with an idea for a new weapon, a high-ranking officer concerned about the state of our defenses and anxious to advance his service interests and possibly his own career, a labor leader with a large union membership in the manufacturer's plant, where current defense contracts are about to be completed, and the Congressman whose district includes the plant, may all find a common interest in the inclusion of funds for development of the new weapon in the next fiscal year's budget. The manufacturer can discuss his idea informally with military and civilian officials who he thinks may be interested. The high-ranking officer can propose a "reprogramming action" to include the new budget item in the budget submission from his service, and he may even be able to bring together representatives of the manufacturer and of the union to argue the substantive case with other officers and civilian officials in his military department. The Congressman may express his concern to department officials that the defenses of the nation will suffer if the new weapon is not developed. But, at least within the establishment as it is currently organized, the issue of inclusion of a new weapon in the budget will rapidly reach a level of decision-making to which its supporters have only limited access—or more likely it will have been abandoned by its proponents, despite their interest, because of the resistance they encounter at an early stage of discussion.

If the proposed budget item is eliminated before the budget reaches the Secretary of Defense or the President, there is no practical way in which the interested parties can get it back in, except through the very limited device of persuading the secretary of the military department or the Chief of Staff to "reclama," i.e., to seek a re-examination of the issue at the next highest level, and the record on reclamas is not much better than the record on petitions for rehearing in the United States Supreme Court. On the other hand, the proponents of a new weapon may be able to postpone the issue, or even to advance the likelihood of its being included in a future year's program, by finding funds within the research and development budget to continue at least the preliminary development of the weapon.

If a controversial item survives, and is included in the budget as it goes to the Congress, the interested Congressman and his allies in the interested military department and in the private sector can and will be active in trying to avoid its elimination at the authorization and appropriations stages of congressional review. In this respect, he and his friends are following a practice similar in kind—if not in degree—to what would be expected with budget requests from the Bureau of Public Roads or from any other government agency.

The most significant difference between congressional handling of the military budget and its handling of other agency budget requests is that the military budget ordinarily goes through the authorization and appropriations processes without stimulating any significant counterpressures for over-all budget cuts. Occasionally there will be a George McGovern or a Wayne Morse to attack some of the underlying premises of the administration's military budget, but until recently these moves rarely attracted more than a handful of votes. In the last several years, of course, congressional attacks upon basic military assumptions have become frequent and widely publicized, if generally unsuccessful.

If, however, an item is not included in the administration's budget proposal, the odds that the Congressman can persuade his congressional colleagues to insert it are very low indeed. Occasionally, two or three budget items are added by the Armed Services Committees, but these "add-ons" are rare exceptions within the over-all budget, and thus far the executive branch has resisted such instructions from the legislative branch. One famous recent incident was the Rose Garden episode of March 1962, in which President Kennedy took the then chairman of the House Armed Services Committee, Carl Vinson, for a stroll in the White House Rose Garden in order to persuade him to abandon his committee's insistence on tripling the funds which the President had requested for the RS-70 bomber. This situation contrasts sharply with the pork-barrel practices that are customary with the annual Rivers and Harbors Bill, in which individual Congressmen and Senators are able to make major additions to the budget by the process of mutual agreement.

It would be easy to conclude that the surrender of responsibility for reviewing and/or revising military plans and programs stems from some shabby relationship by which the favor of lawmakers is bought with awards of military contracts or military installations. But one man who strongly doubts this is a former official of the Department. Reflecting on the source of the political strength of the military establishment, he concluded that it would remain a stronger force than it need be and unrepresentative of the views of the majority of the American people, for so long as the Congress retained the seniority system. The critical decisions on Pentagon spending, he argued, are made by committees whose membership is determined to a considerable degree by their chairmen, and whose chairmen are selected solely on the basis of seniority. What this means, he reasoned, is that conservatives, often with militaristic, chauvinistic, and/or nationalistic tendencies, tend to occupy the critical committee chairmanships because conservatives tend to come from so-called safe seats, and safe seats, in turn, are quite obviously the stuff of which seniority is made. This more often than not has brought Southerners into positions of enormous influence on matters having to do with the military, and, by and large, Southerners tend not only to be good soldiers when they join the military but promilitary when they become members of Congress.

An outstanding example is Congressman L. Mendel Rivers of South Carolina, chairman of the House Armed Services Committee, probably as well-rewarded a partisan of the Pentagon as any House member; his Charleston district bristles with nearly a dozen important defense installations and he is faithful to a fault in his support for more and more military spending.[12] Yet the rewards in his district for this support probably had nothing to do with his violent response when the North Koreans shot down an American reconnaissance plane over the Sea of Japan in April 1969. "There can only be one answer for America: retaliation, retaliation, retaliation," Rivers cried, and he took this martial line, in all probabilty, for no other reason than that he believed in it.[13] The militant turn of mind is

12. On August 12, 1970, Congressman Rivers was given the first "Distinguished American Award" of the Air Force Association together with a lavish celebratory luncheon.
13. Quoted in the *New York Times,* April 20, 1969, sect. IV, p. 1.

not, of course, a uniquely Southern characteristic. Congressman Arends for instance, the senior Republican on the committee, is from Illinois, so that the common denominator may be conservatism and a safe seat.

Another problem reinforcing failure to review is the weakness of the staffs of the Armed Services Committees. These staffs are not large enough or specialized enough to conduct major independent analytical studies of the Defense budget or of the budgetary processes. Given the realities of patronage politics, creating first-rate intellectual capacities in congressional staffs is not an easy effort. But the caliber of the Senate Foreign Relations Committee's professional staff is evidence that it can be done. There have been suggestions that a corps of budget and systems analysts be created within the legislative branch, perhaps attached to the Legislative Reference Service of the Library of Congress, to be available to help individual Senators and Congressmen. This sort of function, however, does not tend to attract first-rate talent (particularly when it is in high demand elsewhere), in part because of an unhappy tradition of using Legislative Reference Service people only to gather evidence in support of previously established congressional positions.

One promising proposal calls for a permanent joint congressional committee—or at least a temporary congressional commission—to examine the relationship of military to other spending, and to establish priorities between them. Examination of the issue of national priorities would provide a context in which particular technical issues would be intelligently addressed, and it would encourage comparisons between domestic and security needs, which the Armed Services Committees are inclined to regard as irrelevant, if not impertinent.[14]

The President may be able to find additional support for an independent review of military requirements in the congressional forum, if he seeks it in other parts of the executive branch. For example, the Secretary of Defense has exercised the prerogative of delivering to the Armed Services Committees of the Congress, and (in declassified or "sanitized" form) to the public, an annual statement on the military posture of the United States. There is no reason why a similar statement on the foreign policy posture and commitments of the United States should not be prepared and delivered by the Secretary of State. The Defense posture statement is reviewed, in the normal course, by the Secretary of State, before it is delivered. But it is a familiar principle of political gamesmanship that the person or the

14. The 1969 Report of the Joint Economic Committee devotes a major section to proposals for "formal and comprehensive study of national goals and priorities with a view to establishing guidelines for legislation and expenditure policy." Report of the Joint Economic Committee, Congress of the United States, on the January 1969 Economic Report of the President, April 1969, Part IV (pages 33-43) "National Priorities and Effective Public Policy." The Brookings Institution has undertaken its own full-scale analysis of the same problem: *Setting National Priorities: the 1971 Budget,* Charles Schultze (Brookings, 1970).

organization preparing the first draft of the statement has an almost un-beatable advantage. This review is by no means equivalent, therefore, to the independent preparation of a posture statement within the Department of State, especially given the limitations on the relative effectiveness of State versus Defense, described in Chapter 3.

An effective, imaginative statement, coming out every year, and incorporating a view of the military establishment as one among many instruments of United States foreign policy, issued by the powerful foreign policy adviser to the President, could make an enormous contribution to public and congressional understanding, and to the instruction of the bureaucracy in the executive branch. No current testimony by the Secretary of State nearly attains this objective. A similar annual posture statement from the Arms Control and Disarmament Agency might be dismissed out of hand by some Congressmen as a "bleeding-heart" product, but it might still be worth getting on the record. The Foreign Policy Statement (*State of the World* address) issued in February 1970 by President Nixon, if instituted on a regular basis, may come to play a similar role.

National priorities are the central issue for Congress, not only because it holds the power of the purse, but also because the complex and technical nature of Defense budgeting can only be made comprehensive if the parts are seen in relation to the larger whole. Otherwise the legislator (or the congressional committee) is likely to be held up by some highly technical and complex issue of fact. A particular issue of fact may be critical to a policy decision. But unless that issue is placed in a matrix of available policy choices, the Congress cannot effectively inform itself or the electorate.

A rigorous examination of national priorities will, of course, involve the Congress in a number of difficult and technical issues of fact in such nonmilitary areas as agricultural subsidies, the preservation of the United States merchant marine fleet, the desirability of a supersonic transport, and the terrestrial value of voyages into interplanetary space. But such issues cannot be ignored or left to specialists alone, especially as the frequent incommensurability of the variables demands the judgment of the generalist.

In the spring of 1969 Senator J. William Fulbright, chairman of the Senate Foreign Relations Committee, was discussing such questions. Senator Fulbright saw the debate then in progress as significant primarily in terms of the far broader question of congressional influence over the Defense budget, foreign policy, and national security. Beyond congressional prerogatives, he expressed anxiety about the larger question of civilian influence over the military establishment, in the executive branch as well as on Capitol Hill. The establishment, he believed, was "presently out of control, but this is due, not to the lack of procedures or the power to do it. It is due to development of circumstances that have led to a nonuse of those controls."

He blamed the Secretary of State and the President, and he blamed himself. "I must confess that I have not really exerted myself as much as I might have in an effort to control the military," he said. "Actually I have been under the feeling that it was useless and utterly futile, that nothing could be done, for example, to cut an appropriation for the Defense Department no matter what I did. This is something that started with World War II. The Congress simply does not review or investigate or exercise control over Defense spending. They vote these bills through with hardly any debate. You get five minutes to ask questions in the hearings and nobody really wants to ask questions. The majority of Senators doesn't want to take responsibility for second guessing the military. But maybe if we can defeat them once, on the ABM [antiballistic missile], just possibly this will encourage Senators and Congressmen to believe that they can exercise some influence across the board. If we can show a majority, if we can demonstrate that it can be done, then maybe we can begin to treat military spending the way we treat all the other kinds of spending. That's why the ABM is important."[15]

Although the fight against ABM was narrowly lost in 1969 the exhilaration of the battle has not been entirely dissipated. Senator Hart described the mood:

When it became clear that Congress would not automatically buy anything put on the counter, a number of things were suddenly no longer for sale. I know that this reasoning sounds suspiciously like someone trying to make defeat sound like victory—a practice not totally unknown in politics. . . . But at least the Congress during the ABM debate fulfilled its assignment to take a critical look at military proposals—an assignment largely ignored for years. We established the fact that questions about military proposals do not indicate any disloyalty to the nation or lack of confidence in military experts.

It is nonsense to pretend that we can buy absolute military safety, just as it is really very poor economics for a family to build a shelter that offers ultimate protection against every contingency. But someone must take the architect's proposals, lay them next to the food and clothing requirements, and strike some reasonable balance. That job belongs to Congress. . . .[16]

15. Interview with Gene M. Lyons, May 1969.
16. See Note 2 above. In the summer of 1970 Senator Edward Brooke of Massachusetts proposed an amendment to the military procurement bill, renouncing as a point of policy a strategic "first strike" on the Soviet Union. Secretary of Defense Laird objected on the grounds that it would "set the precedent that Congress will establish the general characteristics of U.S. military systems" (sic). Senator Brooke replied that "unless Congress addresses the composition and characteristics of the armed forces, its constitutional power is very nearly meaningless," but withdrew the amendment when its defeat became certain. New York Times. August 28, 1970.

5

The Military-Industrial Alliance

The Bureau of Public Roads, a substantially autonomous organization formerly a part of the Department of Commerce, and since 1966 a unit of the new Department of Transportation, administers the Highway Trust Fund, which is currently providing $4.4 billion annually to build and maintain some 900,000 miles of the United States highway network. The Bureau has financed (on a 50-50 basis or, for the 42,500-mile interstate system, on a 90-10 basis) the building of over 225,000 miles of roads in the last twelve years, and expects to finance as many miles in the next twelve years. It is a magnificent engine for its purpose. The only complaint of those who observe its activities from a somewhat broader perspective is that it is perfectly capable, unless restrained, of covering all the open space in the United States (plus a good deal of space now being used to house and otherwise to serve human beings) with eight lanes of concrete (or asphalt) highway. In this endeavor, the bureau would, of course, have the enthusiastic support of the concrete and asphalt industries, the unions of operating engineers, the automotive industry generally and, since roads go everywhere, a good many Congressmen and Senators, as well as state and local public officials.

For many—if not most—of the people who work there, the Bureau of Public Roads is very much like the Department of Defense. They have the same kinds of jobs. Indeed, most civilian employees of both organizations, if asked what they do, would reply, "I am a GS-5 clerk-typist," or, "I am a GS-7 punch-card operator," not "I am a road-builder," or, "I am a defense worker." They have the same kinds of problems, too, the same kinds of near-term goals, and the same sharp focus on tasks that can be accomplished within the organization—more roads or more arms—while the side effects of these accomplishments, or the tasks that are beyond the competence, mission, or legislative authority of the organization, tend to look rather dim and fuzzy. The same kinds of alliances tend to be formed with outside political and economic interests, in spite of the restraining efforts of conservationists or arms controllers.

Some of the differences between the Bureau of Public Roads and the Department of Defense are differences of degree: The bureau is smaller, by two orders of magnitude. Because it is a domestic agency of the federal government, it is limited by the express powers conferred by the Constitution in domestic affairs, as well as by the greater visibility and political exposure of a domestic agency. It does not actually build roads, but only finances and advises on their building. It has no uniformed corps of road-builders, set off dramatically from the rest of the bureaucracy, and heir to a particularly colorful and emotional tradition. Its industrial suppliers are perhaps not quite as specialized to road-building, nor do they command the same wide range of skills as defense contractors. The technology of road-building is a good deal less complex, and the research and development component is small. They have substantial other markets even for their road-building skills as such, in state and local government. And the vital interests of the United States are not, or do not appear to be, as much involved in roads as in defense. The differences in kind are not so much internal as external to the two organizations. They have different impacts on society because they are in different businesses, not primarily because they do business in different ways. In fact, they do business in rather similar ways. This is not to suggest that the existence of a highway-industrial complex justifies or explains away the existence of a military-industrial complex.

The roots of the military complex go back before World War II, when the military could not help but play a key role in public policy, to World War I. Paul Koistinen wrote in the *Journal of American History*[1] that the military moved reluctantly into the alliance with government and industry because it was "suspicious of, and hostile toward, civilian institutions." It had faced involvement in foreign policy decisions in World War II with similar reluctance. Koistinen maintains that Congress and President Wilson compelled the Army to integrate its personnel into the War Industries Board. In the 1920's and 1930's industry and the military collaborated in procurement and planning under the Defense Act of 1920, setting up the Office of the Assistant Secretary of War, which guided planning for total mobilization. The Industrial Mobilization Plan was formulated in 1930 under War Department sponsorship. Businessmen and industrialists were

1. Paul A. C. Koistinen, "The 'Industrial-Military Complex' in Historical Perspective: The Inter-War Years," *Journal of American History*, March 1970, pp. 819-839.

also enlisted in planning, Koistinen says, through such devices as an Advisory Board to the Army Industrial College, and a Business Council; by 1931, roughly 14,000 corporation executives and representatives were reserve officers assigned to the office of the Assistant Secretary of War.[2]

No survey of the failure of the political system to apply countervailing power to the military establishment would be complete without scrutiny of the way in which the interests of the Defense Department, or services or factions within it, mesh with interests and activities of the private corporations that supply that establishment. The development after World War II of what H. L. Nieburg[3] calls "the contract state" built a wholly new engine into the American economy. It has had a considerable bearing on the defense establishment and its relationship to the public weal.

In the mid-1950's, the services found that their "in-house" research and development capabilities were not extensive enough to handle the new generation of immensely expensive and complex weapons systems being purchased. Although the services had been relying on private enterprise to produce most weaponry, they now found that they had to turn there for development of the systems as well.

Nieburg wrote in the *Bulletin of Atomic Scientists* (March 1966) that this erosion of in-house capabilities of all the services was due largely to the growth of Air Force missile-contracting procedures in effect during the 1950's. "The generosity of Air Force contract procedures quickly inflated the technical manpower market," he wrote, "depleting the government's in-house pool and demonstrating great political efficacy. In a sense, the Air Force, through contracting, financed a powerful constituency to advance its interests in Congress." Nieburg said Congress had "served these constituencies well . . . creating a new and powerful kind of political patronage."

Former Pentagon efficiency expert A. E. Fitzgerald claimed that the Air Force, which gained status as a separate service in 1947, "deliberately avoided creation of an in-house capability for the missile age because it wanted to create a big, well-heeled constituency of scientists, organized labor, and industry. It knew that such a constituency would push successfully to keep defense spending high and the Air Force in business." Whether it acted out of such Machiavellian motives, or simply for reasons of greater efficiency, the Air Force in the 1950's began to move far ahead of its sister services in the dominant field of aerospace weaponry, partly by brilliant development of this simple idea—later emulated by the Army and Navy—of nurturing a network of private research and development contractors whose "free enterprise" credentials took the curse off the large use of public moneys. The projects conceived by the R&D "think shops"

2. Koistinen, *op. cit.*
3. H. L. Nieburg, *In the Name of Science* (Chicago: Quadrangle Books, 1966).

in turn produced manufacturing contracts for other private concerns. Large and increasingly important sectors of the private economy were enlisted into the Air Force's program for public recognition and support. Before long, private companies even assumed operations formerly conducted only by the military; they maintained aircraft, fired rockets, built and operated launching sites and missile ranges. Private companies entered into the making of major public decisions, and, in many cases, junior officers and enlisted men of their service sponsors came to serve in such menial roles as liaison agents or clerks.

This "buyer-seller" relationship probably could not have assumed such lavish proportions had it not been for the national-defense-at-any-cost mentality that prevailed during the cold war and was kept alive by naïve faith in the possibilities of nuclear superiority. The result is the widely advertised military-aerospace-industrial complex, sustained for the most part by the $40 billion—half the Defense budget—spent on prime military contracts for the development, production, or deployment of weapons and military equipment.

The ABM program is a solid case in point from its inception. The original "thin" version proposed by the Johnson administration was to cost about $5 billion and would have involved 28 private contractors with plants located in 42 states. It thereby affected the interests of 84 Senators and 172 Congressmen. Even before Robert McNamara announced the decision to build the "thin" system, Arthur Weisenberger & Company, a New York Stock Exchange firm, placed in the *New York Times* financial section a special report on nine companies which took part in the research and development of the ABM's precursor system, the Nike-X; the ad also listed the 28 potential corporations likely to go to work on the ABM, thereby providing jobs for one million or more persons. Before the proposition had been debated, or even presented to the public, the ABM had begun to assemble a constituency too widespread and too strong to be easily headed off.

In the summer of 1969, a full-page newspaper advertisement touted the ABM proposal, and when the *New York Times* identified the signatories, it was learned that 55 of the 340 had defense-industry connections, and a number of these were prominent in companies already engaged in ABM activity under Defense Department contracts.

The ABM case is but one recent chapter in a continuing story. That is how the system works: the interplay of mutual or similar interests, the easy and almost automatic interaction between the military, the manufacturers, the politicians, and the grass-roots community leader, whether he be the mayor or the president of the chamber of commerce. Professor Walter Adams of Michigan State University describes the process and its threat to the countervailing power of government in this way:

the government becomes almost totally dependent on the chosen instruments, i.e., creatures of its own making, for effectuating public policy. Lacking any viable in-house capabilities, competitive yardsticks, or the potential for institutional competition, the government becomes—in the extreme—subservient to the private and special interests whose entrenched power bears the government seal.

This unique buyer-seller relationship, which defies analysis by conventional economic tools, lies at the root of the military-industrial complex and the new power configurations generated by it. . . . Given the political reality of such a situation and the economic power of the constituencies involved, there is little hope that an interaction of special-interest groups will somehow cancel each other out and that there will emerge some compromise which serves the public interest.[4]

The web of linkages between the military, industry, and the government is reinforced by elaborate rituals of lobbying, public relations, and the exchange of mutual favors.

Scientists, technicians, and public relations men employed by a defense contractor spend considerable time at the Pentagon in a task called "market intelligence," that is, checking with Defense Department officials to learn of any potential obstacles threatening rapid approval or funding of a project in which their companies have an interest. If there is trouble ahead, a high-ranking official of the company usually visits the Pentagon official in charge.

In the summer of 1969, a blue-ribbon panel was organized by the Secretary of Defense to recommend reforms in the Defense Department. Senator William Proxmire of Wisconsin analyzed the composition of the fifteen-member panel in a report published in the *Congressional Record* (October 28, 1969) and found that the chairman, Gilbert W. Fitzhugh, was also chairman of the board of Metropolitan Life Insurance Company, which holds roughly $34 million worth of common stock in twenty-four of the hundred largest companies engaged in defense business. Eight of the fifteen held posts with companies with heavy commitments to defense contracts. Contrary to Proxmire's implication, however, the Fitzhugh Report, when it emerged in July, 1970, made a number of reform proposals that were quite radical in their scope and their impact on vested interests within the Department, although it did not attack the problem of countervailing power outside the Department.[5]

Despite the termination of regular Vietnam tours for newsmen, the Pentagon still authorizes military transportation on a "space available"

4. Walter Adams, "The Military-Industrial Complex and the New Industrial State," *American Economic Review*, May 1968.
5. Report of the President and the Secretary of Defense on the Department of Defense by the Blue Ribbon Defense Panel, July 1, 1970.

basis for newsmen, industrialists, and community leaders who wish to visit defense plants or military installations. One of the biggest events of this kind is the annual "Joint Civilian Orientation Conference," in which some seventy business and professional men are treated to an eight-day cross-country tour of military installations. The Aerospace Defense Command recently reported that its distinguished visitor program conducted eighteen to twenty three-day trips a year and exposed 450 to 500 "key community leaders from all parts of the United States to aerospace defense."

The industrial component of the alliance also is adept at winning friends and influencing policy-makers. A former official of the Eisenhower administration, for example, said a common tactic of defense contractors was to formulate a new weapons proposal and approach a key Congressman or Senator before taking the proposal to the Pentagon. Acquiring congenial support, he said, would "position the contractor favorably" with the Pentagon at an early stage of the weapon's consideration. "For instance, an official of an aerospace firm might ask Mendel Rivers to get him an appointment with the Air Force's Chief of Research," he said. "If the Air Force buys the idea, Rivers will claim he didn't influence the decision at all. There's no question, however, that the contractor got in a favorable position to make that sale the minute Rivers made the call."

A 1959 investigation of defense contracting by the House Armed Services Committee uncovered details of a "wining and dining" strategy of persuasion. George Bunker, chairman of the Martin Company, acknowledged that his company had entertained at least twenty-six active duty officers at a weekend retreat in the Bahamas. Bunker denied there was any impropriety involved, saying "a man could neither operate nor compete effectively unless he had a close personal relationship." But spokesmen for the secretaries of the three services agreed that such a relationship "doesn't look well," and could not be condoned.

Another case concerned an invitation to a "small off-the-record party" to discuss the plans and problems of the Air Research and Development Command with its newly appointed chief, Lieutenant General Bernard A. Schriever. The invitation, sent to ten members of Congress (all but two of whom were members of the Armed Services or Appropriations Committees), was issued by three Air Force contractors: Aerojet-General President Dan A. Kimball (a former Secretary of the Navy), General Dynamics' Frank Pace (a onetime Secretary of the Army), and Martin's Bunker. All three men defended the propriety of the proposed party, although it later was called off because of the undue "publicity." Pace defended it as "a means of advancing the interests of the United States of America."

During the years of Defense Secretary McNamara's tenure in the Pentagon, mass entertainment of Congressmen all but disappeared, at least overtly. "McNamara drove the entertainers underground," one Air Force official said. Another Pentagon civilian theorized, however, that "the contractors are just a lot more discreet now. There's still a lot of entertainment going on, but it's usually limited to . . . just one or two Congressmen."

Contacts made at such pleasant occasions and shared interests have led to a more direct relationship with industry for many in the military who find themselves retired after twenty years of service at the peak of their abilities and energy. They are ready for a second career, and defense contractors have been ready and willing employers. The paradox is that the actual influence of retired military officers in industry is far less than their numbers would suggest.

As the number of nationally prominent officers retiring into politics has sharply declined, the role of the military in government policy-making posts has receded. Instead, the public focus of attention has been on the role of the military in defense-related industries and especially in the aerospace complex. There can be no doubt that these industries continuously recruit technical personnel and individuals knowledgeable in the procedures of defense procurement.

The employment of retired officers in defense industry played a direct role in the formulation of President Eisenhower's farewell warning against "the military-industrial complex" and in the genesis of the phrase itself, according to Malcolm C. Moos, who drafted the speech for the President.[6] The issue had first been given some concrete substance three years before by an inquiry conducted by Senator Paul H. Douglas of Illinois into the employment of retired officers by the hundred largest defense contractors. Douglas's inquiry sparked a similar study and extensive hearings in the summer of 1959 by the Hebert subcommittee of the House Armed Services Committee, chaired by Louisiana Congressman F. Edward Hebert. This investigation was part of a bargain to head off an amendment that would have completely barred the employment of retired officers by defense contractors. The amendment failed to pass by only one vote.

It was not until ten years later that the issue arose seriously again with a survey conducted by the Defense Department at Senator Proxmire's request. The 1959 survey found 768 retired officers of the rank of colonel-captain or above employed by the hundred largest contractors. In 1969 there were 2,072. Just ten companies accounted for more than half of the total. The five top employers of retired brass on Proxmire's list were all huge aerospace enterprises. (See Table 5.1.) Proxmire made several additional comparisons between the two lists: the forty-three companies that were among the top hundred both in 1959 and 1969; the ten companies at each point employing the greatest number of retirees; and the ten largest

6. "Moos Recalls Idea for Eisenhower's Militarist Phrase," *Washington Post*, March 31, 1969.

contractors on each list. All of these comparisons showed approximate tripling of retiree hiring during the decade.[7]

TABLE 5.1 A List of the 100 Largest Companies Ranked by 1968 Value of Prime Military Contracts and Number of Retired Colonels or Navy Captains and Above Employed by Them, February 1969

1. General Dynamics Corp	113
2. Lockheed Aircraft Corp	210
3. General Electric Co	80
4. United Aircraft Corp	48
5. McDonnell-Douglas Corp	141
6. American Telephone & Telegraph	9
7. Boeing Corp	169
8. Ling-Temco-Vought, Inc	69
9. North American Rockwell Corp	104
10. General Motors Corp	17
11. Grumman Aircraft Engineering Corp	31
12. AVCO Corp	23
13. Textron, Inc	28
14. Litton Industries, Inc	49
15. Raytheon Co	37
16. Sperry Rand Corp	36
17. Martin Marietta Corp	40
18. Kaiser Industries Corp	11
19. Ford Motor Co	43
20. Honeywell, Inc	26
21. Olin Mathieson Chemical Corp	3
22. Northrop Corp	48
23. Ryan Aeronautical Co	25
24. Hughes Aircraft Co	55
25. Standard Oil of New Jersey	2
26. Radio Corp. of America	35
27. Westinghouse Electric Corp	59
28. General Tire & Rubber Co	32
29. Int'l Telephone & Telegraph Corp[1]	
30. IBM	35
31. Bendix Corp	25
32. Pan American World Airways	24
33. FMC Corp	6
34. Newport News Shipbuilding	6
35. Raymond/Morrison, etc.[2]	6
36. Signal Companies, Inc. (The)	9
37. Hercules, Inc	13

7. Variation in the completeness of reporting by companies in the two surveys and inconsistent practice with regard to the reporting of retired reservists make the reliability of the data questionable. Comparability between companies is also affected because of mergers of companies high on the list (e.g., McDonnell and Douglas Aircraft) and particularly the emergence of the conglomerates (e.g., Ling-Temco-Vought).

Table 5.1. (continued)

38. Du Pont, E. I., de Nemours & Co	3
39. Texas Instruments, Inc	7
40. Day & Zimmerman, Inc	1
41. General Telephone & Electronics Corp	35
42. Uniroyal, Inc	6
43. Chrysler Corp	11
44. Standard Oil of California	6
45. Norris Industries	2
46. Texaco, Inc	4
47. Collins Radio Co	3
48. Goodyear Tire & Rubber Co	6
49. Asiatic Petroleum Corp	0
50. Sanders Associates, Inc	17
51. Mobil Oil Corp[1]	
52. TRW, Inc	56
53. Mason & Hanger Silas Mason	5
54. Massachusetts Institute of Technology	5
55. Magnavox Co	3
56. Fairchild Hiller Corp	7
57. Pacific Architects & Engineering	16
58. Thiokol Chemical Corp	3
59. Eastman Kodak Co	15
60. United States Steel Corp[1]	
61. American Machine & Foundry	7
62. Chamberlain Corp	3
63. General Precision Equipment	23
64. Lear Siegler Inc	4
65. Harvey Aluminum, Inc	4
66. National Presto Industrial Inc	0
67. Teledyne, Inc	8
68. City Investing Co	4
69. Colt Industries, Inc	4
70. Western Union Telegraph Co	5
71. American Manufacturing Co. of Texas	0
72. Curtiss Wright Corp	1
73. White Motor Co[1]	
74. Aerospace Corp	6
75. Cessna Aircraft Co	0
76. Emerson Electric Co	3
77. Seatrain Lines	4
78. Gulf Oil Corp	1
79. Condee Corp	1
80. Motorola, Inc	3
81. Continental Air Lines, Inc	4
82. Federal Cartridge Corp	1
83. Hughes Tool Co	13
84. Vitro Corp. of America	25
85. Johns Hopkins Univ[1]	
86. Control Data Corp	14
87. Lykes Corp	0

Table 5.1. (continued)

88. McLean Industries, Inc	2
89. Aerodex, Inc	5
90. Susquehanna Corp	7
91. Sverdrup & Parcel Assoc., Inc	9
92. States Marine Lines, Inc	0
93. Hazeltine Corp	7
94. Atlas Chemical Indus., Inc	0
95. Vinnell Corp	0
96. Harris-Intertype Corp	4
97. World Airways, Inc	4
98. International Harvester Co	6
99. Automatic Sprinkler Corp	3
100. Smith Investment Co	0
Total	2,072

[1] Not yet reported.
[2] Raymond Int'l. Inc; Morrison-Knudson Co., Inc; Brown & Root, Inc; and J. A. Jones Construction Co.
Source: Congressional Record, March 24, 1969, p. S3074.

Since the Senator's figures were advanced in what armed forces' periodicals regarded as an "antimilitary campaign," they deserve critical scrutiny to determine the extent to which his conclusion of increasing influence between the military and big contractors is valid. The increase noted cannot be explained simply by the increased numbers of retirees in 1969 compared with 1959. The total number of officers retired as colonel-captain and above had only doubled during the period in which prime contractor employment of such men had tripled.[8]

Two factors probably account for much of the increase in the proportion of high-ranking officers working for these contractors. First, in 1959, a higher proportion of all retired Army officers were brand-new retirees and thus still subject to the two-year "cooling-off" restriction on selling to the armed forces.[9]

Second, and more importantly, while aerospace companies account for the majority of jobs, Air Force officers and senior naval aviation officers, particularly those with experience in the advanced systems of missile warfare, did not begin to retire in considerable numbers until the 1960's; only one-tenth of the retired regular general officers in 1959 were Air Force. The aerospace firms on the 1959 list employed several times as many retired Navy and Army officers as Air Force officers. Although the figures

8. The inability to proportion numbers between reserve and regular military components precludes a completely valid comparison.
9. Existing measures relating to avoidance of conflict of interest include cooling-off periods to render obsolete "inside dope" from which an officer might profit, the formulation of a code of ethics by the Department of Defense, disclosures of hiring required in bids and proposals, and the disclosure by retired officers of their employment and duties.

do not exist to prove this conclusively, the big jump in employment by contractors probably took place a few years after 1959 when high-ranking air-age officers began to retire in substantial numbers. Sample survey data on types of employers of retirees suggest that the increase of hirings has leveled off since then.

With the continual increase in the number of retirees and no slackening in the volume of defense industry, the rise in the actual number of retirees employed by the giant prime contractors was inevitable—certainly in the absence of strong external restraints.

It is the absolute number—more than 2,000 ex-brass working for big defense industry—rather than the proportional increase, which carries much of the dramatic impact of Senator Proxmire's disclosure. It is therefore also somewhat immaterial that these 2,000 represent a small fraction of all high-ranking retirees. Even with no allowance made for the reservists who were included by error in Proxmire's tally, only 8.8 per cent of the high-ranking regular retirees were employed by the big defense contractors. We can make a crude extension of this figure to all defense industry since we know that the hundred top companies account for 67 per cent of the value of military prime contracts.[10] If lesser contractors employed an equivalent number of retirees per dollar of their defense prime contracts, the entire prime contractor complex would be employing under 12 per cent of the higher-ranking retirees. This would amount to about 15 per cent of retirees who are working at all (about 40 per cent of retirees above the rank of colonel do not work for pay).

The retired military working in these giant companies are not engaged exclusively in defense-related work, although the majority presumably is. Communications, automobile, and petroleum companies are prominent on the list of the largest defense contractors, as well as a few conglomerates. The figures used by the Senator also overstate the case since part-time employees, board members, and consultants are included, and the same individual may be counted more than once in a number of instances.

In light of the attention to conflict of interest and mutual back-scratching between big defense industry and uniformed personnel, it is noteworthy that only 11 per cent of recently retired officers work in the aerospace and electronic industries which have figured most prominently in such allegations, and only 17 per cent in manufacturing industries of any kind. An exceptionally high number of retired military work outside of the business sector, more than 40 per cent in governmental, educational, medical insurance, or other nonprofit institutions.

On the basis of these data, it is hard to make a persuasive case suggesting that there is remarkable concentration of retired military in war in-

10. This was much less concentration than a decade earlier when the top hundred companies accounted for 80 per cent of the defense contract dollars.

dustries. Indeed, to the extent that there is a military-industrial complex, it does not appear to be taking care of its own as well as it could.

The three lists compiled by the congressional inquiries provide ambiguous evidence as to how important and profitable it is for a defense company to have high-ranking retirees on its payroll. In the main, however, the companies with a large number of retired officers on their payrolls have done quite well in gaining defense contracts. Those with policies seemingly most favorable toward retired officer employment were North American Rockwell, Lockheed, TRW, Inc., Vitro Corporation, General Precision Equipment, and Westinghouse Electric. Other large contractors, however, listed so few retired employees as to be suspect of discriminatory hiring. Curtiss-Wright, for example, was listed with only one retired officer in 1969; Cessna Aircraft with none at all.

The company reports suggest that it is possible to be a big defense contractor and employ few, if any, retired officers. Also, a comparison between the companies in terms of the number of retirees they employed and in terms of changes in their relative standing in volume of defense business reveals that having many retirees on one's payroll has not been an automatic guarantee of competitive success. But neither has it been necessarily a hindrance. For example, in 1959, Boeing, then the largest defense contractor, stood in marked contrast to the two other aerospace firms with the largest volume of contracts, General Dynamics and Lockheed. Boeing employed only a third as many retired officers and less than a fifth as many retired generals as did the other two. As compared with a relatively small company—83rd-ranking Ryan Aeronautical Company—it employed fewer retired generals and only a few more officers in all ranks. But in the 1969 rankings Boeing had slipped to seventh place on the list of defense prime contractors, although of companies in the top group, it had the greatest number of military retired employees per volume of contracts. General Dynamics, which by 1969 had become the largest defense prime contractor with a dollar volume of defense contracts three times that of Boeing, reported 113 retired officers of colonel-captain or above on its payroll— Boeing had 169.

The Martin Company (Martin-Marietta) and General Tire and Rubber had disproportionately large numbers of retirees in both 1959 and 1969, but slipped in their standing on the defense contractor list. United Aircraft, on the other hand, consistently reported few retired military employees relative to its defense business—a third as many as the smaller McDonnell-Douglas Corporation, for example—but moved up from fifth to fourth place in its standing on the list of defense contractors. Bell Aerospace Corporation (Textron) is another example in the same pattern.

The concern of the late 1950's typified by the Hebert inquiry had a different focus from that of Proxmire in 1968-69. In the earlier period, the central issues were ethical ones—were officers reaping ill-deserved personal gains by peddling their influence, were they securing undeserved preferment for their employers, were government dollars being wasted in less-than-optimum defense procurement? A decade later, anxiety about the influence of retired officers rested precisely on the fact that many fewer Congressmen, and fewer influential members of the public, shared the earlier premise about defense needs. As Senator Proxmire put it, the employment of retired personnel by defense industry held grave risks:

> This danger does not come from corruption. Except in rare circumstances this is no more prevalent among military officers than among those with comparable civilian responsibilities. The danger to the public interest is that these firms and the former officers they employ have a community of interest with the military itself. They hold a narrow view of public priorities based on self-interest. They have a largely uncritical view of defense spending. . . .
>
> In too many cases they may see only military answers to exceedingly complex diplomatic and political problems. A military response or the ability to make one, may seem to them the most appropriate answer to every international threat.[11]

In the atmosphere of the late sixties, the military again faced the threat of an outright ban on the employment of retired officers by defense contractors. The national commitment to a defense economy had created defense jobs, validated the legitimacy of employing former military personnel, and given to retired officers the sense of contributing to what they regarded as valued social purposes. Reduced national commitments to defense would not only immediately restrict jobs available for the retired military but could also affect their acceptance by employers and their own prestige. Political pressures against their employment are mounting as the result of the unpopularity of the military during an unpopular war. Some defense industry officials have already indicated that hiring retired officers may pose a serious public relations problem. At the same time, publicized opposition of organized civil servants to government hiring of retired military has become more vehement.

While retiree hiring may involve no conspiracy, some long-term and adverse impacts of the entangling alliance are becoming evident. To some extent, the autonomous nature of major corporations largely dependent on the military market is gradually being reduced. In long-term dealings with its major suppliers, the Defense Department has slowly taken over (either directly or indirectly) many of the decision-making functions which are normally the prerogatives of business management: the choice

11. *Congressional Record,* March 24, 1969, p. S3074.

of which products the company is to produce, the source of capital funds, and the internal operations of the company.[12] This accretion of governmental regulation of the defense industry has been so gradual that on various occasions senior spokesmen for the industry vehemently denied that it is "a captive industry nor is it a tamed one, if these terms convey any idea of relinquishment of managerial or fiscal responsibility."[13]

By awarding massive contracts for research and development, the Department of Defense has come to influence strongly or to determine which new products its contractors will design and produce. The military establishment also uses its considerable financial resources to supply the bulk of the plant and equipment used by its major contractors and a large share of the required working capital. The Department of Defense assumes the managerial decision-making functions of its contractors most pervasively through the standard provisions contained in the procurement contracts it awards. As a result of legislation and regulation, military suppliers are required to accept, on a take-it-or-leave-it basis, many clauses giving the government power of veto on such matters as which activities to perform in-house and which to subcontract, which companies to use as subcontractors, which products to buy domestically rather than to import, which internal financial reporting systems to establish, which minimum as well as average wage rates to pay, and how much overtime work to authorize. In recent years, the role of the military establishment in the internal operations of its contractors has continued to expand.

The trend stems in part from the shift from the general resource requirements for conventional military needs, prevalent during World War II and the Korean conflict, to the highly specialized facilities required for contemporary, high-technology military hardware. A large share of the work currently performed for military programs is carried on in highly specialized facilities specifically built for this purpose, often at the initiative of the Defense Department, which frequently continues to retain title to the factories and equipment. Moreover, many of the companies involved were set up for, and so much of their experience is limited to, the design and production of military weapons systems and related aerospace vehicles. The entangling alliance is further enmeshing both industry and the military. As one former high official in the Defense Department put it: "If you owe the bank ten thousand dollars, the bank owns you; if you owe the bank one million dollars, you own the bank."

All of this has produced a "locked-in" effect wherein major defense companies have difficulty in diversifying into more conventional civilian market areas and thus become further dependent on the governmental

12. See M. L. Weidenbaum, "Arms and the American Economy: A Domestic Convergence Hypothesis, *"American Economic Review,* May 1968, pp. 428-437.
13. Karl G. Harr, Jr., "Experiment in Tomorrow," *Aerospace,* Fall 1965.

customer and suffer further reductions in their ability to compete in commercial markets. The appearance of such government-oriented firms may be significant as a long-run institutional change; such a development may conceivably set a pattern for government programs in other public sector areas. A "demonstration" effect in other parts of the public sector already is taking place. Civilian government agencies that require on occasion large-scale technological and production efforts are also turning to the government-oriented corporations. In most cases to date, these are the same corporations which dominate the military market, and the products that they produce are similar. The two largest examples to date are space systems for NASA—an outgrowth of military intercontinental ballistic missiles (ICBM) programs—and the development of a supersonic transport aircraft (SST) under the sponsorship of the Department of Transportation—an extension of military aircraft development efforts. On a much smaller scale, some of the major defense contractors have become involved in applying advanced technology to education, health, crime control, environmental pollution, and other civil public sector programs. To a significant degree, of course, this represents attempts by these contractors to diversify out of military business.

It would appear that government policy-makers need to take account of the adverse side effects of the use of private industry in defense programs, prior to contracting out to the private sector large segments of new civilian government activities.

On the industry side of the military establishment, the greatest need is to reduce the dependence of defense industry on a single all-powerful customer. To provide a larger market place, defense industry should be encouraged to diversify, even while recognizing that the business style of that industry may not be easily adaptable to the commercial market. Diversification may not, in fact, be feasible below the divisional level within a single company. The same division may not be able to produce (and market) timing devices for warheads *and* washing machines. Within a defense-oriented division, pressures for more business to maintain employment and profit levels will not be affected by the creation (or purchase) of other divisions seeking nondefense business. Still, the fact that an enterprise does not live or die on defense business affects its attitude toward the Defense budget and its role in shaping or trying to shape that budget. It will be less likely to escalate the business-getting struggle.

6

The Civilianized Military Command

The American military man has come a long way from the frontier outposts to the hermit life of Minuteman missile silos. John Wayne, commanding a fort in Indian territory, was required to play an isolated and uniquely martial role; he was in only distant contact with headquarters at Dodge City, and even more distant contact with Washington bureaucracy and urban industrial society. There were few civilians among his professional associates other than the contract surgeon and the Indian agent. He could look forward to a series of assignments of essentially the same character until he reached retirement age, when he would try to supplement his meager pension with other employment, for which he was singularly ill-prepared.

The average officer in the Minuteman missile silo, on the other hand, spends a large part of his otherwise rather dreary working hours on a correspondence course in industrial administration or geopolitics; he lives in a suburban rambler in a community of local civilians; he is in continuing communication with other parts of the country, and even other parts of the world; he has professional contact with civilian technicians, civilian managers, researchers, and consultants. He can anticipate a wide range of assignments, even within the Strategic Air Command. And he can foresee on retirement a number of career opportunities in government, in defense industry, and outside the defense area altogether.

In the new military establishment, military executives behave more and more like civilians. Harlan Cleveland points out:

. . . the men who are running things in our armed forces find little need for a loud voice or a parade-ground manner. They seldom shout; if they want to reach large numbers of troops, they speak quietly, and let electronics do the amplifying. Even with subordinates, an officer seldom raises his voice; some even frame vertical orders as "suggestions," much as a dean would deal with an academic faculty.

A growing proportion of each officer's time is spent in dealing laterally with people not subject to his orders anyway. A captain who calls in air support for his beleaguered company is not dealing up and down a chain of command, but negotiating across several chains of command. The colonel "in command" of an air base may find representatives of fifteen or twenty different United States military organizations camping on the two square miles of "his" base. None of the officers in charge of these operating tasks is responsible to the base commander; they deal with him laterally, as a tenant deals with a landlord.[1]

Not only do military organizations overlap among themselves, leading away from a simple military-style chain of command, but military and civilian organizations often overlap, also affecting the traditional military approach. The defense establishment is so heavily dependent on advanced industrial technology and modern management techniques, which cannot be bought off the shelf and which must be designed to meet special military needs, that military and civilian institutions necessarily interpenetrate, with widening circles of consequences.

These two developments created a need for "military managers," who rival the more traditional "heroic leaders." These military managers in turn became highly civilianized as they faced the problems of research, development, and management found in most large industrial organizations. They are likely in the future to resemble the civilian organization man more than the distinctive and traditional member of the military establishment.

The civilianization of the military has been accompanied by a third complication of the role, which undoubtedly affects the perspective of the military—the entrance of civilian experts into the field of military strategy. This penetration was dramatized by their rise to prominence in the Kennedy administration in 1961 and the subsequent growth in their power. So, too, the centralization of civilian authority in the Pentagon—a continuing trend since the National Security Act of 1947, and later amendments—has been accelerated by the appointment of top level civilians who are applying rational techniques to the problems of defense.[2]

Civilian specialists are, therefore, more and more involved in the day-to-day business of defense. At the same time, military professionals are acquiring new civilian skills in their own self-defense—as in the case of the

1. Harlan Cleveland, "The American Public Executive," in *Theory and Practice of Public Administration,* Monograph No. 8 (Philadelphia: American Academy of Political and Social Science, October 1968), pp. 170-171.
2. Gene M. Lyons, "The New Civil-Military Relations," *American Political Science Review,* Vol. LV, No. 1, (March 1961), 53-63.

systems analysis capacity being built for the Joint Chiefs of Staff, to match the (essentially civilian) systems analysis staff in the Office of the Secretary of Defense.

Defense industry officials need to understand in detail and in depth the military requirements for which they are developing technological solutions, and Defense Department officials need to understand what the defense industry can and cannot do. One of the major problems of the McNamara Pentagon was how to involve senior military officials more deeply in the details of the development process. When Secretary McNamara looked at the source selection process for the TFX, he discovered that the source selection board of general officers, which met to consider the multivolume report and recommendations of the technical staff on the selection of a contractor, had conducted its entire deliberations in only one working day, including the time required to type up their recommendations. The controversy over the role of defense contractors as supervisors and coordinators of other contractors' efforts in developing new weapons systems, and the equally controversial creation of nonprofit "captive corporations" like the Aerospace Corporation, for this purpose, were only stages in the process of increasing interpenetration of the civilian and military sectors. This process does not guarantee either a more efficient or a more effective military establishment, but it is a process likely to continue, and therefore it needs to be taken account of in any effort to modify the impact of the military establishmen on the economy and the society.

A similar process is described (Chapter 3) in the relationship between military and foreign policy decisions. No significant military decision can be made today—on force structure, weapons development, strategy, or operations—which does not have foreign policy implications important enough to require their initial consideration within the State Department, and consultation back and forth across the Potomac. By the same token, many if not most foreign policy decisions require and receive a Defense Department input. This consultation does not determine the relative roles of military and nonmilitary considerations. But it does mean that civilian and military members of the military establishment must increasingly share common concerns about the foreign policy implications of what the military establishment does.

The intrusion of civilians into the "mystique" of military affairs has, at times, bridled the military. They seem to have been denied the very expertise for which they and they alone have been trained. But, at other times, they have responded constructively, by broadening their own capacity to deal with the new range and complexity of military problems. It was the military, for example, who took the initiative in establishing the RAND Corporation in 1946 to harness civilian science to military strategy. And the military have developed a large and expanding program through which young officers are sent to civilian universities for advanced education in the physical and social sciences. Indeed, there is by now a formidable corps of highly educated military officers who, in their knowledge of scientific and political matters, rank among the best-trained men throughout government service and possession of the Ph.D. is rapidly becoming a prerequisite for promotion to the very highest ranks. Men such as these wholly defy any shopworn stereotype of the "military mind."

The growing recognition among members of armed forces that they would be well advised to prepare themselves to assume a civilian second career in their forties may further accentuate the civilianization of the military by channeling their ideological and symbolic attachments in directions they perceive as compatible with their eventual status. The trend toward shorter military careers is in some ways antithetical to the professionalizing developments of the military that have evolved in the recent past. The shorter the career outlook, the more the military career approaches the model of the *Dienst* (service) of the reservist rather than the total life-identity of the professional. With such developments, there presumably may be greater tendencies toward extramilitary professional identification—for example, with specialists in kindred civilian occupations.

The employability of retired professional soldiers has been enhanced by the increased convergence of military and skill hierarchies. Even the troop commander and the military staff specialist think of themselves as administrative specialists. The pressure on military men to de-emphasize the distinctively military aspects of their skill is occurring precisely at a time when the military is trying to defend itself against progressively greater civilian encroachments into its domain. As the civilian scientist, political expert, and administrator have taken on increasingly large functions in the defense realm, the military has been faced with an increasing burden of asserting the claims of a specific military expertise and mystique. But with an eye toward second-career jobs, there is a contrary pressure to emphasize how nondistinctive is military experience. From discussions such as those of Janowitz and Feld, one may infer that the loss of the more objective and apparent bases of a distinctive military identity may not lessen at all the strains toward such an identity that are inherent in the military calling—what Feld refers to as "that intense form of parochial allegiance ... essential to military life."[3] Lacking objectives based on work, organization, and technology for a differentiated self-image, military men may be

3. Morris Janowitz, *The Professional Soldier: A Social and Political Portrait* (Glencoe, Ill.: The Free Press, 1960); Maury D. Feld, "Military Self-Image in a Technological Environment," in *The New Military*, Morris Janowitz, ed. (New York: Russell Sage Foundation, 1964), p. 177.

led to seek it through accentuation of attachments to more rigid ideologies and to symbolic ritualized practices.[4]

The conflict in Vietnam has served to complicate the impact of the military on American social structure, because it has hardened professional perspectives. Moreover, the pressure of international events is certain to lead to continued relatively high levels of fiscal support for the military but with considerable civilian pressure to reduce manpower levels. The military is very likely to seek to rely more and more on "professionals"—that is, longer-term career personnel—and to struggle to cut down on personnel turnover. As a result it is likely to have a greater impact on a smaller number of men who will be serving in a more self-contained agency and in an establishment more separated from civilian institutions despite the presence within its own stronghold of civilian experts.

In recent decades the large numbers and wide variety of kinds of officers needed to accomplish the military mission has significantly broadened the social base of the profession of arms. The service academies cannot supply either the numbers or the range of skills required; hence the services have had to lean increasingly upon recruitment of civilian college graduates and, above all, upon university ROTC programs, for their career officers. The striking and important result is that the decision-making elements within the military structure increasingly come from an essentially civilian social, educational, and cultural background. This tendency has been enhanced by the educational requirements implicit in high-level policy-making. Two students of this phenomenon, Masland and Radway, concluded that "it is likely that [military] officers assigned to [policy] positions will have significantly more formal educational preparation than comparable civilian officials." The implication is that this preparation will improve "an officer's ability to grasp large, complicated situations and to adapt creatively to changing circumstances"—a drastic change from the narrow unadaptability of the stereotyped image of "the military mentality."[5]

The trend toward the professional military both separates and distinguishes the civilian and the military identities. The schizophrenic dual identity is reflected especially in the training of future officers. The service academies, while still highly distinctive, are becoming more, not less, like civilian schools. Convergence, not divergence, is their theme.

The number of academy graduates has risen sharply, along with increases in other recruitment programs. Before the Air Force Academy opened in 1955, academy enrollments totalled about 6,200. When cur-

4. For a more extended discussion of these matters, see A. D. Biderman and L. M. Sharp, "The Convergence of the Military and Civilian Occupational Structures: Evidence from Studies of Military Retired Employment," *American Journal of Sociology*, January 1961, pp. 381-399.

5. John W. Masland and Laurence I. Radway, *Soldiers and Scholars* (Princeton: Princeton University Press, 1957), p. 503.

rent expansion programs end (about 1971), combined enrollments in the three academies will be over 13,000. This increase of more than 100 percent will enable the academies to supply a significantly larger percentage of all newly commissioned *regular* officers. Still, there are recruitment difficulties that must be countered by a rigorous and aggressive public relations campaign.

And recruitment difficulties are compounded by attrition. Attrition is a long-standing problem at the academies, where as many as one-third of an entering class may fail to graduate. The over-all rate of attrition is a bit lower, and it has been relatively stable in recent years, but the stability conceals significant changes in the cause of separations and withdrawals. In the past the major reasons were academic, but now they are motivational. The academies are responding by a tactical retreat on various fronts. Students are now permitted to choose among individual electives and "major" fields of study or "areas" of concentration. The Naval Academy now offers majors in about two dozen fields, e.g., marine engineering, economics, chemistry, and Far Eastern studies, and the option of two degrees—the Bachelor of Science in Engineering or the straight Bachelor of Science; the Air Force Academy offers a slightly larger number of majors, each requiring a somewhat larger number of courses; the Military Academy has been a trifle more circumspect because the prospect of a split curriculum has alway activated fear of a divided Army; West Point now offers four "areas of concentration"—applied and engineering science, basic science, humanities, and national security and public affairs—which are in turn divided into twenty-two "fields." Students who prefer not to choose an area or field may elect a program in general studies; a quota system ensures that not more than 10 per cent will concentrate in the humanities, and not more than 35 per cent in any other area.

These major changes have been accompanied by a great proliferation of course offerings. The number of subjects taught has increased by a factor of from four to seven, depending on the particular academy and on whether 1948 or 1958 is selected as the base period. The result is that curricula are much more like those of civilian colleges than they were before. So are methods of instruction. To be sure, prepackaged materials, texts, recitations, and tests are still more in evidence at the service academies than at the civilian liberal arts institutions with the strongest academic reputations. But the use of paperback books is growing, particularly in the humanities and social sciences, and there is a discernible trend toward fewer and more comprehensive examinations, more seminar instruction, independent research, and honors work. An illustration of the latter is the Trident Program, adopted by Annapolis in 1963, which permits a few midshipmen to be excused from most of their senior year courses in order to undertake a major research project, usually in the sciences or engineering.

Finally, the departmental structure of the service academies—which has important implications for the distribution of power and therefore for the direction of change—is more like that of civilian institutions than it was before. It is true that West Point and Annapolis continue to subsume philosophy, music, and art under literature.[6] But West Point is now divorcing chemistry from physics, and history from social sciences, and Annapolis has divorced History from Government.[7]

The greater availability of advanced courses, taught in more highly differentiated or specialized departments, has helped the academies meet the needs of students who enter prepared for advanced standing (some have had several years at a civilian college while awaiting appointment), or who are able to progress faster than their peers, but who must nevertheless remain a full four years to complete military requirements. The Air Force Academy, for example, has induced selected universities, e.g., Indiana, University of California, Los Angeles, the Fletcher School of Law and Diplomacy, to grant credit toward a master's degree for advanced courses taken at the academy. The Naval Academy adopted a comparable program in 1967.

Vying for institutional recognition in the normal American manner, academy officials often debate which institution has the best balanced program and which is the most innovative. The Naval Academy defends its strong emphasis on science and engineering. As a 1967 study insisted, "The Navy is committed to a technological environment. . . . This is not a State Department-sponsored institution."[8] The Air Force Academy, on the other hand, is proud of its emphasis, greater than at the other two schools, on the social sciences and humanities. Officials there are also likely to observe that they started earlier and went further in such matters as electives, majors, number of offerings,[9] number of specialized departments, graduate credit courses, and the relegation of military training and athletics to a minor place in the student's program.

Unquestionably, the Air Force benefited from the lighter hand of tradition. It also benefited from the career structure of the service, which permits a somewhat greater degree of specialization. But it must also be noted that the first staff of the Air Force Academy drew heavily upon West Pointers who had discussed these matters intensely; that the superintendent of the Naval Academy had requested a study of electives in

6. The Air Force Academy has a separate Department of Philosophy and Fine Arts.

7. West Point separated history from English in 1926, whereas history, political science, economics, and English have always been separate departments at the Air Force Academy.

8. *Report of the Professional Training and Education Committee,* U.S. Naval Academy, November 20, 1967.

9. For example, three times as many as West Point, at this writing, in such subjects as psychology, sociology, and anthropology.

1953; and that in a contest for priority, the palm should probably go to the Royal Military College of Canada, which had introduced a split cirriculum before World War II.

Growing convergence between military and civilian education at the undergraduate level is apparent also in the teaching staff, where generalists are being replaced by specialists able to deal with new curricula. Although the process is incomplete, its direction is clear: greater insistence on graduate work prior to appointment; more opportunity to enhance competence while on the job; and a demand for prerogatives enjoyed by faculty members at civilian institutions. Among its unobtrusive but important agents are junior faculty members, whose ranks are replenished annually. Fresh from civilian universities, they take a lively interest in current intellectual trends. A few years ago junior social scientists pressed for studies of development or modernization of emerging nations. They now offer seminars on poverty, student unrest, race relations, and urban violence. They not only attend professional meetings throughout the country but play host to such gatherings at their own institution.

In the social sciences and humanities the process applies most forcefully to the Air Force Academy; in the basic and engineering sciences to the Naval Academy. But curricular changes at all three academies promise to enhance the influence of professionally specialized faculty. Officer instructors are assigned for periods varying from three years in the case of Army officers to six years in the case of nonflying Air Force officers. Some, however, serve longer, and the number is growing. Most departments have one or two "permanent professors." There now also exists a new category, "tenure associate professors," whose tours of duty are expected to be relatively long. Since World War II department heads at Annapolis have served for an average of slightly less than two years. But the Navy contends that continuity and expertise can be provided by a layer of civilian instructors, and in 1962 the Secretary of the Navy went so far as to imply that all departments, except those that dealt with naval science, would eventually be manned almost entirely by civilians. Although this did not materialize (there was, indeed, serious opposition from naval officers), the number of civilians rose 30 per cent in the next five years.

The concept of departmental autonomy is growing at the academies. So is demand for better office space, more secretarial staff, sabbatical leaves, opportunity to establish closer relationships with students, a larger voice in the determination of educational policy, and that hardiest of all perennials, lighter teaching loads. One or another of the service academies already has a committee on faculty affairs, a faculty forum, a faculty council, even a junior faculty council. It is safe to predict that professional aspirations will be aired in such places with increasing vigor.

Sensitivity to civilian standards and practices in the outside world has tended to inhibit the growth of unique or extreme ideological postures among the faculty at the academies. They are capable, for example, of inviting a guest speaker who proceeds to strongly criticize Dean Rusk's conduct of foreign affairs, condemn the regime in Saigon, express doubt that the Soviet invasion of Czechoslovakia posed a threat to NATO, and describe Haiti's government as "much worse than any Communist government could possibly be."[10]

At the official level the academies project what may best be described as an official view—a conventional, if not actually bland, perspective. In domestic policy this is reflected in the quick reassurance given to Congressmen who inquire whether an academy teaches any "radical new social concepts."[11] In foreign policy it is best reflected in the galaxy of well-known persons who have predominated at West Point's Student Conferences on U.S. Affairs since 1949. The names of Acheson, Dulles, Averell Harriman, Nitze, Nelson Rockefeller, and Rusk are supplemented by those of senior officers, academicians, and foundation officials.

The new trend is reflected in Lovell's findings on differences between fourth classmen and first classmen at West Point. Fewer graduating students believe in the inevitability of all-out war; fewer believe the Korean War illustrated a Communist intent to conquer the world; and fewer think neutralism is the result of lack of moral fiber. More broadly, on the basis of observations made as long ago as 1962, Lovell reported some shift from the late 1950's to the early 1960's from "heroic" to "managerial" orientations and from "absolutist" to "pragmatic" strategic perspectives.[12]

These trends are resisted by some outside forces. In one wide-ranging investigation by a subcommittee of the House Armed Services Committee led by Representative Hebert, already referred to, Hebert expressed satisfaction that the Naval Academy, in his words, was moving from "the academic left" to "the professional right"; he recommended that academic deans, who were ordinarily expected to serve until retirement, be limited to four-year renewable terms, and he expressed anxiety that curricular studies

10. *Proceedings of the Twentieth Annual Student Conference on United States Affairs,* United States Military Academy, December 4-7, 1968. The speaker was Bill D. Moyers, former aide to President Johnson.

11. *Administration of the Service Academies, Report and Hearings of the Special Subcommittee on Service Academies of the House Armed Services Committee,* 90th Congress, 1st and 2nd Sessions, 1967–1968, p. 10582.

12. John P. Lovell, "The Cadet Phase of the Professional Socialization of the West Pointer," University of Wisconsin Ph.D. dissertation, 1962, pp. 149-162. See also the summary in John P. Lovell, "The Professional Socialization of the West Point Cadet," in Janowitz, *The New Military,* pp. 119-157. "Absolutists" believe the Communists are intent on world conquest, that nuclear war is likely, massive retaliation is the soundest policy, and that neutrals are unreliable, if not potentially hostile. "Pragmatists" believe the Communists are expansionist, that some kinds of conflict are likely, that America must be prepared for all contingencies, graduated deterrence is the best course, and that allies may be essential.

were being made by men more concerned with academic content than with professional and military training.

But supporters of the academic program also have powerful external allies. Sometimes an individual intervenes; the most notable probably is Vice Admiral Hyman S. Rickover, one of whose targets is anti-intellectualism. Boards of Visitors composed of private citizens and members of Congress and *ad hoc* committees have been important in reinforcing the academic trend. The Folsom Board, established March 31, 1959, by the Chief of Naval Personnel, composed mostly of civilian academic administrators, served essentially to endorse and legitimize changes already planned at the Naval Academy. A 1966 visit to Annapolis by an evaluation team of the Middle States Association had much the same effect.

An indicator of the prevailing ethos at the service academies is that commandants, whose staffs have in time past been citadels of anti-intellectualism, now contemplate the assignment of prospective "company officers" to graduate school to study behavioral science, either because they feel they must dangle such bait to compete for the men who are often in demand by academic departments as well, or out of a growing conviction that knowledge of psychology, human relations, testing, counseling, and the like will make better training officers.

In a number of other, often subtle ways, the convergence of military and civilian styles is in process at the academies. All academies now discourage sanctions in the form of corporal punishment, denial of food, or humiliation. Training officers testify that it is no longer good form to "pull rank." Though students are still faced by many special requirements, the word has gone out that these are to be "meaningful," "businesslike," and "career relevant." Privileges are related more closely to performance; rewards are substituted for threats. The sensibilities of upperclassmen are also considered more carefully. Reveille comes a bit later at West Point these days; airmen get a slice of unscheduled time in the evening. One academy or another now permits selected students to wear civilian clothes, drink alcoholic beverages, and to drive their own cars under carefully specified circumstances. All academies, moreover, have begun to give students a larger voice in the formation of educational policy. All are more generous with leave, including long weekends. Each supports a flourishing program of extracurricular activities, the most attractive of which—skiing, debating, glee clubs—enable students to leave the reservation. The life-style at the academies more and more resembles that of the college campus—even to a narcotics problem —but there is still a considerable distance between the two.

But as these young men approach graduation, they become more aware of a modifying fact of life—belief in combat virtue exemplified by classical heroes is particularly strong among field commanders, and these values are important to promotion boards. Graduates understandably display increasing interest in electing "line" or combat specialties associated with "the charismatic leaders whose exploits liven the annals of military history."[13] Such elections, in turn, often lead to unusually strong identification with a particular service; and service loyalty may be transformed into service bias. The academies do nothing extraordinary to inhibit the formation of such bias or to lay the foundation for close interservice collaboration. Shortly after World War II, there was talk about merging the institutions, or requiring cadets and midshipmen to take a significant part of their education together. But not much has happened.[14] If anything, there has been retrogression. In the past, graduates of one instituiton could choose to be commissioned in the service of another; today this is impossible unless the student has a special reason, such as family tradition.

The appropriateness of these conditions is questionable. Given the nature of modern conflict, given sophisticated and costly weapons and inexorable political constraints, it is difficult to preserve the priority accorded to combat virtues in an earlier age. Yet it is just as obvious that those virtues are not yet obsolete. Within the military academies this is reflected in competing codes of behavior. As one official statement put it:

The Academy must fuse two potentially conflicting values: on the one hand the spirit of intellectual integrity and inquiry, which may downgrade deference to authority unless rationally supported, and on the other hand the spirit of military loyalty and discipline, which sometimes accents deference to authority without rational justification.[15]

The dimension of social background intersects with that of Academy experience. Though most Army generals no longer come from rural backgrounds, the majority of today's West Pointers come from small or medium-sized towns rather than great metropolitan centers like New York, Chicago, Los Angeles, and Detroit. Actually, the metropolises are seriously underrepresented. If cadets from military (and mobile) families are excluded, 65 per cent of all entrants come from towns of fewer than 50,000.[16]

At West Point, where figures are available for the period since World War II, the proportion of cadets from business and white-collar families has dropped; the proportion whose fathers were skilled or unskilled laborers has risen significantly.[17]

These indicators of middle or lower middle-class origin are supported by

13. Lovell, in Janowitz, *The New Military*, p. 125.
14. For a Canadian contrast, see Richard A. Preston, *Canada's RMC* (Toronto: University of Toronto Press, 1969).
15. *Five Year Plan for the United States Air Force Academy*, Headquarters, United States Air Force Academy, May 1968, pp. 7-8.
16. John P. Lovell, "The Cadet Phase," pp. 80-83. See also Morris Janowitz, *The New Military*, p. 21.
17. Lovell, p. 84.

data on religion. Only 30 per cent of West Point plebes (freshmen) belong to those denominations (e.g., Episcopal, Presbyterian, Congregational)
which include many high-status families. Most belong to Protestant denominations (e.g., Methodist, Baptist, etc.) or to the Roman Catholic Church,
many of whose members are of lower middle-class origin. The proportion of
Catholics has risen steadily since World War II and now stands at 33 per
cent. Two per cent of all cadets are Jews, a figure well below the national
average for all college students (8 per cent) and even further below the
average (12 per cent) for institutions of comparable selectivity as measured
by entrants' test scores.

Between 1870 and 1961 West Point enrolled an average of less than
one black student each year; and Annapolis had even fewer. But recruitment of blacks is now a major goal of each academy, and determined efforts,
including the use of already enrolled blacks to search for others, are beginning to bring results. Not all academies will publicize detailed figures, but
the number of blacks at each is now measured in the dozens, with most of
the increase taking place since 1966.

Each of the academies compares favorably academically with national
averages,[18] but compared to more selective colleges such as Dartmouth, on
the other hand, the academies received fewer students who stood in the top
tenth of secondary school classes, and significantly fewer who scored over
700 in College Board aptitude tests. West Pointers are far more likely than
civilian freshmen to have held top office in high school, to have won a
varsity letter (70 per cent) and to have been captain of a team (33 per
cent). Of those who came to West Point in 1969, an astonishing 51 per
cent had played varsity football in school.[19] They are more ambitious, forceful, hard-driving, and dominant than civilian undergraduates. They are less
likely to be "turned off" by an emphasis on authority, conformity, tradition,
or patriotism. They are less introverted and artistic.[20]

It is not surprising that the Military Academy students are less libertarian than contemporary civilian undergraduates. According to a recent
survey, West Pointers are more likely to feel that college officials (a) have
been too lax in dealing with campus protesters; (b) should be authorized
to clear student publications; (c) have the right to bar persons with extreme
views from speaking on campus; and (d) have the right to regulate student
behavior off campus. Fewer West Pointers feel that students should have

18. Hebert, *Hearings,* p. 10384.
19. Arthur E. Wise, *A Comparison of New Cadets at USMA with Entering
Freshmen at Other Colleges,* Office of Research, United States Military Academy,
March 1969.
20. Lovell, "Cadet Phase," pp. 96-98. The American Council on Education's
survey found that they were 50 per cent more likely than civilian undergraduates
to think it important to have administrative responsibility for the work of others.
Wise, *op. cit.*

a major role in specifying curricula or that faculty promotions should be based in part on student evaluations; they are less likely ever to have argued with a teacher in class. They are twice as likely to have chosen their institution in the belief that "most other students there are like me."[21]

Nor is it surprising that such a group should have "hard-nosed" views on foreign affairs. When West Pointers were compared with a set of Dartmouth undergraduates weighted toward the military by the inclusion of ROTC students, a higher proportion of the West Pointers believed that total war between the United States and Communist forces was likely in the next fifteen years; more also believed that limited nuclear war was likely. Although the contrast was less striking, the cadets led in believing that neutrality is caused by Communist influence in neutral nations, or by lack of moral fiber; that the Korean War illustrated the desire of Communists to conquer the world; and that United States forces were unnecessarily denied victory in that conflict.[22] But one cannot conclude that the cadets held exceptional views. As Lovell notes, a comparison with Gallup Poll figures on the likelihood of major war suggests that on this particular question the Dartmouth group was deviant and the West Point group was closer to the mainstream of American opinion.

Such differences become significant, however, in view of the fact that graduates of colleges like Dartmouth often hold senior posts in the national security establishment. There are other important differences between senior civilian appointees and potential military leaders. Civilian federal executives are much more likely to come from urban or suburban upper middle-class families. More than 50 per cent of the under secretaries and assistant secretaries appointed by President Kennedy were born in metropolitan areas.[23] Over 20 per cent of a much larger group of political executives who served between 1933 and 1965 had attended one of eighteen famous residential preparatory schools in the East, and the proportion rose to 30-40 per cent when the analysis was confined to national security agencies.[24] The civilian appointee is less likely to be Catholic, twice as likely to belong to a high-status Protestant denomination, and twice as likely to be a Jew.[25] Because so many political appointees are lawyers—44 per cent in the survey just cited—the odds are that they rank high in verbal skill; on this attribute West Point entrants do not rank high; at least they score below students in university-related colleges.

Finally, modest but suggestive data are available on differences between

21. Wise, *op. cit.*
22. Lovell, "Cadet Phase," pp. 155-160.
23. Dean E. Mann, *The Assistant Secretaries* (Washington D.C.: The Brookings Institution, 1965), p. 291.
24. David Stanley, Dean E. Mann, and Jameson Doig, *Men Who Govern* (Washington D.C.: The Brookings Institution, 1967), p. 20.
25. *Ibid.,* p. 14.

entering cadets and new Foreign Service officers. While the latter now come from families of approximately the same economic status, they are twice as likely to come from urban areas and only half as likely to be Catholic. When they describe themselves they use such phrases as "cultured," "intellectual," "sophisticated," "less likely to be middle-brow," "rebellious," and "less likely to be cooperative." This is clearly different from the image West Point cadets have of themselves.[26]

Recent social developments have introduced a new factor into the situation. The growing unpopularity of all things military among American young people means that a narrower range of individuals is likely to apply to the service academies. Increasingly it is predominantly the highly motivated and determined young man from a distinctly conservative social background who will be able and willing to buck peer-group pressure and choose a military career. In this sense the anti-military bias of the youth culture ironically may be generating a more "militaristic" military profession in the future. In any case, this new trend toward a more conservative student body at the service academies runs counter to the liberalizing trend within the academies' faculty, administration, and structure. The net result may be that at least for the foreseeable future, military men on academy faculties will be more civilized than the plebes in their classes.

For various reasons, then, to strike a proper balance among goals in military education is not easy. Morris Janowitz points out that "current indoctrination in the armed forces is designed to eliminate the civilian contempt for the 'military mind.' " He elaborates:

> The "military mind" has been charged with traditionalism and with a lack of inventiveness. The new doctrine stressed initiative and continuous innovation. The "military mind" has been charged with an inclination toward ultranationalism and ethnocentrism. Military professionals are being taught to de-emphasize ethnocentric thinking, since ethnocentrism is counter to national military policy. The "military mind" has been charged with being disciplinarian. The new doctrine seeks to deal with human factors in combat and large-scale organization in a manner conforming to contemporary thought on human relations.[27]

Still, there are countervailing forces in the demands of the military role that encourage indoctrination along lines that are more conservative, chauvinistic, and authoritarian. Certainly, as Janowitz points out, military atti-

26. John E. Harr, *The Professional Diplomat* (Princeton: Princeton University Press, 1969), pp. 175-193. Harr also notes (p. 183) that three-fourths of all mature Foreign Service officers described themselves as "somewhat liberal" or "liberal" in political orientation, while the proportion of military officers doing so ranged from one-fourth in the Navy to one-third in the Air Force.
27. Janowitz, *The Professional Soldier*, p. 13. See also Chapter 5 above.

tudes about political and social issues are influenced by the nature of the military system and the background of the officer corps as well as by the demands of combat.

Although the changes in operating environment, recruitment, and education are influencing the nature of military attitudes, there are important limits on how far the military can become civilianized or nonmilitarized. According to Janowitz: "The military establishment has not lost its distinctive characteristics. . . . The need for heroic fighters persists. The pervasive requirements of combat set the limits to civilizing tendencies."[28] Whatever new and challenging tasks the military have to assume, their ultimate responsibility is to the demands of combat.

But not all students of military affairs have looked upon the civilianization of the military as a blessing, even from the viewpoint of strengthening civilian control. One important analyst, Samuel P. Huntington, has argued that military professionalism should be strengthened as the most efficient means of ensuring unchallenged civilian control. In his influential book, *The Soldier and the State,* Huntington concludes after detailed historical analysis that military professionalism by its nature involves the acceptance of, even the desire for, civilian control. It is only when military professionalism is diluted by "civilianizing" influences that it can begin to entertain ambitions of mastery of, rather than service to, the goals and purposes of the state. On these premises, Huntington erects a distinction between two kinds of control of the military. "Subjective control" aims at forestalling the military from defying civilian authority by instilling within the military the same values and social philosophy as the civilian authority possesses. "Objective control," which Huntington argues is more efficient and more sure, aims at thoroughly reinforcing the values and culture of military professionalism, with its inherent respect for the constitutional sovereign.[29]

Indeed, whether the considerable overlapping of military and civilian functions within the military establishment makes for a more open or a less open relationship with the outside world is a debatable issue. By analogy to Huntington's distinction between "objective" and "subjective" civilianizing of the military, it can be argued that absorption of functions formerly conducted outside the organization makes it less rather than more responsive to outside influences.

On balance, the contrary is perhaps more likely to be true. The presence of individuals and groups in the establishment who are directly concerned with problems formerly considered outside the establishment cannot help but open windows on the great world. At the same time, an organization that has internalized a large part of its needs and requirements presents a

28. Janowitz, *The Professional Soldier,* p. 33.
29. Samuel P. Huntington, *The Soldier and the State* (Cambridge: Harvard University Press, Belknap Press, 1957), pp. 80-97.

more formidable aspect to the outside world, once it has made up its collective mind on a course of action. The professional military and the civilians make their bargains first inside the walls of the Pentagon. And the very fact that the professional military is no longer a race apart makes its activities seem a more natural and less prominent part of the landscape. One must explore the impact of the military on the civilian as well as of the civilian on the military. It is certainly possible that the civilian society has become more militarized than that the military has become civilianized.

Huntington's theories raise other disturbing questions for the contemporary practice of civil-military relations in the United States. Huntington implicitly suggests that civilianization of the military via "subjective control" necessarily implies the militarization of the civilians—precisely the historical reality of the current period. Yet in America the civilianization of the military has been only partially a product of the reigning ideologies. It has been also partly a response to the realities of the national security problem. The highly technological nature of modern warfare makes it imperative that the military acquire scientific, engineering, and managerial skills that have little to do with traditional qualities of military leadership. Pursuing the development of the military establishment in competition with nonmilitary demands for resources involves the military in the predominantly civilian political processes by which priorities and choices are decided upon. The intrinsically interlocking questions of military and foreign policies have made it impossible to prevent the military from considering the political aspects of alternative strategies. In some ways, Huntington's "objectively controlled," purely professional military seems feasible only in the pre–World War One universe. For better or worse, we now are all quasi—civilians in a quasi-military, quasi-civilian, society.

7

The Military, the Budget, and National Priorities

Since the days when the student radicals of the thirties chanted "schools not battleships," public debate has attempted, with little success, to find a common calculus for the benefits of military and nonmilitary spending. The debate has failed in part because no one has yet devised a framework in which the need for an additional battleship (or a nuclear carrier, or a fighter wing, or a division) can be effectively measured against the need for an equivalent dollar value of schools or hospitals or job training programs. Lacking such a framework as well as a clear national commitment on priorities, the division of national resources between military and nonmilitary needs has proceeded on the basis of a political struggle among the various contestants, shaped by shifting popular concern about the state of the world and the state of the country.

In the post-Korea period, difficulties arose when the military budget remained at such a high level that the political contest between Defense and other claimants became an uneven one. Budgetary changes from year to year are incremental, and calculations begin with the level of the current year's budget. Of the approximately 33 per cent of gross national product accounted for by public spending, 9 per cent goes for defense against 24 per cent for all other federal, state, and local programs. In the fiscal year 1971 budget, about 8 per cent of GNP goes for defense and another 1 per cent could be considered to be for related needs. The Vietnam war in fiscal year 1970 cost $17 billion; two years previously it was costing $23 billion a year. Some $35 billion was spent on NASA's "man in space" programs (Mercury, Gemini, Apollo) over the last ten years, in part to carry on cold war competition. In contrast, in 1971 $5 billion was budgeted for public housing and $11 billion for public health, from the federal budget (although states and localities make substantial expenditures in these areas), or 3 per cent of the budget for public housing and 6 per cent for public health compared to 35 per cent for defense (but this compares with 43 per cent for defense in 1969).

To take one seemingly peripheral category of military expenditures—the pay for retired military—in 1967 these expenditures were greater than the expenditures of each of nine of the fifteen federal departments. Military retired pay in that year was $300 million greater than the expenditure for the Office of Economic Opportunity's war on poverty program, and cost four and a half times as much as all operations of the Department of State or the Labor Department. Considered as political constituencies, the retired military are just a handful (707,000) as compared with some 24,000,000 veterans in the population. But in 1966 retired pay was equal to about one-fourth the sum spent for all veterans' benefits combined. So far, no easy answers have been found to the staggering rise in military retirement costs. Retired pay costs exceeded $2 billion in 1968. A recent estimate for 1970 is $2.57 billion and for 1980 $4.15 billion.

The dilemma on priorities in the United States reflects and stimulates a similar dilemma internationally. The U.S. Arms Control and Disarmament Agency published a survey showing that 120 nations in 1967 spent $182 billion for their military needs, more than 7 per cent of the world's total gross production of goods and services.[1] This is the equivalent of about 20 per cent of global industrial production and 75 per cent of total world trade. The world's spending for armaments and other military costs is 40 per cent greater than its spending on education and more than three times the total spent on public health. According to ACDA, by an admittedly rough estimate in the first two-thirds of this century the world had spent the equivalent of more than $4,000 billion on wars and military preparedness. At the current rate of increases in arms spending, war and weaponry would consume an equal amount in the period from 1967 to 1980.

Recently there has developed a painful public awareness that in a period of high military spending the federal budget has a limited capacity to accommodate to the problems of the cities, minority group needs, pressures for improved crime prevention, the consequences of environmental contamination, and similar domestic problems. That limitation magnifies the consequences of allotting a marginal 1 or 2 per cent of the gross national product to defense purposes or to particular civilian purposes, when that one or two percentage points can amount to $8-$16 billion. Although the electorate has accepted defense increases in the past with relatively little grumbling

1. *World Military Expenditures and Related Data, Calendar Year 1966 and Summary Trends, 1962–1967* (Research Report 68–52) (Washington, D.C.: Government Printing Office, 1968, pp. 1, 3.

about the justification, there are indications that the extended—and expanded—conflict in Southeast Asia is now being seen in a different light. For
a great many people, the social needs of the country have assumed at least
as high a priority as the upper layer of military cost. Forced to choose
among a reduction in military spending, a sharp limitation on the effort
devoted to resolving vital social needs, and a tax rate increase large enough
to avoid having to choose, the electorate appears now to favor the first of
those options. One obvious influence on that choice is recent criticism of
military spending that is either clearly wasteful or that seems to have
resulted from indifferently validated requirements for specific weapons
systems.[2]

The Eisenhower administration attempted to resolve the problem by
putting an "arbitrary" ceiling on defense spending, but this ceiling was more
effective in freeing the military from civilian guidance on the components of
the military budget than in juxtaposing civilian and military requirements.
President Kennedy took the alternate tack of instructing his Secretary of
Defense to determine military requirements "without regard to arbitrary
or predetermined budget ceilings," on the assumption that the nation was
rich enough to afford the defense it needed.[3] This new policy had the effect
of forcing a more analytical and coordinated approach to Defense budgeting. But, while it improved the quality of the budgetary product submitted
by the Secretary to the Budget Bureau and the White House, it increased the
imbalance between defense spending and other government spending. No
such presidential instructions or requirements "without regard to arbitrary
or predetermined budget ceilings" had been given to other Executive departments. And, by the time the so-called draft presidential memoranda embodying the budgetary proposals of the Defense Department reached the
White House, internal priorities had been argued out and settled within the
department, and inconsistencies eliminated. No such process took place
within the domestic establishment, and the claims of the domestic departments and agencies were even less effectively marshaled, in contrast to
the claims of the military.

By the time Secretary McNamara departed in 1968, the budgetary reforms he introduced had been institutionalized and presented a cohesive
front among conflicting military interests to observers from the other side
of the Potomac. None of President Nixon's organizational innovations

2. A recent Gallup survey showed that 49 per cent of the American public desired
a reduction in defense spending; 10 per cent desired an increase and 34 per cent
considered it about right. *New York Times,* Sept. 24, 1970.

3. President Kennedy said in a Special Message to Congress on the Defense
Supplemental Budget, March 28, 1961: "Our arms must be adequate to meet our
commitments and ensure our security, without being bound by arbitrary budget
ceilings. This nation can afford to be strong; it cannot afford to be weak." *New York
Times,* March 29, 1961, p. 16.

have produced agreed-upon policy goals or quantitative program guidelines across the spectrum of domestic agencies.[4]

It is the cumulative effect of the growth of defense institutions and innovations, especially in the absence of concomitant growth on the civilian side (until quite recently), which has aroused apprehension of undue military influence.

The confusion over budgetary priorities and policy goals is both a reflection of ambivalent national attitudes toward the military and a stimulus to such ambivalence. On the one hand, there is the national preoccupation with world leadership and power, with national security, with fear of the Communist enemy and dread of the potential proliferation of nuclear weapons —and the respect for the military attitudes of duty, order, authority, and patriotism that often accompanies this preoccupation. On the other hand, there is the national preoccupation with the quality and survival of the nation's own internal life, with the decay of the cities, the polarized races, the ecological crisis—and the preference for the values of freedom, compassion, individualism, and creativity that tends to accompany it.

Until World War II, military ideals had, on the whole, been viewed by this society as highly authoritarian and antithetical to democratic practice. Even during the war, most Americans, like those portrayed by Norman Mailer in *The Naked and the Dead,* saw military life from the perspective of the civilian soldier. The professional officer was often cast in a mold of inflexible sternness, frequently a figure of loneliness in his unquestioning obedience to the demands and obligations of his station. But the war also gave the military new and enhanced stature in the nation's eyes. Other works of fiction—*From Here to Eternity* by James Jones, *Guard of Honor* by James Gould Cozzens, and *The Caine Mutiny* by Herman Wouk— shared the earlier portrait of an aloof military. But they paid tribute to military qualities of sternness and obedience and their contribution to the national effort. At the end of *The Caine Mutiny,* for example, Greenwald, the defense attorney, who had successfully won acquittal for the leader of the mutiny against the career officer, Queeg, spoke with regret and even repentance of his destruction of Queeg:

. . . While I was studying law 'n old Keefer . . . was writing his play . . . and Willie . . . was on the playing fields . . . all that time these birds we call regulars—these stuffy, stupid Prussians, in the Navy and the Army— were manning guns . . . . [They were] standing guard on this fat dumb and happy country of ours . . . . So when all hell broke loose . . . who's gonna stop [the Germans]? Not [me]. Can't stop a Nazi with a law book . . . Captain Queeg . . . Yes, even Queeg, poor sad guy, yes, and most of them

4. In his press conference of July 20, 1970, President Nixon noted that he had cut the defense budget $7 billion in two years (including Vietnam cutbacks) and said that it would be "very difficult" to cut it further. *New York Times,* July 21, 1970.

not sad at all . . . a lot of them sharper boys than any of us, don't kid your-self, best men I've ever seen, you can't be good in the Army or Navy unless you're goddam good. . . .

In the years immediately following the war, the military emerged with heightened political prestige. Generals Eisenhower and MacArthur, the two most popular heroes of the war, appeared as potential presidential can-didates, men who, it was claimed, would bring the soldier's qualities of courage and good faith and his capacity for making clear decisions to the complex problems the country faced, the lack of confidence at home, the threat to security abroad. General David M. Shoup, former Marine Corps commandant, pointed out that in 1968 living veterans of the United States military service totaled about 24 million, or about 20 per cent of the adult population. From this fact, Shoup reasoned that most middle-aged men— most business, government, civic, and professional leaders in this country —have served some time in uniform, that for many it was the most exciting and adventurous time of their lives, that for most the military codes were "powerful medicine," compounded of patriotism, service to country, honor among fellow men, loyalty to organization and leaders, discipline. He described the various veterans' organizations, numbering more than four million members, as a concentrated force for militarism. Shoup contended, "Their memberships generally favor military solutions to world problems in the pattern of their own earlier experience, and often assert that their military service and sacrifice should be repeated by the younger genera-tions."[5]

Even among those who have high respect for the military establishment, there is a divergence of attitude which has created a serious tension in the military itself. On the one hand, the traditional combat responsibility of the military tends to lead to a political orientation that is highly nationalistic and "hawkish." On the other, this orientation strains against opposing forces; the historic admonition against political participation and the broadening technological and educational structure of the military, which pushes the profession toward a more internationalist, less ethnocentric world-view.

These conflicting forces split the military between the two wings in American political life, the wings Huntington calls the "Establishment" and the "fundamentalists"—the "Establishment . . . East Coast, Ivy League, Wall Street, big business and executive branch oriented," and the "funda-mentalists . . . rural, Midwestern and Southern, small business, small town, and Congress oriented."[6] It is not surprising that so many "cold war" sem-inars were held in the South and Midwest, that so many participants were

5. David M. Shoup and James A. Donovan, "The New American Militarism," *Atlantic*, April 1969, pp. 51–56.
6. Samuel P. Huntington, "Power, Expertise and the Military Profession," *Daedalus*, Vol. 92, No. 4 (Fall 1963), p. 803.

small businessmen, that the opposition to ROTC and military research exploded in prestigious Ivy League universities and the more urbanized state university campuses, and that the military role in public education has for so long been protected by congressional committees dominated by a Southern and largely rural-based majority.

In the eyes of the public, the military professional is not a figure of high prestige, despite the frequently expressed national perspective of the military-as-hero-and-patriot. The National Opinion Research Center occupation prestige study of 1947—a time of much military influence in public policy—found that the captain in the Regular Army had comparatively low prestige. He was ranked below physician, lawyer, and minister, and even accountant (although above public school teacher). This finding may be misleading, however, since the prestige of a captain, as a comparatively young officer, is far lower than the officers whose rank puts them in positions of public power. A study in 1963 showed that the military officer was one of the few who had increased in prestige, though not markedly, in the interim.

The relatively low prestige in good part derives from the presumed low pay, or at least lack of opportunity to make a "fortune" in the military establishment, in part from the presumed hardship of military life, especially the constant rotation of assignment. Even more fundamental, however, is a complex ambivalence to the function of the military; reliance on the professional military is mixed with a skepticism about the value of such a profession. There is an apparent lack of interest in the civic spirit and personal dedication which the regular sees in his own calling. Coupled with this relatively low prestige is a pervasive feeling of the excessively hierarchical quality of military life. The American style is simultaneously to respect authority and to resent it.

The traditional antimilitary bias did not disappear during the years of military resurgence after World War II. Successful novels (and their film adaptations) such as *Fail-Safe* by Eugene Burdick, about a nuclear war, and *Seven Days in May* by Fletcher Knebel and Charles W. Bailey, about a military conspiracy, reflected the latent fear in many Americans of the power of a large military establishment and the unknown perils of a thermonuclear age. But the pressures of two wars since 1945 have sustained the power of the military establishment and, generally, have suppressed or subordinated expression of antimilitarism through public policy. But each of these wars, in Korea and Vietnam, became increasingly unpopular. The attrition of support for the decade-long Vietnam involvement, combined with the growing awareness of severe and growing domestic needs, has revived the traditional American suspicion of the military and stimulated a counteroffensive against the power of the Pentagon and the military establishment generally.

The extent of popular reservation about the war in South Vietnam emerges from a comparison of public opinion about Vietnam with attitudes toward World War II and Korea. On the basis of data collected by the American Institute of Public Opinion, shortly before Pearl Harbor, dissent about involvement in World War II was expressed by about 34 per cent of the population; but with the outbreak of hostilities dissent dropped to and remained at about 7 to 8 per cent. In the Korean conflict, data from the same source indicated that 20 per cent dissented at the beginning (1950), when it was seen as a supportive operation in behalf of the United Nations and an action against classic aggression, compared with about 50 per cent in 1954 at the conclusion of hostilities. The same pattern of increased disaffection has characterized the period of involvement in the South Vietnam war. After the Bay of Tonkin action, dissent against involvement was about 23 per cent. It rose to 45 per cent by the middle of 1968, and to 55 per cent at the end of 1969.

Appeals from draft classification were much lower in World War II than in the Korean and Vietnam wars. The appeals initiated declined as World War II progressed, reflecting the relatively high legitimacy of the war; in the Korean and Vietnam wars the trend went up as the conflict continued.[7] Perhaps paradoxically, the higher the level of popular legitimacy, the more successful were appeals from Selective Service classification. The percentage of successful appeals in World War II was higher than in Korea, while appeals in the Vietnam war have been systematically unsuccessful. Finally, it should be noted that dissent from military service was more external to the military in Korea and especially Vietnam, while during World War II it was more internal and on a more personal basis— the desertion rate was much higher during World War II than in the Korean or Vietnam conflicts.[8]

Desertion is in part a response to the intensity of battle conditions, the geographic locale, and feasibility of escape, but it seems that the military hardens in its intolerance of attempts to seek relief from Selective Service when the national commitment is confused, and responds to individual cases when the commitment at home is united; further, that individual dissenters in the military find the need to reject service, through desertion, less compelling when organized dissent speaks for them at home. If, in Korea, the

7. Prior to Pearl Harbor, there were 26 voluntary appeals per 1,000 I-A registrants, compared with only 3 per 1,000 at the end of the war, according to a report by Robert B. Smith, "Disaffection from War, Legitimacy and Combat Effectiveness," unpublished, August 1968. For Korea in 1950, there was only one voluntary appeal per 1,000 I-A registrants compared to 47 per 1,000 at the end of the war; in Vietnam prior to large-scale American participation there were only 4 appeals per 1,000 registrants compared to 45 per 1,000 by the middle of 1967.

8. At the height of World War II, the desertion rate was 63 per 1,000 while in Korea it fell to 22.5 per 1,000. For Vietnam, the figure rose from 14.7 per 1,000 in 1966 to 29.1 per 1,000 in 1968.

weakness seemed to the military to lie in the lack of ideological conviction among troops in the field, in the case of Vietnam there must seem to the military to be a similar but more broadly based and dangerous lack of understanding among the general public, and particularly in the articulate, urban, youthful elites that serve in the forefront of the antiwar movement.

Acts of direct opposition to the policies of the war are buttressed by the wider trend of American public opinion which, especially since 1965, has increasingly turned from support of the Vietnam war to an attitude against escalation of the military effort and disillusion with the United States involvement. In this shifting set of political forces the professional military faces the dilemma of having served as an instrument of political leadership that is under serious public indictment. The growing dissent and restlessness with the Southeast Asian war and the power of the military are concentrated —though by no means exclusively—in the young. By 1968 large numbers of moderate students were working in the election campaigns for candidates who were committed to ending the Vietnam war and who were closely scrutinizing the Defense budget. In 1969 and again after the Cambodian escalation of 1970, middle-class, moderate (and many otherwise apolitical) students, young professionals, and others repeatedly "marched on Washington" to seek a peaceful redress of grievances and organized politically to support antiwar candidates.

This kind of expression from the solid center of student opinion in the major universities is mirrored in the widespread acceptance by students of the goals, if not always the methods, of protest movements that oppose the draft, that seek to terminate ROTC contracts, military-supported research on campus (whether classified or unclassified), and visits by recruiters from defense industry. (See Chapter 19.) These attitudes serve to alienate a sizable portion of young people from the military establishment, even to the extent that anything connected with that establishment is automatically under suspicion. There is a defensive reaction, particularly among middle Americans, to this youth protest and the antiwar movement, equally intense in its expression. It has made a primary symbol of the American flag with ardent patriotic decals and bumper stickers advising "Love it or leave it." Each group provokes the other to increasing rage. The ambivalence of the general public toward the military is increased by this passionate evidence of polarization and alienation. The danger of two societies described in the Kerner Report[9] in terms of white and black is repeated, in certain respects, in the confrontation over the role of the military and the responsibilities of citizenship.

The convergence of military and civilian styles will also undoubtedly affect future public attitudes toward the military. It will make it difficult to

9. Kerner Commission's *Report of the National Advisory Commission on Civil Disorders* (Washington, D.C.: Government Printing Office, 1968).

sustain either stereotype of the military—as persons motivated solely by patriotism and personal sacrifice, whose plans and actions should not be questioned, or as men on horseback threatening the democratic foundations of the republic. Opinion-makers go through alternating cycles of idealizing and of muckraking the military. Both the hero syndrome and the devil syndrome inhibit realistic analysis of the internal bureaucratic pressures, the organizational biases, and the utility calculations that enter into military decision-making. As the military character of the military establishment becomes less distinctive, absolutist perceptions may be replaced by more realistic ones. The military may come to be regarded as any other part of government—as an agency with an assignment that is to be made and controlled and evaluated by the elected representatives.

The future course of any organization, even the largest and most powerful in the world, is likely to be shaped more by outside events and attitudes than by its internal dynamics, and the most powerful shaping force on the military establishment is the climate of American opinion about the role of the United States as a world power. This climate in turn is a resultant of two major elements: concern about external dangers and preoccupation with domestic problems, two concerns that are in many respects interdependent. When Senator Gerald P. Nye of North Dakota initiated the 1934 hearings which popularized the "merchants of death" thesis, he was motivated as much by isolationist views as by concern over the activities of munitions manufacturers. When Franklin Roosevelt announced that "Dr. Win the War" had taken the place of "Dr. New Deal," he was able to do so not only because of the clear threat of Nazi-Japanese aggression but also because the exigencies of the international situation had produced a level of federal spending that had somewhat alleviated the domestic economic crisis of the thirties.

When it is argued that the requirements of national security have a natural primacy, the issue is usually put in terms of national survival, which it is claimed must necessarily come ahead of all other considerations. In a hostile world, according to this view, there is a level of military expenditure below which the security of the nation is significantly threatened. But the apparent simplicity of this formulation is blurred by several complications. The hostility of the outside world may be, in part, a function of perception, in part of reality, and the distinction between them is not always clear. Certainly many of America's allies have held a less fearful view of the post-World War II world. Nor is the external threat an independent variable. American survival as a free society is challenged not only by external threats to which a military response is appropriate but also by internal threats of disunity and decay to which a military response typically is inappropriate. Moreover, there is no fixed point or threshold above which "security" exists and below which there is mortal danger. Questions of marginal utility and opportunity cost are involved.

The danger to the United States from the spread of violence in the world is largely a function of world social and economic problems that increase the likelihood of violence. American social and economic policies can have a considerable impact on those problems that may decrease the potential for violence more than military expansion could do. The United States can affect its security, for example, by the level of its own international development activity and its own trade policies, both directly and through the example it sets for other nations. As Robert McNamara put it in his famous Montreal speech, "Security is development, and without development there can be no security. A developing nation that does not, in fact, develop simply cannot remain secure for the intractable reason that its own citizenry cannot shed its human nature."[10]

Objective definition of the external threat to national security is complicated by the fact that, to some extent, it is itself determined by American military policy choices. The real threat is affected by America's actions as they appear to potential antagonists, and as those antagonists react to American actions; the threat as perceived by the United States government is even more drastically affected by reactions to the actions and policies of the United States by the rest of the world. This is not to suggest that the United States is likely to be motivated by considerations of territorial expansion or economic gain in its military actions toward other countries. Rather, it is to suggest that America's perception of what threatens national survival—from the "yellow peril" to "monolithic world Communism" —and what must be done about it cannot help but affect in turn the degree of hostility the United States encounters in the world, and the military capabilities that may be mobilized in counterdefense. The wind that drives the sailboat is not the true wind but the apparent wind, which includes the wind produced by the movement of the boat itself through the water.

The second complicating factor is that it increasingly appears that "survival" rests on domestic as well as foreign developments. The simple survival argument for the primacy of military requirements may be called into serious question over the next decade—survival may relate more directly to containing civil disorder at home, or to preventing disorder through fundamental institutional change, requiring substantial reordering of public spending priorities.

There is a further complication: when one speaks of national attitudes, there is a temptation to take them as expressions of some kind of national consensus. In fact, the crucial question is likely to be, Which view of the contemporary predicament prevails? Is the country in more trouble at

10. Robert S. McNamara, *The Essence of Security* (New York: Harper & Row, 1968), p. 149.

home or abroad, and where should resources be concentrated to deal with those troubles? The relative strengths of differing interests, both inside and outside government, largely determine the accepted definition of what are the major national problems. Even the power of the President to identify dangers and to chart a course around them is severely limited, although confident leadership can guide a nation's choice of priorities. He must, however, take some account of the conflicting charts thrust at him—including the charts offered by the military establishment itself. It matters who gets to define what is a threat to the survival of the country.

Unhappily, in postwar America it was only in the guise of national defense that Americans could be persuaded to undertake certain long necessary domestic programs. The momentum of national defense obviated the necessity of engineering the large-scale democratic consensus that would otherwise have been required. Federal support of higher education gained support in the demand for military research. School curriculum reform, long overdue, was justified after Sputnik on the grounds that engineers and scientists must be better than their Soviet counterparts. A gigantic interstate highway program was undertaken partly as a support for national defense. The study of international affairs and the development of foreign area research was fostered because a great power would need this knowledge to maintain its power position. Many people today are saying if you do the right things for the wrong reasons for too long you may end up with a society incapable of understanding what is truly necessary for the longer run. By cloaking domestic needs in requirements of national defense the nation risks sacrificing domestic progress when national defense loses its urgency in the public mind. And, at a time of high antimilitary feeling, useful programs may be jeopardized through guilt by association with the military even when that relationship is artificial and easily broken. Perhaps most important, the nation may find that its sense of priorities has become rusty and inflexible for the public debate by which such priorities are selected and implemented in the context of national purpose.

III

THE USES OF

MILITARY POWER

8

Nuclear Equilibrium
and "Worst Case" Planning

The primary, indeed the ultimate, utility of American military power is to deter potential enemies from launching a nuclear attack on the United States or from resorting to the use of force below the nuclear threshold in such a way that nuclear war might result. To deter a nuclear attack, the United States maintains a nuclear force of 1710 missiles (plus some 500 bombers). In preventing nonnuclear adventures that might flare up into a nuclear conflagration, the United States maintains more than four division equivalents—some 310,000 men—in Germany, some two divisions in South Korea, and in the United States a mobile force of more than three divisions, deployable overseas relatively rapidly together with major tactical air support all quite apart from American forces in Southeast Asia.

The employment of nuclear weapons—conceded to threaten an all-out nuclear holocaust and hence human survival—has been unacceptable in the major military crises faced by the United States since World War II: in Korea,[1] in the Middle East, in Vietnam. When President Truman, in a press conference remark, suggested that he had not ruled out the use of nuclear weapons in Korea, the British Prime Minister, Clement Attlee, hastened to Washington in alarm. For the first time in human history, men had invented weapons too terrible to use.[2] War had, by necessity, become "conventional" again.

1. A mistaken notion that the United States intended to rely solely on a nuclear response to aggression may possibly have led the North Koreans to invade South Korea, calculating that their action would be below the threshold of nuclear retaliation, and that no other response would be forthcoming.
2. Poison gas, first employed in World War I, never saw extensive operational use, because of problems in tactical employment. By World War II, when gases had become much more effective and their delivery systems more reliable, the assumption

Over the decade of the 1950's, the United States and the Soviet Union both came to recognize extraordinary limits on the usefulness of nuclear weapons. The celebrated NSC-68 policy paper (still classified), produced under the direction of Paul Nitze, then head of the State Department policy planning staff, predicted in 1950 a Soviet attack capability with nuclear weapons by 1954. The appropriate United States response, NSC-68 pointed out, was to upgrade its air defense to limit damage to the United States, and also to upgrade American conventional capability, especially in Europe, so that any Soviet ground attacks might be countered with less than all-out nuclear war.

The NSC-68 rationale was somewhat eclipsed by the "more bang for the buck" philosophy of the Eisenhower administration, but it was reaffirmed when, in response to the Soviet military buildup in Europe and Asia, a series of presidential messages to the Congress, during the winter and spring of 1961, called for strengthening of nonnuclear military forces (along with additional funds to increase the size and security of second-strike nuclear forces), and particularly emphasized the counterinsurgency function. The green beret of the Special Forces, authorized by President Kennedy over some military opposition, became a symbol of the "new wave" in military doctrine. The apparent discovery that warfare could be reduced from the level of unimaginable mass slaughter to the level of personal combat produced a surge of relief about our ability to deal with local conflict without inciting nuclear war. War could once again continue.

The Soviets' zeal for "national liberation" and the American zeal for counterinsurgency soon proved naïve. The Soviets found that providing support for local insurgencies could involve them with clients they could not adequately control but whose mistakes—or defeats—could be an enormous embarrassment politically and financially. The Americans eventually learned that even a small commitment of military advisers could rapidly escalate into a war so big that rash action might produce a direct confrontation with the Soviets, yet so costly and apparently indecisive that it could drag on beyond the limits of patience of the American people.

Even though conventional war took on a new lease, the shadow of the possibility of nuclear war still falls over every conflict in the world, although most heavily on conflicts directly involving nuclear powers. The notion that nonnuclear military adventures can be carried on with impunity under a kind of protective umbrella of nuclear power, or even numerical superiority in nuclear power, seems a dangerous will-o'-the-wisp. Yet the nuclear powers have not been deterred from action below the threshold of nuclear

---

on both sides that the other possessed an effective chemical capability generated a situation of mutual deterrence. It was this, rather than any feeling that the weapons were too terrible to use, which forestalled their employment.

response when vital national interests are involved. Nor has the United Nations proved effective in control. But the Soviet Union and the United States in their encounters with each other move with great caution. In the Cuban missile crisis, Nikita Khrushchev risked a direct confrontation with the United States over the highly sensitive issue of the secret deployment of nuclear weapons ninety miles off the coast of Florida, but when the crisis came to a head, both sides acted with extraordinary care and delicacy, the United States controlling even the smallest details of military action directly from the White House; and when the burden of escalation had been shifted to the Soviets, they chose to back down. Even in much less direct and dramatic military confrontations, a double calculation must be and is attempted. What will be the immediate military consequences of a proposed action; and what effect will that action have on the possibility of escalation toward nuclear war?

These changes in military strategy have in turn had profound effects on the military establishment. They have made every putative participant in a nuclear war a loser. They have made participants in a nonnuclear conflict acutely conscious of the nuclear war danger. They have, therefore, increased both the demands and the frustrations of military life. Specifically, they have increased the requirements for readiness, flexibility, and control of military forces, nuclear and nonnuclear as well.

The requirement of readiness demands an extremely high standard of training and discipline in the strategic nuclear forces. An officer on duty with the Strategic Air Command, for example, must be reachable by the third ring of the telephone twenty-four hours a day. He knows he cannot depend on forces in reserve or on industrial capacity in the so-called mobilization base. A nuclear war can be fought only with weapons already in place.[3]

Readiness means alertness combined with inaction. An Army general described the Air Force of the future as "the silent silo-sitters of the seventies." So, too, the Navy submariners wait, six weeks at a time, below the surface of the sea, the officers taking their meals in a wardroom with real curtains covering fake windows. The Army, apparently, will be sitting in the ABM sites. Even more frustrating, they wait for what? A nuclear war whose possibility the world cannot even entertain. The military is aware that violence must be contained early, so that the cost of containing it will be lower, and so that it does not escalate toward nuclear war. Its new function is, logically, preventive.

In this situation, flexibility becomes a particular requirement for nonnuclear forces, in part because readiness is not possible without it. It stands

3. This is not to deny the critical importance of civilian industrial capacity that could be converted to weapons production on accelerated timetables if necessary, as a deterrent to the other side expanding its weapons production. Nor does it deny the importance of industrial capacity in a prolonged "phony war" situation.

to reason that an arsenal consisting of a relatively large number of highly specialized weapons is more difficult to mobilize rapidly or at reasonable cost for a particular purpose than one consisting of a smaller number of flexible, multipurpose weapons. This requirement creates a built-in conflict between the natural desire of each military department to protect its own specialized weapons, and the over-all needs of the establishment. Hence the controversy over the introduction of the TFX as a common Air Force-Navy airplane. The range of possible situations in which nonnuclear forces might be employed also calls for the development of flexible forces like the new Strike Command, established in 1961, as a central pool of force that could be rapidly deployed to any part of the world.

Responsiveness is as essential as flexibility. Advancing technology makes possible rapid long-range communication with distant military commanders, so that closer control can be exercised from the Pentagon and from the White House. Communications can be relayed within the theater to and from the most remote outposts. There is still a good deal of vitality in the tradition that operational decisions should be left to the field commander, but commanders at every level are subject to more restrictive constraints than at any time in the past. The logic of the immediate military situation may seem to call for hot pursuit of the enemy into his own (or someone else's) territory—as MacArthur wished to do in Korea and General Creighton W. Abrams in Vietnam and in Cambodia—or expansion of an attack to take advantage of the enemy's confusion; the logic of the political situation—as seems clear in Southeast Asia—may be to avoid the greater dangers that might result from changing the rules and limits under which the conflict is being fought.

But it is at least doubtful in a nuclear world whether any great-power military establishment can be ready enough, flexible enough, and responsive enough, so that its own size, dynamism, and structural complexity will not get in the way of its adjustment to the requirements of nuclear strategy. There is always tension between the need to maintain a credible threat and the need to avoid, so far as possible, situations or actions that might precipitate the threat into actual destructive violence. For nuclear weapons, with their sophisticated delivery vehicles—intercontinental ballistic missiles launched from dispersed sites or from submerged nuclear-powered submarines—mark an entirely new era in warfare. Man's technological capacities have made it possible for both sides, in a great-power conflict, to destroy or to cripple each other, no matter which side takes the first round. Both sides are put on the defensive, because both sides can be overwhelmed.

Technology has developed to the point at which both sides possess a secure second-strike capability (or, in equivalent jargon, an assured destruction capability), that is to say, the capacity to absorb the most violent nuclear attack that could be launched under ideal conditions of surprise, and still be able to strike back with sufficient force ("survivable force") to inflict unacceptable damage on the attacker's economy and society. Both sides are vulnerable, and each side's security depends on the other side's ultimate vulnerability. This is a development particularly shocking for the United States, because no foreign enemy has touched the continental territory of the United States since the War of 1812—and shocking for the Soviet Union, because the ancient Russian strategy of trading space for time may no longer be a serious option. Clearly, it confronts the military establishment with a permanent dilemma in the uses of military power.

A nuclear great power could, by systematic neglect of research and development, permit its antagonist to achieve a technological breakthrough in defensive or offensive weapons—e.g., an antiballistic missile system or a multiple independently targeted re-entry vehicle system (MIRV)—that would threaten a new imbalance. A nuclear great power could, by continuing neglect, permit the antagonist to deploy the new system, without itself taking the countermeasures necessary to maintain a secure second-strike capability. But major technological breakthroughs take a relatively long time to develop, leaving time to devise and construct counters to them, and such an unbalance is unlikely.

The so-called missile gap issue in 1959 and 1960 was, in part, a result of misapprehension about the rate at which the Soviets were expanding their missile force, but in part also an expression of justifiable concern about the adequacy of precautions being taken to "harden" American bomber forces and missile sites, i.e., to protect them against an enemy's first strike, and to develop a properly hardened system of command and control, linking the bomber bases and missile sites with the highest civilian authority. The greater part of the Kennedy administration's efforts in improving the nuclear arsenal was devoted to perfecting a secure second-strike capability, yet those efforts continued to be plagued by the missile gap issue.

The demand for security continued. During the test-ban treaty debate, congressional skeptics demanded strong assurances that effective, well-staffed laboratories could be maintained without the opportunity for atmospheric testing. (See Chapter 9.)

The capacity for mutual destruction has been described as a state of nuclear parity, or sufficiency, or even of nuclear equilibrium, but these phrases may be more misleading than accurate. Mutual destruction could, for example, be associated with chemical or biological weapons—or with as yet unimagined nightmares of science fiction—not merely nuclear weapons. Chemical and biological weapons can, of course, be engineered for a wide variety of effects—from nausea and weeping to long-term incapacitation and death—and a wide variety of employments—from riot control to battlefield tactical to strategic, population-destroying uses. Unlike chemical weapons, however, biological weapons carry a high inherent risk of loss of control, and are widely believed, even in military circles, to be unusable for this reason. Resistance by the American military to President Nixon's decision in the autumn of 1969 to phase out United States biological warfare capability was therefore quite light, and, in the end, ineffective. A great power could still achieve a technological break-through with yet another weapons system that could require a major countereffort in research and development in order to reach a similar standoff. Military stability requires continuing research and development.

The state of "nuclear equilibrium" does not provide a ready answer, on either side, to the question, "How much is enough?" Simplistic opponents of so-called "overkill" calculate the megatonnage in the United States (or the Soviet) arsenal, divide by the number of inhabitants on the other side, and come out with a horrendous percentage of unnecessary weaponry. The appropriate calculation is a good deal more complicated, and spotted with a number of uncertain estimates. It begins with the number of weapons that survive the most severe enemy attack that could be launched against them, so that they can be employed in a second strike; it then considers the number of weapons that misfire or fail to penetrate enemy defenses; and finally it asks what degree of destruction of lives and property from such a second strike would deter an enemy from launching a first strike— under conditions of less than perfectly rational judgment by a less than perfectly understood (or even identified) set of decision-makers, acting in circumstances that cannot be fully imagined.

A further calculation may then be made of the number of millions (or tens of millions) of lives that might be saved, under varying conditions of attack, by further increasing the nuclear arsenal. And a still further calcula-tion might go to improving what is called the war-fighting capability of the surviving weapons (and people) again under varying conditions. The utility of the latter two calculations is a matter of considerable controversy. The Department of Defense, for instance, has published figures indicating that any kind of "thin" ABM system would at best save only ten to twenty million of the 120 million Americans expected to perish in a nuclear ex-change. The Soviet figures are comparable. Even a much heavier, full-scale ABM system, which might cost $50 billion or more, could save only forty to fifty million Americans, and that only if the Soviets made no offsetting improvements in their offensive forces—an unlikely presupposition. Secre-tary McNamara's formula defining "unacceptable" (hence deterring) damage—a quarter of the population killed and half of industry destroyed —can be achieved by either of the nuclear superpowers against any reason-able level of ABM systems.

Whatever the outcome of these calculations, they will be different for the prospective victim of an attack than for the prospective attacker. The victim will assume the attacker to be less cautious than the attacker will be, so that the calculations can never be true reciprocals. If both sides, in their capacities as potential victims, make these conservative calculations, each side insuring against the worst case for him, their reciprocal actions can become an infinite series.

Equilibrium implies a kind of steady state. But in a so-called nuclear equilibrium, each side will pursue new developments, as has been suggested above, for fear that the other side will spurt ahead. Some advances may have the effect of making arms-limiting agreements difficult to arrive at—for example, the development of MIRVs. One "multiple" missile in a launching silo can contain a number of separate nuclear warheads to be released after firing, each tagged for a different target. Counting your antagonist's missile silos, therefore, does not reveal how many effective warheads there are; agreed limitations on numbers of missiles are complicated accordingly.

But the participants in the nuclear arms race are learning that however fast they run, they are only running to keep in place. What one side can achieve through new technology, the other can frustrate through the same means. A case in point is the antiballistic missile: There may possibly be some increase in international stability through the deployment of the so-called thin ABM.[4] But a "thick" ABM system could be neutralized if the other side built enough offensive missiles and penetration aids to saturate it. And a thick system that promised to save enough lives so that the other side's secure second-strike capability was threatened, would have to be—and would be—neutralized. Should both sides deploy an antiballistic missile system, and should both sides concentrate on improving the capabilities of their offensive forces to penetrate such defenses (as they almost certainly would), it is doubtful whether the consequences of a nuclear war would be predictably different from what they are now. Billions of dollars and thousands of missiles later, both sides would still face each other in the same nuclear stalemate. Unfortunately, there is nothing about the so-called nuclear equilibrium that guarantees against this kind of mutually defeating arms race.

If more nations acquire nuclear weapons, the problems multiply, making agreements and understandings less probable and less feasible. As nuclear

4. The argument is also made that a country like Communist China, after it acquires a limited ability to reach the United States with a few intercontinental missiles, and before it acquires a second-strike capability, may be irrationally tempted in a crisis to launch a suicidal attack, on a "now or never" theory, and such an attack could be intercepted by a thin system. Also, it is argued that a thin system around American missile sites could be used to trade off increased protection of offensive missiles against increased numbers of such missiles. It could substitute for increased hardening of missile sites, or even for mobility of missiles. And it could minimize the consequences of accidental or unauthorized attacks.

weapons spread, the possibilities increase that one small nation will be able to destroy a small rival without itself being destroyed, or even before the other side acquires its own small, vulnerable capability. But the proliferation of nuclear power expands the possibilities of a nuclear Armageddon as well. As additional nations acquire relatively small, primitive, vulnerable nuclear arsenals, the danger rises of a pre-emptive strike, by or against the new nuclear power, setting off a major military exchange. And new members of the nuclear club are unlikely to be willing or able to invest in the elaborate and expensive safeguards against accidental or unauthorized weapons launches that the nuclear superpowers have installed.

The great-power nuclear standoff puts severe constraints on the use or threatened use of nuclear weapons by even the strongest nuclear power. Thus, the Dulles doctrine of massive retaliation, declaring that "local defenses must be reinforced by the further deterrent of massive retaliatory power,"[5] was overtaken by events. Once the Soviets had achieved a secure second-strike capability, the United States could believably assert that it would use nuclear weapons only in a situation in which its most vital interests were involved (the limiting case presumably being a massive non-nuclear invasion of Western Europe by the Soviets), since the consequences of using those weapons were too drastic to contemplate under any other circumstances. Nuclear weapons are an effective deterrent only when the other side believes that if it challenges the deterrent on a specific issue, it will descend upon them. And they will not believe it if we do not believe it ourselves. A wide range of possible actions by an antagonist, therefore, must lie below the threshold of nuclear deterrence. It is unreasonable to suppose that if the Soviet Union sent a battalion to probe across the central front of Western Europe, the United States would unleash nuclear war. Therefore it takes something other than nuclear weapons to deter such a foray.[6]

But here, again, there is an insistence on planning mostly for very large wars against very capable, well-armed opponents. Thus, when NATO was formed, the intelligence appraisals indicated that it was improbable that Europe would be overrun, but for military planning purposes a large-scale invasion of Europe was taken as the "official" threat.

Further, the kind of organization that can maintain the research and development effort required to keep up with remote possibilities that might

5. John Foster Dulles, *Evolution of Foreign Policy: Speech Before the Council on Foreign Relations, Department of State Bulletin*, Vol. XXX, No. 761, 1954.

6. It has been suggested that so-called tactical nuclear weapons might be used below what would otherwise be the nuclear threshold. But tactical nuclear weapons cover a range of destruction that overlaps with the range of strategic nuclear weapons. Employing a 400-kiloton so-called tactical nuclear weapon is no different from using a strategic nuclear weapon, and using a 30-ton tactical nuclear weapon may have no more practical effect than using a conventional iron bomb, while at the same time it has all the dangerous consequences of breaching the nuclear barrier.

upset the nuclear balance has some difficulty restraining its people from trying to transform the products of their imagination into immediate reality. Since it is geared to respond effectively in a wide range of complex and unpredictable situations, it is inclined to opt for maximum control of the total environment, even where overriding political considerations call for a narrowly defined military effort, with the role of the United States clearly subordinated to the authority of the host government. A military organization would be altogether extraordinary if it treated a politico-military problem as more political than military; its natural role is to treat all problems as primarily military. But treating it as primarily military may make the problem more difficult to resolve, particularly without escalating the level of violence to a point that heightens the danger of nuclear conflagration.

This is especially so in a limited war situation, where the political authorities may find that the amount of military power they were willing to employ is insufficient, or that the limits under which they chose to fight are too restrictive to accomplish their objectives; they face the decision whether to escalate the conflict, to seek a compromise end to the war, or to withdraw. (The impact of the military establishment on the original decision to intervene is not an issue here; it is discussed in the next chapter.) But a political decision to compromise or to withdraw, based on an awareness that at some level of conflict general nuclear war may break out and that both sides will be losers, can have an extremely disturbing effect on the military, who have been accustomed to the idea of all-out commitment to complete victory. This strain will necessarily be reflected in civil-military relations.

If the conditions of warfare in the nuclear age, at all levels of conflict, tend to strain relations between the military establishment and its political masters, the conditions of force planning and weapons procurement produce similar strains. These strains are primarily related to the difficulties in answering the key question, "How much is enough?" A significant first step was taken when President Nixon shifted the focus of the discussion at the level of presidential utterance from "superiority" to "sufficiency." But, as has been suggested, there is no simple way of telling when a nuclear standoff has been reached. We may feel deterred by the other side's nuclear arsenal. We also may believe that if we were on the other side we would feel equally deterred. But how do those on the other side feel? They may know something we do not, or they may be ignorant of—or unwilling to accept—some critical facts that we know. For safety's sake, we tend to underestimate the extent to which they do feel deterred. But if we underestimate too far, so that we build up a force that seems to them significantly stronger than their own, we then set off another round in the nuclear arms race, raising the same issues again at higher force levels.

The natural inclination of the military establishment is to seek an expansion of the nuclear arsenal. But if this inclination is not controlled, the process of reciprocal escalation can proceed indefinitely, adding to the costs and the dangers on both sides, augmenting the role of those whose primary concern is with military rather than political solutions. The problem is further complicated by the need each side feels to pursue an intensive and extensive research and development program, so as not to be caught unawares. Research and development is relatively inexpensive, although R&D experts are skilled at imagining remote possibilities in the other side's R&D programs (e.g., waging war behind the moon), and devising elaborate schemes to frustrate these possibilities. What is demonstrated in the laboratory need not, necessarily, be duplicated in the field. But four factors come into play here, all tending to convert the nuclear research and development race into an arms race. The first is the difficulty of ascertaining whether the other side has in fact moved beyond the research and development stage, by going into production and deployment. For some two years, Western intelligence was unsure whether the so-called Soviet "Tallinn line" was a new antiballistic missile defense system, or something rather less ambitious. More troublesome is the question of what one's antagonist's intentions are for future development or expansion of existing systems. The second factor is the uncertainty of how one's own new development will work out in actual operation—an uncertainty that may require some form of operational test to resolve. The closer one gets to operations, the greater the costs, and the greater likelihood that one's antagonist will be challenged to move closer to action.

Third, there is the tendency, sometimes referred to as the American syndrome, "If you can do it, do it." One of the most difficult tasks for defense establishment management is to insure that technological possibilities are subordinated to military requirements. The idea of a nuclear-powered airplane, or a long-range missile launched from a bomber flying at stratospheric altitudes, has almost irresistible technological appeal, quite apart from its military usefulness. Both were in development for extended periods at very great expense until they were scratched as not militarily worth the enormous effort involved. And, fourth, there are the interests of defense industry, and its political allies, in moving from the laboratory bench to the production line, where the material rewards for effort are primarily to be found.

And there are no automatic counterpressures to these factors. The notion that no additional amount of nuclear weaponry will buy immunity from the nuclear threat is still resisted by substantial elements within the American military establishment. Each side seems impelled to try to steal a march on the other; the effects are mutually reinforcing.

It may be assumed that the civilian leadership both in this country and in the Soviet Union has become increasingly aware that an arms race is self-defeating, and that a nuclear war must at all costs be avoided. But, although civilian leaders may consider the avoidance of a nuclear war their first priority, military leaders live in fear that the other side will suddenly acquire a position of real strategic dominance. Their first priority is not avoidance of war, but preparation for war if it comes. The central impetus to the arms race in this country has not been the capabilities the Soviets actually possess, but anticipations of what they might acquire. The long lead times of the weapons acquisition process have obliged military planners to project in terms of the opponent's future capabilities rather than his present ones.

This planning process could conceivably culminate in all-out nuclear war—although it need not. To stabilize the size and character of nuclear arsenals—not to speak of achieving mutual reductions in opposing forces—will require massive, sustained effort. But the contemplation of nuclear war, even the maintenance of nuclear arsenals, is abhorrent to most Americans and to much of the rest of the world. It is ironic that the preparation to avoid war serves to bring the possibility of war closer, one side considering war as an option for the other side, and therefore an option, in counter-response, for itself. It used to be widely said that, in view of the prospect of nuclear war and the threat to human survival it would entail, large-scale war was no longer tenable. But the great powers behave militarily as if it is.

We are learning that to overestimate enemy strength—real or potential—may be even more dangerous than to underestimate it. Under circumstances in which knowledge about the opponents' capabilities and intentions is uncertain, planning for the worst case may seem to provide cheap insurance, for much the same reason that it is wise to overengineer bridges and dams. But this perspective may not take sufficient account of the escalatory effect of worst case planning on the enemy's intentions, and it may thereby actually increase the risks. According to official military doctrine, forces designed to fight large wars will have the inherent flexibility to deal with lesser contingencies. The course of the Vietnam war suggests some doubts about the correctness of official doctrine on this score. But the great danger of worst case planning is the effect that such planning has on an arms race; the worst fears involved in such planning are rarely if ever realized, but the forecasts are likely to be self-confirming. At any given time an acute danger can be predicted for the period immediately ahead.

Standard military briefings begin with a section entitled "The Threat." The great nuclear powers have so far restrained themselves from destroying "The Threat," real or imagined, that each other represents. Each has so far been ultimately inhibited by the knowledge that it cannot destroy the threat without being destroyed itself in the process. It might be useful to underline this concern by prescribing as a sequel to the threat section in every American military briefing a section on the threat that the United States presents to its potential antagonists.

9

Military Involvement in Foreign Policy

During the last thirty years, the military establishment has exerted much more influence on the making of American foreign policy than in any previous period. As indicated earlier, the Chiefs of Staff have acted as presidential advisers, often with a voice on foreign policy issues equal to or greater than that of key Assistant Secretaries of State. Since civilian Secretaries of Defense have continued to give advice on foreign policy and have at the same time acquired increased independent authoritativeness, the military establishment has sometimes dominated presidential councils. Such occasions have become all the more frequent partly because so much discussion of foreign policy concerned actual or imminent warfare or the complicated and compelling issue of nuclear balance, partly because foreign policy questions were posed by overseas commands or military aid or advisory missions.

Yet, even more important, policy-makers, civilian and military, became obsessed with the problem of the nation's security and gave to it the highest priority. In Europe, Asia, and the Middle East, successive American administrations opposed the expansion of Communist states and Communist political strength, taking the position that any such expansion would adversely affect the balance of military power, encourage the Soviet Union (or the Sino-Soviet bloc) to initiate war, and put the United States at a disadvantage if war came. Policy-makers adopted military staff habits of reckoning contingencies in terms of the capabilities rather than the intentions of potential enemies and, as has been pointed out, emphasizing readiness for the worst contingencies that might arise. These characteristics were slightly less in evidence in periods when the professional military had least access to the White House—the later Eisenhower years and the interval between the Cuban missile crisis and the Johnson decision to bomb North Vietnam—periods that saw the opening of dialogue between Washington and Moscow, the limited test-ban treaty, and American pressure for more broadly based and politically responsive regimes in Seoul and Saigon. But, in substance and in character, United States foreign policy has become substantially militarized.

It was not, however, the military establishment alone that gave the policy this cast. Basically, it was done by civilians. Civilians in the White House, the State Department, and in other policy-making and opinion-making centers shared the military establishment's view of the Soviet Union as an aggressive and threatening force. They also shared awareness that long-range aircraft, missiles, and nuclear weapons had brought to an end America's long era of what C. Vann Woodward called "free security."[1] They were strongly influenced by lessons alleged to be taught by recent history. Above all, they believed, with some justification, that Congress and public opinion would apply those lessons only if convinced that the continental United States faced danger. And to be convinced, Congress and the public had to hear testimony from those whose judgment they regarded as most detached, trustworthy, and authoritative—the spokesmen of the military establishment. The prominence of the military in the policy-making process has been a function of the priority of military security in American policy. It is essential to look for factors that explain *both* phenomena.

The impact of the military establishment on political decision-making is very much a function of the tasks assigned to the military establishment by the political decision-makers. Early in 1961, it became clear that the balance of payments problem would be an acute and continuing one for the United States, and that a major contributing factor to the big deficits registered by the United States was its overseas troop deployments, particularly the troops stationed in Europe under NATO commitments. While some reduction in the numbers of troops stationed overseas might have been achieved in the long run, through improvement of airlift and ingenious rotation policies, the immediate need was to reduce the outflow of dollars to Europe without reducing the number of troops.

After some investigation and experimentation, the Department of Defense concluded that the most effective way to reduce the military impact on the balance of payments was by agreements with the countries on whose territory the troops were stationed, principally Germany and Britain, to purchase military equipment in the United States in amounts approximately equal to the dollar expenditures arising out of the costs of American troops. The department pursued this policy so vigorously that it had some un-

---

1. C. Vann Woodward, "The Age of Interpretation," *American Historical Review*, October 1960.

anticipated consequences on American relations with Great Britain and Germany, even to the extent of indirectly encouraging sales of second- or third-hand military equipment by Germany to Third World countries. The Department of Defense arms sales policies and programs were monitored by the Department of State and by the National Security Council staff in the White House; but the creation of a vigorous and aggressive sales force within the Department of Defense, assisted and encouraged by the private sector of the defense establishment, developed a momentum that the political decision-makers had not anticipated and could not fully control, until finally it produced the congressional investigations of 1967, which resulted in congressional curbs on the credit mechanisms that were the principal instruments of foreign military sales promotion.

When Japanese troops seized Shanghai in 1937, it was the commander of the Pacific fleet who submitted a recommendation that the United States government reaffirm its intention to protect American nationals and reinforce its garrison in the international settlement as proof of its determination. The recommendation became for several days the focus of State Department and White House debate.[2] As a rule, however, before World War II, military and naval officers figured as quite minor characters in major diplomatic decisions.

With World War II and the elevation of the Chiefs of Staff to virtual supercabinet status, the reverse became true. General Eisenhower managed relations with the French regime in North Africa, and later he handled negotiations for Italy's surrender. Other American military commanders functioned with even greater political independence. Communication with De Gaulle was as much the responsibility of Admiral Harold R. Stark, the commander of American naval forces in Europe, as of any American ambassador. And in the Far East, General MacArthur, General Joseph Stilwell, and General Albert Wedemeyer dealt with the British Dominions, the Republic of China, and the Chinese Communists as the ranking representatives of the United States. Field commanders and their staffs had much to do with determining which foreign policy issues would be raised in Washington. The service staffs and committees of the Joint Chiefs recommended solutions. After the President made a decision, his instructions went back to the field commanders. From beginning to end, military men were involved in wartime foreign policy.

After 1944, relations with the U.S.S.R. became the most important foreign business of the United States government. These relations had not at any point been managed by the military. The small military mission in Moscow had remained subordinate to the embassy, and President

2. Dorothy Borg, *The United States and the Far Eastern Crisis of 1933–1938* (Cambridge: Harvard University Press, 1964), pp. 321-323.

Roosevelt had communicated with Premier Joseph Stalin either directly or through the American ambassador or special civilian emissaries. President Truman used similar channels. In dealing with liberated countries in Western Europe, Truman relied on the embassies, and he used Marshall in a civilian capacity in 1945-46 as a special envoy to China. Management of foreign affairs lay with the military only in occupied areas, although enough major problems arose so that General Clay in Germany, General MacArthur in Japan, and Lieutenant General John R. Hodge in Korea remained among the principal American agents abroad.

In civilianizing the foreign policy machinery after 1948, Truman attempted to change arrangements in Washington and overseas. In 1949 he replaced Clay with a civilian high commissioner, and in 1950 he opened negotiations for a Japanese peace treaty which, when completed, would mean the end of MacArthur's proconsulship. However, he concluded that the North Atlantic Treaty would not in and of itself deter a Russian attack on Europe, and the result was the organization of NATO forces under an American supreme commander. And, of course, the eruption of war in Korea meant that the American commander in the Far East—first MacArthur and then Ridgway—also had a great deal to do with fixing the terms in which Washington would debate foreign policy problems.

Through most of the 1950's and 1960's, the NATO command played a central role both in posing foreign policy issues and in championing particular policies. Successive supreme commanders and their staffs had much to do with establishing a case for German rearmament, promoting formation of a European Defense Community, defining the challenge involved in Khrushchev's proposal to sign a separate peace treaty with East Germany, and advocating creation of a multilateral nuclear force. Although President Johnson's final rejection of the multilateral force (MLF), followed by France's virtual withdrawal from NATO, reduced the stature and influence of the command, it retained a voice equal to that of any civilian agency on such matters as, for example, a means of reducing American expenditures in Europe in order to compensate for balance of payments deficits.

When President Eisenhower reorganized the defense establishment in 1953, he provided for a number of unified commands. After the Korean War, a commander in chief, Pacific, assumed control of Army and Marine units in Korea, Japan, Okinawa, Taiwan, the Philippines, and island areas, the Seventh Fleet, and United States Air Force groups stationed in the region. He, his headquarters staff, and subordinate commanders played a prominent role in defining the policy issues involved in French reversals in Indochina, Chinese Communist threats to Chinese Nationalist-held offshore islands, civil warfare in Laos and South Vietnam, and Communist movements in the Philippines and Indonesia.

As the level of American engagement in Vietnam increased, the Military Assistance Command, Vietnam (MACV), developed more and more of a separate identity while its influence in foreign policy debate was amplified by transmission through the Honolulu headquarters of the Pacific Command. Other military organizations, of course, figured in the foreign policy process. The Strategic Air Command, for example, participated in debate over the policy issues involved in test-ban negotiations. The issues on which policy-makers had to act were posed as often in cables from SHAEF, SCAP, SHAPE, SACEUR, COMPAC,[3] or MACV as in cables from American embassies or notes presented by foreign governments.

Aid funds earmarked for military purposes in the mutual security

TABLE 9.1 Percent of Foreign Assistance Program 1950–69 Represented by Military Assistance ($ millions)

Fiscal Year	Total Foreign Assistance Program	Economic Assistance	Military Assistance	% of Program for Military Assistance
1950	$ 5,042.4	$ 3,728.4	$ 1,314.0	26.1
1951	7,485.0	2,262.5	5,222.5	69.8
1952	7,284.4	1,540.4	5,744.0	78.9
1953	6,001.9	1,782.1	4,219.8	70.3
1954	4,531.5	1,301.5	3,230.0	71.3
1955	2,781.5	1,588.8	1,192.7	42.9
1956	2,703.3	1,681.1	1,022.2	37.8
1957	3,766.6	1,749.1	2,017.5	53.6
1958	2,768.9	1,428.9	1,340.0	48.4
1959	3,448.1	1,933.1	1,515.0	43.9
1960	3,225.8	1,925.8	1,300.0	40.3
1961	4,431,4	2,631.4	1,800.0	40.6
1962	3,914.6	2,314.6	1,600.0	40.9
1963	3,928.9	2,603.9	1,325.0	33.7
1964	3,000.0	2,000.0	1,000.0	33.3
1965	3,325.0	2,195.0	1,055.0	31.8
1966	3,933.0	2,463.0	1,545.0	39.5
1967	2,935.5	2,143.5	792.0	26.8
1968	2,295.6	1,895.6	400.0	17.4
1969	1,974.1	1,599.1	375.0	19.1
Total	$78,777.5	$40,767.8	$38,009.7 Avg.	48.6

Sources: 1950–1968 in *Military Assistance Facts*, October 1968, Department of Defense, Office of the Assistant Secretary for International Security Affairs, 1968, p. 25. 1969 in *U.S. Code Congressional and Administrative News*, 90th Congress, 2nd. Sess., 1968, Vol. III, p. 3973.

3. SHAEF, Supreme Headquarters Allied Expeditionary Force; SCAP, Supreme Commander for the Allied Powers; SHAPE, Supreme Headquarters Allied Powers (Europe); SACEUR, Supreme Allied Commander, Europe; COMPAC, Commander, Pacific.

program made up almost half of United States foreign aid between 1950 and 1968. (See Table 9.1.) The figures tell only part of the story, since economic aid itself had to be justified to Congress primarily in terms of its contribution to effective military aid. The establishment of military advisory missions was a natural consequence. By 1968, missions were stationed in at least fifty countries. Military advisers, serving at least as quasi-diplomatic agents of the United States, outnumbered State Department personnel stationed abroad by almost two to one.

Like overseas commands, military aid missions contributed regularly to the policy process. Their cables framed questions that policy-makers had to answer. And to some extent this has been the case regardless of the degree to which the officers involved were technically subordinate to ambassadors or other civilians. For in countries where the military dominated political life, members of United States military missions almost inevitably had special entree. In the Dominican Republic between 1961 and 1965, for example, military aid constituted less than 4 per cent of American assistance; the military mission never numbered more than forty-five, and presidential instructions plainly made the ambassador captain of the country team. Nevertheless, when civil warfare broke out in 1965, members of the Military Assistance Advisory Group were regarded in Washington as having better information about both warring factions than the embassy. Where the major stakes in a country's relations with the United States government are military aid funds, as was the case in Vietnam under Ngo Dinh Diem, American military personnel can become the chief focus of attention on the part of local politicians, with civilians in the embassy routinely playing second fiddle.

Major overseas commands and military missions have exerted an influence simply by their existence. The Seventh Army and Sixth Fleet in Europe constitute an important element in the balance of payments problem. Their estimates of increased force or supply requirements call forth high-level policy debate in Washington. American bases and garrisons in Spain, Turkey, North Africa, the Caribbean, Southeast Asia, Taiwan, Okinawa, and Japan have been the causes of comparable debates, either because they provided a focus for political agitation in the host country or because base or other rights had to be negotiated or renegotiated.

The military establishment has thus participated not only in counseling the President but also in putting foreign policy issues before him and, at least on occasion, in creating these issues. For example, there was evidence that an Air Force general, who was in charge of negotiations with his Spanish opposite numbers in Madrid, had acted in a high-handed fashion toward the American Embassy, while making all kinds of commitments in the name of the United States government to defend Spain in return for the base rights. The Congress (particularly the Senate) was alarmed, but not necessarily for the right reason. For it soon became apparent that the Air Force had been delegated the responsibility to pursue bogged-down negotiations in large part as a tactical move initiated by the State Department and warmly encouraged by Secretary Rusk, who handed over responsibility to the Defense Department, in particular to Deputy Secretary of Defense Paul Nitze, who delegated it to the Joint Chiefs, and its chairman, General Earl G. Wheeler, who wound up calling the shots, with Air Force General David Burchinal doing the actual negotiating.

The international posture of the United States has changed since 1940, and the change has coincided with an expansion of the policy-making role of the military. Until then, Presidents and Secretaries of State said ritually that the United States had three foreign policy objectives: the preservation of the Monroe Doctrine, the maintenance of the Open Door and the territorial and administrative integrity of China, and the avoidance of entangling alliances.

The first of the objectives embodied some concern for military security. The Monroe Doctrine rested on an assumption that the United States would be endangered if any foreign power increased its holdings in Latin America. The development of Pan-Americanism, culminating in Franklin Roosevelt's "Good Neighbor" pronouncements, however, subordinated this specific American interest to the collective interest of the inter-American community.

The Open Door doctrine contained no security component. Except for devotees of Homer Lea,[4] feverish about a yellow peril, few Americans imagined that barriers to trade in China or even the takeover of China by Japan or the Soviet Union would put the continental United States in danger. In fact, military planners and others who thought in security terms tended to side with a minority that voiced doubts about the traditional policy. Protests against Japanese encroachment on China, they held, needlessly irritated the Japanese and thus increased the risk of Japan's attacking the Philippines or Hawaii.

The third principle, nonentanglement, expressed a traditional belief that no change in the balance of power elsewhere would affect America's safety. But the United States emerged from World War II with a somewhat altered set of principles. The American government promised to cooperate with the other victors as it had not cooperated with its allies after World War I. Through the United Nations, it accepted responsibilities it had refused earlier. Collective security replaced nonentanglement as a watchword.

The Monroe Doctrine and Open Door policy were by no means dis-

4. Homer Lea (1876–1912), American soldier and publicist; military adviser to Sun Yat-sen; author of *The Valor of Ignorance*, Harper & Brothers (1909), a detailed prediction of a U.S.-Japanese war.

carded, as the Chapultepec and Rio conferences of 1945 and 1947 and the Marshall mission in Asia demonstrated. But a new element entered American policy when Truman called for aid to Greece and Turkey in 1947 in the name not only of collective security but of American security; he argued that ". . . totalitarian regimes imposed upon free people, by direct or indirect aggression, undermine the foundations of international peace and hence the security of the United States."[5]

Although the Marshall Plan, as originally proposed, did not preclude aid to the Soviet Union and other Communist states (Marshall said the program would not be "directed against any country or doctrine but against hunger, poverty, desperation, and chaos"),[6] once the Communist nations refused to take part, Marshall and other administration figures argued before congressional committees that United States economic aid could reduce the danger of Communist revolutions or electoral victories in the countries of Western Europe and hence make it less likely that these potential powers would line up against the United States in a new war. Significantly, the Secretary of Defense joined the Secretary of State in asking for the European recovery program. "Peace and security are not to be viewed merely in terms of great military power or wealth in the hands of the United States," said James V. Forrestal, adding that

France had its Maginot line . . . and ancient Rome had her legionnaires, but none of these gave real security. . . . In our own case the security of our nation has to be viewed not merely in the light of our military strength but in the light of the restoration of balance throughout the world.[7]

By 1949, spokesmen for the administration were stating this point more emphatically. Immediately after ratification of the North Atlantic Treaty, they sought funds for building up the military forces of the new allies. Dean Acheson, now Secretary of State, described Western Europe as America's first line of defense. So long as it remained militarily weak, he declared, "the United States is open to attack on its own territory to a greater extent than ever before."[8] American policy-makers began to take a similar attitude toward areas other than Europe after the outbreak of the Korean War. Almost immediately after authorizing American air and naval forces to defend South Korea, Truman announced that the Seventh Fleet would protect the Chinese Nationalist regime on Formosa. He also proposed to aid the French in their struggle against Communist-led guerrillas in Indochina.

5. Statement of President Truman to a joint session of Congress, March 12, 1947.
6. *State Department Bulletin,* June 15, 1947, pp. 1159-1160.
7. *Hearings, European Recovery Program,* Congress, Senate, Committee on Foreign Relations, 80th Congress, 2nd Session, p. 480.
8. *Hearings, Military Assistance Program,* Congress, Senate, Armed Services and Foreign Relations Committees, 81st Congress, 1st Session, p. 7.

Since the Indochinese rebels had support from the Chinese Communists, observed Dean Rusk, then Assistant Secretary of State for Far Eastern Affairs, in testimony before Congress, their war against the French was tantamount to Chinese aggression. "If that aggression succeeds in that area," Rusk declared, "it would bring added strength and impetus to Communist aggression in other parts of the world and it would seriously affect the basic power situation upon which our own security depends." If the Chinese prevailed, they would acquire new resources—"the bread basket of Southeast Asia." The "free world" would suffer "a sapping of sources of strength . . . ; strength in terms of raw-materials resources; strength in terms of strategic position; and strength in terms of potential manpower." Rusk went on to claim that "the loss of the province of Tonkin, where active operations are now going on . . . would make it extremely difficult to retain the remainder of Indochina. The loss of Indochina would make it extremely difficult to retain Burma and Siam in the free-world system."[9]

From 1950 onward, America's stand in Asia resembled its stand in Europe. The truce line finally established in Korea, the Formosa straits, and the line drawn in 1954 between Communist North Vietnam and the rest of Southeast Asia were treated as military frontiers. The United States engaged itself by treaty to defend South Korea against another attack, and some 50,000 American troops remained in the country. Similarly, the United States signed a mutual defense treaty with Nationalist China. In 1955 and 1958, when the Communists shelled Quemoy and the Matsus, President Eisenhower and Secretary of State Dulles warned that seizure even of those tiny islands situated just off the mainland harbor of Amoy might constitute a threat to the United States. By the Southeast Asia Treaty of 1954, the American government meanwhile committed itself to the proposition that any Communist aggression against South Vietnam, Laos, Cambodia, or Thailand would "endanger its own peace and safety."

In the Middle East, the United States gravitated to a position of defining as its vital interests the territorial and political integrity of non-Communist states. The Eisenhower Doctrine of 1957 pledged United States aid to any government in the region menaced by Communist attack or subversion. A memorandum prepared by various hands in the State Department and submitted by Secretary Dulles to the Foreign Relations Committee explained the logic behind this doctrine.

The Soviet Union aspires to control the Middle East, not because it needs or is dependent upon the resources or the transportation and communications channels of the area, but because it sees control of the area as a major step

9. *Hearings, Mutual Society Act of 1951,* Congress, Senate, Armed Services and Foreign Relations Committees, 82nd Congress, 1st Session, pp. 533-537.

toward eventually undermining the strength of the whole free world. Africa might well be the first major objective. Control of the oil of the Middle East would almost insure control of Europe. . . . The Middle East offers an avenue for aggression against India, West Pakistan, and the Asian countries which lie to the east of them. Successful Soviet aggression in the Middle East could flow to the eastward as gains were consolidated.[10]

Concern for American security had clearly replaced concern for collective security. As Dulles saw it, the world situation has to be viewed in simple balance-of-power terms, because ". . . our national security cannot rest on the strength of the United States alone. We must have allies to join their strength with ours and we must also prevent their strength from falling into Soviet hands. . . . If the Soviets take over the great land masses of Europe, Asia, and Africa, the scales of world power would be heavily weighted against us." He told Congress that subversion posed an even greater danger than overt aggression, for successful subversion of a free government could give the Soviet Union control of a country with "its population unharmed and its industries and resources intact."[11]

All continents were viewed as arenas of competition. In the Western Hemisphere, the Eisenhower, Kennedy, and Johnson administrations were prepared to forgo inter-American cooperation in order to minimize the risk of a Communist gain. The United States acted in Guatemala in 1954, at the Bay of Pigs in 1961, and in the Dominican Republic in 1965 without prior consultation with other American republics. In Africa, the United States government supported United Nations intervention in the Congo on premises expounded later to the House Foreign Affairs Committee by one of Kennedy's Assistant Secretaries of State: ". . . when it comes down to a question of whether the Russians will put in the steel structure of government in the Congo or whether we will, I think we have to work for our doing it because of the danger to a world order of having country after country operated as responsive puppets to a central world Communist movement run out of Moscow."[12]

From the late 1940's until the late 1960's, American thinking about foreign policy was substantially military in character. The globe was conceived as a potential battleground between Soviet Communist forces on one side and American and "free world" forces on the other. Any

10. *Hearings, The President's Proposal on the Middle East,* Congress, Senate, Armed Services and Foreign Relations Committees, 85th Congress, 1st Session, pp. 30-31.

11. *Hearings, Mutual Security Appropriations for 1954,* Congress, Senate, Committee on Appropriations, 83rd Congress, 1st Session, p. 77.

12. *Hearings, United Nations Operation in the Congo,* Congress, House, Committee on Foreign Affairs, 87th Congress, 1st Session, p. 21.

addition to the land or resources of any Communist nation (except possibly Yugoslavia) or any political successes by Communists or Communist sympathizers would, it was assumed, add to the relative strength of the Soviet Union and diminish correspondingly that of the United States. American statesmen were not only preoccupied with elements of military potential; they also adopted military habits of thought. One such habit is to avoid estimating a potential enemy's intentions but instead to appraise his capabilities and to assume that he will do whatever mischief he can. Dulles's adherence to this way of thinking was evident in his response to a Senator who asked whether he possessed actual evidence of Soviet designs on the Middle East. "No one can reliably predict whether, and if so, when, there would be Communist armed aggression," he replied, "but three things are known: (1) the Communist capability, (2) the temptation, (3) the lack of any moral restraints."[13]

A second, closely related habit is to emphasize readiness for the worst contingency that might arise, a rule best illustrated by American policy in Europe, in which priority consistently went to preparedness for a massive assault mounted in secrecy and launched suddenly and surprisingly by the Soviets. It was much more difficult, as a result, to test whether the U.S.S.R. might be willing to settle some European issues. Between 1950 and 1953, the Truman administration rejected all Soviet suggestions for negotiations on an all-German peace treaty. In 1957-58 the Eisenhower administration rejected Polish Foreign Minister Adam Rapacki's scheme for making Central Europe a denuclearized zone. On both occasions, as cautious and hard-eyed Western analysts now read the evidence, the Soviets may have had a geniune desire for some kind of agreement.[14] The United States did not follow up Soviet overtures in large part because if agreements were reached, it believed NATO would be less able to lay preparations for the worst contingency.

In other rimlands American diplomacy has concentrated on building up ready military force to the exclusion of almost all other considerations. Between 1953 and 1963, more than half of all United States aid in Asia went to Korea, Nationalist China, and South Vietnam. Each of these three states was ruled during all or most of this decade by dictatorial governments. Though President Eisenhower and President Kennedy both affirmed belief in principle that popularly based governments possessed much greater strength in the long run, neither mentioned this principle in connection with these Asian states until Kennedy in 1963 uttered some cautious criticism of the tottering Diem regime. American thinking was concentrated here, too, on a "worst contingency"—a full-scale North

13. *Hearings, The President's Proposal on the Middle East*, p. 5.
14. Adam B. Ulam, *Expansion and Coexistence: Soviet Foreign Policy, 1917–1967* (New York: Praeger, 1968), pp. 504-514, 610-613.

Korean, Chinese, or North Vietnamese invasion—and such thinking precluded the diplomacy of looking toward a longer run.

It is now a fashion among writers identified with the New Left to suppose that the postwar Soviet menace was invented in Washington.[15] Bent from the beginning on extirpating Communism, these revisionist writers contend, American officials provoked the cold war by attempting to install anti-Soviet regimes in Eastern Europe. This reconstruction ignores almost completely the cooperative spirit which Truman and his agents displayed time and again at Potsdam, in meetings of the Council of Foreign Ministers, and at sessions of the United Nations and its committees. It ignores the steady accumulation of evidence that Soviet-backed Communists not only brutally suppressed all potential political opponents in Eastern Europe but also did their utmost to provoke disorder and seize power in Italy and France. It ignores, too, the evidence of Yugoslav and Bulgarian aid to Communist rebels in Greece, the demands of the U.S.S.R. for a strategic trusteeship in Tripolitania and for territorial and other concessions from neutral Turkey, and Soviet support for separatism in Azerbaijan, coupled with failure of the Red Army to withdraw from that Iranian province. Anyone looking open-mindedly at the cables and memoranda crossing the desks of Truman and his key advisers between 1945 and 1947 can hardly fail to understand why they reached the conclusion that the Soviet Union aimed at control of Western Europe, the Mediterranean, and the Middle East.[16]

The subsequent refusal of Russia and her satellites to participate in the Marshall Plan, efforts by Western European Communists to defeat that plan, the Czech coup, and the Berlin blockade necessarily seemed confirmation of the original judgment. The solidarity with the Soviet Union shown by the triumphant Chinese Communists, together with guerrilla or subversive activity by other Communists in Korea, Southeast Asia, and India, appeared to be evidence that Soviet imperial ambitions ranged even more widely. The sudden North Korean attack on South Korea

15. As examples, see Denna F. Fleming, *The Cold War and Its Origins, 1917–1960*, 2 vols. (New York: Doubleday, 1961); Gar Alperovitz, *Atomic Diplomacy: Hiroshima and Potsdam—The Use of the Atomic Bomb and American Confrontation with Soviet Power* (New York: Simon and Schuster, 1965); David Horowitz, *Free World Colossus* (New York: Hill and Wang, 1965); and, as the most responsible statement of such a position, Walter LaFeber, *America, Russia, and the Cold War, 1945–1966* (New York: John Wiley, 1967).

16. Some of this correspondence is now published in *Foreign Relations of the United States, 1945*—Vol. I: *General: The United Nations* (Washington, D.C.: Department of State, 1968), Vol. II: *General: Political and Economic Matters*, Vol. III: *European Advisory Commission, Austria, Germany*, Vol. IV: *Europe*, Vol. V: *Europe*, Vol. VIII: *The Near East and Africa*, and *Foreign Relations of the United States, 1946*, Vol. V: *The British Commonwealth; Western and Central Europe*, 1969.

added final proof, for there existed no doubt that Soviet authorities dictated policy in Pyongyang and directed, through advisers at every major command level, the operations of North Korean military units.[17] A riot in Bogotá in 1948, allegedly inspired by Communists, suggested that Soviet ambitions extended to the Western Hemisphere. Meanwhile, unwelcome evidence that at least a few clandestine Communists had infiltrated the British, Canadian, and American governments made it seem that even during the period of the wartime alliance, the Soviet Union had regarded the English-speaking nations as enemies.

To apparent evidence of Soviet expansionism and hostility, American leaders need not, of course, have reacted by deciding to interpose American power. Aid to Turkey and Greece, the North Atlantic Treaty, the arming of NATO, the Southeast Asia Treaty, the Eisenhower Doctrine, and the use of American forces in Lebanon and Vietnam reflected judgment not only that the Soviet Union had imperialistic aims but also that it was so important to prevent those aims from fulfillment that it justified the risk of a large-scale war. To explain why Americans drew this conclusion, it is important to take into account not only the prevailing view of Soviet behavior but also another factor—awareness of advancing technology.

On the eve of World War II, Roosevelt and his civilian advisers believed that German bombers based in Brazil or the Azores could reach targets in the United States, and this belief heightened their concern about Nazi activity in Latin America and the Iberian Peninsula. By the end of World War II, intercontinental bombers were almost in production, and long-range guided or ballistic missiles were a possibility. The sense of peril grew as one generation of nuclear weapons gave way to a second, as tests proved the workability of a hydrogen bomb. Intelligence showed the Soviet Union rapidly catching up in nuclear technology. The threat of possible direct attack by the U.S.S.R. disturbed Truman and his civilian advisers. In the Eisenhower administration, when the Soviets demonstrated an intercontinental bomber fleet and a long-range missile capability, the anxiety of the White House grew.

Awareness of advancing technology could have led instead to less concern about geographic positions, manpower, and natural resources— elements of power which had determined the outcome of World War I and World War II. But a future war could be imagined only in vague outline while past wars could be recollected in detail. American participation in the two world wars had followed inevitably, it seemed, from crises in faraway places—the Balkans, Manchuria, Czechoslovakia, Poland. It

17. Roy E. Appleman, *South to the Naktong, North to the Yalu, June-November, 1950,* (Washington, D.C.: Office of the Chief of Military History, Department of the Army, 1961), p. 7.

seemed, therefore, that Americans could not—and should not—in the future ignore episodes abroad that reminded them of Sarajevo or the Manchurian affair or Hitler's descent on Czechoslovakia.

In the two world wars, moreover, Americans had had time to muster their resources while others held the enemy at bay. The new technology made such a grace period unlikely. Acheson, Dulles, Rusk, and others repeatedly argued that rather than take the expensive course of turning America into an armed camp of immediate preparedness, it would be wiser to seek allies who might give the United States at least a little leeway for mobilization. This kind of reasoning, mixing supposition about the future with inference from the past, justified many of the changes in American diplomacy. But neither this reasoning nor perceptions of Soviet intransigence and expansionism led inevitably to the policies actually adopted. American statesmanship became preoccupied with military security, with the capabilities of the potential foe, and readiness for worst contingencies. In part, this preoccupation was a result of domestic politics. American political leaders recollected the strength of isolationism prior to World War II, and most officials in the executive branch, many Congressmen, and most members of the foreign policy establishment feared a revival of isolationism. They read signs of its return into the Henry Wallace campaign of 1948, congressional opposition in 1950-51 to stationing troops with NATO, the public support for General MacArthur in 1951, the popularity of Senator Joseph McCarthy in the early fifties, the campaign for the Bricker Amendment, persistent criticism of foreign aid, the activities of such groups as the Committee for a Sane Nuclear Policy, the Goldwater candidacy of 1964, and the upsurge of protest in the sixties against the war in Vietnam.

The most effective exhortation involved warnings that the people of the United States faced immediate danger. If stated convincingly, this argument could subdue any doubts and was, therefore, used in every conceivable context. Witness, for example, administrator Robert L. Johnson's testimony in support of the International Information Administration budget for fiscal 1954:

I think there are bonds that can be developed that are strong, and may prevent a third world war, and I think unless we win the cold war in the next two years we are apt to have a third world war. So I am anxious to use all the tools that honorable people can use to win the hearts and minds of the people of this world.[18]

Reliance on such arguments compelled the executive branch to send representatives of the military establishment to Capitol Hill to support

18. *Hearings, Overseas Information Programs of the United States,* Congress, Senate, Committee on Foreign Relations, 83rd Congress, 1st Session, p. 869.

foreign policy recommendations. Though Truman took pains to separate the issue of subsequent military aid to Europe from the ratification of the Atlantic treaty, he arranged for both the Secretary of Defense and the Chairman of the Joint Chiefs to appear before the Foreign Relations Committee. For the first post-Korean mutual security program, thirteen out of thirty administration witnesses represented the military establishment. Annually, thereafter, about one-third of the executive branch witnesses for any aid program would come from the Pentagon.

The tack taken by the executive branch responded also to the need of other Representatives and Senators to justify themselves in the eyes of their constituents. Even if they themselves regarded the Executive's policies as wise, they had to explain to voters why they accepted the risks involved in alliances and why they contributed money to foreigners. Few felt it adequate to say that they followed the lead of the President or the Secretary of State or the advice of diplomats or other political analysts. Most preferred to portray themselves as defenders of America's security. The fundamental logic of American policy was the belief that the American people would respond first to what could be called the logic of fear.

Although the foreign policies of the United States might have been rationalized in military terms in any case, the actual involvement of the Pentagon and military commands in the policy-making process has had the effect of intertwining with the rationale for certain foreign policies a rationale for increased defense spending. It has also entailed an increase in the number and variety of military options available to Presidents in crises, probably at the expense of making other kinds of options either less available or less visible.

But while members of the military establishment have become much involved in foreign policy, few have regarded this as their primary function. Whether in uniform or not, they continue to regard the protection and strengthening of the military services as their primary function. Of course, military men have sometimes supported foreign policies that worked against their parochial interests. Some officers and Pentagon civilians, for example, advocated the Baruch plan, the test-ban treaty of 1953, and other moves toward arms limitation.[19] Secretary McNamara's Montreal

19. In the case of the nuclear test-ban treaty, however, the Joint Chiefs of Staff attached a set of conditions to their agreement to support the treaty: that withdrawal from the obligations of the treaty be as easy as possible; that the government pursue an aggressive program of underground testing, not barred by the treaty, and that other research and development facilities, for testing in those environments forbidden by the treaty, be kept intact and ready for action should the treaty be broken. *Nuclear Test Ban Treaty*, Hearings before the Committee on Foreign Relations, U.S. Senate, 88th Congress, 1st session, 1963, pp. 274-275. All of the Chiefs testified that, unless their conditions were, in fact, met, they would

speech of 1966 stands as one of the most eloquent appeals for reconsideration of the priority given military security over other national needs.[20] But such instances are exceptions. Most of the time officers and civilians from the military establishment addressing foreign policy issues have taken positions consistent with advocacy of larger investment in military force.

At the end of World War II, these officers and civilians feared a complete dismantling of all American defenses. To an extent, it took place. The Army dropped from over eight million men in 1945 to below 600,-000 in 1950. Officers were conscious not only of the time that had been needed to build up forces for World War II but of the fact that advancing technology made lead-time requirements longer than before. B-36 bombers, ordered in 1940, were not to be operational before 1947. A *Midway*-class carrier would not leave the ways until two years after construction began. Fearful lest the country fail to prepare for an unforeseeable future, officers and civilian secretaries in the Pentagon advising Truman inevitably stressed the military dangers that might arise from the diplomatic intransigence and ideological imperialism of the Soviet Union. Equally inevitably, men from the military establishment interpreted the Soviet moves of 1948—the Czech coup and the Berlin blockade—as steps preparatory to aggression. The alternative interpretation—that the U.S.S.R. was reacting to the Truman Doctrine and the Marshall Plan by building a defensive wall—did not lend itself as well to the case for military preparedness.

At subsequent stages, whenever issues turned on predictions regarding future Soviet or Chinese behavior, the military establishment, as a rule, associated itself with the direst forecasts. Such is the military tradition. It was no coincidence that such forecasts in turn provided a rationale for spending money on maintaining or expanding military installations and developing and producing new weapons. Secretaries of Defense usually tried to hold down service demands for funds, and differences of opinion sometimes arose between civilians and professionals over the degree of danger involved in foreign developments. For example, Gates and McNamara evidently took a more hopeful view than the Joint Chiefs of prospects for Soviet agreement to limitations on strategic weapons; both vetoed JCS proposals to proceed with development of full-scale anti-

---

have to oppose the treaty. During the Senate hearings, for example, General Wheeler, then Army Chief of Staff, reminded the committee that "in the purest sense of the term any agreement or treaty which limits the manner in which we develop our weapons systems represents a military disadvantage." *Ibid.*, p. 355. The treaty was ratified by a vote of 80 to 19.

20. Robert S. McNamara, *The Essence of Security* (New York: Harper & Row, 1968), pp. 141-158.

ballistic missile systems. In the later stages of the Vietnamese war, McNamara and Clifford differed with the Chiefs about the extent of peril entailed in ending that war with something short of victory.

But the range of disagreement over foreign policy between the Secretaries of Defense and the Joint Chiefs has usually been relatively narrow. Though civilian secretaries have fought for economics within the Pentagon, they have still had to go to the Budget Bureau, the White House, and Capitol Hill to demand and argue for immense expenditures. These expenditures have had to be justified in terms of probable perils. Civilians in the military establishment no less than professional officers have felt a positive responsibility to take a pessimistic, foreboding view of actual and potential international issues.

Representatives of civilian agencies should have been able, of course, to discount the biases of the Pentagon just as they might discount those of the Commerce Department or Agriculture Department. To an extent, all Presidents and presidential aides have done so. But, as a rule, they have had to assume that Congress and the public would not do likewise but would instead accept military judgment on foreign affairs as sage, detached, and disinterested. And because Presidents have been aware of the military establishment's prestige with Congress and the public, they have had to pay unusual deference to military opinion, even within their private councils.

The military establishment has gotten from Congress some of what it estimated as the military strength necessary to cope with the foreign contingencies which it forecast. (Not all, to be sure, for Congress has consistently shown a preference for high-technology hardware, involving contracts, profits, and jobs for constituents, over providing the services with manpower or everyday items like machine guns, mortars, and landing craft, and the services have adjusted to this fact by stressing such items in their budgetary planning.) One result has been the military's increasing capacity for suggesting to the President that he employ military force to deal with foreign problems.

At the time of the Berlin blockade, Forrestal and the Joint Chiefs could recommend a limited range of alternatives—send tanks down the *Autobahn* and, if they were were halted, use SAC bombers; test whether the Soviets would stop an airlift; or get out. Despite the Korean War buildup, the Joint Chiefs of 1954 could offer Eisenhower only three choices in Indochina —the use of land-based and carrier-based bombers to rescue the French, followed perhaps by contingents of United States ground forces, or the use of nuclear weapons, or taking no military action at all. In the 1960's, on the other hand, with 10 per cent of GNP being spent on military capabilities, Kennedy and Johnson could be presented with a variety of alternative military moves suited to defending Berlin, reacting to the placement of Soviet missiles in Cuba, coping with a revolution in the Dominican Republic, or supporting Saigon against the Vietcong. Given their possession of F-105's, F-4's, carriers, destroyers, patrol craft, mine-layers, helicopters, Green Beret detachments, etc., etc., the military could, in the latter case, offer a different prescription for each worsening phase.

Theoretically, the President ought to possess the widest possible range of options when dealing with any critical international problem. Such is the meaning of "flexible response." Having on hand a varied mixture of military forces does not make it inevitable or even necessarily more probable that he will use them. It simply provides him the opportunity to do so if he judges such action wisest. But this abstract reasoning ignores at least two realities. In the first place, situations serious enough to entail contemplation of the use of force are almost certainly situations with built-in deadlines. The President cannot spend much time considering all imaginable courses of action; he has to focus on those few which his subordinates are best equipped to carry out. In the second place, the investment required for a wide range of ready military options diverts some resources from preparation and multiplication of other kinds of options. Although one less well-outfitted carrier task force would not convert into one better-equipped State Department country desk, insofar as both demand talent and money (and talent and money are scarce) the one may be had only at the expense of the other.

In practice, therefore, heavy investment in military forces, and most recently, in flexible response, probably has increased the likelihood that a President in a crisis will consider military options above other possible options.

The Cuban missile crisis of 1962 provides an illustration. From the discovery of the missiles on October 14 until October 28, when Khrushchev promised to remove them, the executive committee of the National Security Council (Ex Com) spent at least 90 per cent of its time studying alternative uses of troops, bombers, and warships. Although the possibility of seeking withdrawal of the missiles by straightforward diplomatic negotiation received some attention within the State Department, it seems scarcely to have been aired in the Ex Com. At the same time, scarcely any attention went to possible uses of economic leverage. To be sure, any time spent on options other than a "surgical" air strike or a naval quarantine might have been time wasted. But it seems noteworthy that nonmilitary agencies should have had so few expedients to put before the President, and it seems at least possible that this would not have been the case if State, the Treasury, and perhaps some lesser agencies had also been manned and funded for flexible response.

The existence of a variety of military options has probably had less effect in noncrisis situations, when representatives of civilian agencies have had more leisure to reflect on what they might do if the President assigned them a task. Even in routine handling of foreign policy problems, how-

ever, the massive presence of the military establishment has very likely
had some skewing effects. Officers from the services and the Joint Staff
and civilians from the Office of the Secretary of Defense necessarily concentrate on military aspects of issues that come before them. If involved in
administering a foreign aid program, they focus on military components.
While they can consider and even urge development aid, they must do so
in terms of its contribution to military strength. If they take part in preparing a paper on, say, post-Franco Spain, they have to emphasize security aspects. Otherwise, when sitting at a table with representatives of
State, CIA, the Treasury, and other agencies, they lead from a weak suit.

While representatives of the military establishment may, and perhaps do,
conclude that an economic or diplomatic or other approach to the problem
would be preferable, they are precluded from going very far in developing or
recommending strategies that involve primarily the resources of other parts
of the government since military force is presumed to be their area of competence. Papers from the Pentagon could speak again and again of the
crucial importance of Saigon's winning "the hearts and minds" of the Vietnamese peasantry, but their operative paragraphs necessarily dealt with
more efficient methods for killing, maiming, or starving a battlefield enemy.

Interdepartmental memoranda on relatively routine foreign policy problems usually represent a blend of views and recommendations. On formal
committees, such as assistant secretary level, interdepartmental regional
groups of the Johnson administration or interagency groups of the Nixon
administration, the military establishment has had two representatives,
one from the Joint Staff and one from International Security Affairs. Often,
military capabilities have received heavy emphasis in papers relating to
noncrisis situations. In sum, while the preoccupation with military security
characteristics of post-World War II American foreign policy has to be laid
to events, changes in technology, perceptions of the past, and predilections
of Congress and the public, the extensive participation of the military establishment in the policy process accentuated this preoccupation, keyed
policy to defense expenditures and, in both crisis and noncrisis situations,
tended to focus undue concentration on military responses.

The military establishment's participation in the policy process produced
some distortive effects. It led to an overemphasis on NATO affairs, the
nuclear balance, subversion in Southeast Asia, and other subjects with
special implications for the Defense budget or for contests over roles and
missions among the services or service branches. It also gave Presidents a
richer variety of military options than of other kinds of options, when confronted either with crises or with longer-term problems. In these respects,
the military establishment has had a direct and potent impact on foreign
policy.

But the character and conduct of United States policy would probably have been the same had the military establishment taken no part at all. For the real or apparent preoccupation with military security reflected the attitudes and values of civilian policy-makers, and ultimately of the American people. The conspicuous role of military men and civilian secretaries in framing and defending foreign policy was traceable in part to belief that visible military support was a political necessity. Under the circumstances that prevailed since World War II, had there been no elements in the military establishment concerned with foreign policy, it is likely Presidents and Secretaries of State would have had to invent them.

The recent past has, however, witnessed changes in the basic factors shaping American foreign policy. The Sino-Soviet split, acute divisions among other Communist states, and shifts in Soviet policy toward the United States and the nations of Western Europe have changed the image of the enemy. In addition, Americans have grown used to the shrinkage of the world and the absence of a sense of invulnerability. The "loss" of Cuba and the outcome of the 1962 missile crisis suggested, at least to some, that localized Communist successes need not jeopardize America's safety quite so much as had been assumed. And, most important of all, the force of military logic and the authoritative status of military professionals as spokesmen on foreign policy—or even on military matters—have diminished.

Mere passage of time accounts in part for this last change. Only men and women of middle age and older remember World War II. Many voters scarcely recall Korea. But the prolonged war in Vietnam, where predictions of victory from high military men were once so frequent, has had a decisive impact on most Americans. If they have any image of the contemporary military professional, it is at best that of a technician like General Westmoreland, at worst, a caricature drawn from a novel like *Fail-Safe* or a movie like *Dr. Strangelove*.

Meanwhile, national priorities have changed very critically. Civil rights, the plight of the cities, the needs of urban and rural poor, the restlessness of students, and other such problems have, since the early 1960's, commanded a much larger share of public interest. Although the military establishment's resources occasionally can be used in coping with them, its expertise is largely irrelevant to them. And the war in Vietnam, coinciding with this shift in priorities, and triggering some of them, stirred widespread concern about the expense of policies heretofore vouched for by the military establishment. The spread of this concern and a diminution in respect for military views on foreign policy were registered most visibly in public opinion polls relating to the war and in the surprisingly strong bipartisan movement in Congress against both Johnson's and Nixon's proposals for deploying antiballistic missile systems.

Nor was reaction confined to outspoken "doves." Senator Richard

Russell of Georgia, long considered one of the military establishment's warmest supporters on Capitol Hill, indicated as early as 1965 skepticism about military testimony on the importance of Vietnam. "I don't think it has any value strategically," he said. During a hearing in 1968, Russell further declared, "I guess I must be an isolationist. I don't think you ought to pick up 100,000, or 200,000, or 500,000 American boys and ship them off somewhere to fight and get killed in a war as remotely connected with their interests as this one is."[21] Senator John C. Stennis of Mississippi, another longtime champion of the military establishment, asserted in 1967, "I believe that we are overcommitted. . . . I voted glibly for things around here in the fifties to guarantee this and guarantee that. I am certainly one that did not realize how hard it was going to be to carry them out."[22] Representative George H. Mahon of Texas, the shepherd of Defense appropriation bills, in the House declared that the military had "generated . . . lack of confidence" by their "many mistakes."[23] Issuing from such sources, these pronouncements were more than straws in the wind. They indicated that the authority previously attaching to military opinion had virtually disappeared.

These alterations in circumstances, in national priorities, and in public and congressional respect for military wisdom all suggest that major changes in basic American foreign policy are in prospect. Possibly, of course, the changes will be temporary. The Korean War was followed by a "never again" mood, accompanied by a slight turn of public interest away from international affairs. Yet preoccupation with military security quickly reasserted itself. The same could occur after Vietnam. Some act of belligerence on the part of the Soviet Union or China could reawaken fears subdued or subsiding. So could a number of other events, including, for example, a sudden transfer of allegiance or collapse within a nation accounted a reliable American ally. Possibly, though, the change in United States policy will bring a long pendulum swing back toward isolationism such as that of the mid-1930's. But what seems more probable at this writing is the evolution of a trinity of operating principles superficially similar to those of earlier eras but different from them in scope and substance: first, a security-based but cooperative "Monroe Doctrine" embracing the great non-Communist industrial powers—the nations of Western Europe and Japan; second, an "Open Door" doctrine entailing support in various forms for economic and political development in less-developed countries, but with

21. Interview on CBS television, August 1, 1965, quoted in Theodore Draper, *The Abuse of Power* (New York: Viking, 1967), p. 154; *Hearings, Department of Defense Appropriations for 1969*, Congress, Senate, Committee on Appropriations, Part V, p. 2545.

22. *Hearings, Worldwide Military Commitments*, Congress, Senate, Committee on Armed Services, 90th Congress, 1st Session, Part II, p. 133.

23. *Congressional Record*, 91st Congress, 1st Session, Vol. 115, Part 10, p. 13128.

no actual or implied commitment to defend their governments against domestic or foreign foes; and, finally, a new version of nonentanglement, involving abrogation or modification of existing treaties with the end of insuring that, except for the defense of Western Europe or Japan, the United States will not be in danger of having to employ ground forces or to employ any forces at all except as part of a broad-based multilateral military effort. (Such a forecast must be accompanied by a caveat, that, if history teaches any lesson, it is that those developments which appear most probable at a given moment are rarely the developments that actually take place.)

It is possible to make slightly more confident predictions about the future of the military establishment in the foreign policy process. Even if the future sees simply a return to the policies of the fifties and early sixties, the Pentagon will probably have less to do with the framing and execution of those policies. For no event seems likely to restore the political charisma and air of infallibility which made support by military men seem almost indispensable for public acceptance of any major foreign policy decision. On the other hand, not even a violent swing toward isolationism could deprive the military establishment of all of its influence or function in the foreign policy process. The chances are that, while military professionals and Pentagon civilians will be less prominent and less influential than in the last three decades, they will continue to have a voice in formulating options and a hand in writing some of the cables and memoranda that form the stuff of foreign policy.

Such a prediction seems safe because the military establishment has developed such strong capabilities for dealing with foreign policy issues. The professional military men upon whom Roosevelt depended so heavily had to learn about international affairs while acting as presidential advisers. Of the wartime chiefs of staff, only Leahy, who spent eighteen months as ambassador to the Vichy regime, had had any experience outside his own service. Typically, by contrast, the service chiefs and other senior officers of the present day will have had prolonged involvement in the subtleties of international politics. General Wheeler (now retired), for example, became Chief of Staff of the Army after a career that included attendance at the National War College, three years of occupation service in Europe, four years with NATO, and three years on the Joint Staff. After moving up to the chairmanship of the JCS, he remarked to a congressional committee, "It is very hard to define where the military begins and the civilians leave off in our form of government."[24]

Senior officers not only possess background and qualifications for work on foreign policy problems; they possess a special organizational capability.

24. *Hearings, Department of Defense Appropriations for 1964,* Congress, House, Committee on Appropriations, 88th Congress, 1st Session, Part II, p. 131.

The reliance placed on the military establishment by past Presidents has not been wholly a matter of choice. Truman stated an intention to centralize responsibility in the State Department. After acquiring some experience, he remarked regretfully on June 13, 1945, to Forrestal that "there wasn't much material in the State Department to work with." Kennedy started with a similar notion and came to the same conclusion. In the summer of 1961 he found the State Department a "bowl of jelly."[25]

While Truman and Kennedy did not necessarily judge fairly, it has been consistently the case that the State Department has not produced what the White House has wanted. Traditionally, Foreign Service officers have developed skill in reportage, representation, and negotiation. As a rule, they have not practiced reasoning out contingencies, analyzing alternatives, and planning detailed courses of action. Since professional military men do acquire these arts, the Pentagon can outperform the State Department in staff work on foreign policy problems (as discussed in Chapter 3). Though latent capacity for matching the Pentagon may exist in the Agency for International Development, the U.S. Information Agency, the Arms Control and Disarmament Agency, and certain reaches of State, it seems unlikely that the military establishment will be supplanted in this sphere so long as Foreign Service officers dominate the civilian foreign affairs community.

Furthermore, military men are apt to retain roles in the foreign policy process simply because they have them now. The President and his staff could sharply curtail consultation with the chairman and the Chiefs or with the Secretary of Defense. A simple executive order could decree that the military establishment be represented in interagency groups and other such bodies by a civilian or an officer from the Joint Staff, but not both. The State Department officials who ordinarily chair such committees could invite military representatives less regularly. Commanders overseas and chiefs of military aid groups could be directed to communicate with Washington on any subjects affecting foreign policy through State Department or other civilian channels.

But even if policy-makers would not be restrained from taking such steps by awareness of the unusual qualifications and capabilities of the military, they would probably not succeed in drastically civilianizing the process. At every level in State, CIA, and other foreign affairs agencies, consultation with the Pentagon has become an acquired habit, and the habits of bureaucracies are not easily altered. Similarly, overseas commands and military assistance groups have developed functions and procedures no arbitrary organizational change could quickly alter. It is almost

25. Walter Millis and Eugene S. Duffield, eds., *The Forrestal Diaries* (New York: Viking, 1951), p. 62; Arthur M. Schlesinger, Jr., *A Thousand Days: John F. Kennedy in the White House* (Boston: Houghton Mifflin, 1965), p. 406.

inconceivable that the military establishment could be restored to the kind of marginal or fitful role in foreign policy that it occupied prior to 1940.

Finally, it is more than likely that the military establishment will continue to take part in the policy-making process because, regardless of how basic United States policies may change, many major issues are certain to be ones on which the military cannot be denied a voice. No foreseeable set of international agreements will do away with nuclear weapons or missile systems. No détente with the Soviet Union seems likely to end altogether the need for some American military presence in Europe and Asia. Even if there were no other reason, it would be called for in order to reassure Germany's western neighbors and to permit the Japanese to adhere to the arms limitation clauses of their constitution. In addition, it is a prerequisite for making workable any curb on the proliferation of nuclear power.

The military establishment can, of course, be ordered by the President to tailor strategic and general purpose forces to diplomatic ends. If opposition to military spending continues to grow in Congress, the services could find themselves in pre-1940 circumstances, with only a handful of friends on Capitol Hill. The size and composition of the forces could be determined almost wholly by the judgment of civilians outside the establishment, as was the case with the Navy between the signing of the Washington treaty in 1922 and the beginning of rearmament in the 1930's. Even so, generals, admirals, and civilian secretaries would—as in the twenties and thirties—have an undeniable right to be heard. Since the military establishment is now very different, since it possesses staff capabilities not equaled elsewhere in the government, and since it is inextricably meshed with the foreign affairs establishment, it seems most unlikely that military views will ever again, as in the past era, go unheard and unregarded.

Indeed, there seems little chance that the military establishment will be ignored in the framing of foreign policy. The history of the last three decades warns that the opposite danger is greater. The danger does not stem from the military establishment itself. Except possibly for MacArthur, no professional or civilian with any following in that establishment has sought to determine policy, as did Moltke, Schlieffen, Tirpitz, and Tojo. In the past, "militarization" of American foreign policy has developed because civilians adopted military ways of thinking about political problems. The influence of the military establishment on domestic politics or the domestic economy may be functions of its budget or size or power, but its influence on foreign policy depends on an altogether different variable—the extent to which civilians in the executive branch, in Congress, and among the public bear in mind or forget General Marshall's maxim that political problems, if thought about in military terms, become military problems.

10

Control of Revolution and Counterrevolution

Since the advent of the nuclear age, the United States has used its military power in sporadic attempts to shore up or to put down foreign governments. These attempts have been subjected to intensive critical examination, particularly since one of them—Vietnam—developed into a major war. To the extent that they have involved direct intervention, overt or clandestine, they have been few and relatively ineffectual. The underlying motivation seems to have been shifted over the last decade from fear of an allegedly monolithic and expansionist world community hegemony, to concern about local violence, however inspired, that might spill over national boundaries. After tentative support of the reformist Arbenz regime in Guatemala, the 1954 CIA paramilitary adventure encouraged an army *coup d'état* to replace an increasingly Communist-influenced government with a non-Communist one; the 1958 intervention in Lebanon was intended to contain a conflict not divided on Communist-non-Communist lines, and the 1965 intervention in the Dominican Republic, initially prompted by domestic sensitivity to yet another Castro and probably paranoid fears of local Communism, ended by preventing a right-wing coup.

In the latter part of April 1965, civil disorder broke out in the streets of Santo Domingo. President Johnson was faced with the question of whether to land American troops to forestall the establishment of what he described as the possibility of "another Cuba in this hemisphere." It was not easy to tell, from Washington, whether there was any real danger of a Communist takeover of the Dominican Republic, let alone what the United States might gain from taking sides in the struggle that was under way. There is no way of telling how the issue might have been resolved had it come to the President in its purest form: Do we or don't we apply our power and influence on the side of the Dominican military and the status quo? The fact of the matter is that it did not come to the President in that form because American influence had already been committed against the rebel forces four days before the President actually dealt with the question of whether to land the first detachment of Marines.

The commitment was not made by the State Department or even by the American Embassy in Santo Domingo; for all practical purposes, the initial involvement was undertaken through the military attachés in the embassy. A cable received in Washington on April 25, the day after the uprising began, and signed by William Connett, the chargé d'affaires in the absence of Ambassador W. Tapley Bennett, reported that "the country team is against a show of force by the U.S. at this time." But it went on to say that our military attachés "have stressed to the three military leaders . . . our strong feeling everything possible should be done to prevent a Communist takeover." Elsewhere it was disclosed that Connett had reluctantly agreed to the Los Santos–Wessin (the names of two of the three "loyalist" military leaders) plan to forestall a leftist coup even though it could mean more bloodshed.

It was not until late in the afternoon of April 28 that President Johnson made the decision to send in the Marines, but three days earlier the prestige of the United States government had already been firmly committed on one side of the conflict in a situation and under circumstances which Connett himself described as "extremely confused." It is too simple to say that the military, through some innate predilection for military governments or rightwing elements in Latin America, had forced the President's hand. It would be more accurate to suggest that the local military in a great many Latin American countries holds the effective political power in its hands; that the State Department has a preference for dealing with those who do have effective political power; and that the State Department's Bureau of Inter-American Affairs has habitually ceded an inordinate amount of influence over its decision-making to American military attachés who have close relationships to their Latin American counterparts. The lesson here is at least twofold: the Commander in Chief of the armed forces is not all-powerful in his capacity to order events; but the extent to which the military orders events is very often a function of the amount of leeway the military is given by civilians in one branch or another of the government.

The presence of American military men in other countries, in connection with Polaris submarine bases, or staging areas, or communications stations, tends also to involve them in demonstrations of support for existing regimes, whether through joint training exercises in Spain directed at civil disorder or liberty parties for American sailors while their ships are refueling in Capetown. Even assuming that American forces would maintain strict neutrality in a revolutionary (or counterrevolutionary) situation, their presence cannot help but be a factor in internal politics, either as a buttress for the regime or as a target for the opposition.

The dominant case in any discussion of United States military intervention must be the tragedy of Vietnam.

When it became apparent, at the beginning of the sixties, that the United States could not ". . . depend primarily upon a great capacity to retaliate instantly by means and at places of our own choosing,"[1] to deter other nations from courses of action that were adverse to our interests but that did not threaten our existence as a free society, national security policy-makers by and large heaved sighs of relief. The idea that it was possible to meet force with force at any level, and even to put on the aggressor the burden of deciding whether to escalate or to withdraw, had a considerable appeal to men who had turned away from visions of Armageddon. It was not surprising that the idea of counterinsurgency as a new kind of military skill caught on very rapidly in this atmosphere. It suggested that force could be used on a scale that was no more than human, and even implied that military results could be accomplished by persuasion, technological assistance, and political artistry—including vaccination for village children and bridge-building for their elders.

The lower end of the spectrum of force had previously been the exclusive domain of CIA's Plans Division (or department of "dirty tricks"), which, however, drew heavily upon military personnel and resources. The Plans Division's debacle at the Bay of Pigs in 1961 had not improved the agency's reputation in this area. Following an intensive investigation, a Task Force chaired by General Maxwell D. Taylor recommended divorcing large paramilitary operations from the CIA and the creation of better White House information systems resulting in a White House "situation room." Despite the Taylor report's recommendations, the CIA bureaucracy was able to circumvent the Taylor report conclusions insofar as CIA operated in "war theaters." Further, the CIA apparently was able to interpret "war theaters" as including territory in countries adjacent to war theaters, for certain purposes. The CIA may therefore have been operating on a somewhat larger scale than either reason or experience would dictate. At the same time the Army, which had been the disfavored service in the last half of the fifties, had been developing the Special Forces as units trained for what was called sublimited war, with emphasis on independent operations by a six-man squad, and by the individual soldier on his own,

---

1. John Foster Dulles, *Evolution of Foreign Policy: Speech Before the Council on Foreign Relations, Department of State Bulletin,* Vol. XXX, No. 761, 1954.

winning the support of the people in hostile or potentially hostile territory. The need for this kind of soldier was underlined, in the context of the cold war, by Khrushchev's famous speech to the 20th Party Congress, in January 1961, in which he ruled out nuclear wars and conventional wars, but urged the effectiveness of "wars of national liberation."

Against this background, enthusiasm for counterinsurgency as an instrument of national security policy echoed and re-echoed through the Kennedy administration. Major speeches proclaimed the new doctrine; a "counterinsurgency course" was introduced for military and civilian personnel assigned to Third World countries; the Special Forces were authorized to wear a green beret, despite continuing resistance from the Regular Army. Not surprisingly, the general mood of euphoria that the concept gave rise to made it almost impossible to recognize the inherent limitations of the use of force beyond the reach of national sovereignty.

The limitations are apparent in a poster in the office of the United States military advisory team in the province capital of Hue in South Vietnam. The yellowed sign tacked on the wall declares in elaborate scrollwork: "Our concept—assist the Republic of Vietnam Armed Forces in the conduct of counterinsurgency, train military and paramilitary personnel and units in counterinsurgency operations, and, finally, apply our skills in civic action (self-help) programs conducted under Vietnam government leadership at the village and province (grass-roots) level to contribute to an over-all nation-building effort." This is a reasonable definition of a limited mission in a limited war with a limited objective; apparently it was a definition which the American military advisers had been quite prepared to live with in the days before the massive expansion of American combat involvement. But across this scrollwork an unknown hand, in 1965, had scribbled in large black letters: "P.S. KILL VC, KILL VC, KILL VC."

The times—and the temper of the troops—had changed, with the landing of the first organized combat troops in March 1965, and their heavy reinforcement throughout the spring and summer as American soldiers became engaged in conventional warfare with large units of the enemy. As the scale of the fighting expanded, so did the scale of the mission at all levels: the United States presence was pervasive; nation-building had given way to killing the enemy, and nothing could be more natural than for troops engaged in so conventional a military exercise to come to believe in a conventional military objective and to expect conventional military results. It was not just the generals and admirals in Washington or Honolulu or even the headquarters of Military Assistance Command, Vietnam, in Saigon who thirsted for greater latitude than the President was prepared to grant them to expand their effort and crush the enemy once and for all. Had that been all there was to it, the President might have found this continuing pressure easier to deal with; but the pressure worked its way up in a perfectly natural way, from the front-line troops and the combat officers who were asking them to die in a conventional way for a limited military purpose which they could not understand. The frustration worked its way up the chain of command to the top, found powerful expression in the high counsels, and contributed logically and inescapably to the President's political dilemma; it became a part of the politics of the President's conduct of the war effort and therefore a valid part of the problem of the politics of defense.

A year later, in war zone C in South Vietnam, near an outpost called Suida, the impression of a professional army, moving in conventional ways toward a conventional solution of the war, was even more striking. In one day's operation, Major General William E. DePuy, commander of the First Infantry Division of the United States Army, dropped two of his battalions into a jungle plain for no other purpose than to lure whatever enemy troops might be there into a fight, to draw them in and then kill as many as possible with artillery and air strikes. It was, to be blunt, a military operation based on the simple stratagem of a tiger shoot, with American troops playing the role of the tethered goat. "Killing VC," General DePuy said, "is the name of the game." It was not the business of American troops to think in terms of negotiation or compromise settlements, of trying to strike some kind of balance of force which would encourage the government in Saigon to come to terms with the National Liberation Front or the Hanoi government.

But just as the defenders of United States policy make far too much of the complex and confusing situation in Vietnam as the ultimate test of American determination to resist the advance of Communism, so the critics of that policy may in time be proved to be mistaken in taking it as the pattern for the use of American military power in intervening in local conflicts. In the perspective of history, the Vietnam war may turn out to be a terrible but isolated example—providing we can find our way out of it before it has destroyed the fabric of American society, or involved us in a larger war.

Of greater relevance to a discussion of the uses of American military power are the major factors that have made this kind of use of military power more likely: the legacy of the cold war (discussed in Chapter 9), the shift from the doctrine of massive retaliation to one of flexible response (discussed in Chapter 8), and the development of the military assistance program. If the first is external to the military establishment, the other factors are functions of what has happened within the establishment itself.

The Military Assistance Program, originated in 1950 as a way of speeding up the reconstruction of national military establishments in Western Europe, was expanded to provide assistance to other nations on the borders of what was then the Sino-Soviet bloc. Since 1950, some seventy-eight countries have received $34.6 billion in aid through the Military Assistance Program. (See Table 10.1. All tables are taken from *Global Defense*).[2] Fiscal year 1953 marked the high point of the program with $4 billion expended. Western Europe was the major recipient, but as Europe re-

TABLE 10.1 Military Assistance Program Expenditures (In millions of dollars)

Fiscal Year	Total*
1950	$ 51.7
1951	934.2
1952	2,385.9
1953	3,953.1
1954	3,629.5
1955	2,297.2
1956	2,612.7
1957	2,349.2
1958	2,145.8
1959	2,319.0
1960	1,605.5
1961	1,440.7
1962	1,381.6
1963	1,724.7
1964	1,449.8
1965	1,201.6
1966	1,033.0
1967	898.0
1968	625.6
1969	610.6
Total	$34,649.5

* Excludes military credit sales. Amounts may not add due to rounding.
Source: Defense Department (International Security Affairs).

covered from World War II, emphasis on military aid shifted away from the grant format. In fiscal year 1964 Europe was receiving $176.7 million through MAP and with the exception of fiscal year 1965, the expenditures steadily diminished: fiscal year 1966, $101.6 million; fiscal year 1967, $58.4 million; fiscal year 1968, $42.5 million.

As European recovery proceded and as MAP expenditures in that area, and in general, dwindled, the program tended to focus more on Africa and Latin America, areas which still could not afford to buy military goods from the United States. Thus, the totals for Africa increased as follows: fiscal year 1965, $17.3 million; fiscal year 1966, $22.2 million; fiscal year 1967, $25.2 million; fiscal year 1968, $32.6 million. And in Latin America the figures also increased: fiscal year 1964, $52.1 million;

2. Congressional Quarterly Service Publication, September 1969.

TABLE 10.2 Deliveries Under Military Assistance Program†
(In millions of dollars)

Country	FY 1950–1963	FY 1964	FY 1965	FY 1966	FY 1967	FY 1968	FY 1950–1968
East Asia							
Cambodia	83.2	3.6	.3	—	—	—	87.1
China	1,960.3	128.1	84.8	76.5	70.4	115.0	2,435.0
Indo-China	709.6	—	—	—	—	—	709.6
Indonesia	53.3	7.1	2.1	.7	.6	3.1	66.9
Japan	772.1	18.7	29.6	1.2	29.1	3.6	854.3
Korea	1,706.3	124.3	173.1	153.1	149.8	197.4	2,503.9
Malaysia	—	—	*	.2	.2	.2	.6
Philippines	268.4	10.7	18.2	26.0	21.0	29.1	373.4
Thailand	415.0	52.7	36.4	40.8	44.9	—	589.7
Vietnam	846.5	185.2	274.7	170.0	—	—	1,476.4
East Asia Area **	394.5	40.4	59.3	68.3	84.7	3.1	650.3
East Asia Total	7,209.2	570.7	678.4	536.7	400.8	351.5	9,747.3
Near East and South Asia							
Afghanistan	2.3	.5	.1	.2	.1	.3	3.5
Ceylon	—	—	—	—	—	*	*
Greece	1,044.9	83.1	104.0	78.7	44.0	45.0	1,399.8
India					2.1	.2	
Iran	556.0	27.3	49.9	41.1	41.2	38.7	754.2
Iraq	46.1	*	.2	.2	.1	*	46.7
Jordan	20.6	8.1	4.6	2.8	11.9	2.1	50.2
Lebanon	8.4	.1	.1	.1	.1	.1	8.9
Nepal					.5	.5	
Pakistan					*	.1	
Saudi Arabia	28.8	1.1	.8	1.5	.8	1.0	34.0
Syria	—	*	*	*	*	*	.1
Turkey	1,994.2	101.6	118.4	100.5	118.5	130.9	2,563.9
Yemen	—	—	*	*	—	—	*
NESA Area **	648.0	63.8	62.2	6.6	.2	.1	784.1
NESA Total	4,349.3	285.7	340.4	231.6	219.4	219.1	5,645.5

Country	1950-1963	FY 1964	FY 1965	FY 1966	FY 1967	FY 1968	1950-1968
Europe							
Austria	1,189.6	39.6	4.8	1.6	*	*	1,237.6
Belgium	530.0	12.1	48.1	20.1	7.5	1.9	617.9
Denmark	4,144.5	5.2	3.5	—	—	*	4,153.2
France	900.4	.3	.1	—	—	—	900.8
Germany	2,160.0	40.0	81.6	3.2	4.2	—	2,288.9
Italy	1,153.7	10.7	49.7	*	2.8	—	1,217.0
Luxembourg	8.2	*	*	—	—	—	8.2
Netherlands	701.1	41.1	35.3	42.8	32.6	24.2	877.1
Norway	293.9	5.6	7.5	1.5	2.2	3.2	313.8
Portugal	436.4	20.1	40.6	35.5	8.0	11.8	552.4
Spain	1,034.0	.3	.2	—	—	—	1,034.5
United Kingdom	693.9	—	—	—	—	—	693.9
Yugoslavia	297.1	1.9	3.9	1.4	.9	1.2	306.2
Europe Total **	13,542.8	176.7	275.3	106.1	58.4	42.5	14,201.7
Africa							
Cameroon	.2	*	—	—	—	—	.3
Congo	.1	5.0	2.3	3.6	5.1	3.8	19.9
Dahomey	.1	—	—	—	—	—	.1
Ethiopia	62.3	10.3	8.3	10.7	9.0	17.4	118.0
Ghana	*	*	—	—	—	*	.1
Guinea	—	—	—	.7	.2	—	.9
Ivory Coast	.1	—	*	—	—	—	.1
Liberia	2.0	.7	.5	.5	1.3	1.1	6.0
Libya	4.4	1.6	2.0	1.7	2.6	1.6	13.9
Mali	.9	—	.6	.5	.7	—	2.7
Morocco	10.1	6.0	2.3	3.1	5.2	6.6	33.3
Niger	.1	—	—	—	—	—	.1
Nigeria	*	.1	.3	.4	.2	.2	1.2
Senegal	1.7	.5	.1	.1	.1	.2	2.7
Sudan	.1	*	*	.3	.3	*	.7
Tunisia	10.7	3.5	.9	.6	.7	1.7	18.0
Upper Volta	.1	—	*	*	—	—	.1
Africa Area **	—	—	—	—	—	*	*
Africa Total	92.8	27.8	17.3	22.2	25.2	32.6	218.0

Table 10.2 (continued)

Country	FY 1950-1968	FY 1964	FY 1965	FY 1966	FY 1967	FY 1968	FY 1950-1968
Latin America							
Argentina	2.8	1.5	6.0	6.4	6.8	10.9	34.4
Bolivia	5.4	3.2	1.9	2.4	2.9	3.5	19.3
Brazil	150.6	9.1	11.4	9.5	13.4	12.6	206.7
Chile	52.0	7.8	6.3	8.4	4.7	7.5	86.7
Colombia	39.4	6.2	5.7	8.3	7.9	12.2	79.7
Costa Rica	.8	.5	.2	.1	.1	.1	1.8
Cuba	10.6	–	–	–	–	–	10.6
Dominican Republic	8.2	1.5	1.2	1.6	3.4	2.3	18.3
Ecuador	22.2	2.6	2.3	3.9	3.1	2.8	37.0
El Salvador	1.7	.9	.8	.7	.6	.6	5.3
Guatemala	5.3	1.4	1.5	1.2	1.4	2.3	13.1
Haiti	3.2	–	–	–	–	–	3.2
Honduras	2.6	.4	.7	.7	1.0	1.0	6.4
Jamaica	*	.2	.4	–	.3	.3	1.1
Mexico	.6	.3	.2	.2	.2	.1	1.7
Nicaragua	4.5	1.2	1.2	1.0	1.0	1.3	10.2
Panama	1.1	.2	.2	.4	.5	.3	2.6
Paraguay	.9	1.2	.9	1.0	1.1	1.8	7.0
Peru	41.1	10.0	8.2	7.3	6.6	8.7	81.9
Uruguay	27.5	1.7	2.4	2.5	1.6	2.0	37.8
Venezuela	1.6	1.5	1.3	1.0	1.0	1.3	7.6
Latin America Area	6.9	.5	3.0	1.8	1.3	1.0	14.5
Latin America Total**	388.8	52.1	55.9	58.4	59.1	72.8	687.0
Non-Regional	2,433.1	301.5	-131.6	107.3	50.6	.3	2,761.2
Grand Total	28,016.0	1,414.5	1,235.7	1,062.4	813.5	718.7	33,260.7

* Less than $50,000.
** Includes totals for classified countries.
† Military equipment, training and related support.
Note: Totals may not add due to rounding.
Source: U.S. Defense Department (International Security Affairs).

fiscal year 1965, $55.9 million; fiscal year 1966, $58.4 million; fiscal year 1967, $59.1 million; fiscal year 1968, $72.8 million. By 1969 the entire MAP program amounted to $550 million. Meanwhile, the emphasis on military assistance in general passed to the American Foreign Military Sales program (FMS). Initiated in 1962, it is increasingly replacing MAP, especially in Europe. During fiscal years 1966-68, FMS averaged $1.8 billion while MAP dropped below $1 billion for fiscal years 1967-69.

Military sales became a highly controversial issue in the latter part of 1967. At that time it came to light that the Export-Import Bank had for some time been making "Country X" loans (so-called because the bank was not told the name of the countries) to finance military sales to nations which lacked funds for immediate payment. Credit was guaranteed by the Defense Department. It was widely felt that this device was driving impoverished nations deeper in debt by making it too easy for them to acquire military hardware they could not actually afford. At the same time the United States gained twice—from the sales, and from the interest on the loans financing the sales. The fact that few in the Congress had been aware of this system (though some had been informed) led to suspicions that the Pentagon had been trying to hide its activities. The result was a foreign-aid package from Congress in December 1967 containing provisions that would have all but terminated the foreign military sales program. During the following summer, however, Congress passed a new Foreign Military Sales Act. It abolished any role for the Export-Import Bank (which Defense had tried to re-establish that spring) and imposed a variety of other restrictions, but re-established the sales program on a basis that has proved generally noncontroversial since. In 1969, the administrations of FMS and MAP were brought together in the same office under the Deputy Assistant Secretary of Defense for Military Assistance and Sales, Air Force Lieutenant General Robert H. Warren.

Since its inception FMS has totaled $11.5 billion in sales (see Table 10.3) compared with United States military sales to foreign countries between the early 1950's and 1962, which averaged less than $300 million a year. Again, as in the MAP program, Western Europe has been the prime recipient. Between 1962 and 1968, $8 billion of the total went to Western Europe, with West Germany and Britain getting the largest shares. The total for the Near East and South Asia is $1.6 billion, with Israel and Iran as the major purchasers. In the Far East the amount is $1.4 billion, with Australia, Japan, New Zealand, and Nationalist China leading the list. The total for Africa is $0.1 billion and for Latin America $0.3 billion. These last two areas still rely more heavily on MAP. Since FMS requires more substantial expenditures on the part of the recipient nation, one would expect that the more underdeveloped countries would favor MAP. It should be noted that these figures do not include gifts of "obsolete" equipment.

TABLE 10.3 U.S. Foreign Military Sales†
(In billions of dollars)

Grand Total, Fiscal 1962-68 $11.5 billion

Sales by Type

	1962-1965	Fiscal Year 1966	1967	1968
Commercial sales	$1.8	$ .4	$ .4	$ .5
Government (cash)	3.0	1.0	.7	.8
Government (loan)	.4	.3	.3	.3
Export-Import Bank	.7	.1	.5	.2
TOTAL	$5.9	$1.8	$1.9	$1.8

Sales by Region

Fiscal Year	Europe and Canada	Near East & South Asia	Africa	Latin America	Far East
1962-1965	$4.7	$ .3	*	$ .1	$ .8
1966	1.2	.4	*	*	.1
1967	1.2	.4	*	*	.2
1968	.9	.5	*	*	.3
TOTAL	$8.1	$1.6	$ .1	$ .3	$1.4
1969 est.	$1.1	$ .6	*	*	$ .2

Note: Totals may not add due to rounding.
* Under $100 million.
† Figures pertain to transactions under the Foreign Military Sales program, which was started in 1962.
Source: U.S. Department of Defense.

In addition to the provision of hardware, both MAP and FMS train some 10,000 foreign military personnel annually in 175 centers located in the United States and overseas. FMS data are classified on this subject; but MAP statistics are not. Here, East Asia leads the list with a total of 107,044 men trained from fiscal year 1950 to fiscal year 1968. This total represents, among others, United States commitments to Korea, China, Japan, Vietnam, the Philippines, and Thailand. Next is the European total of 62,386 (with most, by far, from France, followed by Italy and Spain). The Near East and South Asia total is 46,773 (Turkey, Greece, and Iran the leaders), followed by the Latin America figure of 46,479. Africa lags behind with only 5,198 personnel trained under MAP. (See Table 10.4.)

The Military Assistance Program and the Military Sales Program make the use of American military power somewhat more likely for two reasons. The ties that a military aid program creates between the United States and

TABLE 10.4 Foreign Military Personnel Trained Under MAP†

Country	Trained FY 50-63	Trained FY 64-68	Total Trained
Cambodia	334	3	337
China	19,508	3,604	23,112
Indo-China	434	–	434
Indonesia	2,379	485	2,864
Japan	13,790	1,490	15,280
Korea	21,160	7,365	28,525
Malaysia	18	123	141
Philippines	9,141	3,076	12,217
Thailand	7,340	2,796	10,136
Vietnam	10,756	3,242	13,998
East Asia Total	84,860	22,184	107,044
Afghanistan	164	88	252
Ceylon	–	7	7
Greece	9,399	3,351	12,750
India	6	465	471
Iran	6,228	2,782	9,010
Iraq	241	163	404
Jordan	142	203	345
Lebanon	60	1,280	1,340
Nepal	–	15	15
Pakistan	3,498	642	4,140
Saudi Arabia	621	496	1,117
Syria	3	20	23
Turkey	12,894	4,000	16,894
Yemen	–	5	5
NESA Total*	33,256	13,517	46,773
Congo	–	165	165
Ethiopia	1,555	968	2,523
Ghana	33	13	46
Liberia	94	241	335
Libya	58	321	379
Mali	7	49	56
Morocco	4	1,002	1,006
Nigeria	18	298	316
Senegal	3	5	8
Sudan	34	92	126
Tunisia	20	206	226
Upper Volta	4	8	12
Africa Total	1,830	3,368	5,198
Argentina	1,190	1,216	2,406
Bolivia	764	1,432	2,196
Brazil	3,416	2,255	5,671
Chile	2,219	1,448	3,667
Colombia	2,516	1,378	3,894
Costa Rica	208	321	529
Cuba	521	–	521

TABLE 10.4 (continued)

Country	Trained FY 50-63	Trained FY 64-68	Total Trained
Dominican Republic	955	1,419	2,374
Ecuador	2,246	1,549	3,795
El Salvador	304	528	832
Guatemala	903	1,117	2,020
Haiti	504	–	504
Honduras	746	602	1,348
Mexico	240	306	546
Nicaragua	2,366	1,204	3,570
Panama	768	2,106	2,874
Paraguay	204	564	768
Peru	2,820	1,624	4,444
Uruguay	807	607	1,414
Venezuela	724	2,382	3,106
Latin America Total	24,421	22,058	46,479
Belgium	4,809	389	5,198
Denmark	4,129	581	4,710
France	14,312	30	14,342
Germany	1,251	373	1,624
Italy	9,215	148	9,363
Luxembourg	158	18	176
Netherlands	6,085	212	6,297
Norway	5,229	303	5,532
Portugal	2,288	205	2,493
Spain	6,049	1,426	7,475
United Kingdom	3,853	14	3,867
Yugoslavia	844	–	844
NATO Agency	465	–	465
Europe Total	58,687	3,699	62,386
Classified Countries	6,310	13,031	19,341
Total	209,364	77,857	287,221

* Near East and South Asia.
† Figures include personnel trained abroad and in the United States.

the recipient regime may lead to deeper involvement. The scenario has been played out in Vietnam: U.S. military equipment, U.S. military instructors to assemble it and demonstrate its use at U.S. base facilities, U.S. advisers to operate with combat units, U.S. troops to protect U.S. bases, and U.S. retaliatory air strikes, and ultimately U.S. troops in general combat.

Clandestine military aid programs have at times involved no more than the secret transfer of purchasing funds (through so-called Country X loans) and have at other times involved extensive CIA participation in counterinsurgency training programs, or in logistic support through Air America, Air Asia, or other government-subsidized carriers. Some of these aid programs may involve a degree of reciprocity, with resulting United States intelligence collection stations and political complications.

Furthermore, the existence of American military assistance missions in other countries creates a target for attack or harassment by the domestic opposition within those countries, which may become an occasion for a challenge to the regime and to its American ally. This kind of challenge is, of course, not limited to military assistance missions. It applies as well to United States overseas bases—which may in turn be the quo for which military assistance is the quid. The dependence on Portugal for the use of staging bases in the Azores has exposed the United States to at least a limited risk of involvement in Portugal's efforts to retain her African colonies, while probing of North Korea's electronic warning systems apparently exposed the United States to a significant risk of military involvement, a risk that was avoided only by cool heads in the Pentagon and the White House. Without judging the benefits from these risks, it must be concluded that they do increase the likelihood of United States military involvement in conflict situations inside other countries.

The reach of overseas activities by the United States military extends to scholarly research conducted in other countries on behalf of the military establishment. The rationale for defense involvement in social science research was set out in the hearings of the Fulbright Committee in the early part of 1968. When asked by Senator Fulbright why the Department of Defense should support studies of the social structure of foreign societies, Dr. John S. Foster, Director of Defense Research and Engineering, replied that ". . . simply because at the outset of hostilities or the possibility of hostilities, the Defense Department is frequently asked to consider just what kind of action it might take in the interests of the country affected —in supporting the United Nations allies, or friends associated with that possible incident. So it is in our interests to understand the nature of such instabilities, as well as the various countries in which instability might occur."[3]

And Secretary McNamara in his Montreal speech of May 18, 1966, stated: "There is still among us an almost ineradicable tendency to think of our security problem as being exclusively a military problem. . . . We understand that our military mission to be most effective requires understanding of the political, social, and economic setting in which we fulfill our responsibilities.[4]

This seems essentially an enlightened recognition on the part of the military that the application of force in international affairs is an exten-

3. *Defense Department-Sponsored Foreign Affairs Research*, Hearing before the Committee on Foreign Relations, U.S. Senate, May 9, 1968, p. 11.
4. Robert S. McNamara, *The Essence of Security* (New York: Harper & Row, 1968), p. 142.

sion of political action, and the way in which force is applied and the circumstances in which it is used cannot be separated from the nonmilitary aspects of the problem. In a sense it is a reaction against the simplistic concepts of "unconditional surrender" or "massive retaliation" or "fighting to win" which had dominated much American thinking about military problems until the 1960's. It is a logical outgrowth of emphasis on concepts of "limited war" and "counterinsurgency" which, as noted earlier, emerged largely from the thinking of a segment of the intellectual community in the 1950's.

The antiwar critics cite such statements as evidence that the United States government, and particularly the military, is engaged in the systematic suppression of popular revolutions and self-determination throughout the world. But it can be argued that the same kind of knowledge is needed to decide when potential revolutions constitute a genuine threat to valid American security interests and when they do not. Such knowledge could as well be used to justify nonintervention as intervention.

The military establishment has also become involved in the large-scale application of social science research techniques to the study of counterinsurgency. Defense funding of this kind of research has been a significant although now a diminishing source of support for the social sciences. (Its significance for the academic community is discussed in Chapters 18 and 19.) The uses of social science research range from handbooks for American soldiers assigned to, say, Vietnam or Korea, to studies of the potential for revolutionary activity in countries where the United States is not militarily involved, as in the ill-fated Project Camelot, which illustrates the major problems associated with military sponsorship of foreign area research.

Project Camelot, as described in a document issued by the Army's Special Operations Research Office in December 1964, was to "devise procedures for assessing the potential for internal war within national societies"; and to "identify with increased degrees of confidence those actions which a government might take to relieve conditions which are assessed as giving rise to a potential for internal war, and finally, to assess the feasibility of prescribing the characteristics of a system for obtaining and using the essential information needed for doing the above two things."[5] It was "conceived as a three-to-four-year effort to be funded at around one and one-and-a-half million dollars annually," and recruited social scientists from several leading universities.

At this funding level, Camelot would have been one of the largest

5. Irving Louis Horowitz, ed., *The Rise and Fall of Project Camelot: Studies in the Relationship between Social Science and Practical Politics* (Cambridge: M.I.T. Press, 1967), pp. 47-48. The quotation is from an official description of the Project released through the Special Operations Research Office of the American University in December 1964.

social research projects in the United States. But it never came into existence. It was abandoned six months later, after a major flare-up in Chile, a country not included in the original planning design, when a Chilean-American consultant to the project group made apparently unauthorized approaches to the University of Chile for assistance. As a result there were outcries in the Chilean Senate and the left-wing Chilean press about "intervention" and "imperialism." The reverberations began with an outraged cable from the American ambassador to Chile, who had known nothing about the project until the situation exploded, and culminated in a decision by the Secretary of Defense to cancel the project because the Chilean reaction had shown it would be impractical in any of the other Latin American countries for which it had been scheduled. A presidential memorandum followed, instructing the Secretary of State to establish procedures so that "no government sponsorship of foreign area research should be undertaken which in the judgment of the Secretary . . . would adversely affect United States foreign relations." In December 1967 the State Department, in conjunction with other agencies sponsoring external research, promulgated a set of regulations designed to protect the government from similar embarrassments, while significantly restricting freedom of sponsored "foreign area" researchers.

The rise and fall of Project Camelot can be traced in a simple syllogism. The military establishment is rich and powerful enough to be able to launch a foreign areas research program to supplement its military contingency planning in the Third World; the program attracts social scientists who have been unable to find support elsewhere in government, where funds for social science research are tightly limited; the image of the rich and powerful military establishment makes the military-sponsored research unacceptable in the countries where they propose to gather material—and has a chilling effect on all United States foreign research, university- as well as government-sponsored. The syllogism can be elaborated. The initial unsophisticated enthusiasm of the military for what this new tool can accomplish called forth a naïve research design, full of implicit major premises about the need to maintain established governments, and the efficacy of standard palliatives for domestic unrest in the developing countries. Not surprisingly, it led some commentators to inquire why Third World investigators should not be funded to study the prospects for "internal war" in the United States. In finding an institutional home for Camelot, the military used the academy—in this case American University in Washington, D.C.—as the merest administrative convenience, rather than as a source of guidance on how to organize and conduct research.[6]

Concern within the academic community was divided between those

6. Irving Louis Horowitz points out that on the project stationery, "Special Operations Research Office" was printed in larger type than "American University." See Horowitz, p. 25.

who felt that future Camelots threatened the independence of academic research, and those who felt that their own future overseas research activities were threatened by the fact that Camelot had failed. The Camelot fiasco was in a sense a product of the same enthusiasm that swept in counterinsurgency and beatified the Green Berets. Despite the negative controls exercised by the State Department, Defense has continued to supply the major funds for foreign area research. But just as the military is learning to respect the independence of the domestic scholar, and of the Third World subjects, the Congress has cut back very sharply on Department of Defense funding for social science research, and the academic community, under student pressure, has turned away from Defense funding even for unclassified basic research. Both problems have been exacerbated by the newly imposed congressional requirement that research projects be directly related to military objectives. The uses of military power to support social science research on examining the propriety or impropriety, the effectiveness or ineffectiveness of United States military power in revolution and counterrevolution control now appear to be severely limited.

The Central Intelligence Agency is a natural object for unparalleled speculation, feeding on secrecy, and generally overstating its very considerable resources. Its errors of commission, in which the dagger has emerged from behind the cloak, have attracted more attention than its errors of omission, although, with the notable exception of the Bay of Pigs, they have probably been less serious. The independence that concealment provides to CIA station chiefs, vis-à-vis American ambassadors around the world, has increased the general estimate of their influence—and the suspicion that they are up to no good.

In fact the bulk of CIA activities, at home and abroad, is concerned with the collection and coordination of information, much of which could easily be gathered by a reasonably practical academic researcher. Furthermore, the prodigious outpourings from the intelligence community engulf any policy-maker who indicates an interest in such products as National Intelligence Estimates (NIEs), Special National Intelligence Estimates (SNIEs), various "current intelligence" reports—and, for those with special "clearances," the results of intelligence obtained by exotic methods. Published intelligence estimates are not always read, nor are they always published for informational purposes alone. The White House may ask for a SNIE when it already anticipates the likely contents and has a target group (perhaps a congressional committee or the press) in mind.

Presidential reading is scarcely confined to the intelligence reports, selected and assembled in the White House "situation room." President Johnson was occasionally angered to learn of major developments through the wire services rather than through his intelligence services, but like other Presidents, he was an avid reader of commercial tickers and newspapers. National Intelligence Estimates provide agreed, and important, working figures for Defense budget planning, and fodder for calculated press "leaks" supporting budget advocacy. But formal information channels merely complement the mainstream of informal personal communications. The quality of intelligence activities, as of the operations on the covert side of the organization, is as varied as in the Foreign Service proper, or in the military establishment. More important, the covert operations of the agency are conducted under close political supervision, in greater detail, and at higher levels of government than are comparable overt operations of other agencies. But secrecy is the *raison d'être* of a clandestine service. It insulates the presidency from its activities until such times as "cover plans" unravel. Even then the public image often disconnects the agency from the political authority which directed it.

Within the executive branch there are elaborate control procedures, beginning in the Central Intelligence Agency itself, extending to regional reviews under the chairmanship of various Assistant Secretaries of State, and ending with the scrutiny of an interdepartmental committee at the under secretary level. The President's Special Assistant for National Security Affairs sits on this committee, and if necessary an appeal is taken directly to the President himself.

Most of the supervisory failures have involved inadequate attention to matters of detail in execution, although with hindsight one can also pinpoint gross policy errors as well. Given the clandestinity and compartmentalization of the activities under scrutiny, we should not expect any form of executive review to eliminate all of the snafus. Covert instruments of foreign policy have inherent limitations.

There have been, for example, seemingly trivial failures in technical intelligence missions which have led to political complications. CIA's hitherto remarkably successful U-2 project, photographing Soviet bases from a high-flying plane, ended in political embarrassment in 1960, when a pilot was captured and confessed, while naval vessels working for the National Security Agency (not the CIA, as is sometimes reported) were involved in the Gulf of Tonkin incident of 1964 (the U.S.S. *Maddox* and U.S.S. *Turner Joy*), the Six Day War of 1967 (the U.S.S. *Liberty*), and difficulties with North Korea in 1968 (the U.S.S. *Pueblo*).

The focal point of political supervision must be in the executive branch, which is less susceptible to the selective withholding of information that can undermine congressional scrutiny. Moreover, the four congressional committees which review CIA activities (Appropriations and Armed Services Committees of the House and Senate) tend not to question basic policy objectives. Since the late 1960's, the Senate Committee on Foreign

Relations has obtained partial representation on the watchdog committee under Senator Stennis, and has conducted extensive hearings of its own. But it is difficult to envision rigorous congressional control of the CIA under these circumstances. The Stuart Symington subcommittee of the Committee on Foreign Relations encountered executive secrecy, less than candid testimony, and obstinacy in State Department security review, which almost prevented the release of its report on the secret "Project 404," U.S. Air Force reconnaissance and air-ground bombing support in Laos.[7] Even now, little is known about the relationship between this aerial interdiction project and covert operations on the ground. Even with the help of the press, congressional supervision of clandestine operations can be only sporadic and largely *ex post facto.*

Despite the decisions of 1961 to transfer large paramilitary operations to the Defense Department, some of the paramilitary operations in Vietnam and supporting operations in adjacent countries—including support of the Meo tribesmen in Laos—appear to have been under CIA control. It would be tempting, but unwarranted, to conclude that CIA has been operating under such loose controls that it can circumvent presidential decisions. On the contrary, it appears that after close scrutiny the CIA has been directed to mount a variety of supporting operations in "war theaters" despite the calculated risks of exposure.

7. U.S. Senate, Committee on Foreign Relations, Subcommittee on United States Security Agreements and Commitments Abroad, *Kingdom of Laos,* Part II, Art. 20, 21, 22, 28. 91st Cong., 1st Session, 1969.

11

The Traditional Federal Role
in Domestic Disorders

In 1792 Congressman John Francis Mercer of Virginia rose in the new House of Representatives to denounce a bill to permit use of federal troops to control civil disorders. "In no free country," he said, "can the [military] be called forth, nor martial law proclaimed but under great restrictions."[1] In April 1968 Mayor Jerome P. Cavanagh of Detroit spoke before a television camera:

"No more disastrous consequence for this city or this nation could take place than if we had to maintain a prolonged military presence on our streets. If the National Guard were to become part of our daily life, our freedom would not survive. If military-police power patrolled our streets every night from now until the leaves turned brown and fell from the trees, we would find our liberties just as dead as those leaves, just as brittle, and just as easily trampled."[2]

Both statements, separated by 175 years of American history, reflect the nation's enduring insistence on civilian control of the military, its distaste for a national police, and its scrupulous delegation of law enforcement to the states and local communities. Yet today, as perhaps at no other stage in our history, the pressures for the use of the military in domestic situations are insistent and, perhaps, growing stronger.

Of the eighteen major occasions when Presidents have granted requests by the states for federal troops to suppress civil disorder, four occurred in one nine-month period between July 1967 and April 1968. Between the end of World War II and the end of 1968 a total of 197,759 National

1. *Annals of Congress,* v. 1. 3, p. 575.
2. "Detroit: A New Direction," television broadcast, April 12, 1968, transcript supplied by Mayor Cavanagh.

Guardsmen were called up to deal with civil disorders. Of the total for these twenty-three years, 149,348—about three-quarters—were called up in the years after the Watts riot in August 1965.[3] In 1967 alone, a total of 31,991 federal and National Guard troops were used to combat civil disorders, and in one month, April 1968, the aftermath of the assassination of Martin Luther King, 68,915 were called up and 41,639 committed to use.[4]

In tracing the development of this erosion of traditional restraints on the federal use of military power in domestic affairs, one can observe the patterns that led to restraint in the past and which are making for intervention in the present.

President Washington, confronted by the Whisky Rebellion, wrote in 1794, "Not only the Constitution and laws must strictly govern, but the employing of the regular troops avoided if it be possible to effect order without their aid. . . . Yet if no other means will effectually answer, and the Constitution and laws will authorize these they must be used as the dernier resort."[5] In the end he called out 12,950 militia troops from four states. But he did so with an injunction—carefully enforced—that made the history of the Whisky Rebellion a model for federal conduct in subsequent disorders. As he put it, "Every officer and soldier will constantly bear in mind that he comes to support the laws and that it would be peculiarly unbecoming in him to be in any way the infractor of them. . . . The dispensation of . . . justice belongs to the civil magistrate, and let it ever be our pride and our glory to leave the sacred deposit there unviolated."[6]

A generation later, when the Buckshot War between political rivals in Pennsylvania in 1838 threatened to turn into an assault on Pittsburgh, President Martin Van Buren resisted a state request for federal force. Such a request would be justified, he said, only when local and state authorities had made every effort and had demonstrably failed. Federal intervention under any other circumstances "would be attended with the most dangerous consequences to our republican institutions."[7]

Still later, during President Rutherford B. Hayes's incumbency, the country was beset by its first wave of industrial strike violence. When

3. See Tables 11.1 and 11.2.
4. These data were supplied by the office of the Deputy Attorney General, U.S. Department of Justice in 1968. "Riot Data Review," Lemberg Center for the Study of Violence, Brandeis University, August 1968, p. 60, gives figures of 32,500 in 1967 and 58,600 in April 1968.
5. John C. Fitzpatrick, ed., *The Writings of George Washington* (Washington, D.C.: Government Printing Office, Vol. 32, 1939), p. 153.
6. *Ibid.*, Vol. 34, p. 6.
7. Bennett M. Rich, *The Presidents and Civil Disorders* (Washington, D.C.: Brookings Institution, 1940).

disorders spread in 1877 from West Virginia to California and demand for federal intervention rose to a clamor, Hayes was constrained, nevertheless, by the small number of federal troops available and by a sense of propriety about their use. He demurred to a number of requests and in others dispatched troops only to protect federal property, evidently assuming (correctly as it turned out) that the mere presence of federal troops would suffice. Requests for troops from several states less seriously struck by riots were rejected, though troops were sent to West Virginia and Maryland, where violence was severe and state forces insufficient. Hayes won extensive applause for his prudence, care, and firmness.

Again, in 1907, when widespread disorder was reported in the Nevada mining fields, Theodore Roosevelt sent a blunt coded message to the troop commander on the scene: "Do not act at all until President issues proclamation. . . . Better twenty-four hours of riot, damage, and disorder than illegal use of the troops."[8] Such presidential inhibitions have had firm foundation in law. Use of the National Guard is for the states to determine. But use of federal troops is circumscribed by five United States statutes. Federal troops may be used, under presidential order, in response to state requests, to enforce the federal judicial process, and to enforce federally guaranteed civil rights that state authorities are unable or unwilling to protect.[9]

Apart from legal limitations, most Presidents have, as a matter of policy, adhered to Washington's admonition that federal troops be "the dernier resort." In some instances, state requests for federal military assistance have been denied outright. In most other cases, the requests have been granted, but only after cautious delay. In only four situations were troops dispatched immediately.[10]

But in several episodes of serious civil disorder, Presidents were less

8. *Ibid.*, p. 129.
9. The three principal statutes are sections 331, 332, and 333 of Title 10, United States Code. The first two date from enactments of 1792. Section 333 was passed in the wake of massive Ku Klux Klan violence against Negroes in South Carolina in 1871. Section 334, also dating from 1792, directs the President to issue a proclamation ordering insurgents to disperse whenever he decides to use federal troops in a civil disorder. An additional relevant statute is 18 U.S.C. 1385, the so-called *posse comitatus* law, enacted July 18, 1878. It was designed to overturn opinions of two attorneys general that United States marshals could call on military personnel to help enforce various Reconstruction enactments. The statute makes it a felony to use "any part of the Army or the Air Force" as a posse without express constitutional or statutory authority. See *Opinions of the Attorney General* (Washington, D.C.: Government Printing Office, 1963), Vol. 41, pp. 330-331 (November 7, 1957). Probably the most lasting impact of the statute is its effect on military—and civil—personnel. While few of them may understand the statute in detail, its simple existence has been inhibiting.
10. The first instance, in 1871, put down the widespread Klan terrorizing of Negroes in South Carolina, pursuant to the newly enacted 10 U.S.C. 333. The other cases, discussed below, were several disturbances at Coeur d'Alene; the 1919 race riots; and the dispersal of the Bonus Army in Washington, D.C.

restrained in their response than their predecessors. During 1894 President Grover Cleveland dispatched troops to pursue Coxey's Army, in their hijacked trains, and troops were used extensively during the Pullman strike later in that same year.[11] Governor John Altgeld of Illinois not only did not request such use; he vigorously protested it, but the federal government intervened anyway, citing a need to enforce sweeping federal injunctions against the American Railway Union.

Lack of caution was charged to President William McKinley in 1899 after a mine was dynamited in Coeur d'Alene, Idaho, and a train (the "Dynamite Express") had been commandeered. McKinley acceded immediately when the governor asked for aid, and though there can be little question that federal force was required, since the tiny state militia was away serving in the Philippines and the federal troops were assigned to regular nonmilitary work, such as guarding prisons, they were allowed to remain for a needlessly long period. Some contingents were still in Coeur d'Alene thirteen months later, and despite the length of time, McKinley made no effort to press the state legislature to validate the governor's emergency troop request.

President Wilson followed contradictory policies—restraint, in his first term, precipitate action in his second. In April 1914, after the "Ludlow Massacre," in protracted Colorado mine violence, Wilson delayed responding to the state's request for federal troops until a last effort could be made to induce John D. Rockefeller, Jr., owner of the largest mining operation, to take conciliatory steps. When Rockefeller refused, Wilson finally sent troops, with orders to observe strict neutrality. But, by the end of his second term, in the summer and fall of 1919, a chain of racial disturbances rocked the country. Federal troops were employed quickly in Washington, Omaha, and Gary, and at least in Gary they went to such lengths that public confidence was undermined—for instance, by arresting and searching the house of an attorney for defendants in a federal case.

In 1917, President Wilson signed an order requiring all National Guard commanders to respond to any state request for troops. This devolution of a solemn presidential responsibility represented, in Edward S. Corwin's words, the "most complete, sustained, and altogether deliberate neglect of the formalities required by [the Constitution and laws] that has thus far occurred."[12] There are several likely explanations: One, that the National Guard had been ordered into federal service, leaving the states without adequate protection against civil disturbance; two, Wilson's emo-

11. F. R. Dulles, *Labor in America* (New York: Crowell, 1955), pp. 176 ff.
12. Quoted in Rich, p. 158. Not until Harding's early months in office was the 1917 wartime order requiring continental military department commanders to respond automatically to state calls for aid rescinded.

tional breakdown two days before disorder spread to Omaha; three, government apprehension of widespread Communist-stimulated disorder in the fall and winter of 1919-20.[13] And fourth, there is the suspicion that readiness to employ troops in racial disorders was harsher precisely because the issue was race.

Perhaps the most controversial use of federal force occurred in the summer of 1932, when President Herbert Hoover authorized the use of troops, in response to the request of the commissioners of the District of Columbia, to disperse the ragged Bonus Expeditionary Force. This "army" of perhaps 15,000 Depression-affected veterans and their families had come from all over the country to seek financial assistance from Congress. For two months they lived in tents, shacks, and partially demolished government buildings. When disorder followed a Treasury Department effort to repossess one of these buildings, the city commissioners requested troops. Hoover immediately agreed. Within hours, a force of cavalry, tanks, and troops equipped with tear gas commanded by MacArthur (with Eisenhower as his aide), marched on the unarmed, predominantly peaceable "army." During the night the principal encampment was completely destroyed, and the pitiful Bonus Army was dispersed within twenty-four hours.

In this instance, troops were by no means the dernier resort. Hoover, as critics pointed out, could have instructed the Treasury Department to take legal rather than military action against the sick, dispirited squatters. Even after the decision to use troops, he could have issued the usual warning proclamation. Instead, his hasty use of troops provoked what Arthur Schlesinger has described as "national dismay":

> There seemed no excuse for his refusal to see their leaders; no excuse for resorting to arms when the B.E.F. was breaking up of its own accord; no excuse for forcing pell-mell evacuation in the dead of night. . . . "What a pitiful spectacle," said the Washington *News*, "is that of the great American Govern-

13. Acting on fears of Communists, the War Department promulgated contingency "War Plans—White," superseded in October 1921 by the "Emergency Plans—White," declassified in 1963, which appears to have served as the military's basic civil disorder plan until it was revised in 1940. The revision and subsequent plans remain classified. But, even the 1923 version partially available at the National Archives is, despite a certain stridency, scrupulous in its attention to presidential authority and discretion. The memorandum described among other things the anticipated closing off of food deliveries around the country. Labor was not explicitly mentioned as the source of the disorders, but the organizers allegedly hoped ". . . not to have the strikers use violence of any kind, but to force the public through lack of food to institute mob law and seize stocks of public food supplies. It is at this stage that the plan is for the organized force to step in, seize all food depots and make distribution to the starving people, thereby getting them as friends and in the same way to get control of the local government. This is in general the method whereby the Reds in Russia succeeded as they succeeded in Hungary, the Ukraine, and to some extent in Poland, Siberia, Turkey, and many other places. . . ."

ment, mightiest in the world, chasing unarmed men, women, and children with Army tanks. . . . If the Army must be called out to make war on unarmed citizens, this is no longer America."[14]

Clearly, the use of federal force in a domestic situation had been impelled by reasons of politics or policy and not by imminent danger to law, life, or property.

Eleven years later, a fist fight on a Detroit bridge set off a riot that, in President Roosevelt's view, endangered not only law, life, and property, but also war production. He deployed federal troops in the last such deployment until 1967, when troops were also sent, once again, to Detroit.

Paradise Valley, an ironically named ghetto area, was dotted with fires and looting in the 1943 Detroit riot. Maurauding whites were shot at by Negroes. Negroes were pulled off streetcars and beaten by crowds of whites. White and black gangs roamed the streets overturning cars, stoning people, burning houses. After twenty-four hours, Roosevelt ordered in troops.[15] Their arrival caused—or at least coincided with—an abrupt halt of the rioting. Even so, the riot toll totaled thirty-four dead and more than $2 million in property losses.

In 1957, federal force was used, for the first time since Reconstruction, to resist state violation of federal court orders or state incapacity to enforce them, rather than in response to state requests to put down disorder. After the Civil War the federal government's role had shifted from regional repression of slaves to national protection of freedmen through force— particularly against the Klan in South Carolina in 1871—although white vigilantism, with public and private support, harassed Negroes in much of the South without federal intervention for decades thereafter. The federal government intervened militarily in racial unrest in the first half of the twentieth century only to put down riots, as in 1919 and 1943. But with the end of World War II, and the landmark Brown decision of 1954 against school segregation, the executive branch was forced into intervention in behalf of Negroes in order to carry out the mandate of the Supreme Court.

The support of law in behalf of court-ordered justice, not merely in behalf of public order, was a significant precedent, although public order, in these cases, could only be maintained by compelling state obedience to federal law. It was ironic that this role had to be assumed by a President, Dwight Eisenhower, whose personal philosophy was nonintervention. He dispatched federal troops to Little Rock, Arkansas, in September 1957 after the governor thwarted a federal court order admitting nine Negro pupils to

14. Arthur M. Schlesinger, Jr., *The Crisis of the Old Order* (Boston: Houghton Mifflin, 1957), pp. 264-265.
15. See Robert Shogan and Tom Craig, *The Detroit Race Riot* (Philadelphia: Chilton, 1964).

Little Rock High School—but he did so with considerable reluctance and only after public pressure outside of the South. Rioting was ended and order restored by one thousand men of the 101st Airborne Infantry Division.[16]

In the Kennedy and Johnson administrations federal force was applied in the South in a number of preventative acts of administrative intervention, with the use of federal emissaries and federal marshals, and in acts of troop intervention, all with federalized National Guardsmen and federal forces.

When George Washington authorized the first use of federal troops during the Whisky Rebellion, he did so on the condition that the United States district judge and United States attorney accompany the army, in order to insure adherence to mandates of law.[17] Later Presidents took similar action, sending special civil representatives to report personally on the execution of presidential orders. Such missions were common in the South in the early 1960's, when President Kennedy and President Johnson designated representatives of the Department of Justice as field commanders: Byron White at the time of the freedom rides in 1961; Nicholas Katzenbach at the desegregation of the University of Mississippi and the University of Alabama; Burke Marshall during demonstrations in Birmingham in 1963; and Ramsey Clark and John Doar during the 1965 Selma-to-Montgomery march. They developed close relations with civilian Defense Department officials, among them Cyrus R. Vance, at first general counsel of the Department of Defense, then Secretary of the Army, and then Deputy Secretary of Defense, and later President Johnson's "eyes and ears" in the Detroit ghetto riot of 1967.

Attorney General Robert F. Kennedy had committed the new administration to enforce the law "vigorously." If "circumvented . . . we will not stand by or be aloof," he said. "We will move. . . ."[18] The Justice Department moved a few weeks later when freedom riders were beaten with the police standing by. Although Alabama Governor John Patterson promised state protection, unimpeded white mob violence resulted, so 600 deputy marshals and other federal officers were ordered to the scene by the Attorney General.

A more direct federal-state confrontation took place in September 1962, when a federal court ordered James Meredith admitted to the University of Mississippi. After initial obstructionist moves by the uni-

16. Governor Orval Faubus called out 635 members of the National Guard from September 6 to 20, 1957; on September 24, the National Guard was federalized; 1,800 were used through May 29, 1958; of the total of 9,873 called to federal service, all but 900 had been released from active duty by November 10, 1957.

17. Rich, p. 15.

18. Speech at the University of Georgia, Athens, Georgia, May 1, 1960 (Law Day).

versity, federal marshals escorted Meredith to the campus a day early in a surprise move. In the riot that followed the discovery of this ploy, first the marshals and later a company of federalized National Guard found themselves under severe attack by hundreds of rioters, many using firearms. At this point, the President ordered to the scene units of the U.S. Army, 81st Airborne Division. In a nationwide television address on the night of September 30, 1962, President Kennedy said:

"I deeply regret the fact that any action by the executive branch was necessary in this case, but all other avenues and alternatives, including persuasion and con-conciliation, had been tried and exhausted. Had the police powers of Mississippi been used to support the orders of the court, instead of deliberately and unlawfully blocking them, had the University of Mississippi fulfilled its standard of excellence by quietly admitting this applicant in conformity with what so many other Southern state universities have done for so many years, a peaceable and sensible solution would have been possible without any federal intervention."[19]

In 1963, when Alabama Governor George Wallace threatened to block admission of Negro students to the University of Alabama, once again the National Guard was federalized. In 1965 federalized National Guardsmen were summoned to Selma by President Johnson to enforce a court order protecting civil rights marchers on the fifty-mile route to Montgomery, after brutal repression by local law enforcement officers. As the 20,000 civil rights supporters approached the capitol at the end of their march, they were ringed with troops not facing outward, as protectors, but inward as though the marchers represented the threat of violence. Military officials on the scene, some of whom saw their task as prevention of a riot by the marchers, disregarded the stance of the troops as trivial. But federal officials told Washington, which recognized the symbolism instantly, and the order was given to turn the troops around.

From these and other instances of federal troop use in civil disorders, it is possible to identify four limitations under which most Presidents have operated: popular, practical, political, and legal. In almost every instance, these factors have provided a powerful force for the operation of the federal system and against the use of federal troops.

The *popular limitation* has been the public's distrust of and distaste for the use of military force in domestic affairs. Washington referred to this anxiety bluntly in the early stages of the Whisky Rebellion, when he argued against using regular troops unnecessarily, "otherwise there would be a cry at once, 'The cat is let out; we now see, for what purpose an army was raised.' "[20] President Eisenhower and President Kennedy, seeking to

19. *Public Papers of The Presidents, John F. Kennedy, 1963* (Washington, D.C.: Government Printing Office, 1963), p. 727.
20. *Writings of Washington*, Vol. 32, p. 153.

avoid a use of troops against the states, created small plainclothes armies of United States marshals, hastily deputized prison guards, border patrolmen, and other federal officers, as a tactical substitute more acceptable to the South, though in several instances, as we have seen, they were compelled to resort in the end to federalizing the National Guard. And even that was a partial response to local sensibilities—the Guard was preferred to federal troops.

The *practical limitation* through much of our history has been the simple lack of federal troops or an inability to transport them quickly. When President Franklin Pierce refused, in 1856, to send troops to help control a San Francisco Vigilance Committee, there were, at most, fifty soldiers in all of San Francisco. In the 1892 disorder in Coeur d'Alene, a Senator from Idaho wrote acidly: "We are unable to understand why it should take twenty-four hours to get troops from Sherman to Wardner in time of War when it takes five hours in time of peace."[21] Even as late as 1962, troops dispatched to relieve the small force of embattled United States marshals at the University of Mississippi found that it took nearly eight hours to cover the eighty miles from Memphis.

The *political limitation* is the natural reluctance of local leaders to admit their own executive and political shortcomings by having to appeal for help from Washington. It may reasonably be supposed, for example, that this factor weighed heavily with Governor George Romney in July 1967 when he at first skirted direct admission of incapacity to maintain order. Even Romney's subsequent request, to which President Johnson agreed, said, *"There is reasonable doubt* that we can suppress the existing looting, arson and sniping without the assistance of federal troops."[22] (Emphasis supplied.) Earlier Presidents had refused to act on similar assertions of mere apprehension of violence (for example, Theodore Roosevelt's initial refusal of Governor John Sparks's request for federal troops in disorders at the mines of Goldfield, Nevada, in 1907).

Mayor Richard J. Daley of Chicago offered a pithy explanation of the political limitation: "No mayor wants to call the National Guard. Some people think it's a reflection."[23]

The *legal limitation* has been the strongest deterrent of all. Presidents have been almost uniformly scrupulous about limitations on use of federal troops in domestic disorders, as defined by the Constitution, by statute, and by precedent. Each of these limitations has been in jeopardy in the last five years of urban violence, a period of unrest perhaps without parallel—apart from the Civil War—in the nation's history.

21. Quoted in Rich, p. 111.
22. "Final Report of Cyrus R. Vance Concerning the Detroit Riots (1967)," Department of Defense Release 856-7, September 12, 1967.
23. Interview with Walter Cronkite, CBS News, August 29, 1968.

When Northern ghettos began to erupt, following the example of Watts, the thrust of civil rights progress, already weakened by commitments of resources to the Vietnam conflict, slowed down further. Many of those in the North who had brought pressure for federal intervention in behalf of the nonviolent struggle for justice in the South, assumed a more cautious stance in the face of Northern urban unrest.

In the twenty years prior to Watts, from September 1945 through July 1965, National Guard troops, summoned by state or federal authority, had intervened in at least forty racial incidents, civil rights demonstrations, civil disturbances, and crises in law enforcement (often a euphemism for racial incidents) in ten states and the District of Columbia (the massive peaceful March on Washington of August 28, 1963). Of these ten states seven were in the South, where thirty-five of the forty episodes occurred.[24]

After 1945 and before 1960 most of the major incidents where National

TABLE 11.1 Uses of the National Guard in Domestic Situations
      (By Type of Situation)
      September 1945 to August 1965 (Excludes Watts)

Type of Situation	Troops Called[a]	Instances
Civil Disturbances		
Civil rights and integration (demonstrations with a specific focus of grievance, e.g., Selma voting rights march	14,835[b]	10
Racial disorders and other civil disturbances (outbreaks of violence of a nonspecific and random nature, e.g., youth riots)	14,177	41
Other law enforcement (e.g., sabotage of microwave stations)	1,006	5
Total	30,018	56
Other Uses		
Industrial disputes	11,151	13
Prison riots	1,375	7
Miscellaneous and unknown (e.g., disturbances following natural disasters)	2,383	7
Total	14,909	27
Grand Totals	44,927	83

[a] In many cases, fewer—often many fewer—troops were actually committed to use than were called to duty.
[b] Not included are the 5,000 territorial troops called up during the 1950 uprising against the Puerto Rican government.
Source: Table 11.3.

24. See Table 11.3. The others were in Rochester, New York, in 1964, Cicero, Illinois, in 1951, and Bussel's Point, Ohio, in 1965.

Guard force was used involved industrial disputes (Little Rock in 1957 was the sole exception); after 1960 every one involved racial disturbances and, until 1965, most of these were in response to acts of resistance by state governments to federal court orders, or acts of state unwillingness to deploy state forces to protect Negroes' constitutional rights. After 1965, when the series of urban rebellions began, the primary utilization of military power came in a more traditional pattern—in response to state requests to restore civic order.

In the three years 1965-68, 184,133 troops were called up on thirty-eight occasions in numbers of 1,000 or more and 154,865 of them in civil rights demonstrations or racial disorders. (See Table 11.2.) In the previous twenty years, only 44,927 troops had been summoned to duty, 29,012 of them in civil rights demonstrations or racial disorders. (See Table 11.1.)

The pattern of change is clear. Massive disruptive resistance was no longer pursued by state officials. (Governor Claude Kirk of Florida finally submitted to federal court orders in 1970 after resisting school integration,

TABLE 11.2 Uses of the National Guard in Domestic Situations
(By Type of Situation)
August 1965 (Watts) to December 31, 1968

Type of Situation	Troops Called*	Instances
Civil Disturbances		
Civil rights and integration (demonstrations with a specific focus or grievance, e.g., Poor People's March)	8,986	9
Racial disorders and other civil disturbances (outbreaks of violence of a nonspecific and random nature, e.g., Watts; Detroit and Newark disorders in 1967)	145,879	110
Other law enforcement (e.g., Vietnam protests, public funerals)	7,876	7
Total	162,741	126
Other Uses		
Industrial disputes	300	1
Prison riots	1,367	4
Miscellaneous and unknown (e.g., natural disaster and other emergencies—plane and train accidents, manhunts, explosions)	7,999	48
Total	9,666	53
Grand Totals:	184,133	179

* In many cases, fewer troops were actually committed to use than were called to duty.
Source: Table 11.3.

and no troop involvement was needed). Instead, there were random but massive rebellions in Northern city ghettos and organized antiwar demonstrations between 1965 and 1968. The latter brought about the first federal prepositioning of troops—Chicago, 1968—in American history without evidence of local inability to keep the peace. A further consequence was the antiriot act ("Safe Streets and Crime Control Act") of June 19, 1968, which sought to punish inciting and planning of disturbances, and whose constitutionality is being tested in the appeals of the Chicago riot defendants.

The disorders which were the occasion for the deployment of massive federal military power throughout American history in no circumstance, except the Civil War and in Puerto Rico in 1950, dealt with attempts to overthrow the power of government, at the local, state, or federal level.[25] None was related to crime, as it is customarily understood. Rather, what military force was employed for was to contain social unrest—among prisoners, between labor and management, among racial minorities and among students. All were reflections of failure of the nation's institutions to respond adequately to urgent social need.

Industrial unrest has tended to subside with the rise in power of labor unions. Antiwar demonstrations presumably will ebb with the cessation of combat, whenever that comes. Urban riots appear to be declining. But as any of these kinds of unrest continue, the danger of increasing resort to federal military power will remain acute.

25. The uses of federal troops to conquer and suppress the American Indians are usually regarded as acts of control following the wars with the Indians, whose lands were under federal not state control.

Federal troop use in domestic disorders from the close of World War II to July 1965 is shown in table 11.3.

TABLE 11.3 Uses of the National Guard in Domestic Situations, September 1945 to July 1965 (Specific Cases)

Date	Place	Nature of Disturbance	Number of Troops
1945			
Sept. 29-Oct. 3	Indiana	Industrial dispute	1,480
Sept. 21-Oct. 21	Gulf Coast of Texas	Unknown	174
Dec. 3-6, 17	Jackson, Decatur, Miss.	Unknown	91
1946			
Feb. 25-28	Columbia, Tenn.	Race riot	755
March 1-5	Nashville, Tenn.	Unknown	879
Aug. 4-6	Connersville, Ind.	Industrial dispute	About 1,000
Aug. 17-22	Mankato, Minn.	Unknown	About 600
Oct. 7	Jackson, Miss.	Unknown	39
1947			
Oct.	Arizona	Industrial dispute	Unknown
May 14-22	St. Paul and Newport, Minn.	Industrial dispute	2,500
May 19	Waterloo, Iowa	Industrial dispute	1,000
Oct. 30	Loudon, Tenn.	Threat to local sheriff	About 50
1949			
July 19	Groveland, Fla.	Racial disturbance	200
1950			
May 19	South Amboy, N.J.	Disturbance following natural disaster	400
May 29	Morristown, Tenn.	Industrial dispute	300
Oct. 30-Nov. 6	Puerto Rico	Uprising against government	About 5,000
1951			
July 12-17	Cicero, Ill.	Race riot	500

TABLE 11.3 (continued)

Date	Place	Nature of Disturbance	Number of Troops
1952			
April 20-24	Jackson, Mich.	Prison riot	40
May 20	Columbia, Mo.	Student riot	About 100
Oct. 31-Nov. 6	Columbus, Ohio	Prison riot	700
1954			
June 18, 1954-Jan. 17, 1955	Phenix City, Ala.	Crisis in law enforcement	About 500
Sept. 23	Jefferson City, Mo.	Prison riot	Unknown
Oct. 11-12	Sioux Falls, S.D.	Prison riot	120
1955			
Aug. 16-21	Lincoln, Neb.	Prison riot	About 300
Aug. 27-31	Whiting, Ind.	Disturbance following natural disaster	200
Sept. 9	Gulfport, Miss.	Crisis in law enforcement	40
Oct. 5-20	New Castle, Ind.	Industrial dispute	1,000
1956			
Jan. 11-14	Pensacola, Fla.	Industrial dispute	315
Feb. 26-27	Daytona Beach, Fla.	Teenage riot	About 200
Sept. 2-11	Clinton, Tenn.	School integration crisis	600
Sept. 5-11	Sturgis, Ky.	School integration crisis	200
Sept. 12-22	Clay, Ky.	School integration crisis	300
1957			
Jan.	Prentiss County, Miss.	Civil disturbance	69
Jan.	Benton County, Miss.	Civil disturbance	9
Feb.	Portsmouth, Ohio	Industrial dispute	76
Aug.	Marion County, Miss.	Civil disturbance	39
Aug.	Simpson County, Miss.	Civil disturbance	26

TABLE 11.3 (continued)

Date	Place	Nature of Disturbance	Number of Troops
1957 (continued)			
Sept. 6-20	Little Rock, Ark.	School integration crisis	635
Sept. 24, 1957- May 29, 1958	Little Rock, Ark.	School integration crisis	1,800 federalized NG used (9,873 NG were called to federal service). All but 900 released from active duty Nov. 10, 1957.
Oct.	Parchman, Miss.	Civil disturbance	37
Oct.	Prentiss County, Miss.	Civil disturbance	53
1958			
March	La Mar County, Miss.	Civil disturbance	11
June	Prentiss County, Miss.	Civil disturbance	96
June	Sharkey County, Miss.	Civil disturbance	14
Dec.	Hancock County, Miss.	Civil disturbance	47
1959			
Feb.	Lauderdale County, Miss.	Civil disturbance	70
March	Lauderdale County, Miss.	Civil disturbance	12
March	Quitman County, Miss.	Civil disturbance	41
April 18	Deer Lodge, Mont.	Prison riot	200
April 24-May 1959	Hazard, Ky.	Industrial dispute	2,000
June 4-25	Henderson, N.C.	Industrial dispute	305 (includes ANG)
Aug.	Parchman, Miss.	Civil disturbance	68
Dec. 10, 1959-Jan. 4, 1960	Albert Lea, Minn.	Industrial dispute	275
1960			
July 2-3	Newport, R.I.	Jazz Festival	500 (50 Marines)
1961			
May 14-29	Anniston, Birmingham, Montgomery, Ala.	Racial disturbance (Freedom Riders)	800

TABLE 11.3 (continued)

Date	Place	Nature of Disturbance	Number of Troops
1961 (continued)			
May	Meridian, Miss.	Civil disturbance	163
May	New Mexico (statewide)	Sabotage of microwave station	216
May	Cedar Mountain, Lindover, Utah	Sabotage of microwave station	200
Aug.	Nashville, Tenn.	Prison riot	About 10-20
Aug.	Coeur d'Alene, Idaho	Teenage riot	425
Dec. 14	Albany, Ga.	Racial disturbance	About 150
1962			
June	Harrison County, Miss.	Civil disturbance	5
Sept.	Seaside, Oregon	Labor Day riot	55
Sept. 30, 1962-	Oxford, Miss.	University integration	2,700 federalized NG in area.
July 24, 1963		crisis	10,400 federalized NG at one time available
1963			
May 12	Birmingham, Ala.	Bombings, race riot	About 3,000 deployed to Ala. base but never moved to Birmingham
June	Jackson, Miss.	Racial disturbance	153
June 11-Nov. 20	Tuscaloosa, Huntsville, Ala.	University integration	16,463 federalized 4,000 NG on duty after 3 days; only 300 on duty by Sept.
June 14, 1963-	Cambridge, Md.	Racial disturbance	800 initially. Lesser personnel rotated during period
July 15, 1964			
July 1963	Garnett, Kan.	Auto race riot	45
Aug. 28	Washington, D.C.	Civil rights demonstration	2,000
Sept. 10	Birmingham, Mobile, Tuskegee, Ala.	School integration crisis	Governor called about 400 NG; 16,000 NG federalized; about 400 NG on active duty in 3 armories

TABLE 11.3 (continued)

Date	Place	Nature of Disturbance	Number of Troops
1963 (continued)			
Sept.	Seaside, Ore.	Labor Day riot	55
Nov.	Lincoln County, Miss.	Civil disturbance	76
1964			
Jan.	Jackson, Miss.	Civil disturbance	72
May 28	Hillsdale, Mich.	Industrial dispute	900
July 26-28	Rochester, N.Y.	Race riot	1,300
Sept.	Seaside, Ore.	Labor Day riot	150
Sept.	Hampton Beach, N.H.	Teenage riot	714
1965			
March 20-April 3	Selma to Montgomery, Ala.	Civil rights demonstration	2,200 NG in active role. Entire Ala. NG federalized
June	Columbia, Miss.	Civil disturbance	7
June	Weirs, N.H.	Motorcycle riot	250
July	Bussel's Point, Ohio	Civil disturbance	975
July	Geneva, Ohio	Teenage riot	135

Note: When a guard unit is ordered to state active duty by the governor, it is under his command and is paid from state funds. When called to active duty by the President, it is on federal active duty and is paid from federal funds. The President's call to active duty supersedes that of a governor. "Civil disturbance," often refers to a disturbance of racial or civil rights character. "Race riot" usually refers to what is more commonly called "urban" or "ghetto" riots; generally they did not involve racial clashes.

Source: Compiled from National Guard Bureau data.

12

Use of Troops in Recent Domestic Disorders

An elaborate command center in the Pentagon's north basement houses the 180 employees of the Directorate for Civil Disturbance Planning and Operations. Established on July 1, 1968—several months after a series of riots following the death of Martin Luther King—the directorate derives its guidelines from a 15-page document.[1] Its joint staff is headed by Army Lieutenant General W. J. McCaffrey and Air Force Major General Courtney L. Faught, a former airlift commander. Troops in the field continue to be directed by task force commanders, but the directorate has responsibility for supervising all other aspects of federal military involvement in civil disturbances, including the use of airlifted troops.

In a small "city" at Fort Gordon, Georgia, riots erupted weekly for a two-year period starting in February 1968. There were snipers, looters, and fires. But the bricks were made of rubber, the fire came from smoke grenades, and the rioters were soldiers in civilian clothes.[2] This was the training component of the directorate—SEADOC—the Senior Officers Civil Disturbance Orientation Course. Here regular and reserve personnel joined with civil law enforcement officials for forty hours of riot training. The curriculum ranged from community relations to arson; the dominant themes were minimum force and maximum planning. More than 1,800 military and 900 civil law enforcement officers had completed the course before it was suspended.

A senior army officer (who asked not to be identified) described its function: "This is ugly duty for the army. But it looks like we're going

1. Department of Defense Directive 3025.12, June 8, 1968.
2. "Riotsville, USA," *Army Digest*, August 1968, pp. 24-28.

to have to live with rioting for quite a while, so we might as well make up our minds to do the job and try to do it well."

The directorate and the course at Fort Gordon, Georgia, are both striking illustrations of the growing use of military power in domestic affairs, the developing paramilitary character of local law enforcement services, and the increased interconnection through training, joint research, and shared styles of the civilian and military authority. Civilian law enforcement officers, in conjunction with the military, are now planning for the worst contingencies, just as the military has traditionally done in preparing its responses to foreign enemies.

In the past, any oversolicitous or overzealous Commanders in Chief would have been restrained from excessive use of military power in domestic crises by limitations of public support, insufficiency of resources, reluctance of local public officials to admit incapacity, as well as by legal protection, all described in greater detail in Chapter 11. But past guarantees now appear inadequate to serve as countervailing power. Pressures for less inhibited domestic use of federal force are mounting from many directions.

It was the common experience of the federal officials who went to Detroit, Washington, Baltimore, and Chicago in 1967 and 1968 that both black and white citizens responded to federal troops with warm welcome. Far from resenting or mistrusting them, ghetto residents "swarmed around them as though they were the Allies liberating Italy," in then Attorney General Ramsey Clark's words.[3] His view is seconded by another federal official: "Hostility when we went *in?* My God, they didn't want to let us go. We had to *leave* very, very carefully. They wanted us to stay forever."[4]

The knowledge that federal troops had been used in the South in behalf of black minorities and the visible evidence of integration among the units were conducive to black support for federal troops in the North. But whites also could regard the troops as protectors of the majority, assigned to keep a rioting minority from engulfing their cities, although Southern whites had regarded federal troops earlier as protectors of black minorities. In any event, the shock of widespread disorder, reinforced by televised scenes of violence elsewhere, may have conquered the historic antipathy to the use of federal force.

Further, the practical limitation of insufficient resources has been resolved to some extent. Federal troops are available for riot duty in a number of cities. In addition to the 23,000 federal troops used in April

3. Interview with Jack Rosenthal, Washington journalist, September 10, 1968. Subsequent quotations in this chapter are drawn from this interview.
4. Daniel Z. Henkin, Deputy Assistant Secretary of Defense, in an interview with Jack Rosenthal, September 9, 1968, regarding the role of federal troops in Detroit during ghetto rioting in July 1967.

1968 when rioting occurred after Martin Luther King's assassination (see Table 12.1), the army had approximately 22,000 more troops standing by.[5] And, unlike 1906, when, at the time of impending violence again at Coeur d'Alene, two troops of cavalry covered the 310 miles from Fort Walla Walla in eleven days, troops on riot duty can now be delivered anywhere in giant transport planes in a matter of hours.[6] Under present conditions, according to former Attorney General Ramsey Clark and former

TABLE 12.1 Summary of Data Concerning the April 1968 Disorders in Which Federal Troops Were Used

	Washington	Chicago	Baltimore	Total
National Guard troops called	1,848	6,973	6,765	15,586
Federal troops called	13,682	5,005	4,321	23,008
Total	15,530	11,978	11,086	38,594
Deaths	12	11	7	30
Injuries	1,201	922	1,096	3,219
Arrests	7,640	3,124	5,504	16,268
Property damage	$24 million	$13 million	$12 million	$49 million

Note: National Guard figures given here do not agree with those in Table 12.2 because they are based on a later federal review of the disturbances in these three cities.

Source: Office of the Deputy Attorney General, Department of Justice, Washington, D.C.; property damage estimates, American Insurance Association.

Under Secretary of the Army David E. McGiffert, it takes from twelve to twenty-four hours after a call-up for federal troops to begin arriving in a riot city. An exception is Washington, D.C., which is one of the few major cities with a nearby concentration of trained troops.

The earlier reluctance of local political leaders to admit an inability to cope with disorder also seems to have eroded. Governor Spiro T. Agnew, for example, was quick to admit his inability to control the April 1968 disorder in Baltimore and to ask for federal assistance. Public officials seem increasingly willing to summon National Guard assistance as well. Guard units were called for civil disorder duty more times in 1968 than in the three years preceding.[7] Perhaps the most vivid illustration occurred in Wilmington, Delaware, where National Guardsmen, called up during April 1968 rioting, remained on patrol until January 1969. Despite the heated objections of the mayor, Delaware's Governor Charles

5. "Reinforcements Are Put on Alert," New York Times, April 9, 1968, p. 36.

6. The jet C-141 Starlifter carries 154 troops at 565 miles an hour, and the piston C-130E Hercules carries 92 men at 360 miles an hour.

7. See Table 12.2.

TABLE 12.2 Uses of National Guard in Domestic Situations, August 1965 to November 1968 (Specific Cases)

Date	Place	Nature of Disturbance	Number of Troops (ARNG & ANG)
1965			
Aug. 13-22	Los Angeles, Calif.	Watts race riot	13,393 (ARNG & ANG)
Aug. 22	Springfield, Mass.	Civil rights demonstration	2,299
Aug.	Chicago, Ill.	Civil disturbance	2,970
Sept. 3-6	Natchez, Miss.	Racial disturbance	753
Sept.	Indianapolis, Ind.	Civil disturbance	99
Sept.	Seaside, Ore.	Labor Day riot	150
Sept.	Washington Ocean Beach, Wash.	Civil disturbance	500
Oct.	Berkeley, Oakland, Calif.	Vietnam Day Committee	400
Nov.	Berkeley, Oakland, Calif.	Vietnam Day Committee	470
Dec.	Vallejo, Calif.	Civil disturbance	450
1966			
Feb. 8-11	Elkhorn-Platte rivers, Neb.	Flood	150
Feb. 12-27	Elkhorn-Platte rivers, Neb.	Flooding and ice jam	57
March	Richmond, Calif.	Civil disturbance	500
March	Los Angeles, Calif.	Civil disturbance	500
March 22-24	Entire Neb.	Blizzard	16
March 25-April 5	Entire Neb.	Power and generator failure	30
April	Claiborne County, Miss.	Civil disturbance	588
May 17-18	Shade Gap, Pa.	Manhunt	297
June	Los Angeles, Calif.	Civil disturbance	500
June 26	Jackson, Miss.	Racial disturbance	364
June-July	Los Angeles, Calif.	Civil disturbance	34
July	Gary, Ind.	Civil disturbance	100
July 4-6	Omaha, Neb.	Civil disturbance	1,051
July 8-12	Kansas City, Mo.	Firemen's strike	300

TABLE 12.2 (continued)

Date	Place	Nature of Disturbance	Number of Troops
1966 (continued)			
July 12-24	Chicago, Ill.	Filmore race riot	4,300
July 19-31	Cleveland, Ohio	Hough race riot	2,000
Aug. 6-7	Falls City, Neb.	Airline crash	12
Aug. 12-15	Central Neb.	Flood	107
Aug. 28-31	Wauwatosa, Wis.	Racial disturbance	765
Aug. 31-Sept. 5	Benton Harbor, Mich.	Racial disturbance	400
Sept. 1-7	Dayton, Ohio	Race riot	1,142
Sept. 3-6	Lincoln, Neb.	State Fair incident	67
Sept. 4	Cicero, Ill.	Civil rights demonstration and racial disturbance	2,850
Sept. 27-Oct. 2	San Francisco, Calif.	Race riot	3,118
Oct.	Berkeley, Calif.	Civil disturbance	29
Oct.	Oakland, Calif.	Civil disturbance	27
1967			
Jan. 18	Michigan	Flood	180
April 3-19	Clinton, Iowa	Flood	150
April 7-16	Dubuque, Iowa	Flood	46
April	Eau Claire, Wis.	Flood	25
April 23	Belvidere, Ill.	Tornado	800
April 28	Cloud Croft, N.M.	Forest fire	25
May 1	Albert Lea, Minn.	Tornado	100
May 1-3	Mason City, Iowa	Tornado	81
June	Prattville, Ala.	Civil disturbance	300
June	Tampa, Fla.	Civil disturbance	475
June 5-24	Eastern Nebraska	Flood	762 ARNG; 29 ANG
June 14-24	Central Nebraska	Flood	199
June	Rio Arriba, N.M.	Civil disturbance	400

TABLE 12.2 (continued)

Date	Place	Nature of Disturbance	Number of Troops
1967 (continued)			
June	Cincinnati, Ohio	Civil disturbance	900
June 20-28	Halsey Forest, Neb.	Beetle epidemic	47
July	Durham, N.C.	Civil disturbance	400
July	Birmingham, Ala.	Civil disturbance	400
July	Cairo, Ill.	Civil disturbance	150
July	Cambridge, Md.	Civil disturbance	1,200
July	Newark, N.J.	Civil disturbance	4,400
July	Plainfield, N.J.	Civil disturbance	400
July	Minneapolis, Minn.	Civil disturbance	650
July	South Bend, Ind.	Civil disturbance	300
July 2-4	Lake Geneva, Wis.	Civil disturbance	888 called / 647 committed
July 23-Aug. 2	Detroit, Mich.	Civil disturbance	8,262. 10,253 Federalized
July 31	West Palm Beach, Fla.	Civil disturbance	276 (not used)
July 31-Aug. 7	Milwaukee, Wis.	Civil disturbance	4,297 called / 4,126 committed
Aug. 13-24	Nenana, Alaska	Flood	77 called / 77 committed
Aug. 14-15	Fairbanks, Alaska	Flood	170 called / 64 committed
Aug. 14	Jackson, Miss.	Expected emergency (march)	167
Aug. 18-21	Baton Rouge, Bogalusa, La.	Civil rights march	1,735 called
Aug. 17-28	Des Moines, Iowa	Possible civil disturbance at State Fair	235
Aug. 20-27	Des Moines, Iowa	Possible civil disorder	172
Aug. 25-26	Heflin, Ala.	Flood	95

TABLE 12.2 (continued)

Date	Place	Nature of Disturbance	Number of Troops
1967 (continued)			
Sept. 19	Midway, Ala.	Haul water because of a broken pump	5
Sept. 20-Oct. 1	Texas: Rio Grande Valley (Alice, Corpus Christi)	Hurricane	1,336
Oct. 15-23	Oakland, Calif.	Civil disturbance	21 called
Oct. 3	Spooner Summit, Carson City, Nev.	Forest fire	125
Oct. 20-23	Washington, D.C.	Civil disturbance	2,575
Oct. 26-27	Underhill Range, Vt.	Possible civil disturbance	23 called
			23 committed
Oct. 28-Nov. 1	Grambling College, La.	Riot for academic excellence	646 called
Nov. 1	Birmingham, Ala.	Civil disturbance	500
Nov. 2	Winston-Salem, N.C.	Civil disturbance	About 500
Nov. 7	Gary, Ind.	Possible civil disturbance	3,283
Nov. 8	Kearney State College, Neb.	Civil disturbance	Unknown
Nov. 9	Wetumpka, Ark.	Search for missing child	26 committed
Nov. 13	Wilberforce, Ohio	Possible civil disturbance	944 called
			820 committed (includes ANG)
Dec. 5	Pocohontas County, W. Va.	Search for missing deer hunter	98 committed
Dec. 10-14	Fort Walton Beach, Fla.	Tornado	258 committed
Dec. 15-17	Grants, N.M.	Snowstorm	66
Dec. 17-23	Lordsburg, N.M.	Snowstorm	17
Dec. 18	Tucumcari, N.M.	Snowstorm	2
Dec. 19-26	Huntsville, Ala.	Tornado	139 called
			102 committed
Dec. 19	Prescott, Globe, Phoenix, Flagstaff, Ariz.	Snowstorm	20 committed

TABLE 12.2 (continued)

Date	Place	Nature of Disturbance	Number of Troops
1968			
Jan. 11-15	Wayne County, N.C.	Ice storm	10 committed
Jan. 13-15	Chadborne, N.C.	Ammunition train wreck	115 committed
Jan. 22-27	Audubon, Iowa	Leak in water reservoir	14 committed
Feb. 6-March 6	Orangeburg, S.C.	Civil disturbance	1,433 called
			750 committed
Feb. 8-9	Indianapolis, Ind.	Airplane crash	2
March 13-14	Columbia, S.C.	Civil disturbance	325 called
			35 committed
March 28-30	West Memphis, Ark.	Civil disturbance	202 called
			202 committed
March 28-April 14	TENNESSEE	Civil disturbance	9,716 called
March 28-April 14	Memphis	Civil disturbance	3,431 committed
March 28-April 3	Memphis	Civil disturbance	3,383 committed
April 4-14	Nashville	Civil disturbance	2,902 committed
April 5-9	ALABAMA	Civil disturbance	813 called
April 6-8	Tuskegee	Civil disturbance	594 committed
April 4-10	ARKANSAS	Civil disturbance	603 called
April 6-10	Pine Bluff	Civil disturbance	390 committed
April 5-6	CALIFORNIA	Civil disturbance	190 called
April 12	CALIFORNIA	Civil disturbance	17 called
April 5	CONNECTICUT	Civil disturbance	25 called
April 9-17	DELAWARE	Civil disturbance	1,496 called
	Wilmington	Civil disturbance	800 committed
April 5-16	WASHINGTON, D.C.	Civil disturbance	Federal: 1,854 called
			1,854 committed
April 4-10	FLORIDA	Civil disturbance	467 called
April 5-7	Tallahassee	Civil disturbance	333 committed
	Gainsville	Civil disturbance	127 committed

TABLE 12.2 (continued)

Date	Place	Nature of Disturbance	Number of Troops
1968 (continued)			
April 9-10	GEORGIA	Civil disturbance	2,675 called (includes ANG)
April 5-13	ILLINOIS	Civil disturbance	9,367 called
April 5-11	Chicago	Civil disturbance	6,749 committed
April 6	Evergreen Park	Civil disturbance	98 committed
April 5-11	Joliet	Civil disturbance	297 committed
April 7-11	Chicago	Civil disturbance	Federal: 7,174 committed
April 6-8	INDIANA: Richmond	Explosion	190 called 190 committed
April 7-10	IOWA	Civil disturbance	450 called
April 9-14	KANSAS	Civil disturbance	1,178 called
	Kansas City	Civil disturbance	185 committed
April 6-14	MARYLAND	Civil disturbance	6,994 called
	Baltimore	Civil disturbance	5,960 committed
	Cambridge	Civil disturbance	178 committed
April 7-12	Baltimore	Civil disturbance	Federal: 5,783 committed
April 5-11	MICHIGAN	Civil disturbance	10,506 called (Includes ANG)
	Detroit	Civil disturbance	2,584 committed (includes ANG)
April 4-10	MISSISSIPPI	Civil disturbance	1,620 called
April 9-17	MISSOURI	Civil disturbance	3,126 called
April 9-16	Kansas City	Civil disturbance	1,591 called
April 8-15	NEW JERSEY	Civil disturbance	548 called

TABLE 12.2 (continued)

Date	Place	Nature of Disturbance	Number of Troops
1968 (continued)			
April 4-11	NORTH CAROLINA	Civil disturbance	8,757 called
	Raleigh	Civil disturbance	1,669 committed
	Greensboro	Civil disturbance	1,168 committed
	Durham	Civil disturbance	510 committed
	Goldsboro	Civil disturbance	126 committed
	Wilmington	Civil disturbance	1,156 committed
	Wilson	Civil disturbance	323 committed
April 8-13	OHIO	Civil disturbance	2,395 called
April 8-12	Youngstown	Civil disturbance	500 called
April 8-12	Cincinnati	Civil disturbance	1,080 committed
April 6-12	PENNSYLVANIA	Civil disturbance	8,161 committed
April 8-12	Pittsburgh	Civil disturbance	4,458
April 9	RHODE ISLAND	Civil disturbance	15 called
April 7-16	SOUTH CAROLINA	Civil disturbance	991 called
April 7-15	Columbia	Civil disturbance	463 committed
	Hampton	Civil disturbance	69 committed
	Spartanburg	Civil disturbance	31 committed
April 23-28	Wheelersburg, Ohio	Tornado	181 called
			181 committed
May 5-10	Caffney, S.C.	Civil disturbance	127 called
			127 committed
May 6-7	Selma, Ala.	Poor People's March	81 called
			81 committed
May 7-8	Montgomery, Ala.	Poor People's March	326 called
May 7	Montgomery, Ala.	Funeral of Gov. Lurleen Wallace	76 committed
May 12-13	Charleston, S.C.	Poor People's March	310 called
			84 committed
May 16	Jonesboro, Ark.	Tornado	300 called
			300 committed

TABLE 12.2 (continued)

Date	Place	Nature of Disturbance	Number of Troops
1968 (continued)			
May 20	Fairfield, Ala.	Possible civil disturbance	200 committed
May 15-19	Delaware State College, Dover, Del.	Civil disturbance	124 called 124 committed
May 15-23	Fayette, Floyd, Howard Counties, Iowa	Tornado	660 called 626 committed
May 19-26	Salisbury, Md.	Civil disturbance	829 called 809 committed
May 20-22	Athens, Ohio	Civil disturbance	517 called 517 committed
May 24-26	Athens, Logan, Ohio	Flood	17 committed
May 24-28	Laureville, Ohio	Flood	91 committed
May 20-22	Delaware State College, Dover, Del.	Civil disturbance	60 called 60 committed
May 22-Aug. 18	Dover, Del.	Assist local police nightly on patrol	5 called 5 committed
May 26-June 2	Louisville, Ky.	Civil disturbance	2,201 called 2,042 committed
June 7-10	Highlands, N.C.	Search for missing child	348
June 8-9	Washington, D.C.	Funeral of Sen. Robert F. Kennedy	1,248 ARNG 106 ANG
June 13-15	Tracy, Minn.	Tornado	352 called
June 14-16	Loudon, N.H.	Possible civil disturbance (motorcycle race)	164 committed 191 committed
June 19	Washington, D.C.	Solidarity Day march	1,401 ARNG 123 ANG
June 24	Washington, D.C.	Dismantling Resurrection City	1,479 ARNG 104 ANG

TABLE 12.2 (continued)

Date	Place	Nature of Disturbance	Number of Troops
1968 (continued)			
June 24-30	Columbus, Ohio	Prison riot	642 called 642 committed
July 9	London, Ohio	Prison farm riot	234 called 234 committed
July 12-14	Washington, D.C.	Release of Rev. Ralph Abernathy	345
July 13-14	Vicinity Bellows Falls, Vt.	Possible civil disturbance (motorcycle race)	815 called 200 committed
July 18-25	Akron, Ohio	Civil disturbance	1,066 called 950 committed
July 19-Aug. 3	Columbus, Ohio	Prison riot	341 called 341 committed
July 23-28	Cleveland, Ohio	Civil disturbance	2,481 called 2,262 committed
July 28	Grand Rapids, Mich.	Civil disturbance	115 called
July 28-30	Carson City, Nev.	Forest fire	582 called 282 committed
Aug. 8-14	Miami, Fla.	Republican Convention	950 called 239 committed
Aug. 9-14	Little Rock, Ark.	Civil disturbance	981 called 981 committed
Aug. 10-11	Rossville, Kan.	Flood	30 called 23 committed
Aug. 14	Urbana, Ohio	Ammunition train wreck	232 called 232 committed
Aug. 17	Owensboro, Ky.	Civil disturbance	175 called 100 committed
Aug. 22-25	Wichita, Kan.	Civil disturbance	458 called 359 committed

TABLE 12.2 (continued)

Date	Place	Nature of Disturbance	Number of Troops
1968 (continued)			
Aug. 23-31	Chicago, Ill.	Democratic Convention	5,606 called
			5,332 committed
Sept. 1	St. Paul, Minn.	Possible civil disturbance	250 called
Sept. 5-10	Oakland, Calif.	Civil disturbance	187 called
Oct. 1-3	Columbia, S.C.	Prison riot	150 called
Nov. 2-3	Washington, D.C.	Civil disturbance	692 called

Note: When a guard unit is ordered to state active duty by the governor, it is under his command and is paid from state funds. When called to active duty by the President, it is on federal active duty and is paid from federal funds. The President's call to active duty supersedes that of a governor.

See also note to Table 11.3.

Source: Compiled from National Guard Bureau data.

L. Terry, Jr., ordered the maintenance of nightly patrols by Guardsmen, carrying loaded rifles, in radio-equipped jeeps. Their continued presence, however, provoked sharp community opposition and may have contributed to Governor Terry's defeat. In any case, the National Guard's removal was one of his sucessor's first acts.

Even when local leadership is unwilling to ask for federal troops, reliance on military support seems to be growing. In April 1968 Mayor Joseph Barr of Pittsburgh determined to control the situation without requesting federal troops, but 4,458 nonfederalized National Guardsmen were promptly called out and another 3,703 were held in reserve.

Cost may contribute further to reliance on federal assistance, since a governor who calls the Guard has to pay them; federal troops are free. In Tennessee, to take one example, nearly $650,000 was required to cover costs of the Guard in the sanitation strike of early 1968, which brought Martin Luther King to Memphis, where he was assassinated.

The precedents of legal limitation against the use of federal troops have changed in significant ways. While there have been no recent changes in either constitutional or statutory authority, authority has been differently applied. One such new use of executive authority was reflected in a proclamation signed by President Johnson in the early hours of March 20, 1965, after weeks of harassment of Negro voting rights demonstrators in Selma, Alabama. The fifty-mile march to Montgomery was about to begin under the protection of a detailed federal court order, and violence against the marchers seemed probable. Governor George Wallace had refused to call up the National Guard to help enforce the court order, on grounds of cost. In a wire to Wallace President Johnson said: "Both you and the Alabama legislature, because of monetary considerations, believe that the state is unable to protect American citizens and to maintain peace and order in a responsible manner without federal force."[8] Adhering to the precedent of minimum possible force, the President did not call out federal troops, but federalized (and hence paid for) the same National Guard that the governor had refused to use. One of the statutory tests for federal action had been met—Alabama was unwilling to provide the protection envisioned by the federal court order. But the fundamental test—actual disorder—could not sensibly be awaited. The President's preliminary proclamation was grounded on *"a substantial likelihood* that domestic violence may occur." [Emphasis supplied.] Yet his reliance on the prospect rather than the reality of violence represented a significant departure from tradition, one which could be resorted to under different circumstances in the future toward different ends.

Pre-positioning—the advance dispatch of troops to sites near potential

8. *New York Times,* March 21, 1965, p. 70.

disorder, for rapid availability—is another serious new precedent. At the time of the San Francisco Vigilance Committee troubles in 1856, President Pierce—although constrained by lack of troops—ordered two or three national vessels to San Francisco Bay.[9] At the time of civil rights turbulence in the streets of Birmingham, Alabama, in 1963 and the police-dog and hose incidents, President Kennedy ordered federal troops to stand by at military bases near the city. In 1967, President Johnson stationed paratroops near Detroit in advance of the decision to use them in the ghetto riot. Yet each of these precautionary steps was taken only after disorder had actually begun. The only prospective issue was whether they would be used—whether local officials could regain control unaided —not whether violence would occur. But when President Johnson ordered 6,277 federal troops to bases near Chicago before the 1968 Democratic National Convention, no disorder had begun—nor had local forces proved incapable of maintaining control. This pre-positioning in advance of possible violence may have been the first such completely precautionary action taken, with a force of significant size, in our history.[10]

Protection of a party convention, an integral part of the national political process, is essential. But having been taken once, such a step will be harder to avoid in the future. Contingency planning may develop self-enforcing momentum. And the decision to pre-position may be the inevitable precursor of a subsequent decision to deploy. The presence of pre-positioned federal troops might well encourage their use, although they were not used in Chicago, or in New Haven, in May 1970. Local officials have everything to gain—effective force at no cost, additional protection against the spread of violence, and vindication.

Severe rioting is hardly new—the 1863 New York City draft riots resulted in at least 1,250 deaths[11]—and neither are chains of riots—the 1877 railroad strike riots quickly spread to fourteen states, and the 1919 racial disorders spread throughout the East. But the present combination of intensity *and* contagion, attributable, in part at least, to rapid means of vivid communication, may have introduced a serious new factor. The Kerner Commission identified media coverage and rumors of major riots as the specific triggers to disorders in four cities.[12] And, according to the Lemberg Center "Riot Data Review," 203 disorders occurred within the week following rapidly spreading news of the assassination and the funeral of Dr. King.

9. Bennett M. Rich, *The Presidents and Civil Disorders* (Washington, D.C.: The Brookings Institution, 1940), p. 70.

10. Washington, D.C., is a clear exception. As a federal city, it does not possess the state and local law enforcement manpower of other cities.

11. See James McCague, *The Second Rebellion* (New York: Dial Press, 1968).

12. *The Report of the National Advisory Commission on Civil Disorders* (Washington, D.C.: Government Printing Office, 1968), p. 70.

Tactical pressures also contribute to demands for federal aid. One of the lessons of control in April 1968 was, as a *Washington Post* survey put it: "Manpower, not firepower, contained most of the riots that swept the nation in the past week."[13] The International Association of Chiefs of Police agreed with this in a report on the April 1968 disorders prepared for the Department of Justice: "One of the traditional principles of disorder control is the rapid deployment of significant numbers of trained and equipped police. The recent riots once again verified the basic soundness of this principle."[14] Police departments with access to manpower could probably contain disorder quickly, but where police have not planned, or lack personnel, the "manpower, not firepower" formula might well—in direct proportion to its humaneness and success—generate increased demands for federal troops. Arnold Sagalyn, who served on the Kerner Commission staff as associate director for public safety, described the problem:

Few of our police departments have either sufficient manpower themselves or available trained reserves to call on quickly enough to control a large disorder at its incipient stage. . . . Nor can the local police turn to state police forces to provide manpower in sufficient numbers and in the quick response time required. . . . Of the 49 states that have state police forces, 28 have less than 500 policemen in the entire state. Only 7 states have more than 1,000 men. In more than half of the states the police are essentially highway patrolmen who are widely dispersed. . . .[15]

Nor is even maximum use of the National Guard necessarily enough. Mr. Sagalyn reported that, in the April 1968 disorders, Delaware used more than 90 per cent of its Guard, Maryland 92 per cent, Illinois 79 per cent, and the District of Columbia 100 per cent.

Further, although it is not likely to be a major factor in the decision to seek federal help, the greater likelihood of tragedies like the ones enacted in 1970 at Kent State and Jackson State, with the employment of state police or unfederalized troops, may further reduce the resistance of those whose primary concern is with individual rights and liberties.

These diverse pressures lead to an increased probability of use of federal troops, associated with decreased resistance to such use from those who historically have opposed it. As then Attorney General Clark said some months after the April 1968 disorders:

The ghetto residents want federal troops—they're desegregated, they're professional, they're fair. The *police* want federal troops; many police believe

13. "Containing Riots," April 13, 1968.
14. "Civil Disorders: After-Action Reports, Spring, 1968" (multilith) (Washington, D.C.: International Association of Chiefs of Police, undated), p. 3. 1.
15. In "Riots Control Is a Numbers Game," Remarks to the National Symposium on Law Enforcement, Science and Technology, Chicago, April 17, 1968, in its Proceedings, ed. S. I. Cohn, IIT Research Institute, Chicago.

they should not have to engage in riot duty. The *sophisticates* want federal troops; they say riot duty destroys the police-community relations that are essential in the ghetto. The *mayors* want federal troops; they're under tremendous heat from their communities to keep order. And the *governors* want federal troops; some have had to appropriate extra funds for past uses of the National Guard.[16]

When violence erupted in Detroit in July 1967, the worst of 164 significant civil disorders of the year, Cyrus Vance, who had just resigned as Deputy Secretary of Defense, agreed to President Johnson's request to go to the embattled city. Meanwhile, 4,700 paratroops were moved to nearby Selfridge Air Force Base.[17] At first, Vance recommended against using the troops, since sniping and looting had abated, substantial National Guard forces were still uncommitted, and Negro civic leaders feared the deployment of federal troops might exacerbate tension. But later the violence intensified, and he recommended that federal troops be sent into the city. Vance wrote an extensive report on his experiences.[18] His "Detroit Book" has become the source of a series of recommendations directed to more efficient riot control, most of them now implemented.

In addition, three special military boards were convened after the Detroit riot to evaluate the roles and functions of active and Reserve Guard units in civil disturbances, to recommend ways to improve the qualifications of Guard and Reserve officers and to study Negro participation in the National Guard and Reserve. The reports of all three boards are complete but have not yet been declassified.

Experience in Newark and Detroit in 1967 has disclosed lack of training, indiscriminate firing, inadequate discipline, a low proportion of blacks, and frequent lack of equipment among National Guardsmen. Vigorous but largely unsuccessful efforts have since been made to correct these shortcomings. Of the 411,000 men currently authorized for the Army National Guard, 365,000 have now undergone special training programs. Summer camp training in some cases has been devoted to civil disorders. Guardsmen have trained regularly with civil authorities, practicing coordination and methods. In Iowa, a civil disorder was "war gamed," using mock rioters.[19]

In a further effort to avert the need for regular federal forces, the Defense

16. Interview with Jack Rosenthal.
17. Kerner *Report*, pp. 53-54.
18. "Final Report of Cyrus R. Vance Concerning the Detroit Riots (1967)," Department of Defense Release 856-67, Sept. 12, 1967 (cited hereafter as Detroit Book).
19. Interviews by Jack Rosenthal with Colonel Milford W. Wood, Colonel Ray E. Porter, Jr., Lieutenant Colonel Robert D. Beatty, Colonel William M. Hon, and Lieutenant Colonel Edward W. Stephens of the Directorate for Civil Disturbances August 20, 1968, and subsequently. It should be noted that at Kent State the Guard acted not within federal procedural rules, but more permissive state ones.

Department has now provided civil disturbance training for at least 204,000[20] of the 260,000 Army Reservists in the country.

Prior shortages of equipment among under-strength Guard units appear to be abating, particularly for communications. The National Guard reorganization has reduced the total number of units from 4,001 (often thin) units to 3,034 units of 90 per cent strength or better. Decentralization of storage from Louisville, Kentucky, and Sacramento, California, to a number of locations has made it possible for commanders to secure equipment with less delay. This equipment consists principally of CS, a finely powdered form of tear gas; armored vests, and other protective gear; and communications equipment (first used in Chicago in April 1968 by the Illinois National Guard).

For its part, the research arm of the directorate monitors a number of experimental plans for new weaponry for civil disorders. Officers emphasize that they have no funds for hardware research—but they closely follow Army research in techniques for control of civil disorder. Among the unclassified ideas, from the bizarre to the merely ingenious, in the hardware testing stage are tranquilizer dart guns, foam barriers, planes spraying extremely slippery fire retardant, nonlethal, long-lasting chemical agents that disorient target demonstrators, water-filled plastic pellets that can be fired from shotguns with bruising but not seriously injuring effect, and ultrabright searchlights that appear to have crowd-dispersing effects. As in the military sphere, civilian research for civil disorders is also under way. The Law Enforcement Assistance Administration of the Department of Justice commissioned a study by the National Bureau of Standards into CS as probably the only truly nonlethal chemical dispersal agent, and financed dissemination to police forces around the country of the model control and mobilization plans developed by the Kerner Commission.[21]

In addition, the military have taken a hand in paramilitary training of local police. Because the police are neither trained nor experienced in paramilitary actions, they have been unprepared for riots where control personnel must operate in tightly disciplined groups, and where discretion and decision are raised to a unified command and control staff level. In ordinary police operations, policemen are dispersed alone or in pairs, in shifts across the city. The Kerner Commission cited Cincinnati as an example: Even if police could be quickly assembled from their seventy-seven square miles of territory, only a hundred uniformed officers would be on duty in Cincinnati during those hours when a riot was most likely to occur.

The Kerner Commission, therefore, recommended to President Johnson that a series of large-scale conferences for police and other local officers

20. Interview with directorate officers.

21. Interview by Jack Rosenthal with Dan Skoler, Director of the Office of Law Enforcement Programs in the Justice Department, September 13, 1968.

be called, under federal auspices, and with the Department of Defense in an advisory role, for the exchange of information on demonstrably effective riot control and prevention policies. The President immediately ordered the Department of Justice to carry out the Commission's recommendation.[22] With the International Association of Chiefs of Police, the department held one-week information-sharing programs for city executives and policy commanders, complementing the military course at Fort Gordon's "riot city." In four weeks, 400 mayors, city managers, and police chiefs and commanders from the 136 largest cities of the country participated. A number of subsequent regional conferences were conducted for police commanders of lower rank.

Police skills in riot control have also been reinforced by the infusion of a number of military police, many of whom find jobs in civilian law enforcement when they leave the service. Military policemen had trained for proper riot control long before ghetto and urban riots forced municipal police to consider specialized riot control training.

Police forces around the country operated with considerable skill during the April 1968 disorders, probably partly in consequence of these federal conferences. In Newark, where policemen and Guardsmen fired 13,-246 rounds during the 1967 riot, police in 1968 were ordered to use minimum force, and reminders to "keep calm and cool" were broadcast frequently.[23] In Washington, police sought to control large mobs only when sufficient personnel were available. " 'We didn't shoot and they didn't shoot,' one police official said."[24]

In August 1968, the International Association of Chiefs of Police completed an after-action study, commissioned by the Department of Justice, of police operations during April disorders in eight selected cities. It asserted that: "Not only did police personnel understand their department's policy regarding the use of fatal force, but all but two of the officers interviewed agreed that it was satisfactory and would not recommend any change in future disorders."[25]

A number of police departments have recently developed special riot control detachments and/or a cruising squadron of tactical police. Six of the eight cities studied for the IACP report had such forces.

Rioting exploded in scores of cities in the wake of the assassination of Martin Luther King on April 4, 1968. During April, the Lemberg Center

22. Commission letter to the President, October 7, 1967; presidential memorandum to the Attorney General, October 9, 1967; Department of Justice press release, November 1, 1967.

23. "Containing Riots," Washington Post, April 13, 1968.

24. "Riot Lesson: Restraint," Washington Post, April 11, 1968.

25. "Civil Disorders, After-Action Report, Spring 1968" (multilith). (Washington, D.C.: International Association of Chiefs of Police, undated), p. 2. 17.

for the Study of Violence at Brandeis University reports, there were 237 disorders, of which 202 were definite and 35 "equivocal."[26] The degree of control which local and federal officials were able to apply is strongly evidenced by three comparisons between April 1968 and all of 1967. The total number of disorders was very close—249 in 1967 compared with 237 in April 1968. But the number of troops, both federal and National Guard, more than doubled, from 31,991 in 1967 to 68,915 in April 1968.[27] There was, according to the Lemberg "Riot Data Review," a 50 per cent increase in the number of arrests, from 18,800 to 27,000, and a striking inverse correlation between the number of troops and arrest totals on the one hand and the number of fatalities on the other. A total of 82 persons was killed in 1967. In the comparable period in 1968, 43 were killed.

Three of the April 1968 disorders involved simultaneous use of federal troops. In all, 23,000 federal troops—the largest number in the history of domestic disorders—were employed, more than half of them in the nation's capital, where city and military officials activated joint command and control plans prepared in advance as part of "Operation Cabin Guard," the code name for antiriot preparations in Washington.

The Kerner Commission had reported extensive and indiscriminate firing during disorders in 1967. But in April, when 34,900 Guardsmen were used in twenty-two communities, they behaved with extreme circumspection. When alerted in Trenton, New Jersey, for example, they operated under rules of engagement carefully spelled out in "OPLAN 2": "Successive phases would be the deployment . . . into riot formation, the use of water if provided by civil authorities, the use of gas and smoke, limited shooting by selected marksmen and finally, full firepower by selected marksmen."[28] In Washington, where the 15,000 federal and National Guard troops were called out, no more than fifteen bullets were fired.[29] Former Under Secretary McGiffert believes that, nationally, National Guard "fire discipline was good. General discipline was good."

In 1968, the summer was short and cool. In June, July, and August 1968, the National Guard was called out six times, compared with eighteen in those same months in 1967. There were nineteen deaths, compared with eighty-seven in 1967.[30] Police generally seemed less likely to incite disorder through unwitting conduct and more capable of controlling disorder when it erupted.

"Controlling a civil disorder is not warfare," the Kerner Commission

26. "Riot Data Review," p. 60.
27. Data supplied by the office of the Deputy Attorney General.
28. "Jersey Guard Tightens Its Rules on Riot Control," *New York Times,* April 14, 1968, p. 56.
29. "Restraint in Riot Control Aimed at Minimum Toll," *New York Times,* April 14, 1968, p. 61.
30. Report by Attorney General Ramsey Clark, released October 3, 1968.

wrote. "The fundamental objective of National Guard forces is to control the rioters, not to destroy them nor any innocent bystanders who might be present."[31] Recommending urgently against the use of machine guns, flame throwers, artillery, and tanks, the commission quoted Brigadier General Harris W. Hollis, Director of Operations, Office of the Deputy Chief of Staff for Military Operations, U.S. Army: "Commanders and their personnel should do whatever is possible to avoid appearing as an alien, invading force rather than as a force which has the purpose of restoring order with minimum loss of life and property . . ."[32]

The theme of minimum application of force was in line with the recommendation by Cyrus Vance in the Detroit Book that "rules of engagement and degree of force" be clarified. Every soldier engaged in civil disturbance operations is now issued a pocket-sized, plasticized card stating eight special orders:

1. I will always present a neat military appearance. I will conduct myself in a military manner at all times and I will do all I can to bring credit upon myself, my unit, and the military service.
2. I will be courteous in all dealings with civilians to the maximum extent possible under existing circumstances.
3. I will not load or fire my weapon except when authorized by an officer in person, when authorized in advance by an officer under certain specific conditions, or when required to save my life.
4. I will not intentionally mistreat civilians, including those I am controlling or those in my custody nor will I withhold medical attention from anyone who requires it.
5. I will not discuss or pass on rumors about this operation.
6. I will to the maximum extent possible let civilian police arrest civilians, but when assistance is necessary or in the absence of civilian police, I have the responsibility and authority to detain or take into custody rioters, looters, or others committing offenses. It is my duty to deliver evidence and to complete evidence tags and detainee forms in accordance with my instructions.
7. I will allow properly identified reporters and radio and television personnel freedom of movement, unless they interfere with the mission of my unit.
8. I will avoid damage to property as far as possible.

Despite increased use of military power in domestic affairs, however, a sustained effort to reinforce historical limitations against indiscriminate use of federal force has continued. President Johnson, for example, followed precedent in dispatching civilian advisers to report directly to him from the scene of the disorders, an informal practice codified in the Letters of Instruction from the Army Chief of Staff to the commanders of task forces used in civil disorders. Cyrus Vance did not go to Detroit in 1967 to serve

31. Kerner Commission *Report,* p. 503.
32. *Ibid.,* p. 504.

as a civilian check on federal forces already in action; he arrived before troop deployment. Similarly, Deputy Attorney General Warren Christopher in April 1968 was on the scene first in Washington and then in Chicago, and Assistant Attorney General Fred M. Vinson, Jr., was the President's senior adviser in Baltimore. When federal troops were pre-positioned near Chicago at the time of the Democratic Convention, the President again called on Christopher.

Then Attorney General Clark re-emphasized the policy of restraint in August 1967, when he wrote to each governor detailing the legal requirements for the use of federal force, enumerating three conditions which must be met before the President would consider calling out the troops: the existence of serious violence, the inability of local and state forces to control it, and a specific request from the legislature or governor. But even such preliminary steps as alerting troops, he said, "represent a most serious departure from our traditions of local responsibility for law enforcement. They should not be requested until there is substantial likelihood that the federal forces will be needed."[33]

During the latter days of the Johnson administration, McGiffert, who, as Under Secretary, had served with the Secretary of the Army, as the interservice "executive agent" for civil disturbance activities, expressed a similar concern about the reliance on military power, noting that ". . . the army doesn't want to play this role. Not only does it involve the army in law enforcement, but it also requires a response—minimum force—which is quite different from that used in combat. We have gone out of our way to stress the state role and to insist on the exhaustion of remedies." But Daniel Henkin, then Deputy Assistant Secretary of Defense for Public Affairs who served with Cyrus Vance in Detroit and Washington (and now Assistant Secretary), took a contrary view, arguing for enhanced control capability, even if this required pre-positioning of troops at federal bases: "It seems to me that the answer keeps coming down on the side of *precaution*. The federal government has a critical potential problem if disorders spread. It must be ready to move in quickly if local authorities lose control and there are no other alternatives. It can't afford to see a major city burning for a day without federal help."[34]

Directive 3025.12, which authorized the establishment of the Directorate for Civil Disturbance Planning and Operations, notes the limitations on the use of military power by the President: "To the maximum extent practicable, local military authorities will encourage the use of local or state resources rather than military resources."

The Civil Disturbance Information Unit in the Department of Justice,

33. Department of Justice release, August 7, 1967.
34. Interviews with Rosenthal; August 9, 1968 for McGiffert, Sept. 9, 1968 for Henkin.

first organized in 1966 and now called the Inter-Divisional Information Unit, has sought to keep senior federal officials informed of outbreaks of disorder. Its task is to collect and collate information on civil disturbances and distribute the information throughout the Justice Department as needed by the various operating divisions. Insistence on high standards of proof of need is a difficult task, most often performed by Attorney General Clark in the last administration. "Someone *has* to ask the unpopular questions," Christopher said; "to ask whether police leaves have been canceled; whether the whole force is being used; whether the force is on twelve-hour shifts; whether assistance has been sought from neighboring jurisdictions; whether the National Guard is out in force; whether it is intelligently deployed."[35] Attorney General Clark observed "There has never been a riot which was not largely under control before federal assistance arrived."[36] National Guard Chief Winston P. Wilson believed wider use of Guardsmen in April 1968 would have been necessary had it not been for "the vast improvements in local police capacities. They have learned to plan for the worst, to employ maximum visibility and minimum force." Like fire, riots can be controlled by a relatively small force if it arrives quickly. If local forces can muster five hundred men, they may well avert the need to ask the federal government for five thousand.

If future disorders do not exceed the scope or intensity of those in the recent past, then significant increases in federal force need not be required. But if disorder escalates, troubling precedents like the Selma Proclamation or pre-positioning may be followed by common use of federal military force in the streets and by cordoning off trouble areas, whether ghettos or campuses. The diligent, patient efforts of federal and local officials to obviate the use of federal force cannot withstand severe escalation of civil disruption.

The evolving reliance on military methology for coping with civilian disorders has many grave implications. Disorder that erupts in the urban black ghettos or on college and university campuses may be contained by efficient means, but may also dam up rage and frustration which will explode in more serious socially destructive ways later on. The continual use of such force will further polarize the black and the white communities, the young and the old, the children of the middle class and the children of the working class, along divisive lines. Furthermore, the reliance on minimal force and maximum planning sounds very much like the flexible response of counter-insurgency techniques which held hope for limited warfare abroad, only to escalate in Vietnam to full-scale war. A similar danger may exist in the new techniques for countering civil unrest. There may be self-enforcing momen-

35. Interview with Rosenthal, September 6, 1968.
36. *Ibid.*

tum in contingency planning for the worst, and in pre-positioning troops in anticipation of disruption. Particularly in Washington, D.C., where the civilian population is increasingly black, the permanent stationing of federal troops nearby may present a constant danger of overreaction by federal officials. The use of techniques applied in foreign wars and in planning for future wars—war games, riot villages similar to the Green Berets' model training village (see Chapter 13), may lead to increased likelihood that certain groups in American society will gradually be regarded as an enemy, with action appropriate to that perception. Despite the increased efficiency of these new techniques, despite the decline of deaths and injuries and the containment of disorder for which these techniques have considerable responsibility, and despite the continued reluctance of federal executive power to employ troops in local crises, the risks and dangers for the future seem considerable. Just as the power of the military establishment must be adapted to appropriate ends and moderated by countervailing power, so the growing efficiency in the use of military power in civil disorder requires thoughtful attention to probable consequences.

13

The Military Public Relations Network

In the fall of 1968 two memoranda were prepared in the Department of the Army and circulated to officers and civilians associated with plans for the Sentinel antiballistic missile system. One was a memorandum signed by Secretary of the Army Stanley R. Resor outlining the need to combat "public confusion regarding the necessity for the Sentinel System deployment decision and of our need to acquire particular geographical areas for use as Sentinel operational sites." The second, prepared by Lieutenant General Alfred D. Starbird, who manages the antimissile program, was labeled "Public Affairs Plan for Sentinel System," and described as part of the Pentagon's "Sentinel System Master Plan."

The two documents called for a countrywide exercise in propaganda, public relations, and persuasion to promote the ABM system, both technically and politically. The program was calculated to counter the activities of scientific and political opponents of the Sentinel project, and to soothe or eliminate the opposition building up in some communities near which sites for ABM missile storage and deployment were to be constructed.

To the embarrassment of Sentinel's champions, the memoranda found their way into the hands of a *Washington Post* editor and, after the resultant news stories, they were "withdrawn." But the campaign for ABM continued, and many of the activities detailed in Secretary Resor's and General Starbird's public relations directives also continued, although on more circumspect and more restrained terms. When the Johnson administration's Sentinel System became the Nixon administration's Safeguard System, the basic work of influencing minds and countering opposition went on.

Drawing from suggestions in the Resor and Starbird memoranda, and from procedures actually carried out, it is possible to reconstruct efforts on behalf of the "Safeguard System Public Affairs Master Plan" over a few days in September 1968. Such a fictionalized reconstruction might look like this:

\#In Washington, the Deputy Secretary of Defense and two Army ABM scientists lunch with a handful of selected Defense correspondents and two syndicated columnists to educate them on the workability of the Safeguard System. The Secretary of Defense "educates" over drinks two Congressmen and a Senator from Massachusetts, some of whose constituents still fear that an ABM silo is to be built near their town.

\#The Secretary of the Army invites the major press associations, newspapers, radio and television networks to witness a Sprint missile firing at the White Sands Missile Range, and orders a press "junket" prepared two months later to the Kwajalein Missile Range in the Pacific (expenses of transport and housing for the journalists to be borne by the government).

\#In response to requests for military speakers at various civic, fraternal, and other special occasions, the community relations office reports to the Assistant Secretary of Defense for Public Affairs that twenty-four officers and eleven civilian officials have traveled to eleven states in the past thirty days, partly at the expense of their hosts, partly at government expense, to deliver talks and answer questions on the ABM.

\#The Audio-Visual Division of Public Affairs endorses the Army's proposal to extend full cooperation, the use of an appropriate site and the loan of enlisted men and officers (when off duty) to John Wayne's Batjac Company, for the production of his projected new film, *The Missile-Men.* As in the case of Wayne's earlier film *Green Berets,* the film producers agree to pay the Army for certain services ($18,623 in the case of *Green Berets*) and to leave for the Army's use for training in guerrilla warfare the installation of a complete Montana town which Batjac will build on the site. At the same time, Audio-Visual denies cooperation to another company for the production of its new film, *The Day the Rockets Collided,* because it fears that it would be (as with the company's earlier film *Fail-Safe*) "detrimental to the national interest" to do so.

\#Producers of "The Big Picture," the Army television series used by more than 300 commercial TV stations in the United States and forty armed forces stations abroad, program ABM material into its future schedule, while Army Audio-Visual prepares to dispatch around the country "a transportable display exhibit which can be used in communities impacted by [Safeguard] sites and before other appropriate group assemblies." The exhibit will use pretaped voice commentaries and various visual aids and models to show how the system would be set up—how it would reduce casualties in the event of a possible enemy ICBM attack against the United States.

\#The Pentagon's Troop Education Division, widely engaged in the preparation and dissemination of public relations films, pamphlets, and other materials, in the office of the Assistant Secretary for Manpower (not the Assistant Secretary of Defense for Public Affairs), orders two training films, one on the system itself, one on its politics, and orders widespread distribution of an illustrated pamphlet, *The Safeguard Story*. These are to be used to educate military personnel, but extra prints of the film and copies of the printed material will be made available for use by veterans' groups, service clubs, schools, and other civilian groups.

#Special pains are taken by the Army's Public Affairs division to co-operate with the Office of Congressional Liaison to provide, in General Starbird's words, "briefings and information fact sheets to members of Congress, local governmental leaders and officials, military audiences, scientific, fraternal, and civic groups and organizations." In addition, Army Public Affairs prepares "informational or educational articles for general news and mass communications media, military, scientific, and professional journals that are service-oriented."

#"All U.S. Army elements and . . . all individual industrial firms and civilian contractors participating in the production and deployment of the [Safeguard] system" are invited to contribute energy and resources to the Safeguard selling campaign.

All of these activities fall within the resources and capabilities of the public relations and propaganda operations of the Department of Defense and the four military services. The ABM case—admittedly a special one—serves to dramatize, better than any compilation of statistics, how the machinery of public information and persuasion has grown with the rest of the military complex in the years since World War II.

All the communications media, the important members and committees of Congress (see Chapter 4), the business and industrial communities (see Chapter 5), a large proportion of the universities and colleges, many high schools, the veterans', civic, and fraternal organizations, the communities that harbor military recruiting stations, and the 1,500 or more communities whose newspapers are serviced by the armed forces "hometown news" services—all are touched in many ways by the Pentagon's informational, educational, and propaganda machinery.

These operations by their nature tend to be varied, diffuse, and frequently difficult to identify or classify. Defense Department officials prefer to talk in terms of categories or compartments, to separate the direct information function ("Public Affairs") from many other activities. The recruiting process, for example, does not fall under the heading of public affairs, but it may exert a definite subliminal influence in extolling the military life and the necessity for large standing forces. The educational and self-promoting activities which the armed services mount in local communities, in the school and university systems, with veterans' and civic organizations, even though not labeled "public affairs" activities, are indeed that. So, too, the widespread public circulation of Defense Department and service films, radio and TV programs, printed material, and visual exhibits. The armed forces' extensive liaison activities with the Congress and some state legislatures may not be labeled as such, but they, too, perform the function of furthering the military's affairs with the public.

The exact costs of this public relations complex have never been determined; when asked for details, one high-ranking Army information officer estimated that it would cost $85,000 to track down the figure on the size of the public relations force for his service alone. In response to an inquiry by Senator Fulbright, the Pentagon late in 1969 acknowledged a public information force of 2,800 men, and salary and operating costs of $27.9 million. Noting that these figures included only the personnel involved full-time in public relations and public information, Fulbright labeled the estimates "conservative."[1]

From 1952 through 1959, Congress placed specific limits on Pentagon spending for public information and public relations activities. The limits were dropped in 1960 and not imposed again. In 1959 public affairs costs acknowledged by the Office of the Secretary of Defense and the military services were $2,755,000. In a decade—by 1969—they had increased more than tenfold.

Military public relations activities—as the public policy role of the military generally—expanded markedly in the years following World War II. When President Truman set an arbitrary ceiling of $15 billion on the fiscal 1950 Defense budget, the services found themselves locked into a life-and-death struggle to sell Congress and the President on their respective roles in the postwar military establishment. To do so, each reinforced its public information apparatus as a means of getting its case to Congress, the President, and the public.[2]

The first indication of increased reliance on public relations by the services was their postwar decision to raise the status of their public information offices. During the 1920's and 1930's public information had been a staff function of the intelligence services of both the Army and the Navy. But both services elevated public information programs to a separate staff status during the war, although it was not until the immediate postwar years that public information and public relations were placed under the direct authority of the Army and Navy Secretaries, and servicemen were encouraged to pursue the public relations field as their service career. After its establishment as a separate service in 1947, the Air Force followed the example of its sister services and set up an office of public relations directly responsible to the Air Force Secretary.[3]

1. *Congressional Record*, Dec. 1, 2, 4, 5, 1969.
2. "Congress and the Nation, 1945–1964," *Congressional Quarterly*, Quarterly Service, Washington, 1965, p. 253; Samuel P. Huntington, *The Common Defense* (New York: Columbia University Press, 1961), pp. 381, 385.
3. Huntington, p. 385.

For most of the Truman and Eisenhower years, the services used their Public Relations programs as a device to deflate the claims of other services about competing weapon systems while inflating their own projects. The first of these interservice battles developed in 1949 when the Air Force sought approval of the B-36 jet bomber as the centerpiece for the nation's emerging "deterrence" strategy.[4] Within the $15 billion Defense budget, there was no room for both the B-36 and a fleet of new "supercarriers" sought by the Navy as a supplementary means of getting nuclear bombers to distant foreign targets. At the height of the controversy, reports began to reach congressional offices that the Air Force's B-36 bomber not only would fail to carry out its assigned mission but also that there were instances of improper exercise of influence on the part of the Air Force officials who were procuring the craft. The allegations, later dropped, led to the stormy B-36 hearings before the House Armed Services Committee in the summer and fall of 1949. It emerged at the hearings that the allegations had been planted with the Congressmen by a former scenario writer in the office of the Under Secretary of the Navy.[5] The Navy memo, which had not been signed, said its purpose was to clear up "a cloud of confusion skillfully induced through fanciful and fascinating tub-thumping in the name of air power."[6] The Air Force got its B-36, but the Navy's supercarriers were denied.[7]

Among the more significant public relations developments of the immediate postwar era was the proliferation of service "backstop" associations—civilian groups organized to support the interests of a particular service. The emerging role of these groups became clear in 1949 when the Navy League, a civilian organization active in the prewar years but never large or influential, launched a massive public relations campaign to "establish the Navy and Naval Aviation as an essential element of national defense." Similar organizations set up by civilian advocates of the other services (the Air Force Association in 1946 and the Association of the U.S. Army in 1950) also established critical pressure efforts to back up their services' policies.

Despite the permissive atmosphere in which service public relations

4. "Congress and the Nation," pp. 253-255; Edward A. Kolodziej; *The Uncommon Defense and Congress, 1945–1963* (Columbus: Ohio State University Press, 1966), pp. 109-111.

5. Kolodziej, p. 109.

6. *Investigation of the B-36 Bomber Program,* Hearings by Committee on Armed Services, U.S. House of Representatives, 81st Congress, 1st Session, 1949, p. 528.

7. Defending his shift to a more centralized information policy almost two decades later, Defense Secretary McNamara cited the B-36-carrier controversy as ". . . an example of how the national interest suffered because of . . . partisan activities. Parochial salesmanship came not only from within the services but also from within defense agencies and elements of the Office of the Secretary of Defense. The public interest is abused by half truths and distortions." Secretary of Defense Memorandum on Public Information Policy, June 30, 1967.

offices were operating, it was more convenient and less risky for a service to permit its "backstop" group to attack the doctrine of another service or to oppose the position of the President or the Secretary of Defense than to do so directly itself. As one author has observed, these groups are

. . . at times more royalist than the king. They do not necessarily identify more intensely with service interests than do the members of the service, but they do have a greater freedom to articulate those interests and to promote them through a wider variety of political means. Journalists, businessmen, retired officers, speak and act with a freedom denied to those on active duty.[8]

The importance of these groups has increased enormously in recent years as information policy became more centralized in the Office of the Secretary of Defense, and it became more difficult for service public relations offices to articulate parochial views. The service associations were under no such restraints.

As the interservice scramble for defense funds continued into the 1950's, public relations activities took on even greater significance. In 1954, Army Chief of Staff General Ridgway called for the "creation of a public relations-conscious Army," and two years later, the Air Force launched an "extended worldwide" campaign on the theme of a "decade of security through global air power." The Air Force campaign was to take advantage of the concept that public opinion was "the most powerful tool of all, more powerful even than war itself."[9] The Navy almost simultaneously announced a six-month press campaign emphasizing the theme that "The U.S. Navy Is More Important Than Ever."[10]

These and other campaigns led President Eisenhower in his 1958 message to Congress on Defense Reorganization to decry "defense dollars spent in publicity and influence campaigns in which each service claims superiority over the others and strives for increased appropriations or other congressional favors." Although the President exercised existing Executive authority to tighten the Defense Secretary's control over service public affairs programs, his move did not deter Army Chief of Staff General Maxwell D. Taylor from delivering a scorching attack on the Air Force's Bomarc surface-to-air missile, which was in competition with a similar Army missile, the Nike-Hercules.

The Defense Department and the armed services have never been very candid about the scope and size of their public relations operations. The

8. Huntington, p. 397.
9. *Availability of Information from Federal Departments and Agencies (Department of Defense), Report by Committee on Government Operations,* U.S. House of Representatives, 85th Congress, 2nd Session, 1958, pp. 248-249.
10. Huntington, pp. 381, 385.

Congress, which is in a better position than any other body to get the facts, has been, in the opinion of many, quite lax about inquiring into the Pentagon personnel and funds devoted to public relations activities, and the lukewarm inquiries that have been made by the House and Senate Armed Services Committees have sometimes been answered in ways so narrowly literal as to be potentially misleading.

In April 1968, for example, a Department of Defense breakdown of personnel assigned to information work as provided to the Defense Appropriations Subcommittee of the House specified only 1,241 military personnel (out of armed forces totaling more than three million) and 1,070 civilians engaged in such work. Only by the narrowest sort of measurement could those figures have been judged accurate, but not until 1969, when Senator Fulbright authorized his staff to press stringent inquiries to the Pentagon, did a more realistic set of figures emerge.

The new breakdown revealed that more than 200 military and civilian personnel were assigned to the Public Affairs office at Defense Department level, and that hundreds more performed similar functions for the military services. In all, the various arms of the Pentagon are spending at least $27.9 million a year on public relations activities. About 200 employees of the Office of the Secretary of Defense spend over $3,500,000; some 1,000 Navy personnel spend almost $10 million; about 610 Army personnel spend almost $6 million; and 944 Air Force personnel spend over $9 million. These figures for fiscal year 1969 must be considered low, since they do not include many personnel engaged in part-time public affairs activities, or the cost of many programs which have some public relations dimension.

Defense officials feel some defensiveness about public relations activities, and often do not concede that a considerable part of service recruiting activities, educational film distribution, community relations, official speech-making and ribbon-cutting, liaison with the Congress and with industry and civic organizations, downtown parades and State Fair fly-overs by the Air Force, are very much a part of the "public relations" process.

Nominally, the Defense public affairs mechanism is guided and controlled from the top, by the Secretary of Defense and his civilian aides through the office of the Assistant Secretary of Defense for Public Affairs, with its 98 civilian and 116 military personnel. According to Department of Defense Directive No. 5122.5, which was issued July 19, 1961, and which superseded others dating back to a memorandum signed by the first Secretary of Defense, James Forrestal, on October 10, 1947, the Assistant Secretary for Public Affairs is assigned the responsibility for "an integrated DOD public affairs program" to provide the public with "maximum information about the Department of Defense consistent with national security." The public affairs operation also is required to "initiate and support activities contributing to good relations between the Department of Defense and all segments of the public at home and abroad," and to plan for censorship of the nation's communications media in the event of "a declared national emergency."

The directive assigned the Assistant Secretary twelve specific areas of responsibility, including development of over-all Pentagon public affairs policies and programs, security review for all Defense-oriented material proposed for publication, review of official speeches and press releases to ensure that they follow policy, and provision of news analysis and information for the Secretary of Defense and the Joint Chiefs of Staff.

Below the Assistant Secretary is a network of supporting facilities:

1. *The Directorate for Defense Information* generates all Defense Department news releases, and normally is staffed with fifty to sixty military and civilian experts.

2. A major subordinate office in the Directorate for Defense Information, the *Audio-Visual Division*, is charged with responsibility for approval and release of all television and movie films, radio transcripts, and other audio-visual material provided by the Department of Defense or the individual armed services for public consumption. The division also provides technical assistance and advice to producers of films and motion pictures. In return for help, producers must submit a completed production to the Public Affairs Office for review; if the Pentagon determines that the production does not project military life accurately, it may refuse to allow the producer to advertise that the film was produced with Pentagon assistance. Navy Commander E. F. Roeder, director of the program, explains that producers always go along because they "really treasure" the Pentagon credit line. The division's over-all director, Norman T. Hatch, says that in his fourteen years at the division he did not note "a single case" when a producer refused to go along.

Three controversial films about the military, *Dr. Strangelove, Seven Days in May* and *Fail-Safe,* were produced without Defense Department assistance; such assistance was not requested for the first two productions but was requested and turned down for *Fail-Safe*. One movie the Defense Department did like and assisted with was the film *The Green Berets,* produced at Fort Benning, Georgia, in 1968 by John Wayne's Batjac Company. It was the story of a skeptical war correspondent who was converted by a Green Beret commander into a staunch supporter of the Vietnam war.

One other recent recipient of assistance from the Audio-Visual Division parted with the Pentagon on less friendly terms. Alan M. Levin, producer of a critical ninety-minute documentary on military spending telecast by the Public Broadcast Laboratory in early 1969, said the division required him to sign papers giving it the right to edit comments of Pentagon officials he would interview. Otherwise, the Pentagon would not permit the officials to participate.

3. The *Directorate for Community Relations* is the focal point of the

Pentagon's enormously successful ties to local communities, with responsibilities ranging from the scheduling of tours, bands, and speakers to the furnishing of liaison to organized labor and the business community. One of the most effective of the Pentagon's local programs is furnishing bands, choral groups, and aerial demonstration teams. During fiscal year 1969, the Community Relations Directorate set up 4,800 band and 262 choral events in the Washington, D.C., area alone, with audiences estimated at more than five million persons. The directorate also sent the Army's Golden Knights parachute team, the Air Force's Thunderbirds, and the Navy's Blue Angels jet demonstration teams to 289 engagements throughout the country for audiences totaling more than fifteen million.

4. A *Veterans and Civic National Organizations Division* exists within the Community Relations Directorate, the Defense Department's point of contact for some 500 national organizations ranging from the Cub Scouts and Boy Scouts to the Kiwanis Clubs and Veterans of Foreign Wars.

5. A *Business and Labor Division* of the directorate is its principal point of contact with business, industry, and labor groups. The division briefs industry on Defense Department procurement procedures and distributes a free monthly magazine called the *Defense Industry Bulletin* at a cost of about $47,500 annually.

6. The Pentagon's watchdog for security leaks in the press is the *Directorate for Security Review,* which monitors Defense Department news releases for security and peruses the press for possible security violations. If the directorate locates an apparent press violation, it passes the information on to the Assistant Secretary of Defense for Administration, who has the sole authority to investigate news leaks. Defense Department regulations prohibit eavesdropping unless "there are reasonable grounds to believe that a criminal offense concerning the national security is involved, or that a felony has been or is about to be committed." Several Pentagon reporters interviewed for this study said they assumed their telephones in the Pentagon were "bugged." Richard Fryklund, who from 1967 to 1969 served as a Deputy Assistant Secretary of Defense for Public Affairs, wrote in 1966 as a Pentagon reporter for the *Washington Evening Star:* "I have been told, and other reporters have been told by people in a position to know, that tapping and shadowing are done." Fryklund also wrote that he once did a story "in which one hundred and twenty persons, by count of the Defense Department, were asked if they would take a lie detector test. The whole thing blew up in public and the Department officials didn't go through with it, but this shows what they are willing to do."[11] Later, as a Defense Department official, Fryklund said he had "no knowledge of any wiretapping of telephone conversations between DOD officials and newsmen."

11. Richard Fryklund, "Covering the Defense Establishment," in *The Press in Washington,* R. E. Hiebert, ed. (New York: Dodd, Mead, 1966), pp. 166-181.

Fryklund the official may be right, but what Fryklund the newsman believed is equally significant for the impact of the Pentagon on the press.

7. Unlike the Department of Defense, the services maintain numerous *field information offices* at major commands throughout the country and the world; in addition, every military base or separate office assigns officers, enlisted men, and frequently some civilian personnel to handle public relations.

8. There also are many other informational activities conducted by the services or other agencies of the Defense Department which have no parallel in the Public Affairs Office. Some of the notable ones:

—*Army "Big Picture":* Probably the most successful audio-visual venture by any of the services, this television series, mentioned earlier, is used by 313 commercial and 53 educational television stations in the United States and 40 armed forces stations abroad. It costs the Army about $900,000 a year.

—*National Guard Bureau:* Extensive public relations activities are conducted by the National Guard Bureau, an active duty agency that serves as the channel of communications between the fifty states and the departments of the Army and Air Force. In 1966 and 1967, the bureau produced two films on the Guard which appeared on local television in most major cities. The bureau has two radio programs —"Guard Session" (a music-interview show) and "Guard Scene" (a rock and roll show), used by about 2,500 stations. By taking advantage of donations of air time and the use of cost-cutting devices, said Lieutenant Colonel James C. Elliott, the bureau's public information officer, his office gets $20 million worth of advertising a year out of its $450,000 budget. His office also distributes elaborate brochures to Congress, prepares outdoor advertising (space-donated), distributes "National Guard" bookcovers at high schools and hands out Guard comic books and lithographs of troops and aircraft.

—*Radio Television Service:* Another major activity is the Armed Forces Radio and Television Service, administered by the office of Armed Forces Information and Education under the Assistant Secretary of Defense for Manpower. As of mid-1969, this service had 396 AFRTS outlets, including 323 radio and 73 television stations. Outlets were in 27 foreign countries, 9 United States territories and possessions and on 71 ships at sea. In fiscal year 1968 this service received free programming (contributions by industry of films and TV shows) of approximately $10 million. Its own expenditure of Pentagon funds ran about $3.5 million a year. By agreement with host countries, AFRTS programs are aimed only at American troops, but they can be and are picked up by civilian listeners and viewers as well.

9. *Press Trips,* or "junkets," in the 1960's for newsmen continued to be a popular practice, with both the Pentagon and defense contractors picking up the tabs. The best known of these junkets was a Defense Department-sponsored program to send four correspondents a month on ten-day trips to Vietnam. During the fourteen-month duration of the program in 1964 and 1965, a total of eighty-three correspondents made the trip. The government paid for all travel, with the correspondents paying only token amounts for food and lodging.

The biggest public relations trip by a defense contractor in recent years was sponsored by General Dynamics Corporation in November 1967, when more than twenty reporters were flown in a company plane to the company's Fort Worth plant, where the controversial F-111 aircraft was being built. The purpose of the trip was to have the press on hand for General Dynamics' counterattack on the critics of the F-111. Paradoxically, the result of the trip was a rash of generally unfavorable stories about the F-111.

10. *Film:* The office of Armed Forces Information and Education, the Defense Department's Public Affairs Office, and various offices at the service level produce a variety of films on military subjects, many available for public showing. Two recent films are *Why Vietnam?* produced by the Office of Education, and *Not for Conquest,* another Vietnam film, produced by the Public Affairs Office, shown since 1966 at about 45,000 public gatherings, with audiences estimated at more than 50 million. *Conquest* cost the Government about $55,000, *Why Vietnam?* cost $18,000.

An activity that recently came in for criticism by Senator Fulbright, who has asked Congress to impose a cutback on Pentagon public relations activities, is the Public Affairs Office's so-called "V-Series" of newsfilms, under which five military camera crews shoot footage in Vietnam and provide it free to commercial television stations. In its justification for the project, the Pentagon wrote Fulbright that the films were necessary "to document, for release to national television, the feature aspects of the military's participation in Southeast Asia often ignored or bypassed by national media film crews because of the pressure of hard news events." Fulbright complained that there is "enough administration propaganda on Vietnam being provided the American public through speeches and statements without providing this traditional outlet in the guise of 'objective' newsfilm stories." He said 118 different films were made under the program in fiscal year 1969 at a cost of more than $87,000.

11. *Hometown News:* Each of the armed services maintains its Hometown News Center, which reviews and distributes all hometown news releases from commands throughout the world. The Navy and Marine Corps alone sent a total of 2,830,000 releases to 12,000 publications and broadcasting media in fiscal year 1968. Combined costs of these operations totals approximately $750,000 a year.

12. *Regional Information Offices:* Each service maintains regional public affairs offices in several key cities throughout the country. The Air Force and Navy have such offices in New York City, Chicago, and Los Angeles. The Marine Corps has six public affairs branches, but they are largely recruiting offices. The total annual cost of these offices is about $250,000.

13. *Exhibits Program:* Another activity is the services' $750,000-a-year program for displaying combat art and other exhibits. The program is used primarily in conjunction with recruiting efforts, but also may be employed, as General Starbird hoped with his Sentinel ABM campaign, to sell the public on new weapons systems.

14. *Defense Information School:* The Defense Department operates a Defense Information School at Fort Benjamin Harrison, Indiana, to train personnel from all the services in public affairs, newswriting, radio and television broadcasting, and internal information activities. The school has an average faculty of 185 and puts about 2,200 students from all services through the course each year.

The public relations mechanisms of the Defense establishment extend beyond the clearly labeled activities of the Pentagon public affairs offices and their many overt public relations programs, and include as well many allied and auxiliary activities. Consider, for example, such things as:

—The extensive pro-Pentagon activities and publications of such related groups as the veterans' organizations and the service alumni "clubs";

—The elaborate public relations and advertising campaigns of defense industries;

—The industrial lobbyists who work in Washington and elsewhere, and their interaction with the men who pass the laws and who publish the newspapers or magazines and run the TV stations;

—The ways in which military and cold war and space themes figure in film and TV entertainment.

Many of the Pentagon's public relations programs are designed to reach the local community, and these programs have met with extraordinary success. But of equal if not greater importance in the local community is the work of "backstop" associations—all enthusiastic partners in the Pentagon drive to create public support for the military point of view. The major groups are the American Legion, the Veterans of Foreign Wars, the National Rifle Association, the Association of the U.S. Army, the Air Force Association, the Navy League, the National Guard Association and the Reserve Officers Association. They are particularly powerful in small and medium-sized communities where the populations are more cohesive.

Perhaps the most important of these supportive organizations are the veterans' groups. The largest is the American Legion, with a membership of 2,600,000 in 16,900 local posts. Approximately one million mothers, wives, sisters, and daughters of legionnaires belong to the American Legion Auxiliary which has roughly 14,000 local chapters. The major aims of both the Legion and the Auxiliary are to "uphold and defend the Constitution ... maintain law and order ... foster and perpetuate a 100 per cent Americanism ... [and] inculcate a sense of individual obligation to the community, state and nation. . . . ." The Legion conducts a wide variety of community relations activities not related to the military, including junior baseball, Boys' Nation and Boys' State, toys for needy children, hospital work, American Education Week, high school oratorical contests. Among other activities, these have helped cement the Legion's position as a leading civic group and a major influence in many communities. The Legion's Americanism Commission mails out great quantities of literature each year and conducts a vigorous antisubversion program. A Legion history brochure says the group "continues to be the outstanding opponent of Communism and other un-American dogma, and it is proud to be known as one of Communism's most dangerous and persistent enemies."[12]

The *Veterans of Foreign Wars* (VFW), limited to male personnel honorably discharged who served in a foreign combat area in which service was recognized by the award of a service or campaign medal, names among its major objectives fostering "true patriotism" and defending the United States from "all her enemies." There are 1,400,000 million members in 10,000 local chapters.

Backing up the veterans groups are the service-related organizations:

1. In this general category is the *Association of the United States Army* (AUSA), a private organization which lists as one of its primary aims the objective of fostering "public understanding and support of the U.S. Army." It received an income in 1967 of about $1.4 million, including $729,000 in corporate and individual members' dues and $387,000 from advertising, most of it from defense contractors, in the association's monthly magazine, *Army*. The association has a membership of about 100,000 with over 60,000 active Army and the remainder consisting of Army Reserve, retired Army, industry personnel, and the general public. It has about 120 local chapters and maintains a separate public relations program keyed to industrial members of the association. At the end of 1967, it had 4,124 defense industry members representing ninety-eight companies. A spokesman said the group played the role of "middleman" between the Army and industry, frequently providing industries with guidelines on contract procedures. He explained that this industry guidance role was necessary because "the Army has to keep arm's length from the contractors. It can't

12. The Legion's 1967 Annual Report emphasized that its publication, *Firing Line,* had carried exposés on activities of the W. E. B. Du Bois Clubs, Students for a Democratic Society, Spring Mobilization, "draft card burners," and persons guilty of "desecration of the Flag of the United States,"

just go out and call on industry and tell them how to work up their contract proposals."

2. The *Air Force Association* is a professional group with a considerably broader approach than that of the AUSA. Geared not only to the support of the Air Force, it is also devoted to furtherance of the general goal of "aerospace power"—civilian as well as military. Its membership is over 90,000, with about 40,000 active duty Air Force personnel in some 230 local chapters. The association is probably best known for its monthly publication, *Air Force and Space Digest,* whose readership includes 98 per cent of all active Air Force generals as well as many Air Force civilian officials. The February 1969 issue of the magazine carried 34½ pages of defense contractor advertising.

General David M. Shoup, now retired, the former Marine Corps commandant who has become an increasingly vocal critic of excessive influence by the military and its contractors, has described *Air Force* as "the official mouthpiece of the U.S. Air Force doctrine, 'party line,' and propaganda."[13] He wrote that the publication "frequently promotes Air Force policy that has been officially frustrated or suppressed within the Department of Defense. . . . The thick mixture of defense contractor advertising, propaganda, and Air Force doctrine continuously repeated in this publication provides its readers and writers with a form of intellectual hypnosis, and they are prone to believe their own propaganda because they read it in *Air Force.*" The AFA also has 261 aerospace companies affiliated with the organization under what it calls the "Industrial Associate Program." The group provides these members with briefings and printed material on Air Force contract requirements.

3. An affiliate group of AFA called the *Aerospace Education Foundation* provides educational materials available for high schools and universities and also holds annual seminars on how to adapt these materials for use in public school systems. Through another affiliate, the Arnold Air Society and its auxiliary, Angel Flight, it supports the college ROTC program. The society, a professional honorary group made up of selected Air Force ROTC cadets, has 7,000 members at 175 colleges and universities. There are 6,000 members of Angel Flight, located on most of the coeducational campuses where there are chapters of the Arnold Air Society. The aim of both groups, as an AFA handout put it, is to "act on the campuses of the nation as a professional motivating force on behalf of the U.S. Air Force and national aerospace power in particular and on behalf of broad civic and patriotic responsibilities in general."

4. The *Navy League of the United States,* like the Air Force Association, is dedicated to broader goals than the support of the service it repre-

---

13. *Atlantic,* April 1969, pp. 51-56. (Also discussed in Chapter 7.)

sents. Although the League describes itself as "The Civilian Arm of the Navy," it puts almost as much emphasis on the nation's commercial maritime posture as it does on military matters. It has a membership of about 41,000 in 300 local chapters. The Navy League, moreover, is the only one of the three service associations that does not permit active duty service personnel to join.[14]

5. The *National Guard Association of the United States,* with a membership of 80,000, is designed to promote the interests of the Army and Air Force National Guard (there is no Navy Guard). The major community-oriented activities of the group include encouragement of the local Guard commander to conduct open-houses to show the public what the Guard is doing, and to line up films and speakers for local civic groups. The association's headquarters in Washington works closely with the National Guard Bureau to try to persuade local radio and television stations to provide time for Guard recruitment announcements and other publicity. The NGA also urges Guard units, whenever possible, to schedule training activities of direct benefits to the local community, such as the use of engineering companies to help build Boy Scout camps or improve beaches.

6. The *Reserve Officers Association of the United States* (ROA) is made up of 60,000 Reserve officers from all the uniformed services, and also represents the Reserve components. The objectives of the organization, as stated in its by-laws, is "to support a military policy for the United States that will provide adequate national security." The ROA has about 600 local chapters in the United States, Puerto Rico, and the Far East. Regarded as one of the more powerful lobbies in Washington, ROA is credited with almost singlehandedly dismantling Secretary McNamara's 1964-65 proposals for a merger of the Army Reserve and Army National Guard under Guard auspices. The combined lobby clout of the ROA and the Guard Association was evident in 1966, when the group persuaded the House to drop a Senate amendment to empower the President to reach into Reserve and Guard units and call up individuals who had performed less than two years' active service. The amendment's sponsor, Senator Richard Russell, said his proposal would have gone through the House except for "strong lobbying efforts" by the ROA and Guard Association, which he said were "among some of the most formidable lobbies . . . in Washington."

7. The *National Rifle Association* (NRA), 1,135,000 strong, has as one of its objectives the promotion of the national defense through increas-

14. Its public relations director, Captain Gilven Slonim (USN ret.), said this made it easier for the League to oppose official Navy policy whenever appropriate. He said it had been "rare," however, for the League to differ with the Navy, although it had found itself "frequently at odds" with the policies of former Defense Secretary McNamara. The Air Force Association's clash with Air Force Secretary Eugene Zuckert is described in Chapter 2.

ing "the knowledge of small arms" and promoting "efficiency in the use of such arms on the part of law enforcement agencies, of the armed forces, and of citizens who would be subject to service in the event of war." The NRA is affiliated with numerous gun clubs representing active duty service personnel. There are about 400 NRA-affiliated military clubs, including about 290 active duty and 110 reserve groups.

Founded in 1871 by a group of National Guard officers, a major purpose of the NRA has long been support of the military. The government's assistance to the organization began in 1903, when Congress created the National Board for the Promotion of Rifle Practice and its implementing agency, the office of the Director of Civilian Marksmanship. Congress in the 1903 Act charged the National Board with responsibility for promoting military-type small arms practice among persons not reached through military training programs. The DCM program, which long provided financing for civilian rifle matches and for sales of excess arms and ammunition to NRA members, was sharply curtailed by the Army in 1967 and 1968 amid the widespread controversy that had enveloped the NRA over its opposition to gun control legislation.

The public affairs program has attracted relatively little criticism from the House and Senate military appropriations committees, whose discussions of the subject accounted for only twenty-six pages of hearings in fiscal years 1965 through 1969. The Foreign Operations and Government Information Subcommittee of the House Government Operations Committee has held a series of hearings on the subject, but its recommendations for curbs on public relations activities have not been taken up by the authorization and appropriation committees that act on the Pentagon budget.

Senator Fulbright, late in 1969, introduced legislation to cut Pentagon public relations spending to $10 million a year, to prohibit government camera crews from filming and distributing Vietnam newsfilms to commercial television stations, and to require detailed semiannual reports to Congress on six major categories of Pentagon public relations activities, including films released to the public, material prepared for use of radio or television, assistance rendered in production of commercial or other nongovernmental films, press releases and photographs released to news media, speeches made by high-ranking Pentagon civilians and military officials to public audiences, and free transportation on military planes or ships for newsmen and other civilians. This proposal never came to a vote.

The media are all dependent to some extent on the good will of the military establishment; and other sources of public information, covering a spectrum from, say, the Foreign Policy Association to the Conference of Mayors of the United States, are somewhat in awe of the establishment's expertise—and generally with good reason. They may conceal their awe —and their ignorance—with sweeping criticisms, but they do not meet the establishment on equal ground. There are notable exceptions from time to time in magazine articles, books and lectures, but these are sporadic and too often available only to relatively limited audiences.

What is badly needed is the kind of independent data base and analytical studies just beginning to be made available by the Brookings Institution, through its Foreign Policy Division and Defense Analysis staff, which is preparing an annual (unclassified) commentary on the Defense budget and the Defense posture statement, making use of full-time professional personnel to do the analytical work. The dissemination of this information to the general public in understandable form will largely determine its effectiveness—and that dissemination will depend largely on the uses made of the material by others. But at least the raw material will be there for intelligent discussion of national priorities. In the meantime, full disclosures to the Congress and to the public of the extent and character of military public relations activities would seem to be in order.

14

The Pentagon's Handling of News

Until it dropped requirements for official accreditation in the fall of 1967, the Pentagon list of accredited news media personnel normally ranged from 2,800 to 3,100 (the peak was 3,800 during the Korean War). The Defense Department deals daily with news syndicates, radio and television representatives, photographic services, the magazines and other periodicals and, to a very important degree, the trade press. The actual Pentagon press corps—those who regularly or with considerable frequency cover events at the Pentagon—is much smaller. The Public Affairs Office "call list"—reporters who cover the Pentagon on a full-time or fairly regular basis—includes seventy-one names, representing forty-three organizations. Inclusion on the list entitles the correspondents to telephone alerts for major developments, and the privilege of holding building passes admitting them after hours and on weekends without the minor annoyance of the company of Public Affairs escort officers to shepherd them through the Pentagon. To this list of newsman accepted as Pentagon "regulars" must be added the principal Washington columnists and the chiefs of each of the major newspaper, wire service, and magazine bureaus in Washington. The direct media clientele of the Pentagon can be estimated at about 250 Washington-based journalists and broadcasters.

The general public relies on the communications media to seek out and disseminate the information the citizen feels a need to know. But, while the media and at least some of the public may view public information chiefly as a servant of the media and the public, many officials do not see it quite that way. Those responsible for conducting the business of defense tend to view the public affairs operation as a conduit through which flows what "can" be told and what the public "ought to know." Beyond that, the information mechanism is viewed as a shield behind which a giant, diffused bureaucracy may do its work, protected from the curiosity and mischief of the press, and insured against the danger of premature publicity and over-zealous or mischievous scrutiny.

The common tendency within the Pentagon, as in most of the government, is to conduct in private the debates over policies and then to present "agreed policy" for public consumption. In most cases, that is how the system works, leaving the media and the public ignorant of the variety of courses of action and the arguments that ultimately were sacrificed to a final decision. The standing policy is: "Once a decision is made, we all close ranks and do it."

There is no question that when the Commander in Chief or his top lieutenants put their mind to it, they can achieve effective control over the news-handling of a major event, or even the public development of national policy. President Kennedy did it with consummate success in the first week of the Cuban missile crisis. His administration, with far less success and probably to the detriment of the public at large, obscured for nearly two years the transformation of American "advisory" operations in Vietnam into growing combat involvement. To a large degree the Nixon administration has done the same with its activities in Laos and, in the early stages, in Cambodia. President Johnson effectively if disastrously concealed the true budgetary cost of the Vietnam War. Partial suppression or the release of material to achieve desired results or counteractions occurs frequently in the conduct of the Pentagon's information business (although many such abuses are due more to happenstance than to calculation).

There is much exaggeration in the complaints of working Pentagon newsmen, but there is a good deal of truth in them as well. Certainly, the government's security classification procedures pose a serious obstacle to the free flow of news and information. The regulations derive their validity from the need to keep military secrets, troop and weapons deployment, strategic plans, and other sensitive material out of the hands of hostile governments or persons. But these regulations have over the years become translated into broader and broader inhibitions on traffic in legitimate—i.e., nonsensitive or nonsecret—information. The procedures by which documents are classified are indiscriminately applied in the Pentagon (and in the State Department and White House as well) and there are cases in which matters already discussed in public have been classified Confidential or Secret. This has happened even in cases of material gleaned from newspaper or radio reports. Once material has been arbitrarily classified, even for nonsensical reasons, a government employee is technically liable to prosecution for ignoring classification, so it is understandable if few officials and officers tend to include among their services to the public that of seeking martyrdom in the name of "the people's right to know." As the simplest mechanism for blocking public exposure or discourse, overclassification is widely employed by civilian as well as military authorities. Once the inhibition has been applied at or near the top, officials in the lower ranks are hesitant to be venturesome when talking to the media or dealing with the public about a classified matter. The disciplinary, chain-of-command system is, of course, an inhibiting factor in itself.

In the case of a strong Secretary like Robert McNamara, the pressures for a tight information program controlled from the center were compelling and constant. The pressures for care and caution are made even greater when a President takes a direct interest in the information programs of all the executive branch, as did John Kennedy, or when he is as sensitive and unpredictable about the timing and the source of major announcements or news breaks as was Lyndon Johnson. Richard Nixon has also, for reasons of both personality and tactics, taken great interest in holding executive branch processes out of the public view. The result of such direction from the top may work in the national interest. One obvious example of this is the way in which the White House during the recurrent tension over Berlin in 1961 and 1962 exerted firm control over the timing and the temper of United States public statements about Russian and East German actions concerning access to West Berlin. Another, as mentioned above, is the government-wide secrecy invoked by President Kennedy between October 16, 1962, the day it was learned that Soviet missiles had been implanted in Cuba, and October 22, the day the President delivered the United States response to the Soviet Union.

Controls can go wrong—and they frequently do—when inhibitions come to be imposed as a matter of course in the routine intercourse between the government and the press. The fact that so much information was classified, concluded a writer from *Newsweek,* made it "very difficult to tell when you're being lied to. They've got the information and you don't. Actually, they could be telling you a bald-faced lie and you'd never know the difference because of classification."[1]

Pentagon press relations were not improved by an internal Defense Department directive, issued during the Cuban missile crisis, instructing officials who gave interviews to newsmen either to ask a representative of the Pentagon Public Affairs Office to be present for the interview, or to provide a brief report on the interview to the Assistant Secretary of Defense for Public Affairs. The purpose of the directive was to give the Public Affairs Office a better picture of the flow of information out of the Pentagon, but this objective, probably unattainable, was interpreted by the working

1. Interview between James Phillips and a *Newsweek* source.

press as an attempt to "control the news" by drying up personal sources regularly relied on by Pentagon correspondents. The policy was dropped in June 1967.

Similarly, Arthur Sylvester, the Assistant Secretary of Defense for Public Affairs during the McNamara years, who had a gift for the colorful phrase, inadvertently poured fuel on the fire when, in the context of withholding of information on missile sightings during the first week of the Cuban missile crisis, he spoke of the government's "right to lie" in national emergencies.

The desire of top management that the department—and indeed all the government agencies concerned—should speak with one voice, conflicts with the understandable desire of reporters and their editors to ferret out differences of opinion in the bureaucratic structure. Fortunately or unfortunately, bureaucracies, including military bureaucracies, seem to be relatively porous structures through which disagreements tend generally to ooze out. The greater dangers to informed public opinion arise when management is unable to stimulate the kind of debate within the system that fully discloses the available options. A 1958 congressional inquiry found that all military commands had been forbidden to talk with the press about satellite and missile programs lest government officials be embarrassed about the lead the Soviets had achieved in space. The relation between the American military and the press, however, is strikingly open and aboveboard compared with that of nearly every other country. Even Great Britain has, in its "Official Secrets Act," a mechanism that is potentially— and often, actually—much more inhibitory to the press function than anything found in American procedures.

Newsmen whose activities irk authorities, or officials deemed to be too cooperative with the media may tend to find themselves punished by retribution. Although precise case histories are almost impossible to document, it is probably true that officers thought to be involved in news breaks that embarrass or anger higher-ups have been transferred or passed over for promotion. Newsmen have been penalized or harassed for producing stories or articles displeasing to persons in authority. Early in the Kennedy administration, for example, Charles Murphy, a veteran specialist in defense matters who writes for *Fortune,* wrote about the Bay of Pigs disaster in a way that angered the President and his advisers. Mr. Murphy became *persona non grata* for a while in the upper echelons of the national security establishment, but he was in particularly good standing with his Air Force colleagues of World War II days and continued to find ways to obtain information and to write about Pentagon activities.

A more recent case developed with publication of a special *Congressional Quarterly* report in 1968 by James Phillips, detailing about $10 billion in spending that some officials thought could be pruned from the Defense Department's $70 billion budget. In addition to preparing a "rebuttal" to the report and inspiring a similar rebuttal by the staff of the House Armed Services Appropriations Committee, Defense officials distributed the *Congressional Quarterly* document through various departments as a part of their inquiry into possible "security leaks," causing many officials to cut off their contacts with Phillips. On further inquiry, he learned from some of his sources that he had "infuriated" some top military and civilian officials because his story showed that he was a "front man" for the Systems Analysis champions in the Defense Department. Several Systems Analysis experts responded by floating into the public domain their anonymous rebuttal of the rebuttal of the report. One military reporter said that for several months after the *New York Times* had broken a story in March 1968 on General Westmoreland's request for 206,000 more troops for Vietnam, the Joint Chiefs of Staff would not "even let me in the door, not even on routine matters." He said he had a "good source" in that office, whom he saw at least once a week, but his source "literally slammed the door in my face the last time I went down to see him. And neither he nor I had anything to do with that leak."

As Secretary of Defense, Robert McNamara was reluctant to enunciate policy through the Pentagon press corps, and was inclined to look to other channels—to speeches and lectures, congressional testimony, presidential messages—for the means to ventilate major strategic, tactical, or military hardware programs and other important policy developments.[2]

Both the press and government, in differing ways and for different reasons, have encouraged the myth that the defense establishment's public relations system is a relatively tight, contained operation capable of managing the flow of information about defense policies and military affairs. There *is* considerable management, though not as successful as the press implies, nor as much as many government officials would like to exert. The bureaucratic vastness of the Pentagon makes for informational chaos, no matter how intense the attempt at centralization. Few but the most junior or inexperienced of these reporters and writers confine their search for information about Pentagon affairs to the office of the Assistant Secretary for Public Affairs or to the service public affairs operations, nor do they confine their investigating to the Pentagon itself. A very high proportion of news about defense, or of the perspective on that news, comes from other quarters—from the White House, occasionally from a corner of the State or Treasury departments or NASA, sometimes from the CIA (the only "secret" intelligence and espionage operation in the world that maintains a

2. An interesting case in reverse is that of Hanson Baldwin, for many years the military analyst of the *New York Times,* whose hostility toward Secretary McNamara and his policies was so intense that Baldwin refused to seek interviews with the Secretary. He relied instead for information on his longstanding intimacy with military and civil service regulars.

public information office), from any of a hundred or more industries that supply or service Defense and, with very great frequency, from the Congress.

The comparative unmanageability of the immense governmental public affairs mechanism, resulting as it does from conflicting interests and needs within the defense establishment, helps to assure that one man's (or one armed service's) secret deal or questionable policy becomes the next man's (or next service's) exposé. Inefficient as this may be as a mode of operation, and confusing as it may be to the public, it provides a certain amount of insurance against a greater evil—a government that actually "speaks with one voice."

Policy is frequently circumvented, moreover, when a branch of the service or an element within one of the services feels that a cause may be served or an unwanted policy decision may be averted by enlisting the Congress and the press in its fight. With the growth of the services since World War II, the direction and control from the top have frequently proved difficult, sometimes unmanageable. The individual services, and even factions within the services, developed increasingly effective mechanisms and tactics for nourishing their own activities, enhancing their individual images, and waging their battles against civilian authorities or rival services. The Navy successfully went to the public to win its fight for the supercarriers in the 1950's; Admiral Rickover scored a one-man tour de force in public relations in winning both his fight for promotion and his fight for nuclear submarines by bold resort to public utterance and news leaks, while he dismissed the formal public affairs mechanism as the "propaganda arm" of the Pentagon's "civilian general staff."[3] The Air Force's success in keeping big bombers, against the better judgment of civilian strategists, was as much due to adroit public manipulation as to its superb liaison with importantly positioned Senators and Congressmen. And in 1963, certain Air Force and industrial advocates of the Skybolt air-to-air missile found that, although they did not have the power to save the missile from Secretary McNamara's budget-cutting ax, their resort to a premature news leak was probably sufficient to precipitate a crisis in Anglo-American relations and to bring about the critical Nassau meeting between President Kennedy and Prime Minister Harold Macmillan.

In the years since McNamara went to the Pentagon and strove to subordinate military ambitions to independent civilian judgment, rivalries have tended to reach the public ear despite attempts to hide them. The military brass, defense industries, and some men in Congress have riposted with sometimes subtle, sometimes savage bureaucratic infighting. Much of the quarreling is carried on privately in the Pentagon, in White House or

3. From Hearings before the Joint Committee on Atomic Energy, Congress of the United States, on *Nuclear Submarines of Advanced Design* (Washington, D.C.: Government Printing Office), Part 2, p. 161.

Budget Bureau meetings, and in closed congressional hearings. But few of the fights are allowed to remain private for long. One antagonist finds that recourse to the public, or to a segment of it, may help his case or hinder his opponent. Earlier, President Eisenhower, for example, could and did accept the finding of his Science Advisory Committee in 1958 that development of a nuclear aircraft was unwise, but the advocates of such a plane, in particular the congressional Joint Committee on Atomic Energy, which had been pressing for this project for several years, were able to build enough pressure to force Eisenhower to stall for two years, and President Kennedy for another year, before cancellation of the nuclear aircraft project was deemed possible. In the interim, more than $1 billion was spent on its development.

Almost every civilian cancellation of a major aerospace project in the early 1960's—the Dyna-Soar space glider, the B-70 bomber—was delayed, or at least made the subject of costly friction by the ability of its advocates to use the media to provoke congressional and public concern, perhaps because cancellation would harm a community's activity, perhaps because it could be made to seem a blow at the nation's cold war readiness.

Too often even the most intrepid of the specialists who cover the Pentagon cannot arrive at truly unbiased, uncensored, undoctored assessments of a complicated situation. The correspondents are obviously not agents for the military or the civilian high command or a key industry, but however independent they are, they deal mostly with things that are real only in an unreal defense universe—one piece of weaponry against another; the movement of this piece or that on a barely understood chessboard. Frequently this process finds them writing mostly for each other and for a small audience, the knowing and the already-convinced. The cause of public understanding is often barely served, if at all.

Take the case of the TFX. No piece of weaponry has been more discussed by the media in recent years than the TFX, the "all purpose" fighter plane which has flown with at best limited success in Vietnam under the designation F-111. The contract for its development and production came to a total of $6.5 billion, the largest tactical aircraft contract since World War II. Some 1,700 planes and 20,000 jobs were involved. This is the plane Secretary McNamara and his systems analysis division pressed on the Navy, which wanted to develop its own fighter. General Dynamics was chosen as the supplier over other bidders, including one allegedly lower bidder, Boeing Aircraft.[4] Newspaper men and magazine writers have devoted reams to it; Robert Art has written a book about it; a congressional

4. The decision to award the contract to General Dynamics rather than to Boeing was not, despite many allegations to the contrary, a resultant of political pressures, but a deliberate choice by the top civilian management of the Department of Defense of the contractor most likely to meet the objective of a common major weapons system for two military services. See Robert J. Art, *The TFX Decision* (Boston: Little Brown, 1968).

committee has held almost a year of hearings on the plane and the methods by which the design was chosen and the contract let. The integrity of officials, of Congressmen and Senators, of planemakers and military officers has been brought into question by dark innuendo and imputations of official impropriety. The search for the facts has taken reporters and investigators across the spectrum of the defense complex—from the civilian high command to the military services, factions within those services, the successful (and unsuccessful) aircraft manufacturers who wanted either a TFX contract or contracts for the other aircraft that would have been built had the Navy won the case for its own choice. The plane performed so badly in combat in Vietnam there has been talk of grounding and perhaps abandoning the design. The TFX case would be a classroom model for discussion of the public aspect of defense decisions, if it were not for one serious flaw: for all the reams of newsprint and hours of airing, the public is left almost as confused and ignorant about the central truth (or truths) of the case as if there had been no discussion at all. Diligent debate and collecting of facts and allegations about an expensive piece of hardware cannot be said to have produced public enlightenment.

The difficulty is compounded, of course, by military jargon. Open almost any page of any volume of hearings before a congressional committee on defense appropriations and you encounter such sentences as: "Extensive RDT & E has been carried out in the Nike-X and earlier Nike-Zeus programs to advance the state of the BMD art, prove feasibility, and for engineering development of selected sub-systems" or "In this connection, it includes the expenditures not only for the Sentinel command but certain amounts for the supporting command such as ARADCOM, CONARC, STRATCOM, and the like." The language in which great matters having to do with national security are discussed nowadays is unintelligible enough when it is presented in full. But more often than not the meat of the matter is presented in executive session behind closed doors, and the transcript when released is so riddled with blanks and dashes, in the alleged interest of security, that the average concerned citizen has little hope of understanding what it is he is being asked to pay billions upon billions of taxes to protect himself with. Consider, for example, the testimony of Lieutenant General Alfred Starbird before the House Appropriations Subcommittee on the Department of Defense on March 18, 1968. He had been asked if it would be "a serious risk" not to push ahead with the Sentinel antiballistic missile system, in the light of the supposed threat from Chinese nuclear weapons in the 1970's, and he replied most emphatically that it would.[5] He described what the risk—"the threat" from China—amounted to:

5. Hearings before a Subcommittee of the Committee on Appropriations, Deputy Defense Appropriations for 1969, Part 3, House of Representatives, 90th Congress, 2nd Session, p. 4.

Using [deleted] recent analyses, the Department of Defense developed a system design threat. Separately, an OSD Committee, chaired by Dr. Richard A. Montgomery, from the Boeing Co., made an intensive investigation of the Chinese People's Republic (CPR) threat against U.S. cities. The two studies are in basic agreement.

In brief, the threat assumes:

(a) A Red Chinese ICBM initial operational capability in [deleted].

(b) As many as [deleted] ICBM's in the mid-1970's.

(c) Their first generation missile would probably be similar to, say, our [deleted].

(d) An ICBM yield in the [deleted] range.

(e) A [deleted] per cent reliability—the defense would have to cope with [deleted] re-entry vehicles after a [deleted] missile launch.

The members of that particular subcommittee who happened to attend that particular hearing can presumably fill in those blanks. The public cannot.

There is some evidence suggesting that Pentagon officials tend to publicize those figures suggesting a maximum Soviet strategic threat while the budget is before Congress, and those figures suggesting a minimum Soviet threat whenever over-all Pentagon competence, or the prudence of a continued arms race, is questioned.[6]

On occasion, secrecy is combined with an acknowledged policy of deception. The initial target of this deception, of course, is the enemy. But the public at home is no less deceived. On one occasion, Secretary McNamara, under fire for cutting too much material out of congressional testimony before its public release, defended himself under questioning from a sympathetic Senator Richard Russell in these terms:

One of the particular points I objected to releasing, and I think we cut it out of the final version, was the cutback in [deleted] forces. Why should we state publicly we are cutting back [deleted] forces? In the first place, we may not cut back. This is a decision we do not have to make at the moment. It is a plan, it is a program. This is one of the options we buy. We can decide a year, two, three years from now not to make these cutbacks. But assuming we were going to make them, assuming it is a final decision, why should we publicly so state? Why should we tell Russia that the Zeus developments may not be satisfactory? What we ought to be saying is that we have the most perfect anti-ICBM system that the human mind will ever devise. Instead the public domain is already full of statements that the Zeus may not be satisfactory, that it has deficiencies. [Deleted.] I think it is absurd to release that kind of information for the public.[7]

6. For a well-argued presentation of this case, see I. F. Stone, "Laird's Lies," in *The New York Review of Books*, Vol. XIV, No. 11, June 4, 1970.

7. Robert S. McNamara's testimony before the Senate Armed Services Committee, held behind closed doors on May 11, 1961. *Washington Post*, May 12, 1961.

As with attitudes toward the politics of defense, notions about the defense establishment's public relations tend to be simplistic. "News management" is discussed as if it is a practical and workable reality, when unmanageability—whether because of complexity of the subject or the uncontrollability of certain individuals or factions within the defense establishment—is even more obvious.

If, as it has begun to seem, the Congress and the public are growing more concerned about the encroachments of defense on the other increasingly pressing priorities of the society, there is a strong likelihood that the money and energies devoted to explaining and selling defense will undergo, for the first time since the advent of the cold war, a critical examination of what the program is for and whom it is serving. In any event, "credibility gap" is frequently mentioned as if a simple willingness on the part of the President or an administration to tell all, and with candor, in a security-minded, secrecy-ridden world climate is an attainable condition, or even desired by those who command national affairs. The desire of the American government to mask the extent and nature of the American involvement early in the evolution of the Southeast Asian misadventure proved eventually unfeasible, but it must be remembered that once the news media were able to examine and report about that involvement, their critical evaluations were, until well into the 1960's, mostly directed not at the political or moral question of American involvement but at flaws in the way the involvement was being executed. The news media proved with a few exceptions to be building inspectors, not architects. Further, the press sometimes censors itself in what it believes to be the national interests.

Attempts by the military at control of the news, outside of wartime situations, have been uniformly unsuccessful. Voluntary agreement to withhold news has been achieved by government during the Cuban missile crisis, and at great cost to the nation in the case of the Bay of Pigs, as President Kennedy later ruefully recalled, but only with the intervention of the White House. The much quoted testimony of Arthur Sylvester, then Assistant Secretary of Defense for Public Affairs, about the government's "right to lie," mentioned earlier, was an unfortunately dramatic justification of the concealment of military movements—and the diplomatic fib about the reason for the President's returning to Washington from a campaign trip—between the discovery of missile sites in Cuba and the President's speech to the nation less than a week later. And even that attempted news blackout was broken by columnists Robert S. Allen and George Scott, whose column was generally discounted as sensational journalism.

Indeed, the record of misestimation and misplaced optimism on the part of government officials, in and out of the military establishment, through the years of Vietnam fighting, has been faithfully compiled by the press, and the rage of administration officials is very much like the rage of Caliban at his image in the mirror.

This is not to say that full candor on the part of the government would not have better served the American public in the early days of the Vietnamese war, as later in Laos and Cambodia. One may question, however, whether a security-minded nation, widely warned that the loss of one part of Southeast Asia would mean the fall of all of it to Communism, would have imposed any greater inhibitions on the government and the armed forces. To a considerable extent, the public gets the information it wants to hear.

15

Ideological Education of the Military and the Public

American society operates in a relatively pragmatic framework, although there are clear ideological themes conditioning the operation of the political party system. The armed forces reflect this relative de-emphasis of ideology. The professional ethos of the military resists the introduction of political indoctrination as a basis of military morale. While some civilian political groups have sought to increase the amount of attention paid to troop indoctrination in political themes, as we will see later, the military profession has received support, in its general resistance to such measures, from social research findings which emphasized primary group solidarity and adequate leadership as the basis of organizational effectiveness.[1]

This resistance was quite positively suggested by the commandant of the Marine Corps during the Senate hearings in 1962, when he said: "The Marine Corps troop information program is an integral part of our training. Our training system has one and only one objective—to produce combat-ready marines to carry out any mission assigned to the corps. All else is included in this one goal. Devotion to country and duty and to fellow marines is inherent."[2]

Even the dramatic events of the Korean conflict have, in the long run, served to reinforce the nonideological posture of the American military profession, although at the time it seemed less likely. Careful re-

1. Edward Shils and Morris Janowitz, "Cohesion and Disintegration in the Wehrmacht in World War II," *Public Opinion Quarterly*, Vol. 12, Summer 1948, pp. 280-315. Samuel A. Stouffer *et al., The American Soldier* (Princeton: Princeton University Press, 1949), 2 volumes.
2. General David H. Shoup, in *Military Cold War Education and Speech Review Policies*, Hearings, Part 1, p. 206.

search by Albert Biderman and others has revealed that, contrary to the claims of a number of psychologists and psychiatrists, the American troops behaved in captivity as well as could be expected given the extraordinary pressures applied.[3] The weaknesses they displayed were due to inadequacy in effective training and not a failure to expose them to ideological indoctrination. Charles Moskos's field study of enlisted men found that even in the special conditions of South Vietnam the ideological dimension in morale was relatively absent; at most only the term latent ideology could be applied to their attitudes and motivation.[4]

Realistically, in the armed forces, the typical American recruit is exposed to a network of communications similar to those he would encounter in civilian life. Especially through the radio, which each soldier personally owns and regulates, he is linked to the mass communication of the civilian world. The response to the limited troop information and education programs conducted officially for enlisted personnel shows a tremendous suspicion of manipulation and a powerful resistance to any official "line." Even the military's effort to indoctrinate and socialize its officer personnel is subject to powerful built-in limitations. Lovell's study of the impact of West Point training on officer attitudes concludes that "socialization at West Point produces only slight impact upon professional orientation and strategic perspectives of the cadet."[5] It appears that self-selection into the officer corps is more important in determining attitudes than the impact of life in the military academies. Most officers tend to avoid political and ideological discussions with enlisted men. The culture of the military is carried by the noncommissioned officers whose ideological orientation is a vague and diffuse anti-Communism and an undifferentiated feeling of the national mission. Not until after World War II was anti-Communism a major factor.

In the fashioning of political orientations and politico-military perspectives, it seems that both the process of self-selection and selection for promotion as well as the impact of professional experience are more important than conscious indoctrination. At each stage in the promotion process, officers continue to have the opportunity to select themselves out. Undoubtedly some officers with strong reservations about United States policies in South Vietnam have selected themselves out. In turn,

3. Albert D. Biderman, *March to Calumny* (New York: Macmillan, 1963).
4. Charles Moskos, "Latent Ideology and American Combat Behavior in South Vietnam," Working Paper No. 98, Center for Social Organization Studies, University of Chicago, January 1968.
5. John P. Lovell, "The Professional Socialization of the West Point Cadet," in *The New Military*, Morris Janowitz, ed. (New York: Russell Sage Foundation, 1964), p. 119. By contrast, important changes occur in the preferences that cadets express for the branch of service in which they hope to serve and for the extracurricular activities that provide them the most satisfaction.

officers who fit in with the official doctrine of their service are most likely to rise.[6]

The notion of the inevitability of war—particularly of large-scale war—is no longer a universal belief of the military profession. This belief has been destroyed by the development of nuclear weapons. However, there is a body of observation and documented research that demonstrates that belief in the inevitability of major war tends to be strongest among older officers with increased length of service.[7] Thus professional service not only influences the attitudes of the officer while on active duty but also serves as the basis of his attitudes in civilian life on retirement. So far, there have been only a few military officers of high rank who have used their military professionalism as a basis for advocating specific military policies during retirement. Their views have been divided, although more frequently on the "absolutist" side of military doctrine. The candidacy of General Curtis LeMay for Vice President on the George Wallace ticket in 1968 is a conspicuous example. Although the professional ethic of political neutrality is still strong in governing behavior after retirement, this ethic is certain to be tested by the events in Southeast Asia.

But despite military resistance to ideological orientation, the military establishment does rally to the defense of ideology when it sees that ideology as supportive of its own institutions. It will even carry its defense directly to the public. The major channels of public education used by the military came under review during the Senate investigation of "military cold war education" in 1962. The investigation had been provoked by three sets of activities that had drawn increasing attention in the press and popular discussion in the late 1950's and early 1960's The first was the use of right-wing literature and films by military commanders in troop information and education programs. The second was the use of military facilities by right-wing groups for "educational" conferences with the concurrence and sometimes the active sponsorship of military commanders. The third was the review by civilian appointees in the Defense Department of public statements of high-ranking military officers.

For a brief period, in the 1950's, the military had tried to establish a program called "Militant Liberty" as a focus for troop and public information activities. It was developed by civilians in the office of the Joint Chiefs of Staff, and sponsored by the chairman, Admiral Arthur Radford. The goal of Militant Liberty was defined as seeking to "motivate peoples everywhere to exercise and collectively demonstrate the

6. See Morris Janowitz, *The Professional Soldier: A Social and Political Portrait* (Glencoe, Ill.: Free Press, 1960), Chapter 7, "Career Development."

7. See Morris Janowitz, *Professional Soldier*, Part VI, "Political Behavior: Pragmatic versus Absolutist."

practices of a positive philosophy of Freedom." Highly ideological both in substance and presentation, the discussion of Militant Liberty sought "to point our basic principles of liberty . . . ; to develop a method by which these principles can be explained versus those of the authoritarian state; to show that the free peoples of the world can create the wave of the future; and to emphasize that victory belongs to those who are militant in their desires and convictions of liberty." The purpose of Militant Liberty was to offer a hard-hitting theme for troop information and public education sponsored by the military services.[8]

Huntington characterized the Militant Liberty program as "a warning symptom of the derangement of American civil-military relations" and "a measure of the civilian abdication . . . and a devastating example of what can happen when generals and admirals . . . abandon their military knitting and venture into political philosophy."[9] Some military presumably took the program with a grain of salt. "Don't worry," one officer was quoted as saying. "This is just another front-office boondoggle."[10] But another, remembering how some American prisoners seemed to have broken under North Korean pressure during the Korean conflict, justified the program in terms of the need for "a new kind of soldier . . . who is spiritually strong. . . . "[11] One officer responded to questions about the Militant Liberty program with the frustrated cry: "We're facing a kind of moral and intellectual vacuum, damn it."[12] It is a problem of potential frustration that has come with the changing nature of war and international conflict in general, the complication that modern weapons have given to the World War II concepts of "victory" and "unconditional surrender," and the ambiguity of the idea of "enemy" under a policy of deterrence and the conditions of guerrilla warfare.

For many military officers, the conduct of American prisoners of war in Korea offered all the reason anyone needed for troop information programs with a high degree of ideological content. In his letter to the Senate investigating committee in 1962, former President Eisenhower confirmed that the Korean experience had led to intensified programs to inform men in the armed forces of the dangers of Communism. "The need for anti-Communist education in the armed forces is self-evident," he wrote. "Your committee recalls, I am sure, our sad experiences in Korea a decade

8. *Militant Liberty: A Program of Evaluation and Assessment of Freedom* (Washington, D.C.: Government Printing Office, 1955). Issued by the Secretary of Defense on November 2, 1955.

9. Samuel P. Huntington, *The Common Defense* (New York: Columbia University Press, 1961), p. 397.

10. Janowitz, *The Professional Soldier*, p. 407.

11. William Harlan Hale, "Militant Liberty and the Pentagon," *The Reporter*, February 9, 1956, pp. 30-34.

12. Quoted in William Harlan Hale.

ago, in respect to the conduct of some of our captured Americans. This gave rise to improved troop information designed to strengthen troop appreciation of the fundamentals of our own and the Soviet system."[13]

A popular version of the prisoner-of-war experience that at the time was widely accepted by the military was provided in a book by Eugene Kinkead, originally an article in *The New Yorker* magazine in 1957.[14] Its assumptions were that Americans had not been able to stand up to the psychological harassment they suffered because they had no clear idea of why they were fighting or of the nature of their enemy. Their weaknesses were weaknesses of American society and reflected a softness that could prove fatal under the pressures of the Communist challenge. Such assumptions were given official recognition in the promulgation of a new "Code of Conduct for Members of the United States Armed Forces" in 1955.[15]

Traditionally, American servicemen had been instructed to respond with their "name, rank, and serial number" to questions put to them by enemy captors. This historic regulation was expanded by the new code, formulated by a committee of both official civilian and military members appointed by the Secretary of Defense. The code required a member of the armed forces to be "prepared to give my life in . . . defense [of my country and our way of life]," "never [to] surrender of my own free will," "to resist [capture] by all means available," and to "keep faith with my fellow prisoners." In prescribing the new code in an executive order, President Eisenhower instructed that "each member of the armed forces liable to capture shall be provided with specific training and instruction designed to better equip him to counter and withstand all enemy efforts against him. . . ."

The new code was employed by some overzealous military leaders to overcome what they perceived to be a dangerous lack of ideological motivation in their men. The problem was dramatized in its most extreme form by the case of Major General Edwin A. Walker, commander of the 24th Infantry Division stationed in Germany, who, in the early 1960's, used right-wing literature in his campaign of troop indoctrination. The

13. *Military Cold War Education and Speech Review Policies,* Hearings before the Special Preparedness Subcommittee, Committee on Armed Services, U.S. Senate, 87th Congress, 2nd Session, 1962, Part 1, p. 6. See Samuel A. Stouffer *et al., The American Soldier* (Princeton: Princeton University Press, 1949), pp. 105 ff. for studies during World War II; for the Korean experiences, see Roger W. Little, "Buddy Relations and Combat Performance," in *The New Military,* Morris Janowitz, ed. (New York: Russell Sage Foundation, 1964), pp. 195 ff.; for a Vietnam case, see Moskos, Note 4, above.

14. Eugene Kinkead, *In Every War But One* (New York: Norton, 1959). For a rebuttal of Kinkead, see Biderman, *March to Calumny.*

15. The committee that drew up the code also took other explanations into account, including deficiencies in the training programs of the armed services.

act that forced his resignation was his attempt to influence the voting of his troops. In an official Army newspaper, Walker published an evaluation of the voting records of members of Congress prepared by the archconservative Americans for Constitutional Action. Not only did he enter an area of political life to which members of Congress are acutely sensitive—their right to vote—but he had broken the professional military tenet of remaining overtly apolitical. In his testimony before the Senate committee, Walker proved to be violent in his criticism of political authority, almost pathologically suspicious of what he saw as a Communist conspiracy aided and abetted by soft-minded liberals. Walker could be dismissed as an eccentric; what could not be dismissed was the official basis on which he justified his act.[16]

A study of the views of a group of senior military leaders on troop information and education, conducted in 1963 after the Walker case, revealed strong concern about the importance of ideology. With few illusions about the time and effort that could be put into troop information work, the officers interviewed continually expressed concerns, such as: "Men coming into the service . . . don't even know why they are in uniform"; "The military person is far ahead of the civilian, at comparable age groups, as to understanding of what the world is all about, what are the values which are important, what we have to fight for and fight against"; and "There is very great need everywhere—everywhere one turns—for more knowledge about the major threat to our society: Communism."[17]

Both the Militant Liberty program (though widely circulated, it tended to flounder) and General Walker's activities might well be seen as cases of deviant behavior. Janowitz regarded such activities as aberrations from the professional code of the military, an attempt by "absolutists" among the military to find an ideological justification for their role as opposed to the "pragmatists" who accepted the primacy of civilian political leadership and adhered to a posture of political neutrality.[18] The military obligation

16. The Senate investigating committee did not reprimand General Walker, stated it would not "retry" the case, and made no judgments on the disciplinary action taken against him by the Army. The Senate reminded the military of its obligation to remain nonpartisan in these words: "The traditional and time-honored concept that the military shall, under no circumstances, become involved in partisan politics must be rigidly adhered to. Military men must not participate or engage in political activities, and, of equal importance, political considerations must not control or affect the civil authorities in the promotion, assignment or appointment of military personnel . . ." *Military Cold War Education and Speech Review Policies,* p. 11.

17. Quoted in Bock, Monroe, and Williams, *Information and Education of Troops as Viewed by Twenty Military Leaders.* Report on an Exploratory Intensive Study submitted to Directorate for Armed Forces Information and Education, Department of Defense, Washington, D.C., Bureau of Social Science Research, Inc., October 1963.

18. Janowitz, *The Professional Soldier,* p. 408.

for supporting troop information and participating in public education, central to the Militant Liberty program, continued nonetheless to be emphasized. It was written into a classified National Security Council directive in 1958 about which former President Eisenhower disavowed any direct knowledge during the 1962 Senate hearings. But Secretary McNamara indicated that such a document did in fact exist, and included, though "indirectly," matters relating to public information programs.[19]

In addition to the troop information program, the 1962 Senate hearings emphasized the seminars, meetings, and general public discussions sponsored by the military, for which they provided facilities, or in which they participated through speakers or presentations but did not originate. Generally, these meetings presented a hard anti-Communist line in a spectrum that ranged from serious analysis to right-wing radicalism.

One of the consistent themes throughout the hearings was the contention that discussion of Communism and relations with the Soviet Union was not "political," or at least did not constitute an involvement in political activities in the sense of partisan politics. The principle of military participation in such affairs was thus never really disputed, except in the original charges brought by Senator Fulbright. Only when the meetings stirred up controversy among local civilian groups was there admission that the military in charge had shown poor judgment.

Putting the study of Communism into a "nonpolitical" category— as a "given"—was a particular concern of Senator Strom Thurmond of the Senate investigating committee. His exchange with Rear Admiral D. F. Smith, Jr., at that time Chief of Information for the Navy, is an illustration:

Senator Thurmond: I think most people, certainly you and I, are in agreement that all military people should not make official expressions or participate in partisan politics, or make official expressions that are inconsistent with the foreign policy of this country.

Admiral Smith: Yes, sir.

Senator Thurmond: Or the national policy of this country. Admiral, statements on Communism, the enemy, is a different situation, is it not?

Admiral Smith: I agree that it is, sir.

Senator Thurmond: In other words, you would not consider speaking against Communism as involving foreign policy, would you?

Admiral Smith: No, sir.

Senator Thurmond: Communism is the common enemy of the United States and the free world, and every true patriot would be against Communism?

Admiral Smith: Yes, sir.

Senator Thurmond: Is that not right?

19. *Defense Secretary McNamara on S. Res. 191,* Hearings before the Committee on Armed Services, U.S. Senate, 87th Congress, 1st Session, 1961, pp. 127-128.

Admiral Smith: Yes, sir.

Senator Thurmond: So that there should be no objection to military personnel making expressions or making speeches on the subject of Communism, the insidious nature of it, their aims and designs, the techniques of subversion and so forth.

Admiral Smith: Yes, sir.

Senator Thurmond: Are you in accord with that?

Admiral Smith: I am completely in accord with it, sir, and I never give a speech but what I throw in a few nasty cracks about Communism.[20]

Generally the committee showed concern in what the military themselves called "quality control." The purpose of "quality control" was to avoid bringing in extremists, since their participation was apt to provoke controversy among local civic and political groups and involve the military in "partisan politics." Deciding which meetings to support and which to avoid was deemed a matter of "good judgment" and "common sense" on the part of the local commanders. A new requirement, promulgated while the hearings were in progress, compelled base commanders to seek permission from Washington to sponsor or cosponsor seminars or public meetings. The effect of such a directive was to take the pressure off base commanders and to apply a tighter set of standards.

The military education programs have, for many years, served as a major vehicle for acquainting important elements of the public with the military view on major issues of defense policy. These programs have included special conferences at the military war colleges, the central forums for professional military education. The purpose of war college conferences has been not public education but, more broadly, public relations; however, the form has almost always been educational, to avoid the charge of lobbying.

The senior war colleges of the three military services—the Army War College, the Naval War College, and the Air War College—have all developed programs of public education, although under different names. Selected groups of civilians, numbering from fifty to one hundred people each year, are invited to remain in residence for about one week and participate in the instruction being given to officers enrolled in the regular courses of study. The topics selected for examination cover large and complex questions in American foreign policy and military strategy. Like the regular military students, the civilian guests hear a number of official and academic lecturers and, most importantly, sit in with small groups of military officers to discuss the problems of military strategy in seminar sessions.

20. *Military Cold War Education and Speech Review Policies,* Part 4, pp. 1819-1820.

The service war college programs do not attempt to urge civilians to convey any message to their communities. The assumption is that they will be sympathetic to the military position on major issues of public policy. In this respect, the service war college seminars are different from the Defense Strategy Seminar at the National War College and the traveling seminars of the Industrial College of the Armed Forces.

First held in 1959, the National War College Seminar has developed into a broad examination of the world political situation with emphasis on military strategy. Like most military programs, there is a continual stream of lecturers and an emphasis on small-group discussion. If a general "hard-line" pervaded the presentation of issues during the early years, it has been moderated more recently, undoubtedly reflecting the temper of the times and a sensitivity to potential criticism among the directors of the seminar.

Throughout the years, reservists have been urged to develop study programs on Communism when they return to their local communities. "All responsible citizens," they were told in the 1968 seminar, "are on the front line of the cold war along with those men who man the missiles and fight our hot-war battles overseas." Due respect is paid to the increasing political maturity of the public and to the existence of alternative sources of information on international problems. One question raised for the members of the seminar is: "How can the United States public be rendered less vulnerable to Communist psychological warfare and more sympathetic to the indigenous values of our allies and other friendly nations?" The reservists are asked to consider "ways and means of assuring that the American public recognizes and understands the 'facts of life' regarding Communist beliefs and the impact upon our national security."[21]

The Defense Strategy Seminar is an annual program limited to reserve officers who are brought to the National War College to meet their two weeks' active duty assignment. In contrast, the National Security Seminars conducted by the Industrial College of the Armed Forces are held several times during the year in communities throughout the country and are attended by private citizens as well as by reservists. The Industrial College seminars consist of lectures by a team of military officers, supported by series of films and other visual aids, mainly of military production. An elaborate set of procedures has been developed for the seminars, usually set in motion by a request from a civilian organization that wishes to serve as sponsor in its community. The invitation can be generated in a variety of different ways: through local military base commanders; through reserve officer groups; through the grapevine of the business

21. Defense Strategy Seminar, June 17-28, 1968, *Syllabus,* The National War College, Washington D.C.

community. Usually, the civilian sponsor has been the local chamber of commerce, which then serves as host, in conjunction with local military authorities, for the military seminar team from the Industrial College.

Guidelines from the Industrial College place considerable importance on preparations and publicity prior to the seminar: a distinguished citizen should be appointed general chairman; committees should be formed; letters should be sent to the governor, the mayor and other dignitaries; an advance officer from the seminar team should visit the city and make public appearances; newspaper, radio, and television announcements should be arranged; and posters, brochures, and window stickers distributed. The seminar itself, moreover, is to be opened with pomp and military ceremony; "stirring music," the guidelines read, "lends an air of importance as well as prestige."

Participants to the seminar are given a complete outline of the program which, with brief summary statements, tables, and simple graphic representations, provides a step-by-step, session-by-session run-through of the two-week exercise. The seminar outline for 1967-68 included a foreword by the President of the United States, confirming that the Industrial College "is a major instrument for instilling in growing numbers of our people the essential principles of a free society." The seminar covers issues from Africa, American Management, Civil Defense, and Communist China to Transportation and Telecommunications, Western Hemisphere, World Agriculture, and World Industrial Development. The members of the seminar team, military officers of colonel or Navy captain rank, usually divide the topics for presentation and offer lectures that they have tried out in other communities. Much of the material is largely descriptive, a roll call of problems and facts with little analysis. If there is cohesion to the whole program it lies in the theme of anti-Communism and the need for the public to become awakened to the dangers that Communism poses for the United States.[22]

During the 1962 Senate hearings, the Industrial College seminars, like the Defense Strategy Seminar at the National War College, were given approval and even special blessing. The impact of the Industrial College seminars (or of any of the military programs) and their effect on public opinion are difficult to assess. Like most military programs, the audiences for the seminars are probably generally sympathetic to the military. Proposals to discontinue the seminars have invariably been countered by citations from community groups—chambers of commerce, fraternal clubs and patriotic societies—that purport to attest to their success. Criti-

22. See National Security Seminar, 1967–68, *Presentation Outlines and Reading List*, Industrial College of the Armed Forces, Washington D.C.; also, *Information Guide*, for the conduct of National Security Seminars, Industrial College of the Armed Forces, Washington D.C., rev. edition, February 1968.

cisms, often from liberal newspapers, are dismissed as the expected, given the source. Thus the seminars continue and presumably will do so as long as the military continues to have authority to engage in programs of public education.

The support for military programs of public education has a broader base in the programs of the Reserve Officers Training Corps, which enable the services to set up military units in colleges and in high schools throughout the country. The college ROTC programs in several hundred colleges[23] serve two purposes, each in potential conflict with the other. On the one hand, the ROTC opens the junior officer class to wide participation, thus serving to preserve the notion of a "citizen-army" while insuring the military access to the large number of young men they need. But the program also gives the military entry into some of the most important educational institutions in the country, in which military courses become part of the curriculum and from which military officers, serving as faculty, make contact with important academic and community groups.

In the late 1960's the ROTC programs came under increasing attack in many colleges and universities. The immediate stimulus for the attacks was certainly the resentment against the Vietnam war, especially by the more politicized of college youth and academic intellectuals. The attack was supported by many academicians who for years had resented the intrusion of military instruction into the college curriculum but who had never made an issue of their opposition, recognizing the ROTC as a source of draft deferment and scholarship assistance for many students.[24] The ROTC issue became a major focus for more radical student groups to challenge the governing structure of their universities. As significant as the anti-ROTC movement was, however, it was relatively limited, affecting mainly the more prestigious private and state universities—at least by early 1970. Indeed, as faculty resolutions from places like Harvard, Yale, and Dartmouth urged that these institutions cut their ROTC ties with the military, the services let it be known that other colleges and universities were

23. The programs are distributed roughly evenly among the states. There is at least one in every state, in the District of Columbia, and in Puerto Rico.

24. The faculty status of ROTC instructors has been a minor but persistent irritant in the general ROTC situation. Unlike other members of college and university faculties, the military men who serve as ROTC instructors derive their academic titles from courtesy appointments based on their selection by their military departments to serve with a particular ROTC detachment, with their academic rank being determined by their responsibilities within the detachment. Since they receive no benefits from their academic appointments by way of salary or tenure, apart from the privileges of the faculty club and the athletic facilities, and they do not normally participate in the business of the faculty, these courtesy titles only became an issue in the context of the general alienation of the academic community from the military establishment, primarily over the Vietnam war. This issue, like the issue of academic credit for military instruction, could have been resolved without significant difficulty if the underlying divisions could have been healed.

waiting to enter the program. Those waiting, moreover, were largely smaller, rural-based universities, representing more of the conservative "heartland" of the country than those universities suffering through internal upheavals.[25] Nevertheless, the ROTC pressure was the focus of the student protest that led to the tragedy at Kent State University in Ohio, part of that conservative "heartland."

The general support of the "heartland" for a military presence in education programs was a factor several years earlier in forestalling an end to the Junior Reserve Officers Training Corps, a program of military instruction in high schools. In 1964, Secretary of Defense McNamara contended that the Junior ROTC, whatever its origins, could not be justified as a manpower procurement program and thus was not essential to defense needs. He therefore proposed its elimination as a modest way of cutting back on defense expenditures. McNamara's proposition was effectively opposed by congressional leaders in the Armed Services Committees and by veterans, patriotic, and professional educational groups in many parts of the country. In the end, the Junior ROTC was not only retained, but expanded. There are now sixty-eight such groups, distributed fairly evenly throughout the country. The only change was the substitution of retired military for active officers and noncommissioned personnel as instructors, and an obligation by the participating schools to cover partial salary costs. Most important, from the point of view of those who protested the Secretary's original recommendation, is the continued military presence in hundreds of high schools and the program of drill, leadership training, and marksmanship designed to contribute to "attributes of good citizenship and patriotism."

The post-Korean era of "Militant Liberty," the Walker case, and cold-war indoctrination programs is now substantially behind us. But the citizen educational programs of the War Colleges, the Industrial College of the Armed Forces, and especially of ROTC, will bear continuing examination and assessment of their appropriateness for the "era of negotiation" we are hopefully now entering.

25. See, for example, the article in the *New York Times*, February 4, 1969, listing new ROTC units to be established by the Army.

IV

THE IMPACTS OF THE
MILITARY ESTABLISHMENT

16

Military Spending in the Economy

In the fifty years before 1930, expenditures for defense were a minor factor in the American economy—except during World War I their average was just about 1 per cent of the gross national product. Military outlay in the 1930's averaged a little over 1 per cent of GNP. But today, the nation's military requirements account for about 7.5 per cent of GNP and 10 per cent of the labor force.

The impacts of military spending on the American economy are too diverse—and some of them too deep—to be fully understood by reference to any simple percentages. The large and rapid expansion in the amount of resources devoted to military programs in the period 1965-1968 tested the limits of the nation's economic and political capabilities in the public sector. The increase in military spending has resulted in cuts in funds that would otherwise be available for housing, education, the campaign against poverty, or other pressing civilian concerns. It has also exerted inflationary pressure and contributed to the deficit in the balance of payments, which has brought the dollar under attack. The relative scarcity of funds for civilian needs has contributed to rising domestic tensions and to heightened political and social pressures. The marginal social costs of defense, given the political difficulties in raising taxes quickly, may be seen to be the domestic government programs—or increases in them—that are forgone in order to avoid further budget deficits and inflationary pressures.

The shift toward a permanently higher—but fluctuating—level of military expenditures began with World War II, when it reached a peak of 48 per cent of GNP. In the Korean War it reached 12 per cent of GNP. In fiscal year 1971, federal purchases for national defense programs (which include pay and allowances of the armed forces) were about $73 billion, or about 7.7 per cent of the nation's total output (see Chart 16.1). As pointed out in earlier chapters, two fundamental and relatively durable factors explain the high and continuing level of United States military spending in more recent years: the revolution in military technology and the fundamental shift in the world balance of power since the 1930's with American involvement in continuing wars.

Even if a high and rising proportion of GNP is devoted to military programs, the nation cannot automatically assume that it is more "secure" as a result. Obviously security depends, at least in part, on defense out-

Chart 16.1: Defense Expenditures as Percentage of GNP, 1971

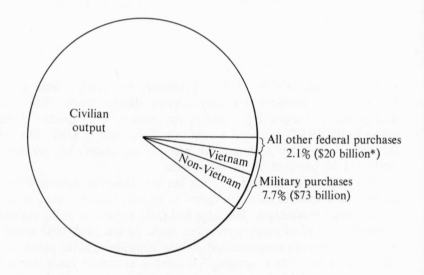

Source: U.S. Departments of Commerce, Labor, and Defense.

* Source: Economic Report of the President (with the Annual Report of the Council of Economic Advisers), United States Government Printing Office, Washington, D.C., February 1970, Table 14, p. 80.

lays of other countries. Since the greatest technological changes have occurred in offensive strategic weapons, the "damage limitation ability" per dollar of expenditure appears to be declining. In other words, while the military power of the United States may be increasing in an absolute sense, its national security may also be declining.[1]

The real cost to society of allocating productive resources to military programs is the unavailability of these resources for other purposes.

1. See Frederic L. Pryor, *Public Expenditures in Communist and Capitalist Nations* (Homewood, Ill.: Richard D. Irwin, 1968), p. 90.

More missiles and tanks mean in general fewer cars, homes, and schools. Of course, such resources might not have been used for cars, homes, and schools, even if they were not being absorbed by the military. Some of the resources might have remained unemployed but for the expansion of defense activities. But if such sacrifices do take place and if the loss occurs in productive investment, the sacrifices will accrue later as society forgoes the returns on the absent investment.

The financing of the military budget—in real terms, the transfer of resources from civilian to military use—also has important economic repercussions for the over-all economy. This transfer is usually accomplished primarily by the imposition of higher taxes. If deficit financing is used instead, the same result is achieved via inflation; the Department of Defense bids resources away from other users, who must pay more for what is available. Higher taxes have various side effects on the economy, many of them harmful to initiative and growth. For example, if military spending were reduced drastically and federal income tax rates cut proportionately, businessmen could then give tax considerations less weight in investment and production decisions.

While resources utilized by defense programs almost always represent a diversion from other sectors, the value of the defense output is not necessarily equivalent to the value of the output diverted from the civilian sectors. For example, when resources shift from production of comparatively low-valued products such as agriculture to high-valued products such as military research and development, the increment of GNP so generated may exceed in value the output yielded by the private sector. Conversely, the operation of the Selective Service System tends to result in substantial economic losses to many men who otherwise would have higher paid jobs in civilian life. The real cost to the economy and to society as a whole is well above the direct cost to the Department of Defense of paying, feeding, and clothing these recruits; it is the opportunity cost of the higher priced goods and services which otherwise they would be producing. An indication of this undervaluation is provided by the estimates of the cost of substituting a volunteer army for the present draft system; according to most available estimates, the extra cost of paying soldiers a high enough wage to attract their voluntary service is in the neighborhood of $4 to $10 billion a year.[2] These estimates compare with $5 billion a year currently spent for housing, or $11 billion spent for health within the federal budget.

There may be another, more qualitative aspect of opportunity cost

2. The Report of the President's Commission on All Volunteer Armed Force, U.S. Government Printing Office, Washington, D.C., 1970. Sources opposed to an all-volunteer Army tend to advance the higher figure; sources favoring it the lower. There are a number of uncertainties, and the calculations are very sensitive to the estimated size of the force required. The President's Commission estimated $4.6 billion for a 3-million-man force.

involved in some of the highly specialized growth-potential resources used by the military establishment. The most striking case is research and development, where half of all the work performed in private industry is financed by the military; as a corollary large proportions of all the scientists in American industry are devoting their efforts to defense work.

Long-term increases in military spending appear to be at the expense of consumer production rather than business investment or civilian government purchases. This appears evident from a comparison of the structure of the GNP in 1929 and today. While military purchases have climbed from 1 per cent to nearly 10 per cent of GNP, as stated above, household consumption has declined from 73 per cent to 63 per cent.[3] To some extent, such a change would be expected to result from the willingness to rely on deficit financing of government spending expansion during periods of relatively full employment. During the initial buildup period of the Vietnam war, for example, the excess government demand that was generated tended, through an intensification of the inflation spiral, to reduce the proportion of national output available to private consumers. In addition, one recent study concluded that military outlays have a statistically significant but still small substitution relationship with civilian government purchases—a displacement of less than 10 per cent.[4] This may reflect the changing priorities within the federal budget between defense and nondefense spending.

In both the Truman administration before the Korean War and in the Eisenhower administration after it, the tendency was to deduct the estimated cost of domestic programs from anticipated federal revenues (or the total expenditures possible within the existing public debt limit) and then allocate the remainder to the military.[5]

At the present time, military spending continues to dominate the federal budget, although it takes a smaller share of the budget than at any time since the Korean War. But it still tends to have first claim, with nondefense programs getting what is left over despite the urgency of their demands. In terms of economic activity, the national security programs account for almost four-fifths of all federal government purchases of goods and services ($73 billion out of $93 billion in fiscal year 1971). Measured in real terms (adjusting the dollar figures to eliminate for changes caused solely by inflation), most of the increase in federal purchases during the last two decades has been accounted for by defense programs. In the aggregate, purchases of all other federal government

3. Kenneth Boulding, "The American Economy: The Many Failures of Success," *Saturday Review*, November 23, 1968, p. 30.
4. Pryor, *Public Expenditures,* p. 124.
5. Samuel P. Huntington, *The Common Defense* (New York: Columbia University Press, 1961), p. 22.

agencies are close to the same real level as in 1940, with the large in-creases in federal civilian spending accounted for by transfer payments and grants, e.g., increases in Social Security payments. These latter two items do not show up directly in GNP since they represent financial transfers—payments for which no goods or services are received in re-turn. The increase of the federal share of GNP from 6 per cent in 1940 to 10 per cent in 1968 has been primarily a result of the spurt in national defense activities. It is clear that security-related expenditures have been the primary medium through which the federal government has expanded its role as a purchaser and consumer of goods and services in the Ameri-can economy.

From six until three years ago a rising share of the nation's resources was devoted to national defense. American citizens increasingly re-ceived a public good, defense, serving their wants indirectly and involun-tarily through the federal budget, rather than private goods, which they voluntarily obtain through market transactions. The voluntary exchange and individualistic nature of American society was proportionately reduced. Although the primary motivations of the great majority of Americans, both as producers and consumers, are oriented to civilian rather than military ends, important shifts in emphasis in recent years have tended to reduce the civilian role somewhat and to increase that of the military.

How much national security spending can the economy afford? Some of the congressional hearings on the appropriations for Vietnam showed concern over the ability of the American economy to withstand the cost of the war. The following excerpt is illuminating.

Senator Symington: My question is, how long can this nation afford to con-tinue the gigantic financial cost incident to this major ground war in Asia, without its economy becoming nonviable?

Secretary McNamara: I think forever, and I say it for this reason. That there are many things, many prices we pay for the war in South Vietnam, some very heavy prices, indeed, but in my opinion one of them is not strain on our economy.[6]

There is no simple or generally agreed-upon method to measure or de-termine the "burden" of military programs on the economy, much less what, if any, economic ceiling exists on such programs. With certain qualifications concerning the opportunity costs of civilian production forgone, economic analysis tends to support McNamara's statement. In

6. U.S. Senate, Committees on Armed Services and Appropriations, *Supplemental Military Procurement and Construction Authorizations*, Fiscal Year 1967 (Washing-ton, D.C.: Government Printing Office, 1967), p. 96-97.

the last few years, it has been apparent that forgoing expansions in certain civilian areas does appear to exact another kind of price, however, particularly in political and social strain. The question is not so much the capability of the economy to produce defense goods but the willingness of society to devote a substantial share of its resources to that purpose, particularly while meeting its obligations in the remainder of the public sector.

Using the GNP comparison, the portion of our national resources given over to military goods and services tended to diminish before the Vietnam war, from 10.5 per cent in 1957 to 8.4 per cent in 1964. During 1967 and 1968, because of the wartime buildup, the ratio rose to 9.5 per cent, still below the 1957 peacetime level. In part, the answer lies in the comparison between the recession year of 1957 and the more recent "boom" years. Obviously an economy with substantial excess capacity and idle resources can absorb a larger defense burden with much greater ease than an economy fully employed.

If necessary for military or political reasons, the American economy can handle an even higher level of defense spending, although it would probably involve increased inflationary pressure and further distortions in the economy. Statements to that effect have come from such diverse groups as government agencies, businessmen's organizations, research institutes, and individual economists. However, authorities have also concluded that the long-term growth and prosperity of the United States would benefit from a lower level of military expenditures. In its report in early 1969 the Cabinet Coordinating Committee on Economic Planning for the End of Vietnam Hostilities, for example, said that the cost of the war has been a load for the American economy to carry and "*not* a supporting 'prop.'" The committee added, "Prosperity has not depended on the defense buildup and will not need high military spending to support it in peacetime."[7]

The Marxist cliché that the American economy depends on military spending still makes the rounds from time to time. Most recently, the *Report from Iron Mountain*[8] contended that the Vietnam war was escalated, in 1965, "in the usual coordination . . . with dangerously rising unemployment rates." The facts of the matter were quite different. The unemployment rate was 5.2 per cent in 1964. Unemployment rates—and total unemployment—were falling all through 1965 prior to the Vietnam buildup at the middle of the year. The rate declined from 5.0 per cent in February 1965 to 4.5 per cent in July 1965. The 1964 tax cut clearly

7. Cabinet Coordinating Committee on Economic Planning for the End of Vietnam Hostilities, p. 187.
8. William Letwin, *Report from Iron Mountain on the Possibility and Desirability of Peace* (New York: Dial Press, 1967).

was the major stimulus to the expansion in economic activity that resulted in declining unemployment. Rather than being necessary to combat unemployment, the war led to cutbacks in many planned civilian government programs, particularly in the welfare and housing areas, and this had a serious deflationary impact.[9]

Because the "market basket" of goods and services bought by the military establishment differs so much from the buying patterns of the civilian economy, military programs produce significant differential effects on the economy.[10] For example,

—Military programs utilize highly specialized resources, absorbing a major share of all of the scientific and engineering talent in the United States.

—Military programs account for the great bulk of all the goods and services purchased by the federal government. In creating this vast market for private industry, these programs have also served as the means of expanding the direct role of the government in the American economy as both purchaser and consumer.

—Because of the specialized nature of military procurement—largely high-technology weapon systems—a relatively few durable goods industries provide most of these needs and have become oriented to meeting governmental rather than commercial requirements. In turn, some of these industries have become the leading growth industries in the country, and the regions in which they are concentrated are among the fastest growing areas.

—Military programs represent a large share of the national economy independent of the level of—or of changes in—private consumption and investment; these governmental programs are relatively independent of forces producing fluctuations in the private sector of the economy because they respond to a different set of demands. Within the domestic economy, defense spending does not exhibit the more predictable patterns of other major sectors, such as consumption and investment. In its relatively autonomous role, defense spending does not regularly act as a stabilizer to counter shifts in private consumption or investment, but neither does it necessarily move in parallel to heighten such destabilizing swings in the private economy.

The impact of defense spending on the economy, however, depends on many factors other than the level and rate of change of spending. Heavy

9. A spring 1969 newspaper report began with the significant statement, "A tentative renewal of peace hopes in Vietnam fueled a stock-market rally yesterday . . ." Vartanig G. Vartan, "Rally Is Fueled by Peace Hopes," *New York Times,* March 27, 1969, p. 65.

10. See M. L. Weidenbaum, "Defense Expenditures and the Domestic Economy," in *Defense Management,* Stephen Enke, ed. (Englewood Cliffs, N.J.: Prentice-Hall, 1967), pp. 315-336.

reliance on deficit financing during World War II, in contrast to the tax financing of the Korean War, produced more serious inflationary pressures and, therefore, called for more complicated economic stabilization measures. Consumer and business expectations may also differ from one period to another, as shown by the jump in consumer purchases of durables at the beginning of the Korean War buildup, but not during the same period of the Vietnam buildup, less clearly recognized as such.

In the period since the end of World War II, defense expenditures have fluctuated far more than either the outlays of state and local governments or of the consumer and business sectors of the economy. Of course, most of these fluctuations, which have been both rapid and large, have been connected with the buildup or cutback periods of World War II, Korea, and Vietnam. For example, during the fiscal years 1965-68, total expenditures of the Department of Defense rose from $47 billion in 1965 to $78 billion in 1968, an increase of better than 50 per cent. No other major part of the American economy has experienced such a large or rapid change, and the problems of economic stability stemming from it have been substantial.

When demand presses hard on a nation's resources, as it generally does in time of war, it becomes very difficult to adjust fiscal, monetary, and government expenditure policies on the large scale needed to prevent substantial rises in the price level. Arthur F. Burns, now chairman of the Federal Reserve Board, concluded in 1968 that the doubling of wholesale prices between 1940 and 1950 "was obviously linked to the enormous expansion of military spending during World War II."[11] And, in his detailed analysis of the first decade and a half following World War II, Stanford University Professor Bert Hickman, another economist, reported that federal purchases (which as pointed out earlier are overwhelmingly defense) have shown "the least short-term stability of all major categories of domestic demand during the postwar years." He also pointed out, however, that the pronounced uptrend in these expenditures after World War II fostered expansion over the period as a whole.[12] Similarly, Paul McCracken, now chairman of the President's Council of Economic Advisers, has emphasized the extreme volatility of the federal sector.[13] An examination of the Korean and Vietnam experiences provides much corroborative detail for these generalizations.

11. Arthur F. Burns, "The Defense Sector: An Evaluation of Its Economic and Social Impact," in The Defense Sector and the American Economy (New York: New York University Press, 1968), p. 64.

12. Bert Hickman, Growth and Stability of the Postwar Economy (Washington, D.C.: The Brookings Institution, 1960), pp. 208-209, 237.

13. Paul W. McCracken, "Review of Our Experience in Administering Fiscal Policy," in Fiscal Policy and Business Capital Formation (Washington, D.C.: American Enterprise Institute for Public Policy Research, 1967), pp. 67-83.

During the first twelve months of the Korean War (the period July 1, 1950-June 30, 1951), the amount appropriated by the Congress was 68 per cent higher than it had been in the previous year. Moreover, contracts and other obligations entered into by federal agencies rose 92 per cent above the level of the previous period. The wholesale price index jumped from 100.2 in June 1950 to 107.1 by September (1947-49 = 100), which represented an annual rate of 28 per cent.[14] This inflationary upsurge was described by one congressional committee as, with the exception of the decontrol period following the close of World War II, "the most rapid and the most widely pervasive inflationary movement" in recent American history.[15]

As it turned out, direct controls were imposed on prices, wages, and materials, but only after much of the inflationary pressures were over. The Korean War showed that the strongest inflationary pressures came during the first year of the military buildup, when the economy was initially adjusting to the increased level of military demand.

The true opportunity cost of the war in Vietnam was obscured during the initial buildup period for a variety of reasons—a major underestimate of the costs of the war, a lack of understanding of the rapidity with which a major increase in military demand affects the economy, and an unwillingness on the part of the administration to face the difficult questions of choice which come under the general heading of guns versus butter.[16]

On the contrary, the January 1966 Budget Message of the President maintained that the nation could afford simultaneously to wage a two-front war (the domestic war against poverty and the war in Vietnam) without raising taxes. That theme was clearly stated:

We are a rich nation and can afford to make progress at home while meeting obligations abroad—in fact, we can afford no other course if we are to remain strong. For this reason, I have not halted progress in the new and vital Great Society programs in order to finance the costs of our efforts in Southeast Asia.[17]

The January 1966 Budget Message called for several steps that would increase federal revenues, notably putting personal and corporate income taxes more nearly on a pay-as-you-go basis and temporarily reinstating the excises on passenger automobiles and telephone service, which had just been reduced.

14. M. L. Weidenbaum, "The Economic Impact of the Government Spending Process," in U.S. Congress, Joint Economic Committee, *Economic Effect of Vietnam Spending* (Washington, D.C.: Government Printing Office, 1967), Vol. II, pp. 645-647.
15. *Inflation Still a Danger*, U.S. Congress, Joint Committee on the Economic Report (Washington, D.C.: Government Printing Office, 1951), pp. 12-13.
16. See M. L. Weidenbaum, *Economic Impact of the Vietnam War* (Washington, D.C.: Georgetown University Center for Strategic Studies, 1967).
17. *Budget of the United States Government for the Fiscal Year Ending June 30, 1967* (Washington, D.C.: Government Printing Office, 1966), p. 7.

On the expenditure side of the budget, despite a good deal of rhetoric on the need for economy and efficiency, the customary pork-barrel items remained sacrosanct. For example, it was recommended that the Department of Agriculture start construction of thirty-five watershed projects and 1,600 miles of forest roads, that the Bureau of Reclamation start work on three new projects with a total cost initially estimated at $1 billion, that the Corps of Engineers start building twenty-five new rivers and harbors projects and begin designing twenty-three more, and that the General Services Administration finance construction of thirty-three government office buildings and design ten more.[18]

Although Johnson chose both more guns (military spending) and more butter (consumer spending), his budget also had the impact—in part as growing monetary tightness affected specific areas of the private economy—of producing less housing and fewer automobiles. Simultaneously, however, the nation was voting for more social welfare programs, so that both the military and civilian portions of the public sector were accelerating spending. As a result of some deliberate decisions and the failure to make others, 1966 was then the most rapid period of price inflation since the Korean War. In striking contrast to the virtual stability in the wholesale price index during the period 1958-64 (the 1-1½ per cent annual rise was mainly due to the rising cost of services), the index climbed more than 3 per cent in 1966. A related result was the collapse of the Council of Economic Advisers' wage-price guideposts, which had been designed to reduce or avoid inflationary pressures by encouraging management and labor to limit wage increases to the over-all increase in productivity. The Council's guideposts were widely violated in 1966 and then ignored in subsequent years.

The basic explanation for the substantial inflationary problem that accompanied the growing American participation in the Vietnam war was that the large and rapid increases in government civilian and military demand, coupled with the continued expansion in business expenditures for new plant and equipment, exceeded the capability of the economy to supply goods and services at then current prices.

To some extent, the inflationary pressures of the Vietnam buildup were accentuated by a liberal—or easy—monetary policy in 1965; as there always is a lag effect in monetary policy, its impact was felt primarily in 1966. In retrospect, it is clear that the rate of monetary expansion should have been braked in early 1965 as the economy regained reasonably full employment; in fact, the rise in the money supply was allowed to pick up speed from a high 8.0 per cent annual growth rate in the first six months of 1965 to an even higher 10.6 per cent rate in

18. *Ibid.*, pp. 192-322.

the second half. Beginning in December 1965, the Federal Reserve Board undertook a series of steps to tighten the availability of credit, and by April 1966, the steep rise in the money stock was halted. Monetary policy was apparently reversed too abruptly; the decline in the money supply that followed resulted in a "credit crunch" during the fall, which hit the housing market and savings and loan institutions disproportionately hard.

Perhaps the fundamental economic stabilization problem of the Vietnam war resulted from the Johnson administration's failure to understand how a military buildup affects the economy or how to take prompt and effective action to curtail the excessive demand that results. In part, of course, the problem was political; Johnson was reluctant to declare war and to demand the sacrifices—increased taxes and tight money, and/or controls—that war would entail. But the experiences during the buildup periods of the Korean and Vietnam wars suggest that it will be difficult to adjust to future changes in military spending of similar magnitudes without economic distortion. It not only takes skillful and timely economic policies; it also demands the political courage to enact policies that call for taxes and restrictions on credit. Still, there are some grounds for greater optimism on the downward side. Reductions in military spending following the end of active hostilities may demand more pleasant economic medicine than during buildup periods —tax reductions rather than increases, monetary ease rather than tightness, and civilian spending rises rather than curtailment. The choices between and within these categories may not be easy ones, however, particularly as each route would entail a different distribution of benefits and costs.

Because the military "market basket" is in marked contrast to the purchases of the civilian sector, it has important differential impacts on the structure of the American economy. If these purchases were similar, the structural impacts would not be of great importance. But so much of its "market basket" consists of fairly exotic equipment (missiles, space vehicles, nuclear-powered aircraft carriers and submarines, tanks, and heavy artillery) for which there are really no private markets that changes in its composition can have a decided impact.

The composition of these military expenditures offers additional insight into the public sector's impact on private activity through defense programs. As shown in Table 16.1, capital outlays—which roughly correspond to plant and equipment expenditures in the private economy—received 42 per cent of the military budget in striking contrast to other sectors of the economy, such as consumer purchases of goods and services. Consumer spending on durables (including residential housing) accounted for only one-fifth of total personal consumption expenditures plus housing. Hard goods or capital items produced for the Department of Defense are currently almost one-third as much as the total production of new plant and equipment for the economy's private sector. Only a relatively few hard goods-producing industries account for the bulk of all military contracts; just four groups—aircraft, electronics, ordnance, and shipbuilding—received about 85 per cent of the awards in recent years. A greater variety of industries and companies participates at the subcontractor and supplier level. This subcontracting partially modifies the tendency toward concentration and also serves to expand the impact of defense programs onto a wider industrial base. Major defense prime contractors subcontract approximately one-half of all the contracts they receive; about 40 per cent of this amount goes to small business firms. But the extent of dependence on defense work

TABLE 16.1 Composition of Defense Expenditures,
          Fiscal Year 1968

Capital Outlays	Billions of Dollars	Per Cent
Procurement of Weapons Systems	$23.3	30
Research and Development	7.7	10
Construction	1.3	2
Total Capital Outlays	$32.3	42
Operating Expenses		
Military Personnel	22.0	28
Operation and Maintenance	20.6	27
All Other	2.5	3
Total Operating Expenses	$45.1	58
Grand Total	$77.4	100

Source: U.S. Department of Defense.

varies widely among industries. It is estimated that 90 per cent of ordnance production is consumed by defense, 80 per cent of aircraft, 60 per cent of shipbuilding, and 35 per cent of electrical equipment. In contrast, the proportion is less than 5 per cent for such important industries as food, clothing, leather, lumber and wood, wholesale and retail trade, services, finance, and construction.[19]

Despite the Pentagon's attempts to disperse its contracts, the market for military goods is a highly concentrated one, with a relatively small group of companies doing most of the business. In fiscal year 1968, the one hundred companies receiving the largest dollar volume of military prime contracts accounted for 67 per cent of the Department of Defense's total outlays (see Table 16.2). The top defense contractor in 1968 was the General Dynamics Corporation, which received $2.2 billion. Four other companies each received total contracts exceeding $1 billion for the year. This concentration is hardly a recent development. In World War II the

19. *Manpower Report of the President, March 1965* (Washington, D.C.: Government Printing Office, 1965), pp. 61-64; Research Analysis Corporation, *A Military Procurement Final-Demand Vector,* 1967, pp. 9-10.

100 largest contractors ranked by dollar volume of contract awards also accounted for precisely 67 per cent of total contract value, while the top 25 companies had 46 per cent.[20] There are many reasons for this concentration—the way the military buys, what it buys, and the nature of the sellers.

There are two fundamental differences between the way military departments and civilian agencies make their purchases. The Department of Defense typically awards a weapons system contract to a company chosen after a lengthy series of negotiations; the typical civilian agency order is given to the company that has offered the lowest sealed bid. The typical civilian agency procurement order is a fixed-price contract; military orders are frequently of the cost-reimbursement type.

The Defense Department maintains that its reliance on negotiation does

TABLE 16.2 Concentration Trends in Military Procurement Shares Received by Major Defense Department Contractors

Rank of Company	Percentage of Military Procurement								
	1960	1961	1962	1963	1964	1965	1966	1967	1968
1-25	54	55	51	52	53	48	43	45	45
26-50	11	11	12	14	13	13	12	12	11
51-75	5	5	6	5	5	5	6	6	7
76-100	3	3	3	3	2	3	3	3	4
All Other	27	26	28	26	27	31	36	34	33
Total	100	100	100	100	100	100	100	100	100

Source: U.S. Department of Defense.

not signify lack of competition. But it is frequently more interested in technical performance than in price. In fact, performance rather than lowest price is the regular basis on which companies compete for military contracts. Clearly, this type of competition is not the price competition that widely occurs in a market situation although nonprice competition is by no means confined to the defense sector in a highly industrialized economy.

It is important to know who are the sellers that do compete for military business. An analysis of the size of the top hundred defense contractors provides some insight into the workings of the military market.[21] Contrary to much that is said about the military-industrial complex, it can

20. U.S. Department of Defense, *100 Companies and Their Subsidiary Corporations Listed According to Net Value of Prime Contract Awards, Fiscal Year 1968*; Merton J. Peck and Frederic M. Scherer, *The Weapons Acquisition Process: An Economic Analysis* (Cambridge: Harvard Graduate School of Business Administration, 1962), Appendix 5A.

21. This analysis is taken from M. L. Weidenbaum, "Concentration and Competition in the Military Market," *Quarterly Review of Economics and Business*, Spring 1968, pp. 8-9.

be seen in Table 16.3 that the giants do not dominate the military market. Rather, corporations with assets over $250 million but under $1 billion receive the largest share of defense contracts; these concerns are hardly industrial pygmies, but neither does this group include such giants as Standard Oil of New Jersey, General Motors, U.S. Steel, or A.T.&T. The major mili-

TABLE 16.3 Size Distribution of Major Defense Contractors,
Fiscal Year 1965

Asset Size	No. of Companies	Share of Defense Contracts to Top 100 Firms
		%
$1 billion and over	27	25
$250-$999 million	30	58
Under $250 million	43	17
Total	100	100

Source: Computed from data in U.S. Department of Defense releases and *Moody's Industrial Manual*.

tary contractors include the key suppliers of large aerospace systems—Boeing, Grumman, Hughes Aircraft, Lockheed, McDonnell-Douglas, and North American Rockwell. Small business concerns are more likely to receive awards for textiles and clothing, weapons, construction, miscellaneous equipment, and purchases of the more conventional defense items.

The available data (for fiscal year 1965) also show that the companies most heavily dependent on military orders are not the industrial giants. For those twenty-seven firms with assets of $1 billion or more, defense contracts in each case accounted for less than one-fourth of their sales; in most cases they accounted for less than 10 per cent. But for the thirty companies with assets in the $250 million to $1 billion range, there were six cases where defense work accounted for more than half of their sales and seven more where defense orders accounted for more than one-fourth of their business.[22] Conceivably many of these thirty would be much smaller—or out of business altogether—without defense work.

Many defense contractors are "locked-in" to military work as a result of dependency on government business. But there is another side to the coin. In the absence of a highly developed arsenal system, the leading contractors represent the backbone of the scientific, engineering, and manufacturing capability to design and produce weapons systems, and the government also becomes locked into or dependent upon them. On the basis of rough calculations, the military establishment currently produces only one-tenth of the aerospace equipment it requires, 3 per cent of the electronics, and main-

22. *Ibid.*, pp. 9-10.

tains no facilities identified as producing motor vehicles, petroleum products, rubber products, engines, or primary metals. In general, the nature of and need for these government arsenals have not been systematically explored.[23]

The Department of Defense reports that almost one-half of its contracts were competitively let in the fiscal year 1968. However, its statistics on contracts are open to criticism. Changes were recently made in response to charges by the Comptroller General that the department was classifying as competitive all awards under $2,500 and all contracts for which only one bid was received, although requests for proposals had been sent out to several firms.[24] What is really needed are comprehensive statistics on individual competitions, showing the actual number of companies that really respond with bids, the nature of the winners, and of the losers.

Meanwhile, indirect methods of analyzing the degree of competition for military business must be relied on. One method is to examine the turnover among the major contractors (Table 16.4 shows the turnover

TABLE 16.4 Turnover Among Major Defense Contractors, 1958–67

Top 100 Contractors FY 1967	1-25	26-50	51-75	76-100	Below 100	Total
1-25	18	3	1	1	2	25
26-50	4	8	5	1	7	25
51-75	1	3	2	3	16	25
76-100	0	1	3	3	18	25
Total	23	15	11	8	43	100

Source: Data from U.S. Department of Defense.

between 1958 and 1967). The entrenchment of the dominant firms is marked: eighteen of the top twenty-five in 1967 also were in the top twenty-five in 1958.

The relatively low turnover among the top companies, which are mainly the large aerospace and electronics companies, results in good measure from the formidable barriers to both entry into and exit from the markets for major weapon systems. Apart from the need for substantial funds, the entry barriers mainly take the form of scientific and engineering capabilities required to design and produce modern aerospace weapons. The exit barriers can be inferred from the many unsuccessful attempts of these companies to penetrate commercial markets (see the next chapter for a related and more detailed analysis of military contractors).

23. See Chapter 17 for an analysis of this issue.
24. U.S. Congress, Joint Economic Committee, *Economy in Government* (Washington, D.C.: Government Printing Office, 1967), Part I, p. 9.

In contrast, there is considerable mobility in the ranking of companies that have large but lesser shares of military business. Of the next 75 firms, 41—more than half—were not on the list of the top hundred defense contractors in 1958. Between 1965 and 1966 alone, 28 per cent of the companies in the top hundred list were replaced. These shifts, primarily among nonaerospace firms, reflect the changing product mix of military procurement and the influence of advances in technology rather than an intensification of competitive forces.

A decade ago, the large missile programs brought many concerns into the military market as suppliers of mechanical ground support equipment, fabricators of silos, and builders of tracking stations. During the period of peak procurement of Army ordnance equipment for the Korean War, the General Motors Corporation, a major producer of tanks and trucks, was the number one military contractor based on size of orders received. It was down to tenth by the fiscal year 1968. The decline in missile procurement and the rise in demand for ordnance needed in limited wars has required a different set of technical capabilities and a new variety of industries.

If, as discussed in Chapter 5, the autonomous nature of major corporations largely dependent on the military market is gradually declining, the Defense Department is playing an increasingly significant role in decision-making normally performed by business management. It is involved in choice of products, source of capital funds, and the internal operations of the company.[25] The trend has been so gradual that senior spokesmen for industry often fail to see or acknowledge it. But the Defense Department's assumption of the managerial role is overtly reflected in the standard provisions in its procurement contracts. Clauses grant the government power to veto decisions on in-house and subcontract activities, on choice of companies as subcontractors, on use of domestic or import products, on internal financial reporting systems, on minimum and average wage rates and overtime. High-technology military hardware, of course, requires highly specialized facilities, and a number have been built to supply it on the initiative of the Defense Department, and the department may retain title to the factories and equipment.

Diversification is understandably difficult under the circumstances. Dependence on the government is, correspondingly, reinforced. This dependence has been further enhanced by the rise of civilian agencies which also require high-technology equipment for which there is no other market. Space systems for NASA and the supersonic transport (SST) for the Department of Transportation (DOT) both rely upon, and later feed back into,

25. See M. L. Weidenbaum, "Arms and the American Economy: A Domestic Convergence Hypothesis," *American Economic Review*, May 1968, pp. 428-437.

the same pool of exotic technologies that the Defense Department has been nursing. But neither space nor supersonic systems can yet be developed by the private market mechanism. The usual result is that high-technology companies trying to diversify out of the defense market do so by "diversifying" into the NASA or DOT market, trading one unique nonmarket relationship for another quite similar one.

The concentration of military design and production activities in certain industries and companies has been accompanied by a rather high degree of geographic cluster. There is a tendency for individual regions to specialize in supplying different types of military equipment. Firms in the east-north-central states— particularly Michigan—supplied over two-thirds of the tanks and related automotive equipment ordered by the Pentagon in the fiscal year 1968; companies on the Pacific Coast, mainly California, and to a lesser degree, Washington, received over one-half of the orders for missiles and space systems in the same year, and more than two-fifths of the electronics equipment was ordered from establishments in New England and the Middle Atlantic States, notably Massachusetts, New York, and New Jersey.[26]

Military bases tend to follow a different locational pattern. A large proportion of them are found in open spaces, relatively distant from large population and industrial centers. To some extent, the geographic dispersion of military activities *per se*—located in large measure in Southern and in other states of below-average incomes—tends to offset the disproportionately large share of defense contracts concentrated in the states and metropolitan areas such as California and New York with the highest income levels.

If military expenditures were distributed across the United States proportionally to each region's industrial base, the geographic impacts of military buildups and cutbacks would be relatively limited. In actuality, however, the regional pattern of defense expenditures ranges from extreme dependency to minor regional influence. Nor are these patterns stable once established; regional impacts of military programs vary as the changing military requirements geographically redistribute prime contracts and military bases.

But certain states and communities, because of their relatively high degree of dependence on specific categories of defense work, are especially vulnerable to shifts in the size and types of defense programs. Missouri represents one such example; military contract dollars increased 53 per cent from fiscal year 1963 to fiscal year 1964, and moved that state from the

26. U.S. Department of Defense, *Military Prime Contract Awards by Region and State*, Fiscal Year 1968.

tenth highest in prime contracts to third. In the same period, Ohio fell back to eighth from third, with a 28 per cent decrease in dollar volume. Texas represents a similar example; in fiscal 1967 it was second in military contracts, rising from a position of eighth during 1950-56.

Often a state's military prime contracts are concentrated in a single procurement category—aircraft in Georgia, Kansas, Washington State, and Missouri, missiles in Colorado, shipbuilding in Maine and Virginia. Moreover, in several cases one or two companies receive the most of the state's defense business—Boeing in Kansas and Washington, Lockheed in Georgia, Martin-Marietta in Colorado, McDonnell-Douglas in Missouri, United Aircraft and General Dynamics in Connecticut, Bath Iron Works in Maine, Newport News Shipbuilding in Virginia.

Three key factors underlie the geographic shift and concentration or dispersion of defense procurement: the kind of products being purchased, the upward or downward trend of a few large individual projects, and the kind of industries (along with their ability to compete) located within each region. In some states with a broad industrial base relatively large amounts of defense work represent comparatively small portions of total employment and payrolls. Thus, shifts in defense spending are cushioned by the depth and breadth of the private sector. One measurement of this dependence is the portion of total industrial activity in a state which is derived from direct military payrolls and from wages and salaries of defense workers in private industry. Virginia, Utah, Washington, California, Alaska, Hawaii, Arizona, Colorado, Maryland, Massachusetts, and Connecticut all depend on defense work for at least 10 per cent of their economic activity (see Chart 16.2). The proportion is less than 10 per cent for all other states.[27]

Within various states the concentration is far greater; important examples are such metropolitan areas as Washington, D.C., Boston, Wichita, Huntsville, Alabama, Cape Kennedy, Los Angeles, San Diego, St. Louis, and Seattle. But most of the communities that are heavily dependent on the payrolls of the military and/or of defense contractors are relatively small towns and cities. In a survey taken in June 1967, the Department of Defense found that of the seventy-two areas where 12 per cent or more of the work force was directly attributable to local defense activity, fifty-eight, or four-fifths, were communities with labor forces of less than 50,000 each. Of the other areas surveyed, most of those with less dependence on defense activity were communities of substantially larger size.[28]

Defense expenditures influence a region directly and indirectly through their impact on income and employment. The cumulative effect depends on the amount of subcontracting coming into and going outside the region.

27. Consad Research Corporation, *Regional Federal Procurement Study*, a report to the Department of Commerce Independent Study Board, 1967.
28. Roger F. Riefler and Paul B. Downing, "Regional Effect of Defense Effort on Employment," *Monthly Labor Review*, July 1968, pp. 1-8.

Adding these direct and indirect employment effects, the total impact expands the effect of defense expenditures on employment to over two-fifths of total employment in the cases of Los Angeles and Seattle.[29]

Roger Bolton, in his pioneering study of the impact of defense on the regional growth patterns, concluded that such spending had its greatest effect on the Pacific and mountain regions. The individual states whose rapid growth rates were most closely related to military contracts were California, Washington, Colorado, and Arizona.[30]

The tendency of defense programs to cluster in a relatively few areas, and in a pattern different from that of American industry generally, is fairly recent. In World War II, the distribution of defense contracts more or less followed the then prevailing pattern of manufacturing activity. The major industrial states—Michigan, New York, Pennsylvania, Ohio, and Indiana—ranked high in prime contract awards. Korea marked the turning point in this pattern, with older manufacturing states declining in relative positions. As aerospace and electronics activities grew in terms of military importance, California displaced New York as number one and Texas appeared in place of Michigan in the number two position. But so long as automotive and conventional ordnance products were a substantial part of defense procurement, the capabilities of established manufacturing companies were drawn upon. With the increasing importance of aircraft, missiles, electronics, and space systems, newer companies became increasingly important and tended to locate in the newer industrial states of California, Texas, Washington, or in rejuvenated New England states.

One specialized economic aspect of the geographic distribution of military activities is the overseas location of many military installations and expenditures. In recent years, the foreign exchange costs attributable to our overseas military operations have come close to approximating the net deficit in the United States balance of payments.

Table 16.5 shows the composition of the United States military balance of payments. There are three main items involved: (1) the foreign exchange cost of the Vietnam conflict, (2) the foreign exchange cost of American military activities in Western Europe and other locations (excluding Vietnam), and (3) the offsetting receipts from the sales of American military equipment to West Germany and other foreign nations.[31]

The largest and most stable of the three items is the deficit due to the stationing of United States armed forces in Western Europe and other

29. Charles Tiebout, "The Regional Impact of Defense Expenditures," in *Defense and Disarmament: The Economics of Transition*, Roger E. Bolton, ed. (Englewood Cliffs, N.J.: Prentice-Hall, 1966), p. 131.

30. Roger E. Bolton, *Defense Purchases and Regional Growth* (Washington, D.C.: The Brookings Institution, 1966), p. 12.

31. U.S. Department of Defense, *The Fiscal Year 1969-73 Defense Program and the 1969 Defense Budget* (Washington, D.C.: Government Printing Office, 1968), pp. 36-38.

non-Vietnam posts. Recent increases in pay rates for members of the armed forces, and for American civilian employees as well, exerted an upward but limited pressure. A bigger swing is likely in the receipts from military sales abroad. The high 1967 level resulted from a bunching of receipts under the offset arrangement with West Germany. Under that arrangement, Germany offsets the bulk of the cost of stationing American troops there by buying an equivalent amount of military goods and services from the United States.

TABLE 16.5 U.S. Military Balance of Payments, Fiscal Years 1961–68
(In billions of dollars.)

Category	1961	1962	1963	1964	1965	1966	1967	1968
Vietnam-related costs	—	—	.1	.1	.2	.7	1.5	1.6
NATO and other non-Vietnam costs	3.1	3.0	3.0	2.8	2.6	2.7	2.6	2.9
Receipts from sales of military equipment	− .3	− .9	−1.4	−1.2	−1.3	−1.2	−1.8	−1.2
Net Deficit	2.8	2.1	1.7	1.7	1.5	2.2	2.3	3.3

Source: U.S. Department of Defense.

The last category in the military balance of payments is Vietnam itself. Southeast Asia deployments in the fiscal years 1968 and 1969 continued to rise above the average for 1967. The military deficit in the balance of payments during fiscal year 1968 exceeded $3 billion. The end of hostilities in Vietnam would be expected to yield a definite improvement in the United States balance of payments. The net effect would depend on the magnitude and timing of economic aid and reconstruction programs in Southeast Asia, which would utilize some of the foreign exchange savings that would result from the end of the war.

The employment resulting from defense activity is another indicator of its economic impact. Military spending has had a double impact on the development of the labor force of the American economy. It represents both a major source of demand as well as of supply, especially for specialized manpower. In 1967, defense-generated activity was responsible for 7,500,000 jobs, representing 10 per cent of total United States employment. A little over half were employed directly by the federal government, either in the armed forces or as civilian employees of the military establishment. The remainder were in defense-generated employment in private industry, working for prime defense contractors, subcontractors, or companies providing materials and services to contractors.[32]

32. Richard P. Oliver, "The Employment Effect of Defense Expenditures," *Monthly Labor Review*, September 1967, p. 9.

About one out of every five scientists and engineers in private industry is employed in defense-related activity. Over-all, defense workers are more skilled than the civilian labor force as a whole. In the fiscal year 1967, nearly 16 per cent were in the broad professional group, compared with 13 per cent of the general labor force. Over 45 per cent were skilled and semiskilled craftsmen, compared with less than 32 per cent for the economy as a whole. In contrast, a smaller proportion of defense employees were in service occupations (4 per cent versus 13 per cent) or in sales (2 per cent versus 6 per cent).[33]

The impact of the defense program has not been limited to the demand side. Both directly and indirectly it has increased the supply of scientists, engineers, and other technical personnel. The direct means include university fellowships, aid to research funding, and training programs. More indirect influences on this supply are exercised by creating a favorable labor market via increased pay rates and employment opportunities. (Chapter 19 contains a more detailed analysis.) There has been considerable mobility of personnel employed by government agencies and by defense contractors. Many veterans of the armed forces are now using skills, such as those in the field of electronics, that were acquired in the military service. The mobility of civilian personnel within the military labor market is shown by the result of the Dyna-Soar space vehicle cancellation: two-thirds of the laid-off employees found jobs in nondefense fields. Other examples include the Martin Company ICBM layoff, where 58 per cent of the released employees found nondefense jobs and the Republic Aviation layoff, where 60 per cent were rehired in nondefense jobs.[34]

Much of the employment impacts resulting from the purchases by the Department of Defense show up in various sectors of the economy. As would be expected, the largest share of the jobs is created in manufacturing industries, notably those government-oriented durable goods producers which receive the bulk of the prime contracts. In addition, however, many civilian-oriented companies serve as suppliers of metal products and other components to the prime contractors. Although defense demands do not form any substantial part of the business of most of these suppliers, the number of jobs indirectly traceable to defense orders is impressive.

Military spending in the United States has been at a high level for almost two decades. While it may level off in the post-Vietnam period and, as it is now, decline somewhat, at least as a percentage of GNP, it will presumably remain as a very substantial element in the economy, absorbing a significant

33. Max A. Rutzick, "Worker Skills in Current Defense Employment," *Monthly Labor Review*, September 1967, p. 17.
34. U.S. Arms Control and Disarmament Agency, *The Dyna-Soar Contract Cancellation*, July 1965, *Post Layoff Experiences, Republic Aviation Workers*, August 1966, and *Martin Company Employees Re-employment Experiences*, December 1966.

share of resources and skills. The demand for resources for military purposes is largely independent of fluctuations in the private economy and subject to significant shifts both in the quantity and the nature of the goods and services required.

To minimize the dislocations resulting from these shifts—and to reduce the institutional pressures to maintain or increase the levels of defense spending beyond the requirements of national security—it seems wise to encourage diversification both in communities and in enterprises with a high proportion of defense business. The high mobility of manpower from the defense to the nondefense sector has already been noted: where that mobility can be achieved without the necessity for moving from one community or one part of the country to another, a good deal of human discomfort and loss of capital investments (public and private) can be avoided. The preservation of individual enterprises is not a high priority public policy goal, but if enterprises can shift their capital and management resources from defense to nondefense activities, they are less likely to become involved in special interest campaigns to shore up military budgets. Variations in dependency, of course, generate noneconomic impacts, particularly political pressures of considerable significance. If defense-generated income and employment were distributed throughout the country proportionally to population or the location of industry, we would expect less localized, less intensified pressures for or against changes in the size and composition of military spending.

Diversification of defense industry to nondefense activities need not mean that the pattern of government/industry relationships that prevails in the defense sector should be carried over into other sectors. The separation of public and private sectors is as critical for countervailing power as the separation of powers in the government itself, and in some ways, more so.

17

Weapons Acquisitions
and Defense Industry

In the present state of the world, so long as the United States maintains a foreign policy that is not wholly isolationist, defense will be costly. National security puts an even heavier levy on American resources because of two separate, but strongly interacting, factors: first, because defense officials (both civilian and military) have been translating American national security objectives and commitments into force structure and weapons requirements based on their perceptions of objectives and their assessment of the capabilities of potential enemies and of the contingencies to be anticipated; and second, because of the methods by which this translation of objectives into specific resource requirements is typically undertaken, and the ways in which research and development procurement is actually managed.

One way of reducing the current diversion of resources from domestic requirements is to improve the efficiency of the process of translating national security objectives into research requirements. It is the thesis of this chapter that the weapons systems acquisition process is a pivotal factor in controlling defense expenditures and in determining the role of defense industry in the military establishment, and that it can and must be modified in fundamental ways.

Why is it such a pivotal factor? There are several reasons:

1. The various individual system acquisition decisions have a dominating and enduring influence on the size of the entire military budget.

2. The demands for military research and development in support of system acquisition determine how a significant portion of the nation's scientists and engineers are employed.

3. The rate at which new technology is adopted has a direct impact on the arms race.

259

4. Because industry is insufficiently prepared to cope with some serious problems that arise through the development and production of new weapons, and because our military institutions are not organized to take greatest advantage of advances that grow from the rather extreme technological orientation of the services, the entire system acquisition process has become of increasing concern both to the Congress and to the executive branch.

Since World War II, research and development have generally accounted for somewhat less than 10 per cent of all military spending, although the proportion has increased in recent years. The way research and development are conducted and motivated determines what kinds of weapon choices the services have, and that, in turn, establishes a large part of the ultimate cost of the defense program: not only R&D cost, but also investment, operating, training, and maintenance costs. It is no small matter to cancel a system development that has cost hundreds of millions (or even billions) of dollars, but the implications of adopting such systems as Polaris, the M-16 rifle, Minuteman, or the B-52 are still more awesome. For example, although development of the B-52 cost less than $500 million, the price of creating and maintaining a B-52 operational capability for the last fifteen years has exceeded $25 billion,[1] and the continued presence of that aircraft in the strategic inventory has vitally influenced decisions on the composition of the national war plan, the character of the probable national response to nuclear attack, relations with various foreign powers (Spain and Japan, for instance), and the structure of the assured destruction strategy on which national defense policy his hinged. Had a different sort of bomber been introduced, or had the B-52 been phased out in the early 1960's, as was planned, the cost, structure, and operations of the entire defense establishment certainly would be different. The behavior of the military services and the character of the national defense effort is directly related to the nature of system acquisition choices and development policies.

The military services and those elements of industry dependent on them have a very large stake in defense. Like all vigorous institutions, they by nature try to expand both their influence on and their share of the national budget. They may meet resistance, in various measure, from the Congress and the President (who are under growing pressure to allocate more of the budget to nonmilitary items), from the electorate (increasingly reluctant to pay the high tax rates required to sustain a generally high level of both civil and military spending), and from other agencies of government that have their own stake in the size and shape of the budget. But, as we have seen in earlier chapters, there is no assurance that the

---

1. Exclusive of any costs incident to Vietnam operations.

traditional checks and balances built into government machinery can in this instance provide the correct amount of countervailing power.

There are two main possibilities for cutting defense spending: (1) a reduction in the quantities of weapons bought by the services based on a more rational balance between stated requirements and real needs; and (2) a reduction in the actual cost of acquiring expensive military hardware, through the appropriate procedures for controlling the system acquisition process itself, for insuring that better use is made of existing technology, so that the new more often replaces rather than simply adds on to the old.

It is also obvious that there are other attractive avenues for cost reduction in defense spending: lessened operating costs, improved supply and maintenance, greater individual productivity leading to lessened manpower needs, and the like. Each of these potential sources of cost reduction is heavily influenced by the weapons acquisition process.

No agency of the federal government has paid greater deference to the cause of economy and efficiency than the Department of Defense. But it not only chooses among alternatives but also decides what alternatives shall be considered, and how, and what standards of economy shall then be used to evaluate the choices. The notion that Congress might take a continuing interest in the department's selection of alternatives and even in its administration of weapons systems acquisition is very new. It represents, in part, belated recognition that there are, in fact, some systematic biases in the Defense Department's internal decision-making processes that tend to limit the spectrum of choices to high cost alternatives, particularly in terms of technology that is added to, rather than substituted for, old technology. Also, the relationship between the military services and the defense industries is not an ordinary customer-supplier relationship, but a special one that tends to discourage an earnest search for low cost alternatives.

The emergence of more rational policies has been impeded by the belief that public monopolies are somehow different from private monopolies. When private corporations possessing a high degree of monopoly power are found to be engaged in activities not in the public interest, they are generally subjected to public regulation of one kind or another. The same kind of logic applies equally to public monopolies. But the degree of control that the President and the Secretary of Defense—to say nothing of the Congress—have over the military establishment is actually much smaller than the degree of control typically exercised by chief executives of business corporations; perhaps it is closer to the degree of control exercised by a university president. For example, while top-level interference in the selection of the leadership is not uncommon in most private corporations (and in some universities), direct intervention in the military establishment's selection process has with relatively few major exceptions occurred only in wartime, and then not always successfully.

Military R&D (including the space and atomic energy programs) accounts for about 60 per cent of all public and private sector R&D spending and employs nearly one-half of all research scientists and engineers.[2] If all these scientists and engineers were efficiently used to open up new exciting avenues of technology, the price to the nation might be regarded as high but probably necessary. Most military R&D spending, however, does not go into exploratory and advanced development activities in which the primary goal is to open up new vistas; rather it goes into acquisition of weapons systems. And the trend over the last fifteen years has been to use more and more scientists and engineers on fewer and fewer projects. Thus, the total number of scientists and engineers engaged in weapons systems development has risen, while the total of aircraft and other weapons systems projects under development has declined by about four-fifths and the total of missile projects by about two-thirds.[3]

One obvious reason for this trend is the increasing complexity of modern weapons technology. But the trend toward increasing complexity may in part have resulted from the habit of using excessively large development teams. Simple and ingenious solutions to problems do not often result from putting 800 engineers on a project that 200 could handle—quite the contrary. The Defense Department tends to assume that development is an activity in which the kinds of results obtained, or the speed at which they are obtained, are more or less proportionate to the magnitude of the development effort. Yet there is no real evidence that heavy manning is highly correlated with the success of development projects.[4]

The ever-increasing amount of government regulation of research and development activities and the significant costs of complying with those regulations have also led to substantial expansion in the expenditure of technical manpower. Manning standards for military R&D projects often tend to be entirely different from those applied to the conduct of non-military R&D. Most companies engaged in both carefully segregate their military from their civilian R&D activities and minimize the flow of people between them. Some of the aircraft companies that have not done very well

2. *Federal Funds for Science* (Washington, D.C.: National Science Foundation, 1965); and *National Pattern of R&D Resources* (Washington, D.C.: National Science Foundation, 1967).

3. Data on projects under way obtained from a special compilation made at RAND; on the number of scientists and engineers, estimated from data compiled by the National Science Foundation.

4. An examination made at RAND of some twenty aircraft and missile projects and ten radar projects failed to disclose a positive correlation between the size of the development team and the success of a project—success in terms of development time, or the cost of the system developed, or its military usefulness relative to alternative systems available during the same period.

in developing and selling transport or business aircraft in the commercial market concede that a primary mistake was in trying to develop and produce commercial aircraft just as they did military aircraft.

To be sure, there have been large spillover effects in the past from this lavish use of scientists and engineers: penicillin, computers, the many non-military applications that came out of the effort to develop the atomic bomb, and so forth. Recent spillover effects, however, have been disappointingly small and seem to be declining—perhaps because of the extent to which military and space R&D is concentrated on kinds of systems that have no very direct civilian analogues.[5] And in any event it is silly to argue that spillover benefits justify the number of scientists and engineers now engaged in military and space R&D; the use of this trained and talented manpower to produce results only marginally beneficial to the civilian economy is, by civilian standards, far from a reasonable disposition of scarce human resources—nor would military authorities be prepared to rely for their own R&D on the spillover from the civilian economy.

For some time to come, however, the Defense Department R&D activities will continue to be the single largest user of scientists and engineers (see Chapter 19), and the really pressing question is how all this talent can be better utilized in order to make defense less rather than more expensive, to encourage the diversion of scientific energy and imagination to questions of direct civil concern, and to diminish rather than intensify the arms race.

The military services tend to push for increases in weapons system performance and versatility beyond what seems sensible in terms of rational military-economic considerations. For example, in commenting on his experiences as comptroller, Charles J. Hitch wrote:

> Virtually every attempt we have made to explain the inexorable logic of relating cost to military effectiveness seems to shatter itself on the argument— "Nothing but the best will do for our boys." And the "best" usually refers to some particular characteristic of physical performance, such as speed, altitude, or firepower, or even unit cost.
>
> Implicit in this challenge is the deeply rooted feeling that national defense is far too important a matter to be inhibited by cost. If one weapon system performs better than another, then we should buy the higher performance weapon system, regardless of the cost; the country can afford it. Indeed, the people who hold this view feel that it is somehow sinful, or at least unpatriotic, to try to relate performance or military effectiveness to costs; that considerations of military effectiveness and cost are antithetical.[6]

It is questionable, however, whether this traditional propensity of the

5. For a further discussion of the spillover question, see R. R. Nelson, M. J. Peck, and E. D. Kalachek, *Technology, Economic Growth, and Public Policy*, a RAND Corporation and Brookings Institution Study, 1967, pp. 82-86.

6. Charles J. Hitch, *Decision-Making for Defense* (Berkeley and Los Angeles: University of California Press, 1965), pp. 43-44.

services to seek the very best can be explained solely by their failure to understand the "inexorable logic of relating cost to military effectiveness." It may be objected that budgets are after all limited, and that one has to compare the risk of not obtaining the very best weapon with the risk of obtaining, say, only half as many weapons. But military organizations do not take readily to the notion of budgetary limits as a serious constraint. Their deep-seated aversion to risk-taking would seem to provide a more fundamental explanation. In being asked to accept something less than the very best, it frequently seems to military officers that it is *they* who are being asked to accept unwarranted risks—the risks of losing a war.

Because the military are trained for operations in which lives are necessarily at risk, they are understandably anxious to minimize risk wherever possible. In many areas this concern is not only appropriate, it is essential. The design of control systems for the launch of nuclear weapons calls for a degree of risk aversion unmatched in civil planning. The danger of accidental firing of a nuclear weapon must be minimized, even at very considerable cost. But risk aversion can also lead the military to fail to recognize opportunities in weapons systems planning that could effect substantial savings in time and money. The issue is not whether there should be elimination of all risk aversion by the military. Rather, attention must be called to the uneconomic, inefficient application of a risk-averting criterion in·situations where it leads to less-than-optimal policies.

Risk aversion indicates an unwillingness to plan in terms of uncertain outcomes. Intolerance of ambiguity, or uncertainty, implies a wish to believe that the outcome of the planning will be more certain than it really is. Ignoring uncertainties when there are ample opportunities for reducing them will lead to irrational conduct almost no matter how the risks are assessed.

Organizations frequently disregard uncertainty because in promoting a new idea it is usually necessary to appeal to higher authority, and the task of convincing higher authorities that an idea is worth serious consideration almost invariably involves convincing them (and the promoter himself) that the prospects for its success are more certain than they really are.

There seem to be wide differences among individuals in their willingness to face and resolve uncertainties, or as psychologists put it, "in their intolerance of ambiguity."[7] And it seems reasonable to assume that persons with a greater intolerance of ambiguity will seek—or will be sought by—organ-

7. The book in which the concept "tolerance of ambiguity" was first introduced is T. W. Adorno's *The Authoritarian Personality* (New York: Harper & Brothers, 1950). Although an authoritarian personality is recognizable in many members of the military establishment, it should not be assumed that this personality characteristic is confined to or concentrated in members of the military establishment.

izations with a greater propensity to engage in uncertainty avoidance. Most organizations are characterized to some degree by an unwillingness to acknowledge the uncertainties that actually face them, and rather than seeking clear answers to replace fuzzy ones, they tend to rely on dogmatism. Like risk aversion, intolerance of ambiguity is a characteristic of many older, well-established military bureaucracies.

Some major policy decisions become understandable only in terms of these phenomena. For example, the strategy of massive retaliation certainly reflected the tendency to plan for the worst. The implicit belief that the world could be neatly divided into Communist-aligned countries and democratic-aligned countries, firm lines drawn, and instant retaliation made a plausible threat to any country that crossed them, indicated a high degree of reluctance to live with uncertainty. Conversely, a good deal of the early resistance of the military services to the doctrine of flexible response may be explained by the fact that as an administrative doctrine it not only left open questions of timing and force levels but also the issue of who would decide such questions—the Commander in Chief, or the Joint Chiefs of Staff.

In a sense, it may seem paradoxical that the military establishment of the United States seems to exhibit a much higher degree of intolerance of ambiguity in almost all its planning than does the army of, say, Israel. The paradox is explained by the fact that the central purpose of the more affluent military organizations like the United States', as their members see it, is not primarily to bring about impressive advances in technology, nor even to support foreign policy, but rather to conduct highly organized, large-scale military operations, the success of which always seems to require firm plans and decisive action. Though only in recent years has the planning of the services been harmonized to make all three of them plan for the same war, each begins its planning cycle with a specific kind of picture of the war that might have to be fought; specific assumptions are made about the size of opposing forces, their capabilities, and how they are expected to be employed. On the basis of such assumptions, calculations are made of the number and kinds of forces needed to deal with the enemy decisively. And on the basis of these "strategic" calculations, detailed plans are worked out for major and minor items of equipment, logistics, training, and so forth. This, essentially, is what is meant by "requirements planning." It is very much like the planning process of a large steel mill, except that those planning the operation of a steel mill can act on the basis of specific and precise information, and those engaged in the planning of military operations cannot.

A detailed military requirement for a new military system is laid down only after the needs of the operational command have been exhaustively studied and reviewed—a process that normally involves the participation of hundreds of decision-makers and may take three or four years to complete. Then, on the basis of the stated requirements, contractors or arsenals are asked to submit detailed designs and specifications, often in the context of a design competition.

Avoidance of uncertainty is also reflected in the insistence that new weapons systems contain completely new and well-matched sets of sub-systems (for example, engines, fire control systems, bombing navigation systems, and so on). This kind of weapons system planning reflects, in part, the tendency to seek nothing but the best because on paper perfectly matched subsystems always perform better than imperfectly matched sub-systems. However, it does not take into account the fact that the beautifully arranged marriages between the various subsystems of a weapons system are seldom consummated. Substitutions are made because as development progresses to the hardware test phase it becomes apparent that some imperfectly matched subsystems will do the job better or more cheaply than those that looked best on paper; or those that looked best on paper will not be available as soon as all the other parts of a total system. The product, in either case, is a combination of theoretically mismatched subsystems which nonetheless (given reasonable designer ingenuity) works as well as the meticulously planned match that could not be achieved.

If, as a result of meticulous planning, weapons systems could be made less expensive both to develop and to procure, there would be nothing to complain about. But such planning seems to have just the opposite effect. The long period of gestation and all that is involved in getting a new weapons system program sold inevitably makes the uncertainties (the variances of the initial estimates) seem much smaller than they actually are. A proclivity for faith in advance planning discourages understanding of what the critical uncertainties really are, and reduces the apparent importance of experiments and early tests required to resolve technological uncertainties. Postponing their resolution until a "final" configuration is well along makes resolution much more difficult and much more expensive, because at that stage many more things have to be changed. This problem is further complicated by the tendency to "stretch" the state of the art in all the subsystems developed. These practices also result in a serious misallocation—or waste—of R&D effort. Relatively less is spent on the more critical items of technology and relatively more on R&D that does not really matter: the enormous coordination problem involved in keeping perfectly matched subsystems from becoming unmatched (although they almost always do).

These built-in practices give birth to some very costly weapons systems. It is frequently impossible to find low cost solutions to problems until hardware, even if in a very rudimentary form, can be seen and tested. The environment in which weapons systems are planned, however, does not encourage a keen search for ways to simplify equipment or to postpone production commitments until hardware can be carefully tested. Nor do the incentives available to contractors promote such behavior. There are additional reasons as well: our lack of good measures of output and consequent reliance on input measures; the natural desire to accept and meet technological challenges; and the American reluctance to accept less than the highest quality in exchange for getting greater quantity in its technological enterprises.

When opportunities exist for reducing the state of ignorance, it is the essence of rational planning to emphasize getting better information and to make plans into which new information can be assimilated at a relatively modest cost. In planning a military campaign it may be necessary to make the best plans one can, and then take whatever action is indicated, however uncertain the information.[8] But good strategy for developing a new weapons system, involving significant advances in technology, requires a different kind of planning and different kind of organization from those typically associated with military development projects.

Since World War II one of the most cherished objectives of military development programs has been to shorten development lead time—to minimize the time between the start of development and the delivery of a new weapons system for operational use. In the 1940's and early 1950's, the technique of "parallel development"—developing two or more systems to do the same job—was frequently used to minimize lead time. The first system to reach operational status was then purchased in quantity. But as weapons systems rapidly became more expensive as the 1950's wore on, this kind of duplicative development became less tolerable. A new strategy, "concurrency," gradually came into favor for projects requiring minimum lead time. "Concurrency" is essentially the simultaneous development of all subsystems of a weapons system. In a missile system, for instance, the upper stages, warhead, etc., are designed and tested without waiting for the first stage design to be "frozen."

This later strategy put less emphasis on a rapid reduction of uncertainty than on a reduction of fabrication and tooling lead times. It emphasized the simultaneous fabrication of all the major ingredients of a weapons system in as nearly "finished" a form as possible. In the Air Force ballistic missile programs, where the most extreme version of the "concurrency" principle was employed, missiles were sent to operational units before their development had been substantially completed. As the development pro-

8. Whether such planning will prove to be good planning in a war obviously depends on the length of the campaign. For a short campaign there may be no alternative but to rely on best estimates. On the other hand, for a longer war (e.g., the war in Vietnam) a much more flexible kind of planning will be desired. Military planners, however, are inclined to place more emphasis on the short and decisive wars.

gram proceeded, the missiles already in operational use were brought up to a more tolerable standard of reliability by an elaborate modification and retrofit program, incorporating changes into already working systems.

A number of systems introduced into military use could probably have been operational sooner rather than later had a different strategy for development and procurement been followed. Especially where a major advance in technology is sought, concurrency is not only costly, but because it involves considerable inflexibility, it may impede timely adaptation of a system to take advantage of new knowledge gained in the development process. Whatever the other advantages and disadvantages of post-World War II procurement practices, there is reason to doubt that they succeeded in achieving one of their principal stated objectives: shorter lead time.

Since 1960, military development programs generally have not reflected the same degree of urgency as did the ballistic missile programs. Yet a high degree of concurrency has come to be accepted, and one that also helps to explain why development and production costs have risen as much as they have. Not only does a concurrency strategy conform to the character of a military service better than a policy of buying technological options, but it offers another apparently important advantage. Policy-makers tend to believe (probably correctly) that it takes more courage to cancel a full-fledged development-production program in the hundreds of millions of dollars category than a prototype program that has consumed only some tens of millions. Larger programs therefore are less likely to be canceled, a situation both the military and its industrial partner recognize and exploit. It is not as widely recognized that in a period marked by fiscal restraint the likelihood of obtaining approval to proceed with a particular system development, for example, the ABM, may be proportional to the cost of the initial investment. Interest in "hardware proof" and "proof of concept through testing" which was noted in the early period of Defense Secretary Laird's tenure certainly stems in part from improved appreciation of that paradox.

The financial interests of concerns that supply unique items to the Defense Department (aircraft, missiles, specialized electronic equipment, for example) are highly correlated to the customers' preferences. Just as the services exhibit a high degree of intolerance to ambiguity, and in their planning invariably insist on getting things quickly, so is it in the interests of defense contractors to make it seem that a new airplane will not be more difficult to develop than next year's automobile, and to secure very large financial commitments from the outset of a program. But, just as the military services prefer nothing but the best in military hardware, so defense contractors find it to their interest to concentrate on high cost items, and tolerate cost-increasing modifications after development has started.

Roughly three-quarters of the profits earned by contractors are earned in production (as distinct from development). Since what they can earn as a percentage of sales tends to be narrowly circumscribed—even with incentive contracts—the main inducement to higher profits is through a larger cost base. And, with relatively few exceptions, the production cost figures submitted as of the time a development program is started are estimates, not bids. In other words, it is not like the market furnished by airline companies for commercial airliners, where any cost escalation must come out of the pockets of the aircraft companies. Finally, for reasons not entirely apparent, the government usually has been willing to make large financial commitments at the outset of programs, and this makes programs much more difficult to cancel and substantially increases the bargaining ability of the contractor.

Better contracting procedures seem desirable, but a normal buyer-seller relationship seems almost impossible to establish—first, because the degree of technical advance sought in military hardware tends to preclude laying down firm requirements and specifications, and second, because the degree of government supervision and regulation almost precludes fixing responsibility. In addition, companies dependent on defense contracts tend to become a responsibility of the government.

In 1961, when the Kennedy administration came into office, two main bodies of evidence on the conduct of military research and development— one gathered by RAND in its studies of R&D decision-making problems, the other by the Harvard Business School's Weapons Acquisition project[9] —agreed that the outcome of weapons systems development projects was highly uncertain. They had abundant evidence to support the contention.

One way of observing the uncertainties in development programs is to compare the initial estimates of development time and development costs with actual costs and time spent in development. The results of such a comparison, made on the basis of data gathered by the Harvard Business School Weapons Acquisition Project, in Table 17.1, show a high degree of optimism, especially in cost estimates. This bears out a major contention of the study: that programs are managed more with a view to fulfilling the initial time estimates than the initial cost estimates. It also indicated a substantial variation in the extent to which costs were underestimated. The uncertainties associated with estimates of production costs are demonstrated by the data in Table 17.2, and the extent of revisions necessary on the basis of later development. The size of the average error is strongly related to the degree of technical advance sought. The variance in the error tends to be substantial and especially so for those systems in-

9. Merton J. Peck and Frederick M. Scherer, *The Weapons Acquisition Process: An Economic Analysis* (Cambridge: Harvard Graduate School of Business Administration, 1962).

corporating "large" technical advances. The final cost estimates for these systems range from about one to ten times the initial estimates.

Something must be said, however, about the methodology used in deriving the factor numbers cited in Table 17.1 and Table 17.2, and in the interpretation of those factor numbers. Very early estimates became the

TABLE 17.1 Ratio of Actual to Predicted Development Costs and Times: Weapons Development Project

Project	Cost Ratio	Time Ratio
A	4.0	1.0
B	3.5	2.3
C	5.0	1.9
D	2.0	NA
E	NA	.7
F	7.0	1.8
G	3.0	1.3
H	2.0	1.0
I	2.4	1.3
J	2.5	1.3
K	.7	1.0
L	3.0	1.4
Average	3.2	1.36

Note: NA means not available.
Source: Merton J. Peck and Frederick M. Scherer, *The Weapons Acquisitions Process: An Economic Analysis* (Cambridge: Harvard Graduate School of Business Administration, 1962), p. 22.

TABLE 17.2 Ratio of Latest Estimated Average Cost to Earliest 22 Weapons Classified According to the Degree of Technological Advance

Small	Medium	Large
1.5	2.8	1.1
1.9	2.5	1.0
0.9	2.0	0.9
1.5	1.2	5.4
0.9	0.9	1.0
1.5	1.3	10.5
		3.9
		3.6
		7.1
		7.7
Means		
1.35	1.75	4.2

Source: A. W. Marshall and W. H. Meckling, "Predictability of the Costs, Time and Success of Development," in *The Rate and Direction of Inventive Activity* (Princeton: Universities-National Bureau Committee for Economic Research, 1962), p. 472.

denominators for many of the derivations, and it is generally understood that very early estimates tend to be extremely optimistic. Most of the factors contributing to optimism have been mentioned: the tendency of new-program advocates to suppress uncertainty and to depreciate risk; the tendency to overlook or to ignore major development problems during the planning phases; and the tendency of programs to grow in scope (and hence in cost and duration) after initial approval. The effect, in each instance, is to cause factor numbers to be large. They tend, however, to shrink when estimates are based on realistic evaluations of program prospects, which generally occurs after development has proceeded to the initial test stages. Factor numbers based on estimates made at the point of what is today called Technical Development Plan approval would be considerably smaller. A recent preliminary survey suggests that the mean of cost factor numbers for one sample of major development programs of the 1960's might be 1.8 rather than the 3.2 of the original studies of 1950-60 programs.

Another circumstance that tended to bias the factor numbers generated in earlier studies was the lack of experience with certain new types of systems—particularly intercontinental ballistic missiles and high-super-sonic aircraft. That such systems would be very much more costly than experimental missiles and subsonic aircraft was not fully understood until the first generation of such weapons had gone into large-scale production.

The moral here is that the apparent size of the estimating error is not as large as once thought, though it is by no means small. Nevertheless, two different general policy conclusions can be drawn. The uncertainties associated with past development projects can be regarded as more or less inevitable, but emphasis on conducting future development programs should be placed on buying information more efficiently and economically than in the past; or development can be regarded as the same kind of activity as production, and more emphasis placed on planning development projects. The proponents of the first point of view would argue, for example, that before going ahead with a one- or two-billion-dollar commitment on the TFX program, the government should have invested $50 or $100 million in constructing and testing two or three demonstrator aircraft that embodied the key features of the F-111 design, and whose essential purpose would be to buy information. A better appreciation of the technical problems and what would be involved in solving them would, in turn, have made possible better estimates of development and production costs. It would also have caused a better appreciation of the feasibility of satisfying both the Air Force and Navy requirements with a common design. The program might have provided a much better grasp of the need for such an airplane, since need cannot be decided independent of cost.

As Table 17.2 indicates, the probability that the costs would turn out to be two or three times the initially estimated figure (which, it appears, they will) is by no means remote.

However, the second conclusion became the accepted doctrine of the McNamara administration. The job of planning the development of a new aircraft or a new missile, it was assumed, was essentially the same kind of task as planning next year's automobile—or could be made so if it were undertaken in the same manner. Programs were to proceed much more in accordance with the initial plan by two main measures: new procedures for assuring the technical planning would be done much more thoroughly, and new procedures would assure that costs would be estimated much more accurately.

The first measure called for more painstaking design studies than had been made in the past and a more stringent review of contractors' proposals (the project definition review). In the case of the C-5A airplane program, for example, some thirty-five tons of documents were delivered to the government at a cost of some $70 million.[10] Nonetheless, even in an aircraft like the C-5A, embodying relatively small advances in technology, unexpected problems did arise, leading to larger procurement costs than anticipated.

Engineering is an inexact science, and a design cannot be fully assessed from studies and wind-tunnel tests of models. A detailed and stringent review process, in addition, can fail to become a means of uncertainty resolution, and become instead a means by which uncertainty is ignored. In the case of the F-111, for example, plans were presented to the Congress for building a force of 1,700 airplanes before a single airplane of this advanced design had been flown. Apparently the efforts of its proponents to win acceptance for the program within the Pentagon, against not always rational opposition, so convinced the proponents themselves, that previous military development problems seemed irrelevant.

Blame for the past errors in cost estimates was not placed so much on the inherent uncertainties as on the incentives provided to industry and the military services to underestimate the costs of new programs. It is true, as Tables 17.1 and 17.2 indicate, that earlier estimates did contain a good deal of optimism. However, there is a substantial variation in the size of the errors. Although cost-estimating techniques can produce estimates of development and procurement costs that may be much less biased than contractor's estimates, they cannot produce accurate estimates of the minimum costs likely to be involved in acquiring a new kind of capability. Cost estimates cannot provide a reasonable substitute for market information. Even in the case of fixed-price contractors for items of aircraft

10. From a public statement of Robert Charles, Assistant Secretary of the Air Force for Financial Management.

technology already developed, the difference between the lowest and the highest technically acceptable bids can average 100 per cent.[11] Since cost estimates are based on relationships derived from past programs, all that independent cost estimates can provide as a yardstick is a means to help insure that the amount of inefficiency associated with past programs—or the rate at which inefficiency has been increasing—will not become greater in the future.

To motivate defense contractors to perform more efficiently, and to encourage them to apply closer cost controls, the McNamara reforms emphasized incentive contracts instead of cost-plus contracts in development, and negotiated-fixed-price contracts in procurement. In development work, the kind of incentive contract that has been commonly used is a "cost-plus-incentive-fee contract"; it differs from an ordinary cost-plus contract in that the size of the fee is controlled by the extent to which actual costs fall below or exceed a predetermined target cost. The size of the fee also depends on the success of the contractors in meeting a specified delivery date and specified performance characteristics. In procurement, the type of incentive contract commonly used is a fixed-price incentive contract. Unlike an ordinary negotiated-fixed-price contract, the contractor here is allowed a higher profit rate if actual costs fall below those initially negotiated.

The effectiveness of incentive contracts is highly sensitive to the government's ability to predict accurately the performance and technical characteristics of new weapons systems, and to predict the minimum costs of new weapons systems. If it were possible to make fairly accurate estimates of cost and performance characteristics, and if once development were started the Defense Department could disengage itself from the development process and leave contractors entirely responsible, incentive contracts could achieve their intended purpose. But the new planning measures have not succeeded in eliminating the uncertainties associated with development. In the case of the F-111 and C-5A programs, actual costs apparently will be about twice those initially estimated.[12] And the government does not become disengaged from the management of such projects.

To be sure, incentive contracts and improved cost estimating procedures have meant that the overruns in development projects are not as large as they were in the 1950's. The arithmetical means of errors in estimating costs was about 3.2; it now seems to be about 2.[13] Even so, a strong

11. G. R. Hall and R. E. Johnson, *Competition in the Procurement of Military Hard Goods,* The RAND Corporation.

12. That there are mitigating circumstances in both cases does not alter the importance of the two outcomes: the scale of the estimating error is large even though extreme measures were taken to avoid precisely that occurrence.

13. Recall the cautions earlier stated about the validity of factor numbers generated in early studies of programs of the 1950's.

tendency still remains to make modifications after the initiation of development projects, and to make them at government expense. A 1968 RAND study based on an analysis of 745 incentive contracts indicated that the cost of modifications and supplemental changes borne by the government actually came to about three times the amounts specified in the initial contracts.[14]

There is nothing inherently wrong with altering goals during development; it can, in fact, make systems less expensive to procure. However, contractors have a strong financial incentive to propose modifications that will result in more costly rather than less costly systems, and the tendency is not materially affected by the kind of incentive contracts used in development projects. Even if the effect of making such modifications were to lower profits made in development, the reduction could be made up several times over from additional profits earned in production. And until fairly recently, almost all procurement contracts were negotiated only after development had been completed, and on the basis of what it would cost to procure what had been developed.

The incentive contracts used in production work supply an incentive not only to reduce costs but also to bargain for higher target prices under circumstances in which the contractor—selected as the sole supplier, and not in a simple price competition—has an important advantage in the bargaining process. It is an open question which incentive plays a larger role: finding ways to reduce costs, or bargaining for higher prices. But if there were a real incentive to reduce costs, there should also be evidence to indicate that contracts providing for larger profit rates (and hence larger incentives to reduce costs) were associated with larger underruns than contracts providing smaller sharing rates. But the RAND study found no evidence of such a relationship, and no other evidence to indicate that incentive contracts make contractors more cost conscious.[15]

To provide better financial incentives for developing systems that are less expensive to procure, and to find a way around the lock-in effect, the Defense Department in the C-5A transport aircraft program introduced the concept of "total package procurement." Under this concept a fixed price incentive contract is awarded, on the basis of competitive bids, prior to the inception of development for the entire development and procurement program. The contract not only provided that the government and the contractor would share in an underrun below the target cost; it also provided that if costs were to exceed 135 per cent of the target cost, any additional costs would be entirely borne by the contractor. Since total program costs have exceeded estimated costs by a good deal more than

14. Irving N. Fisher, *A Reappraisal of Incentive Contracting Experience,* The RAND Corporation, RM-5700-PR, June 1968, pp. 28-29.

15. *Ibid.,* pp. 19-26.

35 per cent, a major dispute has arisen between the Defense Department and the contractors over who should be held responsible. The issue is essentially whether all work ultimately charged to the program was appropriately defined in the original version of the "total program."

Whatever the merits of the specific arguments, it can scarcely be denied that Armed Services Procurement Regulations have provided the services with an increasing amount of authority to intervene directly in decisions ordinarily regarded as the prerogatives of private management: tasks that will be performed by the contractor, and tasks that will be performed by subcontractors, the compensation of employees, the approach to be taken in the conduct of development programs, and the manner in which contractors will make their production preparations. If contractors do not have the technical responsibility for a program, it is difficult to see how they can be made to assume the financial responsibility.

In almost any kind of activity, poor incentives for good performance will almost inevitably lead to centralized direction and control. Hence the Defense Department is heavily involved in management of weapons systems programs. The aerospace industries are not "private" from the point of view of their managements, at least in the generally accepted sense of the word, nor do their profits represent a return on risk-taking. Although incentive contracts may help to maintain the fiction, they do not change the reality of dependency.

How, then, should military research and development projects be planned and organized to make development more efficient, and their products less costly? The drive for major and dramatic technological breakthroughs should be reflected selectively in weapons systems development planning. Not every new system needs to be a significant forward stride in the state of the art. There are, however, occasions when ambitious development programs are warranted—in those instances involving major technical advance. The ingredients of an appropriate strategy for such a program are as follows:

Flexible or Opportunistic Planning.[16] The art of flexible planning consists of three main elements: First, the initial planning is done in terms of broad, yet quite definite objectives rather than in terms of detailed requirements (yet indefinite objectives). Second, substantial emphasis is placed on identifying the major uncertainties and on mounting a carefully planned campaign to overcome them. Third, pending the outcome of the campaign, plans are made that can incorporate new information relatively

16. For a fuller discussion of flexible planning see Burton H. Klein, "The Decision-Making Problem in Development," in *The Rate and Direction of Inventive Activity* (Princeton: Princeton University Press, 1962). For a superb book on the pure theory of opportunistic planning, see Howard Raiffa, *Decision-Making Analysis* (Reading, Mass.: Addison-Wesley, 1968).

easily. Flexible or opportunistic planning has been mainly associated with highly successful R&D organizations. But such a style of planning is congenial to all organizations that are compelled to be risk-takers; they need not be satisfied with initial estimates (criminal law offices, stockbrokers, and the DOD's Special Forces, for example).

Early Testing. The best way to find out about the problems actually likely to be encountered is to get equipment into test early, in however rudimentary a form. Notwithstanding what has sometimes been said about the futility of testing articles that are not truly representative of a production configuration, partial testing is infinitely better than none at all.

Parallel Approaches to Buy Time. Often the success of a program will hinge on overcoming some key technological bottlenecks (an engine with particular performance characteristics, the application to a new airplane of a recently made advance in aerodynamics, the availability of a new kind of tube for a radar). In some cases alternatives can be found in other programs. For example, if United States military aircraft had to wait for the engines initially planned for them, most of them would have been two or three years longer in development. (In Britain, the number of successful matings has actually been less than the number that would be determined by chance.) But in some cases the organization engaged in the development work has to manufacture its own alternatives. And in such instances parallel approaches not only can result in substantial time saving but also, sometimes, money saving. Programs that are missing essential technological ingredients are not always canceled for that reason; rather, they have a tendency to go on and on.

Minimal Manning of Individual Tasks. When a development program turns out to be highly successful (that is, it furnishes a very promising system at a modest cost), the success is not uncommonly due to the ideas of a small handful of key people (usually including the project leaders). But manning military development projects on the scale at which most of them are manned typically involves saturating these more gifted people with co-ordination tasks; in other words, complexity substitutes for ingenuity. Another way of saying this is that organizations that do well in development are discriminating and tend to put their best people on problems that are really important.

An Organization Designed to Live with Uncertainty. If one speaks of organizations in terms of "hierarchical" style of decision-making (Ford, General Motors, and the U.S. Air Force), and "flat" or decentralized style (universities and foundations), a good R&D organization (or any other that must absorb risks and in which rapid learning is possible) contains elements of both. Such an organization must be unstructured and possess a very small group of key people (two or three) who are capable of making a "hard-nosed" evaluation of the results of the research. Psychologists speak of such organizations as having a high degree of internal tension;

sociologists, as having a high sense of mission.[17] Both are right: tension is produced in at least some of the people because they feel insecure about their place in the organization; there are others who prize the mission of the organization above that of the local departments; and of the latter group, there are some who seem positively to enjoy the role of an operator. On the whole such organizations probably attract people with a much greater tolerance of ambiguity than organizations that are more feudalistic in their definition of authority and responsibility.

Although these principles have been listed as separate points, they are, in fact, all part of the same pattern. It seems quite unlikely that an organization can be found that understands the art of opportunistic planning but is opposed to change. Conversely, it is difficult to envision an organization whose leaders decry "wasteful" duplication as more than a general principle, and at the same time possess the requisite mental attitudes to deal with problems of uncertainty.

Over the past twenty-five years there have been frequent, serious, and well-intentioned efforts to improve the way the system acquisition process is managed by the military services. In the main, the tendency has been to enlarge the structure of project management, expand the regulatory and directive literature, and increase both the manning and the duration of major acquisition programs.

As noted earlier, errors in estimating program outcomes are not as high as they were ten or fifteen years ago, but it is not clear that the improvement is real rather than methodological, or that it reflects greater effectiveness in the processes of development management. In some few cases where the principles enunciated in the preceding section have been applied, there have been some striking improvements in cost, time, and success of development. In one interesting recent instance two companies built very similar aircraft in a real if informal competition, but Company A did so under the coverage of a standard development contract sponsored by one of the military services while Company B funded the work privately and honored most of the precepts of unmilitary development. The outcome was roughly the same for both: the first test article did not perform quite as well as predicted and extensive redesign had to be undertaken. But Company A spent about ten times as much as Company B to get that result, and employed perhaps six or eight times as many engineers over a period that was somewhat longer.

The moral would seem to be that it is not planning that needs to be elaborated and refined, as was the conclusion of the McNamara-era Defense Department, but rather that the authorities charged with the difficult and onerous assignments of systems acquisition must learn to live with the uncertainty, ambiguity, and lack of assurance that characterize real research

17. See Tom Burns and G. M. Stalker, *Management of Innovation* (New York: Barnes and Noble, 1961).

and development. Rearrangement of the various boxes to which functions are assigned on organizational charts is not a sufficient remedy: it has been tried with indifferent success for nearly twenty years. Nor is the issuance of new and stricter regulatory orders. What is needed is a striking reformation of both concept and application with two general aims: increasing the establishment's propensity to take risks and to tolerate ambiguity, and carefully disengaging the discrete interests of the supplier (the defense industry) from those of the consumer (the military services).

The establishment's propensity to take risks might conceivably be encouraged in extreme fashion, for example, by reduction of the compulsory retirement age of officers to forty-five, as in the Israeli military establishment, or, taking some highly dynamic United States corporations as a model, by massive top-level civilian interference in the military selection process.

The main danger in these kinds of approaches is that although a high degree of innovativeness is wanted in some DOD activities, a high degree of conservatism may be wanted in others. There is a good deal to be said for a military establishment that is much more flexible in its technological planning; there also may be an inner wisdom in military establishments conducting certain kinds of planning in terms of "worst" cases: it produces a system of mutual deterrence based on each side's grossly exaggerating the capabilities of the other. It should be noted, however, that "worst case" planning can also contribute directly to sustaining the arms race, as argued in Chapter 8.

The problem would seem to consist in finding some way to permit the R&D function to be carried out in a more rational manner, without causing major transformation of the personality of the military establishment. One possibility would be to encourage the services to develop R&D establishments of their own different in personality from their parent organizations. Dozens of committees have reviewed the R&D procedures of the services, and generally agree: what is needed is a planning and management of R&D that places its main emphasis on people rather than on ritualistic patterns of procedure. But military organizations are by nature inclined to favor institutional discipline and formal procedures.

Another alternative would be the establishment of more direct and comprehensive civilian control over the R&D and procurement functions now the province of the military services. There is evidence that civilians in charge of R&D are not as determined to seek "nothing but the best," and much more willing to face up to uncertainties.[18] The danger in creating an

18. NASA, of course, is a major exception, but for reasons that are fairly apparent: by virtue of its failure to accept the truism that safe exploration of space can best be accomplished in unmanned vehicles, it has been forced to become even much more averse to risk than the military establishment. Moreover, it was also caught up in the problem of planning against a highly specific timetable.

agency that would be entirely responsible for the military establishment's R&D function, however, is that it would cease to be independent; that it would be annexed to the military requirements function, as seems to have happened in Britain. Moreover, there almost certainly would be strong political objections to such a far-reaching measure.

A more sensible organizational reform, although it also would run into establishmentarian objections, would be to create an independent civilian organization for the special purpose of conducting exploratory development projects and major weapons systems projects that involve ambitious advances in technology. Were this its purpose, there would be no need to develop a large organization; to a very substantial extent it could rely on existing organizations and test facilities. Such an agency, if properly constituted, could be freer of the traditional service problems of risk aversion and intolerance of ambiguity. The fact of such an organization in the buyers' market for new technology could have a salutary effect on the services, and on the defense industry.

There are also substantial advantages to a deliberate policy of establishing major system acquisition programs as discrete undertakings, each conducted by an organization that will be abolished upon completion of the development-production effort. Such an organization would be capable of accepting ambiguities and of planning for an uncertain technological future because the stake of the participating program personnel would be in the quality of their performance rather than the stability—permanence—of the local organization. Programs could be entrusted to the usual mix of military and civilian engineers, without risk of excessive technological conservatism, if the development organization reported directly to senior civilians—preferably appointed for specific terms rather than tenured—who in the nature of their outlook would be less averse to risk and less likely to avoid uncertainty than senior military officials. Such programs of that general nature have been surprisingly successful in special circumstances in the past:

There is another problem quite as important from the viewpoint of economy and efficiency in defense, which is that of getting the services to make better use of available technology. For example, it may be assumed that one day the tank will become as vulnerable to antitank weapons (if it is not already) as the horse is to a 50-caliber machine gun. It also may be assumed that the day will come (if it has not come) when the large manned aircraft will be made obsolete by the missile. But for the purpose of budgetary planning, when should it be assumed that day has arrived? One way to assure that a decision to innovate will not be postponed for many years is to have the Secretary of Defense or the President appoint a specially qualified commission, which will weigh the evidence and render a decision—in effect, forcing the establishment to absorb more risks.

A decisive effect in increasing the propensity of the services to make hard choices could be achieved also if the President fixed the budget for the Department of Defense as a whole, directing the Secretary of Defense to limit the amounts that could be spent on individual major program packages, at the same time allowing the military services somewhat more freedom to make substitutions within the programs. The fault of the present method of planning and programming is that it constrains the quantity of forces (the number of divisions, offensive missiles, tactical air wings, etc.) more than it does the budget; thus the services have fewer real incentives to make the unit costs of defense less costly. And only by rigid budget ceilings can the rising level of expectations that has dominated so much military thinking and planning finally be halted. To make sure that a sufficiently large number of alternatives was examined, the Congress might insist that alternatives developed in other countries (Swedish tanks and fighter airplanes, French fighters, British aircraft engines and radar, for example) should be explicitly considered before the adoption of a major program in this country.

Three measures—civilian control of R&D (to provide a wider menu of technology), program-oriented development (to protect against the effects of organizational inertia and excessive procedural regulation), and specially appointed *ad hoc* commissions (to ensure a better use of existing technology)—may represent the best currently feasible ways of regulating the defense R&D establishment. There are possible dangers in providing the Secretary of Defense still greater authority, but in the longer run, surely an effective system of checks and balances cannot be based on getting precisely the "right" balance of power between the Secretary of Defense and the Joint Chiefs of Staff. It must be based, rather, on building effective machinery on defense matters into the Executive Office of the President and on establishing a more informed and more effective loyal opposition in the Congress.

The government, the only purchaser of expensive military hardware, is in a good position to drive hard bargains. Defense companies, for their part, at least as indicated by their experience to date, have no very attractive options and are not in a very good bargaining position. If the Defense Department wished to enforce low cost behavior or greater efficiency in production, it has many opportunities to do so. It might use "fixed commitment" contracts for development. The Defense Department officials might say, in effect, to a contractor: "We will give you $10 million to develop some experimental or prototype hardware aimed at meeting this particular need as well as possible. If we like what we see we may do business with you; if not, we certainly won't." The same thing can be and has been done with cost-plus contracts (though it was some fifteen years ago). Or the Department could insist, in advance, on compulsory licensing when development was completed.

More is needed than mere expansion of civilian control. If a civilian agency were engaged in the planning and supervision of such projects, it could reasonably be assumed there would be a difference, but no one can be certain that the civilian agency would not sooner or later become the regulated agency. (The experience of present regulatory agencies is one reason for cynicism.) Further, civilian officials in the Defense Department so far have failed to insist on a toughter set of ground rules.

In any serious public discussion of measures that would alter the present relationship between the military services and the defense industry, two questions need to be carefully examined:

1. If a package procurement concept (i.e., a single contract for development and production) is used for financing the development of aircraft, missiles, or electronic systems, should not the government follow the practices used by the airlines, using fixed-price contracts, with sharp penalties for nonperformance? No government project office would confuse the matter of responsibility. Also, private companies could develop experimental hardware with their own funds to demonstrate the key features of a promising system design. The extent of private risk-taking is uncertain, but there would certainly be more than there has been, and the costs of development would not be the costs of government-financed development projects.

2. Why should not nonprofit corporations or university and government laboratories be used as the preferred instrumentalities for achieving advances in technology that private companies are not willing to finance?[19]

(a) Personnel: The available evidence indicates that organizations like the M.I.T. Instrumentation Laboratory and the Caltech Jet Propulsion Laboratory attract good people; salaries are commensurate with those in defense companies (except for top executive posts). It is true that many of the service laboratories have assumed the personality characteristics of the parent organizations, but new laboratories would be responsive to civilian management of R&D.

(b) Incentives: It might well be possible to avoid the perverse incentives growing out of the interrelationship between production and research and development, with profits essentially a function of the unit cost of the system. Since government laboratories and university laboratories have seldom engaged in systems projects, evidence on this proposition is scanty, but what there is supports it strongly.[20]

(c) Governmental control: If nonprofit organizations do not stand to gain financially by developing more expensive items more expensively,

19. For a paper in which a concept very similar to proposition 2 was advanced some years ago, see Carl Kaysen, "Improving the Efficiency of Military Research and Development," *Public Policy*, XII (Cambridge: Harvard University Press, 1963), pp. 219-273.

20. The Sidewinder versus the Falcon, work done on guidance systems at the M.I.T. Instrumentation Laboratory versus work done in industry, Jet Propulsion Laboratory projects versus similar projects in industry, and the development of the Jupiter at the Redstone Arsenal.

the degree of government regulation and control required might be less than it is with respect to profit-making concerns.

(d) Monopoly: If such agencies concentrate on exploratory and advanced development projects, it might be easier to avoid the danger of monopoly in procurement. Industry spokesmen will question the additional costs involved in transferring the technology to private industry. However, available evidence suggests that economies involved in closely integrating development and production are not great (not likely to be more than an approximate 5 or 10 per cent of total R&D and procurement costs). This question deserves further examination.

(e) Transformation of nonprofit organizations: There is, of course, a danger that these institutions will lose their vitality and be transformed into old-fashioned military arsenals. But does the arsenalization of the aerospace companies represent any less danger?

Probably the most important advantage in separating development from production and in conducting development in an environment protected from production pressures is the substantial minimizing of the incentives to push newly developed systems into the operational inventory. More systems might enter development, but development would tend on the whole to be cheaper, and in the end fewer types of weapons systems could be introduced into operation, production runs of those introduced could be a good deal larger, and production could be concentrated in fewer companies. There is promise of sizable gains in economy and efficiency—at the same time contributing substantially toward a further diminution of the arms race.

18

Military Sponsorship
of Science and Research

The American public has shown its greatest willingness to support science on its own terms when it was most clearly related to national defense and security, or when it could be related to national political prestige. The greatest periods of scientific development in American history, therefore, have tended to follow military crises. New war-generated scientific institutions fostered and developed fundamental science in postwar periods.

The history of the relationship between science and politics can be interpreted as the struggle of the scientific community to retain and institutionalize in times of peace the public support and the institutional independence which have been granted to it in times of military emergency. This relationship has generated great advantages for the development of science but has also exacted a high price in terms of the dependence of science both for financial support and for political autonomy on public interest in and concern with national security and external prestige.

There is a paradox in this relationship. Scientists and scientific institutions have attained greater political influence during wartime, but basic science and scientific education have been subordinated to applied research. Nevertheless, the institutional structure developed in wartime to foster military applied science has been redirected in peace toward the generation of a new level of support for basic science and education and a new status for the scientific community in the national polity.

All this has not always been easy for the scientific community to accept. In the ideology of science, applied purpose is conceived in terms of service to mankind as a whole, rather than to the nation-state. The historical role of military-scientific dependency has been a source of tension between the scientific community and the political structure, and sometimes a serious problem of conscience for the more thoughtful leaders of the scientific community. This tension is especially acute in the contemporary scene because so much financial support, even for the most basic science, comes directly or indirectly from agencies with a military-related purpose, because contemporary scientific technology has eroded what used to be the rather clear-cut boundaries between pure and applied science, and because the potential use of the products of applied science in a nuclear age has compelled many scientists to regard themselves as accessories to a threat to human survival.

Important scientific institutions have been created in times of emergency, or to support military functions, but also to "bootleg" more fundamental science. The history of the Naval Observatory provides such an example; in the words of A. Hunter Dupree, "The Naval Observatory is the classic example of the surreptitious creation of a scientific institution by underlings in the executive branch of the government in the very shadow of congressional disapproval."[1] It was introduced under the guise of a "Depot of Charts and Instruments," ostensibly to standardize chronometers on naval ships for navigation purposes. In 1841 Lieutenant James M. Gilliss, an intense young naval officer who "wished to prove that naval officers could accomplish good work in science," convinced a House committee that studies in hydrography, astronomy, magnetism, and meteorology were essential for the practical business of the Navy, and succeeded in obtaining money for a new building, still under the guise of the Depot. Today the U.S. Naval Observatory, with a new modern telescope in Flagstaff, Arizona, is the world center of astrometric observations—the precise measurement of the positions of stars. It is the source of time and star position standards for virtually the whole world and a leading center of fundamental research on comets.

In the early nineteenth century the scientific exploration of the largely unknown American continent was a frontier of contemporary science comparable to space exploration today. The military services took the lead in this activity from the very beginning. Both Lewis and Clark, for instance, were officers with considerable military experience, although their expedition to the West was not conducted under Army auspices, but under a special appropriation secured by President Andrew Jackson from the Congress. By 1830 the Corps of Topographical Engineers was in process of becoming a scientific corps of the Army with special training and skill in continental exploration. It provided logistic support for private scientific undertakings and frequently turned over its collections to private scientists for further study and analysis. It loaned its officers to help in surveying for

1. A. Hunter Dupree, *Science in the Federal Government* (Cambridge: Harvard University Press, 1957), p. 62.

the railroads, and often made them available to help private enterprise with civil engineering problems. Military expeditions and surveys were better staffed and supported than were most of the civilian projects of the same period.

This pattern of military-civilian collaboration finds its modern counterpart in the United States Antarctic program, for which the U.S. Navy provides the ships, aircraft, and base operations, while the scientific program is conducted in part by civilian academic scientists financed by grants from the National Science Foundation.

The early history of the National Academy of Sciences illustrates how a rather ineffectual war-created scientific institution was converted into the most influential and prestigious body of American science. A conspiratorial atmosphere surrounded the creation of the academy by congressional charter in 1863. A small group of government and academic scientists prevailed upon Senator Henry Wilson of Massachusetts to introduce the bill at the last minute of a lame-duck Congress, and it was passed and signed by President Abraham Lincoln the same night. The principal provision of the bill was that

> . . . the Academy shall, whenever called upon by any Department of the Government, investigate, examine, experiment, and report upon any subject of science or art, the actual expense of such investigations, examinations, experiments, and reports to be paid from appropriations which may be made for the purpose, but the Academy shall receive no compensation whatever for any service to the Government of the United States.[2]

The academy still operates under these provisions today, although it has burgeoned into a large organization with an annual budget of over $30 million, 4,000 scientific advisers, and 400 professional staff members.

The history of the National Academy of Sciences reflects tension between the relative claims of basic and applied science. Although it had been created to advise the government on practical matters of military interest, under the leadership of Joseph Henry after the Civil War the emphasis rapidly shifted from practical service to the government toward the recognition and promotion of "abstract science." Henry proposed that nobody should be "elected into it who had not earned the distinction by actual discoveries enlarging the field of human knowledge."

In each war it became necessary to create a new institutional mechanism to deal with the requirements of military technology, while between wars these new organizations of science tended to revert toward emphasis on basic science. Thus was the National Research Council created for World War I, and the Office of Scientific Research and Development created for World War II. But, as in the Civil War, the institutions created in the heat

2. *Ibid.*, pp. 139-141.

of war emergency hung on in peace, relatively deprived of financial support, but still serving as a nucleus or model for the generation of a broader and deeper national scientific base.

Just as the National Academy of Science was born of the Civil War, the National Research Council was the progeny of World War I. Its creation was sparked by strong pro-allied leadership within the NAS, especially by George Ellery Hale, the astronomer, and Robert A. Millikan, the physicist. The objectives of NRC, however, were not narrowly military. Hale and his group had in mind also a longer-range aim of reforming the research institutions of the country. "It was recognized from the outset," he wrote, "that the activities of the committee should not be confined to the promotion of researches bearing directly on military problems, but that true preparedness would best result from the encouragement of every form of investigation, whether for military or industrial application, or for the advancement of knowledge without regard to its immediate practical bearing."[3] In the organization of NRC, stress was laid on "burying the hatchet" between pure and applied research, and on the potential value of the alliance between scientists and engineers.

A key figure in the success of NRC was General G. O. Squier, chief signal officer of the Army. A graduate of West Point with a Ph.D. from Johns Hopkins, he was impressed with the value of research and filled with the military man's willingness to take responsibility. He asked the NRC to act as advisory agent to the Signal Corps, and before long he had all the members of the Physics Committee of NRC commissioned and in uniform. At this time, in contrast to the situation in World War II, there was no mechanism for channeling funds for military purposes into civilian agencies, and the commissioning of civilian scientists appeared to be the best solution. In 1918, for example, the NRC Division of Medicine and Related Sciences was reorganized under the chairmanship of commissioned medical officers. As a result of the collaboration between civilian scientists and the military, "the record of medicine in the war was so outstanding that it introduced a new era of warfare in which the diseases that had once ravaged armies and civilians alike were kept under control."[4] This was not so much due to research during the war as it was a result of benefiting through better administration and facilities from the accumulated discoveries and knowledge of the prewar years. "The stimulating effects of the war," wrote Dupree, were "to be found in the mass of clinical opportunities and the general shaking up of the whole profession rather than in the research program and resultant discoveries from it."[5]

It was also through NRC and the war experience that psychology

3. *Ibid.*, p. 310.
4. *Ibid.*, p. 316.
5. *Ibid.*, p. 316.

emerged as an independent science. Faced with sorting out the mass of draftees, the Army turned to NRC to develop tests and procedures for selecting men for the specialized tasks required in an increasingly technological style of warfare. The success of these tests and procedures "ultimately converted psychology into a word to conjure with in the United States Army" and provided the foundation of experience and confidence which was to enable the United States to take an international lead in developing psychology and the other social sciences in the period after World War I.

These examples indicate that the wartime NRC became a central directing agency for American science to a degree unprecedented in earlier history. It brought together academic and industrial scientists in a common effort. The problem-oriented, coordinated interdisciplinary approach to large-scale practical problems became a common experience of the leaders and potential leaders of a whole generation of scientists.

Yet, surprisingly, NRC never became a large dispenser of government funds, as did OSRD during World War II. Most of the early work of its committees was done with private funds, and when the promise of practical results appeared, the work was usually transferred to a military service and the scientists commissioned as officers. For the most part, the function of NRC was to mobilize and coordinate existing skills and knowledge at the price of stopping all basic research and robbing the colleges and universities of their best brains. But this was temporary; the organizations created and the new interactions generated brought a new era of scientific advance, which by the 1930's had brought the United States to the forefront of world science.

The wartime NRC, made permanent by executive order in May 1918 under the authority of the National Academy Act of 1863, largely took over the academy's responsibility to advise the government on request. Its membership, however, was not restricted to the NAS membership, selected primarily for contributions to basic research, but became more broadly representative of the national scientific community. The duties of the NRC included the stimulation of research in the mathematical, physical, and biological sciences and "in the application of these sciences to engineering, medicine, and the other useful arts."

However, the country was not yet ready for the intimate marriage of science and government which followed World War II, and NRC became almost wholly separate from government, dependent exclusively on private funds. The Rockefeller and Carnegie foundations became principal sources of support, providing a permanent building and endowment. In its somewhat reduced sphere the NRC did effective work. As a result of discussions in NRC initiated in 1918 by George Vincent, president of the Rockefeller Foundation, postdoctoral fellowships in physics and chemistry, administered by NRC with Rockefeller funds, were established at the same time NRC was set up on a permanent basis by executive order.[6] The NRC fellowships helped the United States achieve a greater place in world science. The leadership of World War II research effort was recruited largely from this group. The NRC also sponsored the publication of a series of reports in basic physical science, and stimulated the rapid assimilation of the new quantum mechanics.

At the time of general public repudiation of internationalism between the world wars, a plan prepared by the National Academy of Sciences led to the formation of an International Research Council, converted in 1931 into the International Council of Scientific Unions (ICSU). Throughout the period of American isolationism Congress paid the small dues of this council through a provision in the State Department appropriation bill.

During the period between the wars military activities were severely contracted, and military research along with them. As late as 1938 more than 40 per cent of federal funds for research were spent by the Department of Agriculture. In 1934 a board headed by former Secretary of War Newton D. Baker recommended increased appropriations for research and development; military research had doubled by 1936. But as the war clouds approached, the Army General Staff reacted paradoxically with a report to the effect that "the Army needs large quantities of excellent equipment that has already been developed," but went on to say that "the amount of funds allocated to Research and Development in former years is in excess of the proper proportion for the item in consideration of the rearmament program." The Army apparently assumed that the coming war would be fought with existing weapons and would not be greatly influenced by technology, least of all science-based technology. No judgment could have been more wrong. This event throws in stark relief the revolution in science-government relations that was about to be precipitated by the advent of World War II.[7]

World War I was essentially a production war. The problems were for the most part those of improvement and adaptation of existing weapons and of organizing technical resources for war on an unprecedented scale—whether for production of weapons and aircraft, the medical care of millions of troops, or the selection and testing of an avalanche of recruits. The course of World War I was not decisively affected by contemporary technology, though it drew heavily on the accumulated knowledge and skill of the recent past. By contrast, in World War II the very course of the war was changed by weapons which had not even been conceived or were in a pristine state of development at the outset of hostilities. At the same time

6. *Ibid.*, pp. 327-330.
7. *Ibid.*, p. 367.

scientists operated much more independently of the military. In part, they defined their own problems and took the responsibility for selling not only new techniques but also new strategies to go with them to the military services. Scientists appeared in the battle zones as civilians, flying with bombing missions to observe the operations of new equipment, nursing experimental equipment on the battlefield or in the war at sea.

Many of the advances of World War II were generated initially in the laboratory. Warner Schilling has christened this style the "whole problem approach,"[8] in which the scientists "were eventually able to persuade the soldiers to inform them of the general military problems involved in order that the scientists might reach their own conclusions about the kinds of weapons and devices the military would need to meet those problems." In many cases the most important contribution of the scientists turned out to be not a specific device but the reformulation of the problem. This mode of operation led to a new "generalist" science known as operations research, the intellectual ancestor of a host of new postwar developments with considerable impact on business management and public policy.[9]

At the outset of World War II the NRC mechanism of World War I was rejected as inadequate, although the academy and NRC themselves played the role of midwife to the new organizational arrangements. The basic weakness of NRC lay in the fact that, as a nongovernmental organization, it could not serve as a channel for the enormous appropriations for a technological war. The device of commissioning civilian scientists into the appropriate military services did not leave sufficient independent judgment to the scientists. Science in World War II was mobilized out of uniform, and its direction was kept firmly in civilian hands. The fact that scientists and military planners collaborated as equals made possible a much greater interpenetration of military and scientific thinking than had occurred in World War I, at least outside the medical area.

The establishment of the National Defense Research Committee (NDRC) in 1940 and of the Office of Scientific Research and Development in 1941 drew together many threads of policy. Although NDRC nominally by-passed the National Academy and the NRC, in practice, it made extensive use of their resources. Following the precedent of the National Advisory Committee for Aeronautics (NACA), it relied on the committee form of organization with a predominance of independent membership,

8. Warner R. Schilling, "Scientists, Foreign Policy, and Politics," in *Scientists and National Policy-Making,* Robert Gilpin and Christopher Wright, eds. (New York: Columbia University Press, 1963), pp. 144-173.

9. Cf., for example, Bruce L. R. Smith, *The Rand Corporation* (Cambridge: Harvard University Press, 1966), esp. pp. 6-14; also, P. M. Morse and G. E. Kimball, *Methods of Operations Research* (New York: John Wiley, 1951). And see Chapter 23.

but with military representation. At the outset it determined not to build or operate laboratories of its own, but instead to develop contracts with universities and industrial firms, selecting the contractor best qualified for the job without reference to geographical considerations. The research and development contract was a new social invention, an open-ended device using the legal form of procurement but without any clear specification of the end product. The principle of payment of full costs, including indirect or overhead expenses, was fully recognized for the first time. The contract device permitted scientists, especially university scientists, to work on military problems within an organizational environment in which they were comfortable, with colleagues whom they trusted and under management they knew and respected.

The weakness of NDRC lay in the lack of a mechanism for transition from laboratory weapons to the battlefield and for coordination of its research with that carried on in military laboratories and the NACA. As a result OSRD was created by executive order in June 1941, and Dr. Vannevar Bush, one of the four dominant members of NDRC, became the full-time head of the new office, within which the NDRC committee structure was incorporated. According to the order, OSRD was to "serve as a center for mobilization of the scientific personnel and resources of the nation in order to assure maximum utilization of such personnel and resources in developing and applying the results of scientific research to defense purposes."

As in previous national emergencies, basic research was largely abandoned and OSRD became the agent for deployment of the accumulated scientific skills and knowledge which had been built up between the wars. It was dominated by the academic science community, especially the nuclear physicists, whose experience in designing and building particle accelerators and in working with high-speed electronics in nuclear instrumentation was ideally adapted to the requirements for work with microwave radar and other weapons requiring sophisticated electronics or a "systems" approach. Nuclear physicists were at home with the "problem approach." They had been their own engineers, with experience in dealing with industrial suppliers, and they were accustomed to tackling technical problems that lay in their path even though outside their nominal field of specialization. What the experience of OSRD contributed to the development of American science was largely an appreciation for what could be accomplished with the resources, scale of effort, and multi-disciplinary collaboration characteristic of the war laboratories. It also made society aware that basic scientists were not necessarily ivory tower scholars remote from the practical world, that on the contrary they could turn their hands to engineering problems often much more effectively than engineers trained more narrowly in existing technologies. The Manhattan

Project, of course, illustrated with particularly dramatic force the relevance of even the most esoteric and theoretical science to the problems of national power.

However, unlike NRC, the Office of Scientific Research and Development and the National Defense Research Committee were never conceived as permanent organizations. They were created with the deliberate intention of being dismantled after the emergency, undoubtedly in part because scientific leaders believed such an organization far too centralized to be suitable for a permanent structure of American science. Its architects felt that the traditional pluralism of the American scientific establishment must be permitted to reassert itself.

Much of the postwar era may be characterized as a struggle to civilianize military science. First, the Atomic Energy Commission, created in the McMahon Act of 1946, sought to civilianize the management of atomic energy. Then much of the military medical research program of NDRC was taken over by the Public Health Service through the embryonic National Institutes of Health, previously primarily an in-house operation. This program remained relatively small until its dramatic expansion in 1956. Then later, when space technology began to emerge from the military programs, under the impact of Sputnik, the NACA was in 1958 converted into the National Aeronautics and Space Administration (NASA) and assumed the mission of developing the new space technology and its nonmilitary applications under civilian management. Most recently, as oceanography and ocean engineering have begun to emerge as significant technologies, moves began to provide an appropriate civilian agency.[10]

Even the earliest move toward taking over the wartime programs of OSRD, the creation of the Office of Naval Research, can be interpreted as an effort to civilianize military research. For the emphasis shifted rather abruptly from short-term military research and development to long-range basic research with a relatively tenuous relationship to military requirements. Indeed, it was the Office of Naval Research (ONR) established in 1945 by act of Congress which set the pattern for the adaptation of the method and style of OSRD to the support of basic research by the federal government. The individual most responsible for defining the research mission of ONR in the legislation, Captain R. D. Conrad, head of the Planning Division of the predecessor Office of Research and Inventions (ORI), inserted into the enabling act the stress on the importance to the Navy of "pure and imaginative" research. ONR was set up with an admiral as chief and a civilian scientist, the "chief scientist," as his principal deputy.

10. President's Science Advisory Committee, "Effective Use of the Sea," The White House, 1967.

The heart of ONR was the research division, staffed for the most part by civilian scientists and engineers attracted by the opportunity of working closely with the outside scientific community, especially the academic scientists who were returning from the OSRD laboratories to their home universities.

In its initial operations, ONR followed closely the pattern of OSRD. It made contracts with private agencies, chiefly universities. But in contrast to wartime, these contracts stressed basic research rather than development. The academic community at first reacted to military support with mixed feelings. The fear of federal control, especially from a military agency, was strong in the scientific community, and wartime experience, despite close working relations between military officers and scientists, had not been an entirely happy one from the standpoint of the scientists. Security restrictions and compartmentalization of research on a "need to know" basis had been especially galling in practice, even though the need for it was recognized in theory. The strong philosophical advocacy of basic research by Navy spokesmen was, therefore, greeted with a certain amount of incredulity. Would the Congress over the long pull permit the military to operate under such a liberal interpretation of their mission?

The Office of Naval Research rapidly became the mainstay of much of American science, especially physics and electrical engineering, and to a lesser extent chemistry, metallurgy, mathematics, and geophysics. ONR also continued to follow the pattern established in OSRD: support the best researchers and the best research proposals without regard to institutional or geographical distribution. And the judgment of what is best was to be made by scientists in the same general field of work, either as program officers within ONR or as outside consulting scientists. ONR quickly achieved a high reputation in the scientific community—indeed, a reputation that was never quite equaled either by one of the other military services, which set up similar agencies, or by the Atomic Energy Commission or the National Science Foundation. When new agencies were formed, especially the National Science Foundation, ONR alumni moved into key positions carrying its philosophy and outside contacts with them. The chief scientist of ONR, Allan Waterman, became the first director of the NSF.

The public debate on the postwar organization for science was opened in November 1944, by a letter from Franklin D. Roosevelt to Vannevar Bush asking him to study how the lessons learned in OSRD could be applied in peacetime "for the improvement of the national health, the creation of new enterprises bringing new jobs, and the betterment of the national standard of living."

The recommendations of the committee established under Bush in response to this request are contained in the report *Science the Endless*

Frontier, published in July 1945. The report stressed the importance of scientific progress to the health, prosperity, and security of the nation. It said that it was "essential that the civilian scientists continue in peacetime some portion of those contributions to national security which they have made so effectively during the war," and it felt this could best be done through a civilian organization with congressional appropriations and "the clear power to initiate military research which will supplement and strengthen that carried on directly under the control of the Army and Navy." It recommended the use of public funds to support basic research in colleges and universities, and to foster "the development of scientific talent in our youth."[11]

The Bush report set forth five principles to govern federal support of research:

1. Stability of funding, so that long-range projects could be undertaken.

2. A civilian agency governed by a board composed of "persons of broad interest in and understanding of the peculiarities of scientific research and education."

3. and 4. Support of research through contracts and grants with universities and research institutes, leaving "internal control of policy, personnel, and the method and scope of the research to the institutions themselves."

5. Assurance of "complete independence and freedom" in the conduct of research to institutions while "retaining discretion in the allocation of funds among such institutions" and being responsible to the President and Congress.

In most respects the Bush report may be said to have charted the course of postwar government-science relations. These principles are the principles which have, at least in theory, animated all the numerous government agencies, military and nonmilitary, set up to support basic research in the postwar years.

In one very important respect, however, the pattern of support which actually developed differed sharply from the Bush blueprint. His report had envisioned a national research foundation as the central agency of United States science policy. It was to have a division of medical research, but these functions were essentially assumed by the National Institutes of Health. It was to have a division of military research, but these functions were, in effect, assumed by the Office of Naval Research, and similar offices in the two other military services. The Bush report had made clear that "there are certain kinds of research—such as research on the

11. Vannevar Bush *et al., Science the Endless Frontier,* a report to the President on a Program for Postwar Scientific Research, July 1945, reprinted July 1960 by the National Science Foundation, Washington, D.C. (document NSF 60-40).

improvement of existing weapons—which can best be done within the military establishment," but had also pointed out that "the job of long-range research involving the application of the newest scientific discoveries to military needs should be the responsibility of those civilian scientists in the universities and in industry who are best trained to discharge it thoroughly and successfully." The basic research establishments of the three military services, although attempting to implement this recommendation, were really a compromise; although they relied heavily on contracting with universities and industry and the programs were managed and administered in detail by civilian scientists, they remained under military command. The military chiefs were responsible for defending their budgets to the Congress and to the higher levels in the Defense Department just as they were for industrial research in competition with other short-range military requirements.

The compromise was not entirely satisfactory. After the Sputnik crisis of 1957, for example, a fourth research service, the Advanced Research Projects Agency, was set up within the Defense Department. It was headed by a civilian scientist and was answerable only to the civilian management of the Defense Department. This new agency did not entirely meet the Bush recommendation; to some extent, it gave less independence to the research function than did the wartime OSRD, but it was a step toward the reconstitution of OSRD to meet what was perceived as a new military crisis of the cold war.

Military research, even basic research, therefore, was not civilianized to the extent envisioned in the Bush report. Two important areas of military-related research, however, did remain in separate civilian agencies, aeronautical research, which stayed in NACA, and, more significantly, nuclear research, which became a federal monopoly under the newly created Atomic Energy Commission. Later, when space technology was brought into the public eye by Sputnik, an organizational pattern similar to the AEC was followed, i.e., a technology originally developed exclusively for military purposes by the military services was shifted bodily into a new civilian agency —in this case the old NACA reconstituted as NASA under a single full-time administrator—with responsibility for development of all aspects of the new technology and its applications.

The Bush committee had not foreseen the great flowering of massive new technologies, apparently convinced that the basic aspects of these technologies could be developed within a single science agency analogous to OSRD and then transferred to the relevant agencies of government for application to their particular missions. The idea of independent agencies built around particular new technologies was not foreseen. A more pluralistic system resulted, with the National Science Foundation playing a relatively minor role, even in basic research, partly as an unplanned pragmatic response to the long delay in the creation of the NSF and its early inability to obtain significant appropriations. It proved easier politically to get research appropriations for agencies that had a significant national security component in their mission. Even today, the NSF accounts for only 17 per cent of federal funds for academic research.

Apart from the more pluralistic administrative setup, postwar science support tended to follow the general principles laid down by the Bush committee. Furthermore, the lessons of the World War II experience created a new pattern, perpetuated in later developments, in many ways representing a sharp break with earlier traditions of American government-science relations. This change was largely dominated by the experience of military research. Its persistence against many natural American political traditions was defended primarily in terms of the necessities of the cold war. The characteristics of the postwar pattern included:

1. Greater reliance on contracting with private agencies for the conduct of research and development. By 1965, only 14 per cent of the $16 billion federal research and development program was conducted in civil service laboratories, and less than 20 per cent in federal contract research centers and civil service laboratories together. Of the remainder more than 70 per cent was performed by industry and about 12 per cent by universities.

2. Along with research and development contracting went extensive use of part-time outside scientific advisers in the planning of programs and—in basic research at least—the actual selection of projects for support. Within the broad objectives laid down for agency missions, research was contracted out to the scientific community on the basis of unsolicited research proposals chosen primarily for scientific merit after review and advice by consultants or panels selected from the general scientific community for expert knowledge in the field of science under consideration.

3. Scientific experts also entered increasingly into the highest levels of policy-making wherever technical issues or their implications were involved. This was an extension of the wartime experience which had revealed the need to bring in scientists not only to answer specific technical questions, but also to help formulate the technical issues. Initially most of the top-level advisers were scientists with extensive war laboratory experience who had returned to academic life, and it is perhaps significant that many of the present generation of scientific advisers are former students of those wartime leaders.

In entering the political process, science was able to retain some of its tradition of political neutrality, as illustrated by the fact that the members of the National Science Board and of the President's Science Advisory Committee are presidential appointees whose tenure in office persists to some extent through changes in political administration.

4. Wartime research established a new pattern of geographical and institutional allocation of resources emphasizing selection of the best agency

or group to accomplish the task at hand, as opposed to the pattern of decentralization and geographical equity which had characterized research activity in old-line federal research agencies such as the departments of Agriculture or Interior. In basic research, as already mentioned, it meant selection of projects on the basis of scientific merit and the record of previous scientific accomplishment of the investigators, with effectiveness of performance given preference over geographical or institutional "equity." A similar pattern prevailed in large development programs with industry, resulting ultimately in large concentrations of technological skills in certain regions of the country, also creating concomitant problems of local economic dependence on defense and space expenditures with consequent political pressures for their perpetuation.

5. The technologies generated initially by defense and national security needs, including the accelerating pace of competition with the U.S.S.R. in advanced technology, tended to preoccupy the technical community as a whole. They probably had a considerable, though hard to specify, influence on the evolution of science itself. They also tended to determine the directions of greatest growth in the economy and to provide the United States with a comparative trade advantage in high-technology products and services such as computers, industrial electronics, and jet aircraft. The trend also helped to accelerate the penetration of technical personnel into strategic policy-making roles in both government and industry, and probably had a much greater influence on the general climate of industrial management than the proportion of defense and space expenditures to the GNP might suggest.

6. The science-based technologies which characterized postwar development tended to cut across the traditional boundaries between government agencies as well as the traditional compartmentalization of scientific knowledge. Before World War II, defense technology drew mainly on mechanical design and engineering; agricultural technology had its own unique supporting science as did the exploration of natural resources.

One of the most striking developments of the 1960's has been the entrance of government on a relatively large scale into the support of the behavioral and social sciences. Of $330 million spent in fiscal year 1968 for research in these areas, about 10 per cent was spent by the military. Of this 10 per cent, approximately 60 per cent was spent on manpower and training, human factors engineering, studies of human performance under stress and other such areas.[12] About 40 per cent was spent on inquiries like the study of cultural and social characteristics of foreign peoples—

12. "Defense Department-Sponsored Foreign Affairs Research," Hearings before the Committee on Foreign Relations, United States Senate, May 9, 1968, p. 11.

of which Project Camelot was the most notorious although not the most typical example—and policy-planning studies. Thus, about 4 per cent of federally supported social and behavioral science research, inside and outside universities, was spent in areas which could be regarded as substantially more sensitive from the standpoint of military involvement than the type of academic research normally supported in the physical and life sciences.

The development of nuclear weapons and sophisticated delivery systems has involved the participation of the scientific community in a way that would have shocked the World War I Army officer who rejected the National Academy of Sciences' offer of assistance on the ground that "the Army already has a chemist." As this participation increased, the number of senior scientists who had acquired expertise in policy as well as the technical problems of weapons development also expanded, as it had never before in peacetime. These so-called weaponeers have played a role in policy formation not only within the Department of Defense but at the presidential level as well. Since the creation of the President's Science Advisory Committee in 1957, and the appointment, beginning in 1957, of a series of distinguished scientists as science advisers to the President, there has been an independent channel for the transmission of policy suggestions from the scientific community directly to the President. During the latter years of the Eisenhower administration, this channel proved increasingly important, and it continued so under President Kennedy, who further strengthened it through the establishment of the Office of Science and Technology within the Executive Office of the President in 1962, with the President's Science Adviser doubling as director of the office. But under Presidents Johnson and Nixon its effective influence has markedly diminished. The committee's concerns have sometimes extended to social science as well as natural science issues, but social scientists (other than economists) have never had the access to the presidential ear which the natural scientists have had. Whether the creation by President Nixon of the National Goals Research Staff within the Executive Office of the President will provide them with better access has yet to be determined.

Because military technology places demands on almost all important areas of science, it is possible to justify a broad range of scientific activities for support. When Defense was the only agency supporting basic science, or virtually so, at least in the physical sciences, hardly any discernible relation to a military mission was necessary to justify support if the work would not otherwise be done at all. The ability of defense agencies to act quickly tended to result in their being able to establish a position in many of the most exciting frontier fields of research—elementary particle physics, computer science, modern control theory, quantitative behavioral science, molecular biology, sensory psychology, satellite technology, radio-astronomy, X-ray and gamma-ray astronomy, cryogenics, and high-pressure physics.

Later, as new agencies were created, certain fields of science were transferred from Defense support to other agencies. For example, by agreement the National Science Foundation gradually assumed responsibility for low-temperature physics after 1954. In the late 1960's an agreement was reached by which ONR's remaining nuclear physics projects in universities were to be largely transferred to NSF. In 1965 NSF was assigned responsibility as "principal agent" for the support of ground-based astronomy, and partly as a consequence, the military services began phasing out of radio astronomy.

Some in the scientific community have argued that this is an unfortunate and short-sighted trend, reducing contact between the military and the frontier areas of science, and lessening in subtle ways its ability to appreciate and exploit the newest scientific discoveries. This is a difficult issue to argue convincingly. It is not too clear whether the administration and funding of extramural research actually improves the intellectual coupling between the technical community supported and those parts of the sponsoring agency which are really responsible for the translation of science into new technology. It is also difficult to separate the question of sponsorship from the total level of activity in a field of science. If the phasing out of Defense Department sponsorship is achieved with no change in the total level of activity, the loss to the development may be small, but if loss of Defense Department sponsorship entails a reduced level of activity or a reduced rate of growth or less flexibility in planning for a field, the long-term consequences may be much more serious.

In terms of applied research, it is not at all clear that corresponding technical resources would have automatically been devoted to socially more productive areas without the massive commitment to space and defense. The demonstration of success in these advanced technologies seems to have been a prerequisite for generating the demand for application of the same techniques in other areas. The governmental programs have, further, served to propel technical personnel into controlling positions in management in both private and public sectors to a degree unmatched in any other industrial nation, except possibly for the Soviet Union. This, rather than the direct transfer of government-generated technology, may have been the most potent mechanism for diffusing technology to the civilian sector, except in a few special areas like nuclear power and advanced aircraft.[13]

13. A sample of 6,000 executives studied by *Fortune* in 1967 showed that of those 55 and over, 35 per cent were technically trained, while of those in the 35-39 age bracket, 53 per cent were technically trained. Since the end of World War II, the number of research scientists, engineers, and technically educated executives in American industry has tripled, and the largest gains in output have occurred in those industries with the highest percentage of scientists and engineers in the work force. In 1950, technically trained persons constituted 52 per cent of industrial employees paid more than $10,000 per year, while by 1965 industrial employees making more than $15,000 per year were nearly 70 per cent technically educated. Between 1930

It is probably true that more than 50 per cent of industrial employment of scientists and engineers is at least indirectly related to space, defense, and nuclear energy, but the struggle of such industries to diversify is ultimately likely to diffuse much of this effort and sophistication toward civilian problems. In this connection it is interesting to note that in the last five years private expenditures on research and development have expanded considerably more rapidly than government expenditures, so that in fiscal year 1968, for the first time since Sputnik, the federal share of support of industrial research fell below 50 per cent.[14] It is still probably true, however, that the most highly educated scientists and technologists, the Ph.D.'s in science and engineering, are in industrial occupations related to defense and space.

Another trend which should be of great importance is the continuing effort to civilianize as many areas of science and technology as is compatible with the maintenance of mission capabilities. After the war, and later, Defense stepped in time after time to fill a vacuum left by the inability of nondefense agencies to obtain appropriations for scientific programs which were needed in the national interest. In the AEC and NASA, both created under strong pressures from the scientific community, major defense-generated technologies were brought under civilian management without sacrifice to their contribution to national defense. In retrospect it is clear that this civilianization greatly accelerated the penetration of atomic energy and space techniques into many aspects of national life.

Some have argued that a Department of Science should be established to nurture the early stages of an infant technology without its having to compete too vigorously with traditional activities of mission-oriented agencies before its full potential and relevance to national goals can be widely known or understood. The application of a new technology cannot be forecast in its early stages, nor can its possible confluence with other technologies be anticipated. Basic science and technology need to be able to define their own missions, unconstrained by past definitions of agency goals. It is also maintained that since defense is likely to remain a dynamic center of new technological and intellectual development, it is necessary to develop methods of rapid spin-off of defense science and technology and management techniques into civil agencies if military influence is not to spread too widely into all areas of culture and scholarship. The problem is not that any particular area of Defense activity is bad. Each of the defense innovations such as, for example, the RAND Cor-

---

and 1965 the labor force grew at an average rate of 1.4 per cent a year, the number of nonproduction workers, 2.5 per cent a year, but the number of scientists and engineers in industry at 5 per cent a year. In 1964, 40 per cent of all scientists and 70 per cent of all engineers in the United States were employed by industry.

14. NSI *Databook*, Table 26, p. 44.

poration, can be justified as necessary and important to defense missions. But it is the cumulative effect of many such institutions in the absence of similar growth in the civilian sector that raises understandable anxieties about undue military impact.

In a typical recent year—fiscal year 1968—the Department of Defense spent $8.1 billion on research and development, almost half of the $16.8 billion devoted to these purposes by all federal government agencies, and about one-third of total R&D performed in the United States. Most of the funds spent by Defense are devoted to the development of weapon systems, however, and not research *per se* (Defense accounts for one-fourth of federal funds for research, but three-fifths of the government expenditures for development). Military agencies (especially the Navy) sponsor more than one-half of the oceanography R&D funded by the federal government, one-fifth of the work in meteorology, and 6 per cent of medical research.[15]

To some extent, these large military expenditures on science and technology can be—and are—viewed as squeezing the amount of funds and resources which can be devoted to civilian needs; certainly the extensive utilization of science and technology may have taken R&D resources otherwise used for civilian purposes. But these expenditures also have exercised a "demonstration" effect on the civilian sectors, which have now begun to devote large expenditures to R&D; while military expenditures for R&D doubled during the last decade, the R&D outlays by the Department of Health, Education, and Welfare grew sevenfold. Thus, the Department of Defense may have demonstrated that science and technology can be important inputs to the conduct of governmental programs, civilian or military.

Among defense R&D impacts is the spillover or transfer of defense technology to other areas of the economy. Transport aircraft, cheap nuclear power, exploration of outer space, high-speed computers and other electronic developments are examples of the legacy of military R&D to the nation's general technological progress. Some of these civilian products are direct outgrowths of government projects; others would not have become commercially feasible without federal investment.

Classified research is definitely open to the criticism that it reinforces isolation of military from civilian technology, and, as a consequence, delays the transfer of promising military technology to civilian applications. Many have noted that government-sponsored research and development have produced far fewer patents per dollar of expenditure than

15. "Federal Research, Development, and Related Programs," *Special Analyses, Budget of the United States,* Fiscal Year 1969 (Washington, D.C.: Government Printing Office, 1968), pp. 135-154; *Special Analysis Budget of the United States,* Fiscal Year 1970, pp. 239-250.

privately financed industrial research, but it is not known whether this disparity is due to the systems character of most military technology, or whether it is due to its isolation from normal commercial markets and market incentives. Most large defense contractors, after all, are organized so that their government business is insulated from their commercial business. The transfer of defense technology to civilian use has occurred much more readily through the small, high-technology firms, where the volume is too small to justify creation of separate organizational units for government and civilian business.[16]

More recent efforts to utilize the "systems" capability of defense contractors in civilian areas have had less success to date. (See Chapter 16.) These efforts are based on the assumption that a company that can design, develop, and produce a military weapons system in all its complexity also should be able to contribute to designing systems dealing with social problems (e.g., urban transportation, environmental pollution, poverty reduction, etc.). Such transfer of military capabilities, at least to date, appears to be more difficult than transfer in the aircraft and electronics industries. But the effort continues.

16. S. I. Doctors, *Technology Transfer in the Federal Agency Setting* (Cambridge: M.I.T. Press, 1969).

19

Military Research and the Academy

In one sense World War II and the subsequent period of the cold war might be characterized as a love affair between the intellectual community and government. Nazism, after all, represented a specific attack on the values most cherished by the academic community, and succeeded in uniting the American intellectual community as nothing else had or could. The reality of its threat was brought home to American academics by a stream of refugees from Europe whose names—Fermi, Wigner, Bethe, Ewald, Franck, and many lesser luminaries—had long been familiar to American scientists. Academic intellectuals were well prepared, emotionally and intellectually, to close ranks behind the American war effort. Natural scientists left their home universities and flocked to the war laboratories set up by the Office of Scientific Research and Development.

An informal and extremely effective system of recruiting for the war effort was established within the academic community. Humanists and social scientists converged on the Office of Strategic Services (OSS) and the various agencies set up to manage the war economy. Just as OSRD in some measure provided the model for postwar natural science, so in some measure the OSS provided a model for the social sciences and an unprecedented involvement of intellectuals in practical affairs. Military intelligence, never considered quite respectable in democratic societies, acquired a degree of respectability among academic intellectuals. The CIA, which inherited the mission of OSS after the war, recruited on university campuses and attracted a number of distinguished academics to key positions on a permanent basis.

It was evident that World War II had left a heritage of intellectual respect for the realities of power politics. Scientists acquired close friendships with military officers, a new respect for the ability of military professionals, and a tolerance—if not admiration—of the military establishment. The favorable climate was reinforced by the experience of scientists with the early academic contracts of the Office of Naval Research. As a consequence of the cold war, and the continuing relationships between the academic and defense establishments, the disenchantment with the military establishment which followed so rapidly after World War I was delayed for almost a generation following World War II. In contrast, following World War I, academic disillusionment with the military came immediately after the military establishment, as a result of rapid demobilization, had lost most of its power to influence public policy and to claim a large share of the resources of American society. After World War II the period of intellectual disenchantment was delayed and, even then, began while the military still held a large share of influence on American policy and a high prestige with the less educated public. This prestige possibly made the intellectual backlash more acute and, at the same time, isolated many in the intellectual community from the rest of the American public, even while unrest over the inconclusive and drawn-out Vietnam war and with high military spending spread in the nation at large and in the Congress.

The discontent among many intellectuals, particularly on the campus, has been manifested in a number of diverse ways. Doubts have increased among scholars about the wisdom of accepting military funds for research, and serious questions have been raised about the influence of such funding on the institution of the university, long regarded as a critical countervailing power to government in a free society. Many scientists, moreover, have been besieged with moral doubts about the uses to which their research is put, in particular toward the further development of a nuclear arsenal and the creation of a biological warfare capability (only recently dismantled). Scholars generally are concerned about the implications of security classification and clearance on free access to knowledge.

Among the students, unrest and protest have assumed dramatic expression. Recruiters for the CIA, and for industries like Dow Chemical, which manufactures napalm, have retreated from campuses after student demonstrations. Students have harassed speakers such as former Secretary of Defense McNamara and Presidential Assistant for National Security Henry Kissinger. Selective Service offices have been attacked and files burned. Students have demanded the ouster of ROTC units from a number of campuses, and, in the case of Harvard and Dartmouth, among others, have succeeded in their demands. Student groups, as well as faculty, have protested campus-based, defense-related institutes, such as the Princeton facility of the Institute of Defense Analysis and the Stanford Research Institute, which have been separated from the university as a consequence. National Guard troops have been summoned to handle such protests on several campuses; tragic violence was the aftermath at Kent State, and Jackson State, where students were killed by troops and police.

It is difficult to separate the funds flowing directly to campuses from defense agencies from those flowing from other sectors of government. Especially in the early postwar days, defense agencies were prepared to support basic research of a nature virtually indistinguishable from that supported by civilian agencies. Most of the research and development supported by the federal government have come from the three national security-oriented agencies: the Department of Defense, the Atomic Energy Commission, and the National Aeronautics and Space Administration. However, the impact of these three agencies on university research has been substantially less since the mid-1960's. The same three agencies in 1967 accounted for 35 per cent of academic research, and, if all federally supported academic science is included, rather than just research, the portion of these agencies is reduced to about 22 per cent. Thus, the portion of research support coming from national security oriented agencies has been declining much faster in the universities than in other sectors.[1] (See Tables 19.1 and 19.2.)

TABLE 19.1 Federal Obligations to Colleges and Universities for Academic Science, Fiscal Years 1966-68

Agency	FY 66	FY 67	FY 68
Department of Agriculture	141.0	144.8	144.2
Atomic Energy Commission	96.9	109.6	110.2
Department of Commerce	2.8	4.4	8.0
Department of Defense	301.5	264.1	243.1
Health, Education and Welfare	1109.2	1251.0	1229.4
Department of Interior	19.1	23.9	28.2
National Aeronautics and Space Administration	142.2	131.5	129.8
National Science Foundation	374.5	394.5	423.0

Source: National Science Foundation, *Databook*, January 1970.

Research in universities proper is generally research carried on in close association with graduate education, mainly by faculty members and graduate students engaged in teaching. Federal Contract Research Centers are separately organized and budgeted research institutes, often engaged in applied or programmatic research and with a higher proportion of full-

1. The actual distribution of academic science support from various federal agencies, over a period of three years, is shown in Table 19.1. Source: NSF *Databooks* for February 1969 and January 1970. (The figures shown are for what the NSF classifies as "universities proper," and includes all colleges and universities exclusive of so-called "federal contract research centers.")

time professional researchers on long-term appointment than in the usual university department. The degree of involvement of faculty or graduate students is small in most FCRC's, although there are exceptions in the case of some on-campus research centers such as the Lawrence Radiation Laboratory at Berkeley or the Stanford Linear Accelerator, which make a significant contribution to graduate training despite being highly professionalized research institutes. (Since most of such FCRC's are in the physical sciences or engineering, the figures shown in Tables 19.1 and

TABLE 19.2 Support from Various Federal Agencies in Fiscal Year 1967
for Research & Development at Universities and for Academic Science

Federal Agency	Research and Development	Academic Science
Health, Education and Welfare	43.5%	54.0%
National Science Foundation	14.5	17.0
Department of Defense	20.0	11.4
Department of Agriculture	4.8	6.2
National Aeronautics and		
Space Administration	8.2	5.7
Atomic Energy Commission	6.8	4.7
Other Agencies	2.0	1.2

Source: National Science Foundation, *Datebook*, January 1970.

19.2 understate federal involvement in academic research in the physical sciences. Most of the discussion which follows excludes the FCRC's, concentrating attention on universities proper.)

The federal involvement in higher education has come largely as a result of its support of research—the proportion of academic funding by the federal government is considerably less for higher education as a whole than it is for research. The heritage of defense involvement in the support of research, which began at the end of World War II, is massive dependence of university education on federal funding, especially at the graduate and professional level. In fact, in the universities as opposed to the colleges, which are not heavily involved in research, the federal share of the total budget is very substantial. In 1964 (the most recent year for which figures are available), 41 per cent of the budgets of private universities was accounted for by federal funding, and the figure is probably close to 50 per cent today. In the same year, 86.5 per cent of their research was supported from federal sources, while 72 per cent of the research budget of public universities came from federal funds. In 1965 in physics, for example, 50 per cent of all enrolled graduate students received federal stipends either directly on fellowships or traineeships, or as graduate assistants in sponsored research.

Although Defense Department involvement in support of academic research has declined significantly as a fraction of the total of all government support—from about 70 per cent in 1954 to only 20 per cent in the mid-1960's—the impact of Defense support on university research is still substantial, especially in the physical sciences. Indeed, much of the relative decline of Defense support is due to the dramatic growth of federally supported biomedical research, mostly in medical schools, rather than to an absolute decline of defense research. Over 30 per cent of all academic research in the physical sciences is still dependent on the Defense Department, and the patterns of Defense support still set the precedents for much of the support from other government agencies.

Defense agencies can provide flexibility to start new programs or to try out new mechanisms of support. For example, the Defense Department, largely through the Advanced Research Projects Agency (ARPA), has pioneered in support of the development of computers and in the development of computer science as a new discipline in universities. It was also ARPA that seized the initiative in following a recommendation of a committee of the Federal Council for Science and Technology to inaugurate a program of long-term support for "materials science" in universities. This program departed from many previous practices in project support by cutting across departmental lines, by providing major research equipment to serve many different groups in a university and not just a single investigator, by providing money to universities with the program management responsibility largely delegated to the university itself over a very broad area of science rather than being funded on a project basis, and by providing guaranteed forward funding over a period of several years in such a way as to permit the university to develop long-range plans for the growth of faculty, facilities, and graduate student enrollment.

ARPA has recently also moved into the field of the behavioral sciences in an attempt to foster a new level of sophistication and scale in the methodology of study of social systems. For instance, ARPA has significantly funded research on so-called "national security indicators," that is, the identification and measurement of different military, scientific, economic, political, and social variables which in combination generate any nation's security posture. ARPA has also taken a long-term interest in studies of information processing by the human mind, and especially information processing and decision-making under stress. The Defense Department has had the money and the administrative flexibility to exercise initiative in support of science, both in identifying and backing new fields of research quickly and on a scale sufficient to explore their real potential from an early stage, and in experimenting with new mechanisms to give greater control to the institution itself.

The Department of Defense and the administrative mechanisms of support later imitated by other research support agencies as they were established have paid not only the direct costs of research, but also other university costs indirectly associated with the expansion of research activity —a portion of faculty salaries, graduate student stipends (out of which in turn university tuitions were often paid), indirect costs including such items as building heat, light, and maintenance, telephone and secretarial services, accounting costs, and research administration costs. The system of indirect cost payments enabled the universities to distribute fixed overhead costs of plant and administration over a wide range of activities, and freed some resources for other academic purposes. Research support, as it grew, became an indirect instrument for the general subvention of universities and helped them accommodate to student and faculty growth, especially in the decade from about 1957 to 1967.[2]

Striking a balance between the benefits and costs of military involvement in the support of science is complicated by the fact that those who argue on different sides tend to start from different premises. Those who emphasize the problems and difficulties brought about by military sponsorship, especially of academic research, tend to argue from the implicit assumption that comparable resources could or would have been channeled into university science from other agencies and by other mechanisms. They argue further that support from nondefense agencies (and particularly from the National Science Foundation, which has no built-in commitments to extrascientific interests) would avoid the difficulties of conscience that trouble so many academicians today. Conversely, those who argue the benefits of military sponsorship point to the tremendous growth in the quantity and quality of academic science, often failing to distinguish between what is due to the growth of resources and what is due to military sponsorship *per se*. The proponents argue that the country as a whole was not ready for the broad-based public support of science, and that the military had intervened in an enlightened and far-seeing way to establish a base of support which has been gradually transformed into a pluralistic approach by many agencies, with the military playing a declining role. They point out that the problems of military technology have often stimulated the development of important new areas of basic research such as mathematical linguistics and nonlinear optics, and have provided new experimental techniques and tools, such as computers and microwave components, which have accelerated fundamental scientific advance.

The practical issue that faces us is whether the public is ready for an entirely different system of support for graduate education and academic research, and what role, if any, the military ought to play in such a system.

2. This is not to suggest that the costs reimbursed in connection with research agreements are not real costs, but only that some of them are costs that the university would have incurred even in the absence of research, and others involve the maintenance of capital plant which might not have been built except in the expectation of sponsored research activity.

For example, with the military supporting only 20 per cent of research in universities and about 10 per cent of academic science as a whole, it becomes feasible to talk of transferring this activity in its entirety to NSF. This would involve roughly doubling the research support budget of NSF and increasing its total budget by 50 per cent—from about $500 million to $750 million a year. The arguments that justified broad-based Defense involvement in academic science when ONR was virtually the only source of support of the physical sciences and engineering cannot be carried over unchanged into a situation where Defense is only one among a number of agencies supporting academic science. But it is possible to argue that either there are certain areas of science, peculiar to Defense needs, which would not receive adequate attention without Defense sponsorship, or that such sponsorship gives the Defense Department a greater access to academic talents and scientific results than it could otherwise obtain, or that Defense has a measure of flexibility for rapid exploitation of new fields of research or new mechanisms of support less feasible in other agencies. All of these arguments are true in some measure, but they are also changing with time, and must be weighed against the negative effects of Defense sponsorship.

It is often alleged by the critics of military-sponsored research that the military has had and is having undue influence on the character and direction of research and training in universities. One body of opinion accuses the universities of having sold their intellectual heritage for a mess of research pottage. The use of the contractual instrument as the principal mechanism of research sponsorship by the military lends superficial plausibility to this argument. The legal arrangements between the services and the universities are closely similar, in form at least, to the arrangements used in the research and development and procurement of weapons systems from industry. An important part of the contract instrument is the "work statement" which defines what the contractor is expected to do. Because research is inherently uncertain, however, such work statements are extremely vague in the case of universities, and much therefore depends upon the interpretation of the contract by the technical monitor in the military agency.

To be sure, the potential for detailed interference in the substance of the work is present, even if it has rarely been applied in practice. Moreover this potential may become stronger as government funds become scarcer and the competition of universities for research support grows keener with the increased enrollment of graduate students and the expansion of faculties. The status of the scholar as a contractor of the agency involved may create subtle psychological pressures on the scholar to yield to his sponsor in the interpretation of the work statement. So long as the total funds for academic research were growing at the rate of about 15 per cent annually, the potential for undue influence on the researcher was probably not serious because almost every agency had a margin of funds for new projects and new investigators, so that dissatisfied investigators could change sponsors relatively easily. In fact, the situation produced a certain amount of competition among sponsors to provide maximum freedom and flexibility.

In the last two years the Defense Department, largely under pressure from congressional appropriations committees, has been more and more insistent on the necessity to demonstrate "relevance" of its sponsored research to Defense needs. And, in 1969, Congress passed the so-called "Mansfield amendment," forbidding any defense research which does not "directly" support military objectives.[3] Academic researchers supported by Defense agencies have been subjected to conflicting pressures to provide evidence to their military sponsors that what they are doing has potential value for military technology, and to convince their colleagues and students in other parts of the university that their research is "free," that *they* have the scientific initiative, and that their research results serve military purposes only in the sense that almost all of science and knowledge has some potential for military as well as other applications. These two viewpoints may not be as irreconcilable as they seem.

It is also argued that military sponsorship has resulted in strong academic emphasis on certain fields, especially in the physical sciences: electronics, solid state physics, nuclear physics, computer science, for example. Some would argue that these fields were exciting anyway, and would probably have attracted equal attention and emphasis from scientists themselves independently of the source of funds. It is pointed out that the evaluation of proposals, and advising on areas of new scientific opportunity, are done largely by members of the scientific community, often from academic life, so that academic scientists have in fact a strong voice in the determination of priorities and projects for support. A related criticism maintains that the universities as institutions have lost control of their own priorities because of the project system—largely introduced by the military and perpetuated subsequently by other agencies. Since individual scientists can negotiate independently with sponsoring agencies, and since university administrations cannot afford to deny the right of a prestigious scientist to seek such support, especially when he brings money to the institution and could easily go elsewhere with his sponsorship if the institution interfered with his negotiations, the institution's research priorities are in effect determined in Washington. It is difficult to determine whether institutional priorities would be substantially different if the support were not project-oriented. Derek J. de Solla Price[4] has examined the relative distribution

3. The "Mansfield amendment" is given in P.L. 91-121, Section 203, Title 2. The appropriate news account appears in the *New York Times,* November 26, 1969, p. 1.

4. Derek John de Solla Price, *Little Science, Big Science* (New York: Columbia University Press, 1963).

of research publications in fields of science in various countries and finds that it differs little from country to country despite vast differences in mechanisms of sponsorship. The relative emphasis between organic chemistry and solid state physics, for example, differs little between Britain and the United States, even though the British universities are supported largely by institutional grants from the University Grants Committee, which is quite independent of the military establishment, while the American universities are supported largely through categorical projects. Perhaps the pattern of world research activity is determined primarily by the pattern in the nation that is the scientific leader, and the activity of the rest of the world is merely imitative of the United States. There is, moreover, a clear if indirect military influence on the employment market for scientists and engineers outside the universities.

A somewhat more convincing case can be made with respect to engineering training. Wartime experience, as we have seen, revealed a weakness in the traditional education of engineers in the United States. Engineering training had been too specialized, too preoccupied with current technology, too shallowly rooted in science and mathematics. The war produced a revolution in engineering education, with greater emphasis on the underlying disciplines and less on the practical aspects of engineering. Engineering schools rapidly became research-minded, and the production of engineering Ph.D.'s boomed while undergraduate enrollments stagnated. In 1935 there were a hundred engineering Ph.D.'s produced in the United States in a handful of schools. By 1968 the production of engineering Ph.D.'s had reached 3,000 per year and was still rising at 12 to 14 per cent a year, as compared with 8 to 10 per cent a year in the sciences. Nearly 50 per cent of these Ph.D.'s were remaining on in academic life, and the Ph.D had become, for the first time, virtually a prerequisite for a faculty appointment even for undergraduate teaching in engineering.

This trend was greatly reinforced by military support. In the early 1960's, 65 per cent of all the research support in academic engineering came from DOD and NASA, and only about 6 per cent from industrial sources. Engineering research tended to emphasize what might be called non-economic technologies—technologies in which technical performance rather than economic strength was the guiding consideration. The balance has been somewhat improved in recent years, and actually civil engineering and sanitary engineering, neglected in the 1950's, are now the fastest growing Ph.D. fields in engineering. Furthermore, both of these fields have benefited greatly from the application of new technologies in materials, in computers, and in systems analysis developed originally largely under Defense sponsorship. In engineering as in science, it is difficult to determine whether neglect of some of the "classical" or traditional fields was due to funding sources or to a temporary lack of exciting ideas, new directions, and dynamic leaders.

Defense sponsorship also has been criticized for its alleged tendency to draw some of the brightest minds into physical science at the expense of other fields. Among undergraduate students, physics majors show consistently the highest scholastic aptitudes and academic records. On the other hand, this has been true since the 1930's and is only now beginning to change gradually as talent is drawn into the social sciences, particularly the more mathematical aspects of the social sciences. In terms of over-all doctoral and bachelor degree output, there has been surprisingly little change in the distribution of students between the natural sciences and engineering on the one hand, and the social sciences and humanities on the other. About 25 per cent of the bachelors and 50 per cent of the Ph.D.'s are in the natural sciences and engineering, and this figure has remained virtually unchanged since 1900, despite a many-fold increase in the number of Ph.D.'s and in the percentage of the population going on to graduate study.[5] The last two years have seen signs of a drop in science and engineering enrollment both at the graduate and undergraduate levels, but this has not yet been reflected in Ph.D. output.

It is certainly true that the sciences are generally more affluent than other disciplines within the university structure. Summer compensation and outside consulting opportunities, secretarial support, travel and telephone money, and semiprofessional research assistance are more available to the sciences. Although academic year salaries are not higher for the sciences at a given academic rank, rates of promotion are faster and teaching loads are somewhat lighter.

But the balance of emphasis in universities may have been influenced less than is popularly believed. In the last ten years at Harvard University, for example, the distribution of total budgetary expenditures among departments of the Faculty of Arts and Sciences has changed very little, taking into account government expenditures. The effects have been rather subtle evolutionary ones, the product of small biases in numerous marginal decisions with a possible large cumulative effect, rather than gross and obvious changes in direction. Since a controlled experiment could not be carried out, there is no way of knowing what would have happened if funds had been available in other ways or from other sources.

One may also argue that a university should be somewhat responsive to the needs and priorities of the society in which it exists and which supports it, although the responsibility of the university to set rather than accept priorities is regarded by many as a primary duty. In the 1950's the American public and a large part of the academic community saw Soviet expansionism and technological progress as a clear and present

5. Harvey Brooks, *The Government of Science* (Cambridge: M.I.T. Press, 1968), p. 195.

danger. The launching of Sputnik led to much reflection about the adequacy of American education and the lag in support of military research as well as of basic research in universities. However, the growing dread of nuclear war has troubled a great many in academic life, and strong opposition in the intellectual community has developed in response to national involvement in the Vietnam war.

Another criticism frequently directed at military support, is that it has led to emphasis on faculty research at the expense of teaching, especially undergraduate teaching. Several recent books have presented evidence which purported to show that federal research—in particular, defense research—has reduced the quantity, and, by inference, the quality, of university teaching.[6]

Complaints about professorial neglect of teaching are hard to evaluate. They were as vociferous in the 1930's, in the absence of federal support, as they are today. They are as strong against the unsupported humanities as they are against the heavily supported physical sciences. Considerable evidence on this subject has been gathered in a study conducted by Parsons and Platt.[7] This study showed that, even in the most research-oriented universities, "most faculty members at most institutions still actually devote more time to teaching than to research" and that they do this by preference. It is worth noting also that the movement for curriculum reform has originated with natural scientists and mathematicians.

Closely related to the question of teaching versus research is the matter of "grantsmanship." It is often asserted that faculty members are selected more for their ability to attract research grants than on their intrinsic merit as scholars and teachers. The university which hires a new faculty member in the natural sciences is seldom in a position to provide him with even the minimum funds required to initiate a research program, and some less affluent institutions have been known to *require* a new faculty member to raise a part of his own salary through external grants. This is one of the most unfortunate results of almost exclusive reliance on categorical research project grants for the support of universities by the federal government. In the last few years, the advent of development grants has alleviated the situation somewhat, at least for an initial period.

Another major criticism of military sponsorship of academic research is that it has resulted in erosion of the independence of the university, especially its role as an independent critic of society. This erosion has

6. For instance, see Harold Orlans, *The Impact of Federal Programs Upon Higher Education* (Washington, D.C.: The Brookings Institution, 1968), pp. 62, 63.

7. Talcott Parsons and Gerald M. Platt, "Considerations on the American Academic System," *Minerva*, Vol. VI, No. 4, Summer 1968, pp. 497-523; also Parsons and Platt, "The American Academic Profession: A Pilot Study," report on NSF Grant #GS-2524.

been facilitated, it is said, by the fierce competition among universities for prestige and for the best faculty and students. They cannot turn down research contracts and grants because students and faculty would simply transfer to other institutions that were more compliant, and they consciously or unconsciously avoid criticizing the government, and particularly the sponsoring agency, because of the fear of reprisal in the form of cancellation of contracts or, more likely, failure to renew a contract after it expires, a hazard greatly increased by the short-term nature of most contracts, particularly those with the Defense Department. Furthermore, many academic researchers working on defense-supported projects also do outside consulting for the Department of Defense or its contractors, and this is said further to inhibit their inclination to criticize government policy publicly.

This sort of charge is even more difficult to evaluate than the problem of research and teaching. If evidence of overt suppression of criticism or reprisals against critics in the form of withdrawal of support cannot be found, it is always possible to fall back on the assertion of unconscious bias, on the reluctance of scientists to "bite the hand that feeds them." In evaluating these charges it must be noted at the outset that there has not been a noticeable lack of public criticism of United States military policies by university professors. Much of this has come from nonscientists who were not involved in DOD support, but much thoughtful and informed criticism has also come from scientists who were intimately involved in military research and privy to classified information as consultants to the government. Dr. Richard Garwin and Professor Hans Bethe, for example, wrote for the *Scientific American* an extremely influential critique of the Sentinel antiballistic missile system (ABM) and strongly opposed its deployment.[8] Many Defense-supported scientists spoke out against the Kennedy administration's civil defense program in 1962. In fact, academic scientists involved in defense research have provided a source of informed criticism of Defense policies which was much more effective in influencing government policy as well as public opinion than would have been more "independent" but less well-informed analysis.

It is true that little of this criticism has been "radical" in questioning the basic premises of American society, but radical criticism generally abounds today, and it is doubtful whether there has been less because of military-supported research. Although coercion by Defense is possible in principle, in practice the Pentagon is extraordinarily sensitive about its role. A flurry was created recently by a group of mathematicians who placed two paid advertisements in the *Notices of the American Mathematical Society*[9] arguing to their colleagues that they were "responsible for the uses to

8. R. L. Garwin and H. A. Bethe, "Anti-Ballistic Missile Systems," *Scientific American*, Vol. 218, No. 3, March 1968, pp. 21-31.
9. *Notices of the American Mathematical Society*, Vol. 15, No. 1, January 1968, p. 277.

which your talents are put" and that "this responsibility forbids putting mathematics in the service of this cruel war." When it turned out that several of the mathematicians who signed the advertisement had research contracts with the Defense Department, a considerable top-level policy discussion was triggered in the Pentagon. The upshot of this discussion was contained in a departmental memorandum from Dr. John S. Foster, Director of Defense Research and Engineering. The essence of Foster's policy was expressed in the following instruction to his subordinates: "Take all necessary actions to preserve our mutually beneficial relationships with the academic research community during this period when there are potentially divisive pressures."

He also said, in part: "Do not emphasize nontechnical issues in your evaluation of the desirability of terminating or renewing. . . . Clearly some members of the research and development community have disagreed with governmental decisions while they contributed significantly to the country." Letters were written to a number of principal investigators asking them whether, in view of their advertisement, they felt they no longer desired to accept Defense support. In fact, all the investigators concluded that their work contributed to all of society, and not just defense, and in consequence no contracts were terminated as a result of this incident.[10]

The incident raises many interesting questions. The letters from the Pentagon were at first interpreted as a veiled threat. Although this appears not to have been so, it is tempting to speculate in the light of the subsequent continuation of the contracts whether its practical effect will not be to embarrass the critics of United States policy so that they will not speak out in public again. The incident also lends credence to those who maintain that the Pentagon derives respectability and public acceptance from its support of prestigious academicians, and puts a very high price in terms of toleration of criticism on keeping the academic community in its retinue of retainers.

Of course, the scientists who administer programs in the Pentagon are themselves members of the scientific community, and their future careers outside of government are in some measure dependent on the good will of that community. Thus the Foster policy of tolerance is not remarkable, but the fact that it was obviously supported at higher levels remains significant. The incident, however, reveals the vulnerability of the academic community to reprisal, and it is interesting to speculate whether, in the absence of an administration anxious to avoid an open break with the academic community just before a national election, the treatment of dissenters would have been so gentle. Clearly the existence of alternative sources of support constitutes the best guarantee against coercion, and the constricted state of

10. Victor Cohn, "Anti-War Scientists Get Choice at Pentagon," *Washington Post*, September 20, 1968.

the NSF budget undoubtedly played a role in the circumstances described.

The contract mechanism of support lends itself to many administrative restrictions which may range from mere annoyance to actual abridgment of academic freedom. The latter has occurred in two major areas—restrictions on publication and interference with the personnel policies of the contractor. Many government research contracts for unclassified research carry a proviso that the contractor must submit proposed journal articles or public speeches to the sponsoring agency for clearance. Many universities have refused to accept such provisions and, in the case of the major research-supporting agencies, they have not been insisted upon. The clearance procedure is apparently often intended to avoid publication of material which would be politically embarrassing to the sponsor. Publication clearance is routinely required of industrial defense contractors, even when only unclassified information is involved, but to date it has proved possible to avoid enforcing this restriction on academic contractors, at least where development or design work was not involved.

Another area of sensitivity involves employment of personnel on contracts. Contractually the university has complete control over personnel: the individuals employed on research contracts are university employees, subject to the same rules and policies as other university personnel of comparable rank or status. But there are opportunities for an informal, unwritten "clearance" mechanism, and there appear to be disturbingly frequent examples of individuals being informally excluded from work on a specific contract because they were *persona non grata* to a particular agency. Such cases are extremely difficult to document. In general they occur most frequently in connection with research activities having strong policy implications, often in the social sciences.

A subject of rising complaint is the administrative restrictions and regulations on research contracts. Many of these are a logical result of the fiction that a basic research contract is the procurement of a specific service from the university by the sponsoring agency. One particularly objectional requirement is for "effort reporting" by personnel working on research contracts. Since a contract calls for reimbursement to the university for a portion of the salary of a particular individual, it is stated that the university must be in a position to present accounting evidence to the sponsoring agency of the fraction of his total effort that the individual devoted to the work. Fortunately, through extended discussions between university representatives and the United States Bureau of the Budget, the problem of effort reporting has been resolved in a manner more consistent with the realities of academic activity.

Administrative restrictions in research contracts usually stem from agency efforts to satisfy congressional requirements for "strict accountability" for taxpayers' funds. They cover a wide range of subjects, including effort reporting, patents, conflicts of interest, reporting requirements and format, advance permission for many types of expenditure, travel, etc. The sanction for failure to meet these requirements is usually nonreimbursement of certain costs to the university, which puts pressure on university financial offices to enforce the regulations locally. This, by itself, creates problems because it comes in conflict with the customary rigid separation between business and academic functions in the university structure. The business officer, often unfamiliar with and less than sympathetic to academic ways of doing things, finds himself enforcing regulations which the faculty member regards as matters of academic, not financial, policy.

The indirect congressional involvement is illustrated by the so-called "antiriot" provisions of recent appropriations to research agencies. In various versions these provisions prohibit the payment of government funds to or for the benefit of individuals on campus who are involved in "disruptive" campus demonstrations. The provisions are rather vague, and the determination of what constitutes "disruption" is left to the university in some cases and to the courts in others. They constitute a new and threatening form of government intervention in the internal operation and administration of the university and have aroused great apprehension in the academic community, although their practical effect has so far been small. There have been widespread protests from university representatives, and several universities have recently turned down federal funds because of these provisions. One commentator has summarized this general area of government-university relations in the following terms:

> The list of administrative restrictions that have led individual investigators and, at times, institutions, to shun various government programs is long but not nearly long enough, for complaints have come more readily than action, the private action of individuals has been more frequent than their united public resolve, and rarely have any institutions jointly refused to participate in a program until designated restrictions were removed.[11]

It should be emphasized that these restrictions are not confined to defense-supported research. They tend to be more onerous in nondefense or defense-related agencies than in defense agencies. For example, attempts to interfere with university personnel policy have been most frequent with NASA, while detailed reporting and accounting requirements have tended to be most onerous with AEC. Until very recently, the Department of Health, Education, and Welfare maintained "blacklists" of scientists who could not be hired by the Department, even to consult on unclassified matters (although the blacklist did not apply to outside researchers sup-

11. Harold Orlans, "Ethical Problems in the Relations of Research Sponsors and Investigators," in *Ethics, Politics and Social Research*, Gideon Sjoberg, ed. (Cambridge: Schenkman, 1967), p. 9.

ported with HEW funds). Publication restrictions are most common in agencies such as Transportation or Housing and Urban Development, where many politically sensitive issues are closely related to research findings. Nevertheless, it is defense research which has set the pattern of reliance on the contractual instrument, imitated by other agencies, and this legal mechanism provides a broad avenue, in principle if not in practice, for government intrusion in university functions and policies. Only forbearance and enlightened administration on the part of government program officers have prevented much more widespread abuses. In a time of rising political tensions and disaffection between the general public and the academic community, the relatively happy experience of the 1945-65 period may not continue in the future.

The elaborate apparatus of security classification and personnel security clearances is largely a new phenomenon of World War II and the cold war, at least so far as it pertains to scientists and to general scientific knowledge. In previous wars only specific military operational plans and battlefield weapons were protected by security, and the notion of long-term security protection of scientific information or formal security clearance for researchers was largely unknown. But the security issue erupted as a fundamental confrontation between the scientific community and the political administrators at the end of World War II. Bush himself emphasized the importance of rapid declassification of the information obtained in war so that it could be used for the benefit of the national welfare and all of mankind.[12] The battle revolved around the important issue of who was to decide on what was classified and what could be declassified. The battle was joined in the newly created Atomic Energy Commission, where the scientific viewpoint emerged triumphant in the sense that the interpretation of broad declassification guidelines was left in the hands of scientists.

The arguments against extensive classification of scientific research, at least in peacetime, are many and convincing. In the first place, classification may and often does have the effect of shielding national policy from informed academic criticism. Even when all the essential facts and issues are actually in the public domain, a suspicion remains that there are secret facts which have an important bearing on policy. Supporters of government policy can use the mere existence of classified information to bolster their case and to erode the credibility of the opposition which is not privy to this information, even though the classified data may actually be irrelevant to the fundamental policy issues. The existence of classified information on the situation in Vietnam in 1965, for example, undoubtedly made it easier for the Johnson administration to escalate the war on the implicit ground that

12. Vannevar Bush *et al., Science the Endless Frontier,* a report to the President on a Program for Postwar Scientific Research, July 1945, reprinted July 1960 by the National Science Foundation, Washington, D.C. (document NSF 60-40), p. 8.

the government was aware of factors that the public did not know. There was a widespread public attitude of "the government knows best," and many people, even on campuses, were unaware that most of the information essential to evaluating government policy could be found in the public press. It is difficult to tell how influential this attitude was in silencing academic criticism, or at least in compromising its credibility—or how far it has persisted in present circumstances.

Furthermore, although the existence of classified information can lead to unquestioning acceptance of government policy so long as the general direction of policy is supported, it can have the opposite effect of rapidly opening up a credibility gap once the public begins to question the general drift of policy.

Another argument, particularly relevant with respect to classified research in the natural sciences and engineering, was that security classification could too easily be used to protect second-rate or incompetent scientific work by shielding it from the customary criticism of the scientific community. Scientists returned from the war effort with many horror stories of blunders and ignorance in research protected by security classification and compartmentalization. The degree to which this protection inhibits research progress is probably strongly dependent on the size of the community that exists inside the fence. After the war, security may have had little inhibiting effect on nuclear weapons development because the community in the know was so large and also at the forefront of their professions. On the other hand, even within the security fence the criterion of "need to know," which was applied with particular stringency by the military, could be quite inhibiting. Who was to be the judge of which piece of knowledge was essential to weapons development? There have been many cases where lack of communication between compartmentalized military research groups significantly delayed the conception and development of new weapons. The conduct of classified research has been a matter of vigorous debate on university campuses. But it is important to distinguish three rather different situations:

1. The conduct of classified research on the campus itself with the participation of regular faculty and graduate students, including even the submission of classified Ph.D. theses;

2. The administration by the university of a separately organized classified research institute (an FCRC), with a separate location and full-time professional research staff, and faculty participation at most only on a consulting basis—as, for example, the Lincoln Laboratory of M.I.T. or the AEC weapons laboratories administered by the University of California;

3. The participation of faculty members as individuals in classified consulting activities with agencies outside the university, including agencies of the United States government.

Many universities in recent years have moved to eliminate or reduce activities of the first type because they are considered basically incompatible with normal academic processes. On the other hand, there has been little disposition to interfere with activities of the third type, on the grounds that such interference would be incompatible with the principles of academic freedom, except insofar as such activities might directly interfere with a faculty member's academic duties or involve him in a conflict-of-interest situation.

Most of the controversy has centered on activities of the second type. Here the problem is that if the classified research is completely isolated from the university, there seems little justification for the university being involved at all, since it contributes little but housekeeping services to the activity, and this consumes the time and energy of an administration which ought to be devoted to more academic matters. On the other hand, to the degree to which the university assumes a genuine management and intellectual responsibility for the enterprise, its continuation as a part of the university is better justified to the sponsor, but questions of appropriateness for the university become more acute. Also, university management of an FCRC which is classified may lend respectability and tacit endorsement to an activity over which the academic community as a whole has little control or influence.

The case for university involvement in all phases of military research has been put by Professor Lawrence O'Neill of Columbia University, in the following terms:

The cure for arrogance is responsibility, especially of a visible kind. . . . In the particular sphere of military affairs, it is hard for me to imagine that our government and our people generally will give much credence to the opinions of academic people if these . . . people insist on refraining from any participation in such affairs. In order to maintain their credentials as commentators upon and influencers of public policy, academic people must, I believe, give some portion of their energies to the ingredients of such policy. This implies . . . that their institutions ought to participate in the processes that build and sustain the nation's military strength.[13]

Many who might agree with Professor O'Neill's sentiments in principle would argue that the requirement of participation is better met by individual rather than institutional participation. But it is also true that such individual participation is less "visible" and so does not convey the same image of participation and responsibility that an institutional commitment does. Considering the contradictions between classified research and the principles of open scholarship, institutional participation in classified research may prove justified only by exceptional circumstances of real national emergency,

13. L. H. O'Neill, "The Relationship of the Armed Forces and American Universities," speech before Army Scientific Advisory Panel, November 1968.

or as a temporary measure until more effective long-range arrangements can be made. Virtually all the university-operated classified laboratories were started to meet what was thought of at the time as a national emergency, and thereafter the arrangement was easier to perpetuate than to modify.

There may be a few exceptional cases in which classified work may have such high intrinsic scientific interest that its continuation on campus might be justified. This would be especially true in instances where most of the work was open and publishable, and where maintenance of the highest scientific quality would require access to classified data or use of experimental techniques that were classified for other reasons.

All the sensitive issues involved in DOD support of academic research become greatly magnified in the social and behavioral sciences. This is particularly true in two areas, "policy" research, and foreign area research, but research in the social sciences generally is more closely related to policy questions, and hence more politically controversial, than research in the physical and life sciences, or in the field of individual, as opposed to social, psychology. Counterinsurgency and "defense research" have become controversial issues in the academy—the abortive Project Camelot (discussed in Chapter 10) and the M.I.T.-Harvard "Project Cambridge" being perhaps the best-known examples. Also, in the physical and life sciences the more general and fundamental types of research have other applications than military and can be regarded as socially beneficial by grantees. When the military application stage is reached, the work is better done for the most part in industry or in separate research institutions organized for the purpose, and there has been built up over the years a large reservoir of specialized competence in military technology in such institutions outside universities. In the social sciences, especially in the study of foreign areas and peoples, almost all the existing competence is in universities, and defense agencies tend to turn to this source for even the more applied research, however closely related to policy determinations.

The basic problem is that the intersection with policy and politics is much larger and much more central to the discipline in the social sciences than in the natural sciences, where the political implications tend to be peripheral to the substance of the discipline and to its fundamental intellectual issues. An additional hazard is that the Defense Department will naturally seek out social scientists who are sympathetic to its viewpoints and policies. These men may acquire increased influence in the university because they are better supported, bringing money and prestige to their institutions, and acquiring a reputation that entitles their opinion to greater weight. What is more, they may have preferential access to facts which support Defense and government policies as well as to data and people denied to other scientists. Defense support could have the effect of arming the supporters and disarming the critics of American policy.

However, it is conceivable that by bringing social scientists into its councils, the Department's fixed positions and prejudices may be moderated by insights of the social science community, even though it relies mainly on its sympathizers. The general cohesiveness and critical standards characteristic of any academic discipline may have a far greater effect than the sympathies of a particular investigator. To the extent that objective evidence and knowledge about foreign nations and societies replace prejudices and stereotypes, there is a net gain which may well outweigh less informed but sharper or more radical academic criticism in influencing policy.

Paradoxically, the extent of military influence on the social sciences may be more a function of the availability of alternate sources of support than of the actual magnitude of military support. Furthermore, given any military involvement in academic social science research, the more narrowly the Defense Department interprets its mission in supporting such research, the greater the danger of its distorting the academic structure, and yet if it goes outside the academic community for intellectual support it tends to cut off the possibility of expanding the research community on which it depends. This is, of course, true of all areas of science support but may be particularly true for the social sciences because of the narrow base which currently exists in many specialized areas of social research.

Although military support of social science research is small in relation to total government support, its relative role in the support of research about certain foreign areas and peoples may be quite large. This poses the problem, among others, that the military will have predominant access to specialized social science information about certain remote areas, and it may be in a position to use this information, interpreted with its own professional biases, to put forth its own views in the national policy debate; it would enjoy a preferential position in interpreting the facts to politicians and nonspecialized executives. This becomes even more significant if the information is classified, or even if defense support creates an inference that there exists an additional classified product beyond what was published. The mere suspicion that such classified information exists may place an aura of "papa knows best" around the policy positions of the Defense Department and of government officials, and may gain illegitimate acceptance for its arguments.

Another serious problem raised by defense support of the social sciences is its possible effect in foreclosing future research opportunities in certain areas. As pointed out by Professor Gerald Berreman of the University of California, Berkeley, "anthropological research depends upon trust, confidence, and rapport which are difficult to achieve and maintain even under the best of circumstances," and this problem is greatly aggravated by association with the military. He also quoted the Committee on Ethics of the American Anthropological Association in a public statement which said:

Anthropologists engaged in research in foreign areas should be especially concerned with the possible effects of their sponsorship and sources of financial support. Although the Department of Defense and other mission-oriented branches of the government support some basic research in the social sciences, their sponsorship may nevertheless create an extra hazard in the conduct of fieldwork and jeopardize future access to research opportunities in the areas studied.[14]

With knowledge so specifically relevant to the formulation and execution of United States foreign policy, the question of the rightness or wrongness of that policy is difficult to avoid. Furthermore, because of the generally conservative bias of the military, the suspicion is bound to arise of the possible use of unique information obtained under military sponsorship to further the suppression of social change in foreign areas, on the unproved assumption that it is inimical to American interests.

Because the social sciences are almost bound to be less politically neutral than the natural sciences—except possibly in highly sensitive (and classified) areas such as biological warfare or nuclear weapons—the support of such research on campus by Defense agencies is likely to have a divisive effect among students and faculty and to upset the mutual respect and confidence which is the basis of the academic social system. Senator Fulbright has raised this issue in quite explicit terms, wondering whether the disruption of campus harmony is worth the results obtained from military-sponsored research.[15] Of course, such a view puts a weapon in the hands of student and faculty radicals which is reminiscent of the banning of liberal or radical speakers from campuses in the 1950's on the grounds that they were "controversial."

The system of military support and decision-making for science and technology, which is the result of a series of pragmatic responses, is being increasingly questioned on the campus and among the concerned public. This is especially true of academic science, where recent shortages of federal funds have revealed, really for the first time since the war, the vulnerability of graduate education and research to short-term fluctuations in policy and funding in government agencies which have no explicit mission to support education or research as such.

It seems likely that no matter how government is organized for support of academic science in the future, some method must be found to channel

14. *Defense Department-Sponsored Foreign Affairs Research*, Hearings before the Committee on Foreign Relations, U.S. Senate, May 9, 1968, p. 59.
15. *Ibid.*, p. 56.

an appreciable fraction of academic science funds to institutions for their discretionary use, in order that they may reassert greater control over their own internal priorities. The project system, with selection of projects by panels of scientific peers, is essential to the quality of American science and to public confidence that the money is being spent responsibly, but the project need not be an all-or-nothing affair; it should return to being what it once was in the early days of the Office of Naval Research—an extra injection of funds to support projects and people of outstanding promise, quality, or mission relevance, rather than the base of support of the entire system of graduate education and research.

20

Military Service and the Social Structure

As an educational and a social institution the military establishment has profound effects upon those whom it controls, and less direct but possibly more potent effects on those civilian institutions with which it, in many respects, competes.

Military service has been justified, in part, in terms of benefits such service entails, specifically a "second chance" for youngsters from lower-class backgrounds, and even for those from the middle class. Both those who do not have access to adequate schools and those who have access but fail are assumed to benefit. Ever since the end of World War II the military establishment has been large enough to supply such assumed opportunities for basic education on a significant scale, and to permit some testing of the assumption.

Even the limited data available[1] suggest that military service assists certain groups not only through specialized training but even more impor-

1. It requires a number of years after service before the consequences of military service on a person's civilian occupational status fully emerges. However, given the magnitude of the number of young men who have served a period of two years in the armed forces, there is strikingly little information available on the impact of their military service. Since 1965, research interest has increased because of the policy questions connected with the renewal of Selective Service and the war against poverty.

The methodological problems in assessing the impact of military experience on basic education or on professional skills represent a most complex research problem. Until recently it was possible only to draw inferences based on data about the characteristics and behavior of those who had actually served in the armed forces. The later surveys involve comparisons between those who served and those who did not, but even for these inquiries the selective factors among those who served are of unknown magnitude, and therefore it is extremely difficult to speak of the comparability of the veteran and the nonveteran group.

tantly through the influence of the military as a social organization. For many young men who spend between two and four years in service, the military tends to de-emphasize or even deny individual social and personal backgrounds and disabilities. Instead, the manpower practices and the organizational life create opportunities for the development of self-esteem and material rewards that are not linked to success based on any particular and narrow vocational or academic criteria. Success in basic education may be directly related to the fact that relative acceptance and involvement in the organization comes before, or at least at the same time as, training in skills.

The more depressed the socioeconomic background of the recruit, the more he seems likely to benefit from the experience in the armed services. This seems true even though recruitment and Selective Service practices since the end of World War II have tended to eliminate young men from the lowest socioeconomic groups, especially those who might benefit most from military service in terms of education.

The military establishment has become the largest vocational training institution in the United States, but only a minority of its personnel receive advanced, complex, technical training, and some of it is not directly applicable to the civilian economy. These technical schools do not, moreover, account for the relevance of the military as an institution of basic education. In fact, the acquisition of many of the skills taught in the armed forces presupposes adequate educational background and specialized aptitudes, and this background is to be found among young men with high school education, primarily from the middle majority of the civilian social structure—stable working-class or lower middle-class backgrounds; it is found less often in the more depressed groups.

On the contrary, precisely because it is a user of unskilled manpower, the military serves as an agency of basic education and youth socialization. Each year it must recruit and allocate vast numbers of personnel and, therefore, it must proceed on the basis of minimum standards and assume the maximum potentials. The result is a system of manpower allocation training that is the reverse of the pattern of civilian industrial enterprise. A task is found for each person rather than a person for each task. In this sense it is a "total" institution, because once admitted, all men have a place. For some, especially those with college degrees, this results in an underutilization of skills and aptitudes. But for persons from the lowest social strata there is a built-in process of upgrading.

The military serves also as a school for mobility from the very lowest ranks into nearly the highest. For some, it operates as the equivalent of the night law school. All the services provide that enlisted men, after a number of years of service, can apply for training as officers and receive the equivalent of college training, and there is reason to believe that promotion from the ranks is as great in the military as in industrial organizations, where entrance with a college degree has emerged as a prerequisite for advancement into managerial ranks.

Although the military inducts new cohorts of young men each year, once a person is admitted there is no question but that the organization must incorporate him into a functioning role. Not all new members adjust to the system, and the institution rejects others. But in contrast to most civilian institutions, and particularly in contrast to the public education system generally, the military establishment is based on the complete availability of opportunity plus a basic standard of acceptance of each member.

In fact, the military's training procedures assume maximum potentials for personal growth. The very notion of basic training implies that there is a set of skills that all members of the institution can and must acquire. Basic training is required of all members as a mechanism of assimilation, with former social characteristics de-emphasized during this period. Individual peculiarities are subordinated to the institution, but social disabilities accumulated during civilian life—such as delinquency records and low academic grades—are also subordinated.

Even more specifically, the training procedures assume that each person can master the contents of basic training; or that it is up to the system to teach each young man the essentials for success in basic training. This does not mean that there are no failures, but rather that those who direct the training develop the expectation that they can teach almost anyone. They are held—and hold themselves—accountable for their failures.

Without benefit of educational psychologists, the basic training systems of the armed services incorporate many so-called "advanced" educational procedures. There is no ability grouping—no tracking that sifts the alleged wheat from the alleged chaff. All recruits are commingled, so that the heterogeneous character of the group will create the optimum conditions for learning and group support. The training cycle is based on the equivalent of the nongraded or continuous educational development scheme. The recruit is not graded at the end of the course, but at the end of each subsection he is evaluated, given remedial help or recycled through the specific phase of his training in which he is deficient. There is extensive emphasis on instruction by an equivalent of the apprentice system, in which instruction is given during the actual exercise or task.

"Project 100,000" is a striking example of the operation of basic training in the military establishment. In 1966, a decision was made to undertake an experimental program for induction of 100,000 men who ordinarily would be screened out primarily because of limited educational background or low educational achievement. The experiment had two objectives—as a new resource for military manpower needs and as an experiment in basic education. If a similar task had been assigned to a civilian educational system, it would probably have segregated these men, devised a special curriculum for them, and cultivated in them a conviction of clear inferiority. But the armed forces included them in its regular training cycle. There was no "compensatory education" program.

As of September 1968 more than 140,000 men in Project 100,000 had entered the armed forces; previously all would have been rejected for induction or enlistment.[2] In fiscal year 1971 possibly 40,000 men will be taken in—about 11 per cent of new servicemen. Over one-third of those who entered were voluntary enlistments. They had completed an average of 10.5 grades of school. About 32 per cent had failed at least one grade of school, and 17 per cent two grades. More than 29 per cent were unemployed and an additional 27 per cent earned less than $60 a week. Their average age was twenty-one years.

There is now sufficient evidence to demonstrate the tragic waste of human resources for which the rigid entry requirements of the past were responsible. More than 95 per cent of the men successfully completed basic training, the discharge rate ranged from a low of 3 per cent in the Army to 9.5 per cent in the Air Force. (The Defense-wide discharge rate for all other men is about 2 per cent. All these rates include medical discharges for conditions other than lack of aptitude.) Equally remarkable is their achievement in advanced training, where the attrition rate was 12.3 per cent, compared with the average Army rate for all men who did not make it of 8 per cent.

After training, these men are not assigned only to "infantry, gun crews," and similar nontechnical specialties (33 per cent); their success in advanced technical training has increased their versatility, and more of them are assigned to tasks which will provide useful civilian skills: electrical and mechanical equipment repair, 25 per cent; service and supply handlers, 18 per cent; and administrative and clerical, 10 per cent.

Their success in some highly complex fields is especially notable: 74 per cent of those admitted to communications and intelligence training completed it; 87 per cent for administration and clerical training; 78 per cent for electrical and mechanical equipment repair training; and 55 per cent for training in electronic equipment repair. It should be repeated that these success rates were not achieved in special courses designed for the academically disadvantaged but under the same requirements established for other men. Success in basic training, with its opportunity for group participation, has become the basis, in part, for further education and advanced training.

2. The Armed Forces Qualification Test is a generalized intelligence and achievement examination, adapted to the military setting. Previously, only a small proportion of men who scored between 10 and 30 on the AFQT were accepted, and then only after they had scored above 90 on two or more aptitude tests. The revised standards permitted the acceptance of all high school graduates in this category without additional testing. Non-high school graduates with AFQT scores between 16 and 30 were accepted if they scored 90 or higher on at least one test; those with scores between 10 and 15 were required to pass two aptitude tests.

Another experiment, "Project Transition," initiated in 1968, represents the emerging approach of the military to technical training. As a response to the task of preparing its recruits for transition back to civilian life and as a contribution to larger societal goals, the armed forces have instituted a program of technical training for enlisted personnel who are completing their term of service and who missed an opportunity for technical training earlier. This is of special importance for recruits from lower socioeconomic backgrounds, who have entered combat units and developed skills that are not transferable to civilian employment. By January 1969, more than 50,000 servicemen had entered this program, and some 33,000 had completed it successfully.

The skill training in Project Transition comes after the recruit develops involvement and acceptance in the military—just the reverse of the civilian society where educational success is first demanded as a criterion for institutional involvement. In the Israeli armed forces also, where all citizens are eligible to serve except a tiny group of the severely handicapped, and there are no social or educational barriers, the recruits are given basic literacy education after mastering basic training and the rudiments of soldiering, and not before. These practices are followed in Project Transition.

The recruit from a lower socioeconomic or minority group soon discovers that the military provides a greater sense of protection than he has had in civilian life. His food and his shelter, his clothes, his medical needs, his welfare and insurance, all are directly available; they are not made available through exchange relations that may lead to a sense of exploitation. The military accepts responsibility for his personal well-being.

Satisfaction of such needs does not mean that recruits lack the resentment toward authority that so many have in the service; it does, however, emphasize the value to many recruits of a stable environment. The fact that the environment is socially integrated is important both for blacks and whites. The military establishment, having made the decision to integrate, assumes the individual will adjust, whatever his personal or family prejudices.

Both the information and the control systems of the military serve to enhance the position of the recruit who enters the military from a low status and disorganized milieu. Specific individuals are responsible for observing and monitoring his experiences and the results. The machinery is elaborate, cumbersome, and at times inefficient, but it engenders a peculiar sensitivity to the needs of a particular individual as they affect potential military efficiency—though the recruit himself may view this absorption with distaste. The professional ethic provides prestige among peers for the officer—both commissioned and noncommissioned—who takes care of his men. In part, also, the accountability results from the information system, which makes possible the follow-up on a particular recommendation or a particular action. The recruit is living in a residential setting, and it is more difficult to avoid confrontation with a human problem or to push aside personal needs. In the military, if a recruit has a medical problem, or is in need of remedial educational assistance—unlike civilian life, where intervention often means referral to an agency without follow-up—a report will be generated on the final outcome. The military's priority is concern with results.

The recruit comes to deal with, to work with, and to soldier with men with diverse backgrounds, styles, and aspirations. He comes to recognize the existence of a larger world. In contrast to many civilian institutions, the military is not based on the notion that the young man must accept himself as he is. The military is a school for fashioning new self conceptions; its system of informal communications explores and tests out these alternatives. Lower-status youths can assimilate new values on a somewhat more equal footing with the more privileged members of the larger society. It is the "underutilization" of the more middle-class groups that supplies an important ingredient for change. What civilian institutions and agencies are prepared to reproduce this sort of environment?

Education and income are direct measures of a person's position in the social structure; therefore, the level of achievement measures the military impact in these areas. A significant percentage of the active duty enlisted personnel have not completed high school; as of February 1965, 28 per cent of the enlisted strength of the Army had not completed at least 12 grades of education.[3] To be actively involved in finishing high school while in the armed forces is not a rare or deviant concern but a normal and relatively widespread practice. The opportunity for the lower socioeconomic groups to complete high school is demonstrated particularly in Table 20.1, which indicates that as of 1961, 27 per cent of the enlisted personnel in the Army completed high school while on active duty.

The ability of the armed forces to encourage young men to complete their high school education is an expression of the educational strategy which seeks to integrate general schooling with occupational responsibility. One of the basic instruments for this function is the United States Armed Forces Institute, which offers correspondence courses and remedial and regular courses on military installations both on and off duty. It is military policy to permit time off from duty to enroll, and the soldier has a continuous opportunity to do so. Often enlisted men become involved in these educational programs after basic training, that is, after they have achieved some status and recognition in the military community. Such educational involvement also reflects the emphasis of military authorities.

Two studies comparing the occupational mobility of veterans and non-

3. Department of Army Sample Survey of Military Personnel, "Survey Estimate of Educational Level of Male Enlisted Personnel by Grade and Component," 550 Report No. 52-65-E.

TABLE 20.1 Education Acquired by Personnel on Active Duty During Their Military Service

Educational Level	Army, August 31, 1961			
	Field Grade Officers	Company Grade Officers	Warrant Officers	Enlisted Men
	Percentages			
Some graduate work	21	8	1	b
Earned college degree	19	11	2	b
Attended college for first time (no degree)	30	23	51	5
Completed high school	5	7	39	27

	Air Force, May 31, 1960					
	Colonel	Captain	Warrant Officers	Master Sergeant	Technical Sergeant	Staff Sergeant
	Percentages					
Some graduate work	21	12	1	b	b	b
Earned college degree	18	18	3	1	1	1
Attended college for first time (no degree)	7	29	35	18	16	10
Completed high school	1	4	21	7	11	4

a Based on difference in per cent who had completed given amount education at present and at time of entry into military service.

b Less than 0.5 per cent.

Source: Based on sample survey prepared by Systems Development Branch, Adjutant General's Office, Department of the Army; Personnel Statistics Division, Comptroller of the Air Force, Headquarters, U.S. Air Force.

veterans show greater social mobility for veterans, particularly for men who completed their military experiences when relatively young.[4] Katenbrink indicates that mobility was concentrated among those who had completed less formal education at the time of their entrance into military service and who were from lower socioeconomic backgrounds. For this sample, occupational mobility was not primarily linked to attendance at technical military service schools, but was concentrated among those draftees who entered

4. One of these studies, by Katenbrink, is based on a careful analysis of the Newburgh, New York, area, and the other, by Otis Dudley Duncan and Robert W. Hodge, makes use of a regression analysis of the Chicago portion of the Six City Survey of Labor Mobility which included the job experiences of some 1,105 males who were 25-64 years old early in 1951 when the survey was taken. Irvin S. Katenbrink, Jr., "Military Science and Occupational Mobility," Center for Social Organization Studies, working paper No. 83, April, 1967, pp. 9-14; Otis Dudley Duncan and Robert W. Hodge, "Education and Occupational Mobility: A Regression Analysis," *American Journal of Sociology*, May 1964, p. 642.

the Army without high school education and who completed high school education by means of the United States Armed Forces Institute programs. The high school diploma is an important symbol in civilian society; it appears that the increased self-respect and increased sense of achievement derived from military service lead many men to complete their education.

In one study based on Social Security and Selective Service records, the relationship between military service and civilian earnings among 556 Maryland Selective Service registrants was examined.[5] Men with low AFQT scores (and correspondingly low levels of education) who had served in the armed forces, were earning up to $500 more a year ten years later than were men who did not serve. This relationship held even for men whose AFQT scores were so low that they should have been rejected (score of 10 or less), but were inducted by accident.[6] The advantage of military experience appears to be greatest for men with AFQT scores between 10 and 20. Above a score of 20, there appears to be little difference in later earnings between men with and without military service.

The most important investigation of the impact of military service on socioeconomic status was a 1964 survey based on data collected by the Current Population Survey and the National Opinion Research Center. Table 20.2 shows a comparison of veterans and nonveterans aged 18-34, classified by census occupational groupings. The relevance of these data rests on the large size of the sample in contrast to other studies: over 5,000 cases are involved. Over-all, the higher position of the veterans can be clearly seen. Moreover, it is striking to note the categories of differences that give a clue to the impact of military service. Laborers and service workers are lower in concentration among veterans than among nonveterans (4.5 per cent versus 10.3 per cent for laborers, and 5.8 per cent versus 7.5 per cent for service workers), while craftsmen, foremen, and kindred workers are higher among veterans (22.4 per cent versus 16.2 per cent). It is at this middle level that the greatest mobility appears to take place. There is also some increase in clerical and kindred workers, and in managers, officials, and proprietors, but of a more limited degree. These data point to the process of upgrading through education and military experience, a process leading those from the bottom to move upward into more middle-level occupations.

This body of data becomes even more revealing if the pattern of social mobility of each man is studied by comparing his occupation with his

5. Phillip Cutright, *A Pilot Study of Factors in Economic Success or Failure: Based on Selective Service and Social Security Records.* U.S. Department of Health, Education, and Welfare, Social Security Administration, Division of Research and Statistics, June 1964.

6. All of the low AFQT men with military service earned more than $3,000 and most were beyond the $4,000 level, but only three of the thirteen men without military service were in this wage range.

father's. Table 20.3, where a summary of these differences is presented in a highly condensed fashion, indicates limited but discernible consequences linked to military service—it seems difficult to attribute them only to selective recruitment. A comparison between white veterans and nonveterans under twenty-six reveals a difference of 5 per cent in upward mobility (36.1 and 31.2 per cent) and a corresponding difference in downward mobility. Among older age groups of whites, the difference is less but the veterans still showed more upward social mobility. (It should be kept in mind that these nonveterans included those who received higher education and therefore should have experienced more upward mobility, but this was not the case.)

Among nonwhites, similar consequences of military service occur. Al-

TABLE 20.2 Full-Time Occupations of Male National Sample
Nonveterans and Veterans, Aged 18-34, Autumn 1964[a]

Occupational Group[b]	Nonveterans	All Veterans
Professional, Technical, and Kindred Workers	13.7%	14.5%
Farmers and Farm Managers	2.0	1.2
Managers, Officials and Proprietors, Except Farm	6.2	11.0
Clerical and Kindred Workers	7.6	8.4
Sales Workers	6.3	6.6
Craftsmen, Foremen, and Kindred Workers	16.2	22.4
Operatives and Kindred Workers	26.1	24.6
Service Workers, Except Private Household	7.5	5.8
Farm Laborers and Foremen	4.0	1.1
Laborers, Except Farm and Mine	10.3	4.5
Total Per Cent	99.9%	100.1%
Number of Cases	(3970)	(2651)

[a] Source for this table is a special survey conducted by the Current Population Survey in November 1964 for the Department of Defense Study of the Draft.

[b] Occupation groups are those listed as major groupings in the 1960 *Alphabetical Index of Occupations and Industries* (Bureau of Census, Washington, 1960). Private Household workers are excluded from the table.

though the number of cases is limited, there is a strikingly lower concentration of downward social mobility among veterans compared with nonveterans.

Because all these data deal with the over-all impact of short-term military experience, one cannot expect change of greater magnitude. But they do suggest the conclusion that the lower the social position, the more positive the impact of short-term military service. Conversely, for men from high civilian social status, short-term service has less effect and even some negative effect.

In addition to basic education, the military extends to young men with limited educational background and from low socioeconomic status the

TABLE 20.3 Summary of Intergenerational Mobility, National Sample
Males Aged 18-34, Veterans and Nonveterans, White and Nonwhite, Autumn 1964

	White								Nonwhite			
	Nonveteran Under 26		Veteran Under 26		Nonveteran 26-34		Veteran 26-34		Nonveteran 26-34		Veteran 26-34	
	No.	%	No.	%	No.	%	No.	%	No.	%	No.	%
Upward Mobility	381	31.2	171	36.1	318	40.9	645	42.1	36	51.4	38	52.1
Stable	379	31.1	145	30.6	281	36.2	526	34.3	15	21.4	22	30.1
Downward Mobility	460	37.7	158	33.3	178	22.9	361	23.6	19	27.2	13	17.8
	(1220)	100.0	(474)	100.0	(777)	100.0	(1532)	100.0	(70)	100.0	(73)	100.0

opportunity to enter professional positions of higher status within the military or in civilian life. One measure of the effect of this opportunity is the social origins of the top military leadership group, brigadier general and above. Table 20.4 shows that the concentration of sons of white-collar and working-class fathers in the top military leadership of the United States has been increasing since 1910. This increase represents, in part, the expansion in the size of the military establishment; but it also stems from a system of recruitment and training that seeks to emphasize achievement criteria. The fact that college-level education is supplied by the profession itself serves to broaden the base of recruitment. As of 1960, 19 per cent of the West Point class of 1960 were of working-class origins,[7] making the military as open a professional group as any in the United States.

TABLE 20.4 Military Leadership, 1910-50:
     Father's Occupation

	Army 1910-20 %	Army 1935 %	Army 1950 %	Navy 1950 %	Air Force 1950 %	West Point Class 1960 %
Business	24	16	29	32	26	15
Professional and Managerial	46	60	45	38	38	50
Farmer	30	16	10	7	15	—
White collar	—	6	11	18	16	13
Worker	—	2	5	5	5	19
Other						3
Total	100	100	100	100	100	100
Number	(37)	(49)	(140)	(162)	(60)	(765)

Source: *The Professional Soldier: A Social and Political Portrait,* by Morris Janowitz (Glencoe, Illinois: The Free Press, 1960), p. 91.

There are, of course, important limiting conditions on this trend toward broader recruitment. Increasingly, a college degree is required for entrance to Officer Candidate School (OCS) or is given priority value among applicants, which suggests that the personnel agencies of the armed forces do not fully recognize the significance of opportunities for occupational mobility as incentives for service. For example, the Air Force controls the entrance to such schools by increasing the amounts of formal education required as a prerequisite, despite evidence that such criteria are of negative value in career retention. Army policies give priority to direct college enlistments for OCS over enlisted applicants. These policies tend to diminish the opportunities for mobility, and reflect the sensitivity of the armed forces to their "professional" image in the larger society.

7. Morris Janowitz, *The Professional Soldier: A Social and Political Portrait* (Glencoe, Ill.: Free Press, 1960), p. 91.

The armed forces do supply a significant agency for the education and development of professional and managerial skills. In terms of sheer numbers, the educational benefits of the original "GI Bill," plus subsequent legislation, are primary. The resources allocated under this legislation could have been distributed by national scholarship programs and thereby have produced a similar contribution to the occupational and professional structure. Working-class men and members of minority groups, while in the armed forces, come into close contact with persons who are college-educated or college-bound. They develop a sense of self-confidence about their ability to succeed socially and intellectually in higher education. Since these educational benefits are based on military service and not on academic achievement, they clearly operate to involve a broader social group than traditional scholarship programs, which have until recently been oriented to students from families of higher social and economic background. So it can be concluded that the experiences of military service itself stimulate young men to seek college education, who in the normal course of events might not have been so motivated.

The armed forces extend college and professional education to officers and enlisted personnel while on active duty. Many hundreds of career officers study at civilian colleges every year for advanced degrees. The services help enlisted men to complete a college education as a channel for entrance into the officer corps. The armed forces also offer master's degrees at two technical institutes. The over-all impact is reflected in the fact that more than one-quarter of all career officers have advanced civilian degrees; and the proportion continues to increase. This schooling is distinct from attendance at the various levels of military professional schools conducted by the armed forces.

Civilian universities conduct educational programs on or near military bases so that enlisted men and officers can pursue college and advanced degrees on a part-time basis. A wide exposure to college-level education is offered through correspondence courses. To these efforts must be added hundreds of specialized technical and professional short and longer courses. The result is that, beyond the fact that the armed forces operate as a vast educational institution supplying basic-level (high school) education, even more resources are committed to college level and professional education.

The impact of the military on the distribution of occupational and professional skills flows not only from the educational enterprise but also from the on-the-job experience and internships that military life affords. The armed forces must extend education and training to men who are destined to spend only a few years on active duty. Each year before the Vietnam build-up, approximately 500,000 personnel left the service for civilian life; at least 50 per cent probably had received some relevant post-high school occupational and professional education and training.

The majority of the military personnel who receive this training are also relatively short-term personnel. The professional affiliations they had before or completed after military service become overriding. In civilian life, they constitute only a limited proportion of their profession and they become scattered throughout the United States. It is rare when the military serves as the major supplier of a specialty; one instance is airline pilots, of whom about 80 per cent receive their basic pilot training in the armed forces. For some professions, as, for example, doctors and lawyers, military experience is a period of intensive internship. In the case of psychiatry, the consequences of military service have been to speed up the development of community and preventative psychiatry in civilian life, since military psychiatrists are often expected to serve an entire community of wives and children as well as men in service. For those without access to technical or professional training in civilian life, military experience may be a turning point. Those already launched may find the military one more step in their career development.

Since 1939, the Selective Service System has been a key element in determining which social groups served in the armed forces.[8] Selective Service not only directly allocates manpower to the ground forces but creates the conditions under which young men enlist into the ranks of the Air Force, Navy, and Marines. Equally critical, its operations stimulate participation in programs of officer education and training.

The over-all impact of the system has been unequal in that the very bottom and the very top of the social structure have been underrepresented among those required to serve. Because of these inequalities as well as administrative rigidities, and uncertainties about military service, extensive criticism of the legitimacy of the draft has developed among college students, reinforced, of course, by the massive dissent about America's military involvement in Southeast Asia. Based on a large-scale sample survey of enlisted men who were on active duty in 1964,[9] it is apparent that extremes in socioeconomic background have been linked to lower rates of military service. At the bottom of the social structure, medical and educational deficiencies result in higher rejection rates; at the top, educational and occupational deferments have led to higher exemption rates.

Sons of fathers with less than eighth grade education and sons of fathers with graduate study are less likely to serve (60.8 per cent and 55 per cent

8. See National Advisory Commission on Selective Service: *In Pursuit of Equity: Who Serves When Not All Serve?* (Washington: Government Printing Office, 1967). See also James W. David, Jr., and Kenneth M. Dolbeare, *Little Groups of Neighbors: The Selective Service System* (Chicago: Markham, 1968).

9. Albert D. Klassen, *Military Service in American Life Since World War II: An Overview* (Chicago: National Opinion Research Center, Report No. 117, September 1966), p. 30, Table III.I.

respectively) than sons of fathers with intervening levels of education, from ninth grade through college graduate (average 69 per cent). Those with highly educated fathers were most likely to be deferred (28.5); those with fathers of less than eight years of school were most likely to be rejected for service (23 per cent).

In Table 20.5 additional data on educational background and father's

TABLE 20.5 Educational Background and Father's Occupation
of Enlisted Men, All Services, 1964[a]

Educational Background *Highest Grade Attained before* *Entering Active Service*		Per Cent
Eighth Grade or Less		7.5
Ninth to Eleventh Grade		30.9
High School Graduate		45.8
Less Than Two Years of College		9.8
Two or More Years of College without Bachelor's Degree		4.3
Bachelor's Degree or Graduate Study		1.7
		———
	Total Per Cent	100.0
	Number of Cases	39,378[c]
Father's Occupation *		
Professional, Technical and Kindred[b]		6.1
Managerial, Officials and Proprietors		10.6
Sales		3.1
Clerical		2.9
Craftsmen		26.7
Operatives		24.0
Service Workers		5.0
Laborers		6.2
Farmers		15.3
		———
	Total Per Cent	100.0
	Number of Cases	39,378[c]

* When respondent was age 15.

Note: [a]Source for this table is the 1964-65 Department of Defense Study of the Draft. The data are from the largest subsample of the survey. The determination of this subsample is described in Albert D. Klassen, Jr., "Subsampling the Survey Data of the Military Manpower Policy Study" (Military Manpower Survey Working Paper No. 7), National Opinion Research Center, University of Chicago, October 1966.

[b] Occupation groups used are the major categories defined by the Census. Note that "Private Household Workers" are excluded, and that the "Farming" group used in the table combines the Census titles "Farmers and Farm Managers" and "Farm Laborers and Foremen," since this distinction was not present in the source data.

[c] Excluded from the table are 10,539 individuals who did not respond to one of the questions, or whose response was inapplicable for miscellaneous reasons. Total enlisted men in the maximal subsample are 39,378+10,539=49,917.

occupation is presented. Enlisted personnel were mainly recruited from the craftsmen and the operatives categories. White-collar managerial and professional groups, and especially service workers and laborers were un-derrepresented. The military serves as a device for integrating the sons of the farming population, who continue to be overrepresented in the armed forces.

The education of the recruit at the time of his entrance into the armed forces also demonstrates the same pattern of underrepresentation of the social extremes. Only 3.8 per cent of the active duty enlisted personnel in 1965 had eighth grade or less education. The better educated are also markedly screened out; only 1.3 per cent of the enlisted personnel had a bachelor's degree or more; only 18.4 per cent had any college education.[10] Since 1966 these inequalities have been reduced. Changed selection stan-dards have meant that the rejection rate at the lower end of the social structure has gone down, while fewer educational deferments have in-creased the incidence of service among higher socioeconomic groups.

The Selective Service System has had pervasive consequences for the population attending institutions of higher education, and, in turn, for college student youth movements in the United States. The impact of military manpower requirements has been not only on those who served but equally on those who do not serve, especially in "defining the situation" for them by means of educational deferments. The number of young men who have entered or remained in college, or until recently, in graduate and professional school, in order to gain an educational exemption cannot be estimated. But the draft has clearly increased the already burgeoning enrollment in colleges and universities. It has also served, so long as occupational deferments were available, to induce students to enter fields such as public school teaching, which they might not otherwise have opted for.

The impact of the military establishment on the domestic social struc-ture is not based primarily on the direct consequences of military operations. Since 1940, the armed forces have operated as a vast training, engineer-ing, and logistical enterprise. They have functioned as a specialized large-scale organization and produced a veteran population of some 24 million persons. The skills that these men have accumulated have produced changes in the occupational and professional structure of the nation, and will pro-duce more. Changes in skill have probably been greater than changes in social and political perspectives caused by the military experience.

If the antimilitary swing of the pendulum continues, and limited wars do not spread, the quantitative impact of the military will be less great

10. Harold Wool, *The Military Specialist: Skilled Manpower for the Armed Forces* (Baltimore: The Johns Hopkins Press, 1968), p. 103.

in the future. Among those who serve, however, the underrepresentation of the class extremes will probably diminish in response to a rising sense of present unjust selectivity. If the nation moves toward military professionalism and a voluntary army, the future impacts on social class structure may be vastly different in quantitative and qualitative terms. (See Chapter 25.)

At present, the potential impact on civilian institutions is wider than the effect on individuals, at least in terms of numbers served. The quantitative scope of the contribution the armed forces can make or should make probably involves only a limited segment of these youths who are now being failed by civilian education. When the armed forces return to the force levels that existed before the Vietnam build-up, they can only offer "a second chance" to approximately 10 per cent, and no more than 20 per cent, of the annual intake of recruits. Paradoxically, the evidence presented here has its main relevance in identifying practices civilian agencies will have to imitate if basic and professional education is to be provided for disadvantaged groups in our society. The greatest impact is an indirect and potential impact on the institutions of civilian education.

21

Military Service and Race

The role of the military establishment in the status of racial minorities in American life has been important throughout the nation's history. At various times the military has followed, and at other times has led, civilian institutions in the implementation of racial policy.

Negroes fought in all of the nation's wars, but until recently—ironically enough in a widely unpopular war—their services were usually unwanted, unwelcomed, and restricted. Negroes struggled to be included in military service from the beginning but won only limited gains. A degree of integration occurred in the War of 1812, but Negro troops were essentially segregated until after World War II. On December 1, 1941, six days before the Japanese attack on Pearl Harbor brought the United States into that war, General George C. Marshall declared that "the settlement of vexing racial problems cannot be permitted to complicate the tremendous task of the War Department. . . ."[1] With isolated exceptions, that view prevailed throughout the war despite the urgent need for manpower. The controversy over the fighting qualities of the Negro combat soldier, which occurred in World War I, was revived in World War II. The armed forces, in effect, followed the restrictive racial practices of civilian society. Not only were military units segregated but Negro personnel were assigned to noncombat units with limited responsibilities. In the prestige system of the military, Negroes were placed in lower-status positions, duplicating their place in the civilian social structure. Some efforts were made to upgrade Negro personnel and to develop all-Negro combat units, but Negro soldiers were systematically underutilized, and segregated units often had low effectiveness. Negro

1. Cited in Ulysses Lee, *The Employment of Negro Troops,* one of a series of special studies of the U.S. Army in World War II (Washington, D.C.: Office of the Chief of Military History, United States Army, 1966), p. 140.

military and civilian morale suffered in response. Only toward the end of World War II were steps taken to develop integrated combat units in the European theater; these units performed with distinction.

The first major step toward integration came on February 27, 1946, when the late Secretary of the Navy, James V. Forrestal, ordered all naval ratings open to all sailors, regardless of race. Three years later, in response to a 1948 executive order by President Truman calling for "equality of treatment and opportunity in the armed services," the Air Force implemented a program of total integration. In 1949, the Army also began to integrate—there were 220 all-black Army units in 1949—and accelerated its efforts in mid-1950 under pressure of the manpower needs of the Korean War.[2] Combat units, in particular, were rapidly integrated. But it was not until 1954 that the Army abolished its last all-Negro units.[3]

As a result of these measures, the military establishment as an institution was more racially integrated than most civilian institutions. The degree of integration varied. Enlisted ranks were integrated more rapidly and thoroughly than the officer corps. Only three blacks had been graduated from West Point prior to 1936, and the first black midshipman did not graduate from Annapolis until 1949.[4] Today West Point has sixty-two black undergraduates, Annapolis has forty, and the Air Force Academy, fifty-two. By 1969, only 2.1 per cent of all officers—8,335 in the Army, Navy, Marine Corps, and Air Force—were black, though blacks are 11.2 per cent of the total population.[5] There are two black brigadier generals in the Army, and one black lieutenant general in the Air Force, but no black admirals. A second black Air Force general recently resigned at the end of his normal career period.

The Vietnam war changed the racial profile of the armed forces dramatically. By mid-1968, Negroes made up 10.5 per cent of American troops in the war zone, including those in Thailand and on naval vessels off Vietnam. The Negro has been warmly welcomed into the armed forces during the Vietnam war. General Westmoreland singled out the Negro for commendation for valor in a speech to the South Carolina Legislature, a posture consistently maintained throughout his command.

Many have expressed concern about the social class basis of United States induction and battle deaths. Deferments of middle-class students and

2. Charles C. Moskos, "Racial Relations in the Armed Forces," in Charles Moskos, *The American Enlisted Man,* (New York: Russell Sage Foundation, 1970); pp. 108-133.
3. The Defense Department announced on October 30, 1954, that there were no longer any all-Negro units. Defense Secretary Clark Clifford said on July 25, 1968, "By 1955 all formal racial discrimination had been eliminated, although vestiges lingered into the early 1960's."
4. Richard Bardolph, *The Negro Vanguard* (New York: Vintage Books, 1961), p. 448.
5. *New York Times,* January 4, 1969, p. 11.

the drafting of lower-status youths have until recently proceeded side by side, and the pressure for equalization has only arisen as the war has dragged on. (See Chapter 20.) It was assumed that the risks of modern war were unequally distributed and, therefore, that the casualty rate as well would fall most severely on the lower socioeconomic classes, on Negroes in particular. The argument of unequal casualties is linked to the technology of war. The heaviest casualties are to be found in the infantry, and the infantry is expected to recruit the greatest concentrations of lower-status personnel since its educational and skill requirements are the most limited. Research conducted on the casualties of the Korean conflict had, in effect, indicated such a heavier concentration of the battle casualties among the lower socioeconomic groups.[6] In the Vietnam war, therefore, a similar concern was raised. Of the 6,644 deaths in Vietnam for 1961-66, 14.6 per cent were Negro. During 1967, of the 9,378 men killed by enemy action, the Negro percentage was 13.5 per cent. In 1970, roughly 9.9 per cent of the troops in Vietnam were Negro; but Negro deaths in April 1970 stood at roughly 14 per cent of the total deaths.[7]

In the Army and Marine Corps, as a whole, however, Negroes amounted to 13.3 per cent of total personnel, approximately the same as the Negro component of the United States population. The proportions of Negroes in the Navy and Air Force were smaller than in the total population. Negro involvement in Vietnam combat has been disproportionately higher for a combination of reasons. According to Thomas A. Johnson, Negroes made up an estimated 20 per cent of combat troops and more than 25 per cent of high-risk elite Army units such as paratroops. He reported: "Estimates of Negro participation in some airborne units have been as high as 45 per cent, and up to 60 per cent of some airborne rifle platoons."[8]

The acceptance—even the seeking—of danger and high risk is itself related to the insidious damage of racial injustice. As a white junior infantry officer told Johnson in Vietnam: "It's an awful indictment of America that many young Negroes must go into the military for fulfillment, for status—and that they prefer service overseas to their homeland."[9] The *esprit de corps,* prestige, and additional pay of combat arms and elite combat units are spurs to acceptance of the possibility of death among soldiers, many of whom have felt that life in "the real world"—GI slang for the United States—offers far less.

Substantial numbers of blacks have chosen to make the military a career, attracted by the opportunity for advancement, job security, pay, the

6. A. J. Mayer and T. F. Hoult, "Social Stratification and Combat Survival," *Social Forces,* Vol. 34, December 1955, pp. 155-159.

7. Thomas A. Johnson, the *New York Times,* April 29, 30, and May 1, 1968. Johnson, a Negro reporter, described his findings on a trip to Vietnam in a series of three articles.

8. *Ibid.* See also *New York Times,* Aug. 17, 1969, p. 54.

9. Johnson, *New York Times* series.

absence of overt discrimination, and the sense of manhood that the military tends to inspire. Re-enlistment rates for blacks are double those for whites and the percentage of black noncommissioned officers is higher than the percentage of blacks in the national population.[10] In the Army, one out of four middle-level sergeants in combat occupation specialties is black, though black soldiers in Vietnam maintain that the number of black junior officers is decreasing.[11]

In a 1964 study of servicemen, veterans, and nonveterans, in the 16-34 age brackets, sociologist Charles Moskos found that Negro enlisted men were more inclined to like military life than were whites. Negro civilians—both veterans and nonveterans—were more favorably disposed toward the military than their white counterparts, and Negro veterans placed a higher value on military training than did whites (53.9 per cent compared to 29.9 per cent).[12]

But the pattern is quite the reverse in the National Guard, where Negro membership is disproportionately low. The *Report of the National Advisory Commission on Civil Disorders* found that the higher percentages of Negroes in Army units, compared with the small numbers in the National Guard, "contributed substantially to [the Army's] better performance" on riot duty; the commission recommended an increase in Negroes in the Guard. In response to such recommendations, the commander of the National Guard Bureau, Air Force Major General Winston P. Wilson, commissioned analysts to conduct attitude surveys, instituted reforms in accord with reports of the special boards, and inaugurated an experimental test of Negro recruitment in New Jersey, where the Guard was authorized a temporary overstrength of 5 per cent—865 extra vacancies. By July 31, 1968, these positions had been filled, 88.7 per cent of them by Negroes so that the statewide proportion of black Guardsmen rose from 2.5 to 6.4 per cent. The Guard then sought to increase Negro recruitment nationally, but Congress rejected a version of the New Jersey plan because it appeared to smack of "discrimination in reverse." By the end of 1969, the low rate of Negro enlistment had shown no change; indeed, fewer Negroes were in the Guard than at the end of 1968—5,487 in 1969, fewer than in 1968 when 5,541 were in service, which was fewer than in 1967 when 5,802 were in service. A perplexed General Wilson commented: "For some reason we haven't been able to get a handle on why they haven't wanted to enlist in the National Guard."[13]

There is little evidence to explain low black involvement in the National Guard. But a variety of such explanations have been given, centering

10. *Christian Science Monitor*, May 18, 1968, p. 1.
11. *New York Times*, January 25, 1970.
12. Charles C. Moskos, *Findings on the American Military Establishment*, mimeographed unpublished manuscript, Northwestern University, 1967.
13. *New York Times*, February 26, 1970.

primarily on two related and racially defined reasons: First, the black conception of the Guard as a white institution, which they see as related more to the states, which are seen as socially limited, than to the federal government, which is seen, under liberal administrations, at least, as more cosmopolitan; and second, the black fear that Guard duty will require them to confront black civilians in an adversary situation. For example, several Negroes on riot details at Fort Knox told interviewers they would not shoot Negroes even if ordered to do so; some said they might even join insurrectionists. (Some whites at Fort Knox also expressed dislike of riot duty, but on grounds of dislike of racial rioting and personal inconvenience.) And a group of Negro soldiers at Fort Hood, Texas, balked at the prospect of going to Chicago for riot duty during the 1968 Democratic Convention; of the dissidents, forty-three were ordered to the guardhouse.

Despite the many positive signs of Negro involvement in the armed services, racial unrest in the armed services, paradoxically, has accelerated. Disruptions have occurred at military bases in the United States and in Vietnam. For example, at Camp Lejeune in North Carolina, in the summer of 1969, a cross was burned on the lawn of a Negro civilian employee of the base. The riot at Longbinh stockade outside Saigon in September 1968 was another serious racial incident. One white soldier was killed and several wounded after a black "takeover" of the stockade.

The most serious tensions exist in the Marine Corps, which has a higher percentage of blacks than the other services, and where iron discipline and uncompromising rules are a matter of tradition and pride. Although they have not been widely publicized, there have been numerous racial clashes at Marine bases and stockades since 1965. These outbreaks often led to harsher rules aimed at preventing communication among blacks, and stronger measures to stamp out what was considered alien black-power influence. The situation became so tense in the spring of 1969 at Camp Lejeune, North Carolina, where 3,500 Marines were stationed, that the commanding general appointed a committee of seven officers, several of them black, to study the situation. The committee reported that "a racial problem of considerable magnitude continues to exist and, in fact, may be expected to increase" and that Marines, both black and white, were being returned to civilian society "with more deeply seated prejudices than were individually possessed upon entrance to service."[14] They found "complete disillusionment of the young black Marine with progress toward the realization of equal treatment and opportunity" and noted racial prejudices in many white officers and NCO's often manifested in stories, jokes, and references; continued segregation of many local community facilities; discrimination against blacks by the MP's;

14. *New York Times,* August 10, 1969, p. 67.

failure of the "mast procedure" to provide effective redress for grievances of blacks; and increased "polarity of white to white and black to black." The command took no action on the report; on July 20, 1969, a white Marine was killed in a fight, according to charges, begun in an attack by 30 black and Puerto Rican Marines on 14 white Marines. The division commanding officer, Major General Michael P. Ryan, said there were "indications" that members of the Black Panthers were involved because some had been seen to give the clenched fist salute. The battalion involved was suddenly sent to the Mediterranean for training.[15]

In August there were large racial brawls at Kaneohe Marine Air Station in Honolulu and Fort Bragg, North Carolina. When the Marine Corps commandant, General Leonard F. Chapman, flew to Honolulu, a number of ranking black enlisted men presented more than a dozen complaints about bias in promotions, harsher punishment of blacks, lack of black toiletries in the post exchange, and absence of soul music in the enlisted clubs. On September 3, 1969, General Chapman issued a message to all Marine commands calling for an end to racial violence and renewed attempts to eliminate discrimination against blacks.[16] The message contained concessions to the rights of blacks to cultural diversity and racial identity. The Afro haircut would be permitted if neatly trimmed and not more than three inches on top. Blacks would not be forbidden from giving the black-power clenched fist salute to greet one another if not given "in a manner suggesting direct defiance of duly constituted authority." Soul music would be provided in the service clubs. Commanders were ordered to review their promotion and mast procedures to insure that there was no discrimination and that blacks' needs were being attended to, and to be available "after hours" to hear grievances.

After General Chapman's order, the Army and Air Force also announced that they considered Afro haircuts within regulations.[17] Secretary of the Army Stanley Resor released a directive to army commanders on racial problems similar to General Chapman's.[18] Thus, at a time when it appeared that official military policies and black nationalism were so far apart that no room could be made for black cultural identity, the services gave ground.

Nevertheless, a few concessions on dress will not remove many of the deep-seated antagonisms of blacks in the military, nor various practices

15. *New York Times,* July 29, 1969, p. 19.
16. *New York Times,* September 4, 1969, p. 39.
17. *Army Times,* September 17, 1969, p. 1. New Army regulations permit three-inch haircuts and neatly trimmed mustaches (goatees and beards are still banned), and decree that hair cannot be cut less than one inch without the soldier's permission. Shaving of heads or excessively short haircuts are described as "degrading or depersonalizing." *New York Times,* June 1, 1970.
18. *New York Times,* October 14, 1969, p. 1.

of subtle or flagrant persecution against black servicemen on and off the base. Two staff writers on the *Los Angeles Times* reporting on racial tensions in California military installations in November 1969 observed that "the troublemaker often cited is the young, single, black serviceman . . . a product of a society increasingly aware of minority civil rights, impatient and assertive in the presence of discrimination" who not infrequently wears an Afro haircut and reads militant black literature. They quoted a black sergeant's comments on young black recruits: "They resent taking orders from whites. First of all they see me as a brother. Right away they get me in trouble."[19] Military demands for conformity seem to the racially conscious black a reflection of white institutional authority generally and an affront to his new sense of cultural racial identity. It remains to be seen whether the militant and the military styles can be reconciled.

An Army study of race relations in United States Army bases throughout the world reported in January 1970 "an increase in racial tensions" was widespread, and warned that "unless immediate action is taken to identify problem areas at the squad and platoon level, increased racial confrontations can be expected." Racial problems had been ignored or covered up in the past and, therefore, "Negro soldiers seem to have lost faith in the Army."[20]

A briefing of commanders in South Vietnam on the study's findings produced some significant comments, as recorded on tape and replayed for newsmen; a sampling from the official briefing follows:

We have found that the potential and the ingredients for widespread racial violence in the Army appeared to be present.

The assessments of the degree of danger vary, but several different individuals of various grades said that if nothing is done there are likely to be widespread disruptions in a year or less . . .

. . . to take an ostrichlike approach to racial fear, hostility and misunderstanding is indefensible, especially when the signs can be read in the racial obscenities written by both groups on latrine walls and can be heard from an alarming number of black soldiers who readily complain they suffer injustice in the Army solely because of their race . . .

. . . the cries of the Negro soldiers—enlisted men and even officers—have never been so loud.

The location of a large number of sizable military installations in the South has encouraged the adoption of discriminatory attitudes among some career military and has increased the tension for the black recruit. Incidents such as the burning of a wooden cross and the flying of a Confeder-

19. William Endicott and Stanley Williford, "Color and Mayhem: Uptight in the Armed Forces," *The Nation*, 464, November 3, 1969.
20. The study, reported in the *New York Times* of January 25, 1970, had been commissioned in the summer of 1969 by Army Chief of Staff General William C. Westmoreland.

ate flag over the base at Camranh Bay in Vietnam on the day Martin Luther King was assassinated attest to continuing affronts to black racial pride. The Concerned Veterans of Vietnam, formed after the Camranh incident, now has a $65,000 grant from the Office of Economic Opportunity, offices in three states, and a veteran's assistance program. To take another example, the Moormen have organized at Quantico Marine Base in Virginia; they wear black berets and dashikis off duty and give each other the clenched fist black power salute. Initially such actions were subjected to Marine discipline, but the Corps regulations have been relaxed to permit them, in an unusual departure from traditional practices.

Most blacks have the common problem of establishing and maintaining identity within the military structure, and although identity is a problem confronting all servicemen, it affects blacks more deeply because the officially sanctioned military ideology rejects attempts by groups, and particularly blacks, to establish their own separate identity within the system. This highly structured way of life is considered by the military to transcend all separate identities, but it is seen by blacks as heavily dependent on traditional white attitudes and cultural identifications. Furthermore, many white officers are still unable to regard the proud young black as other than arrogant, as one who does not know his place, and needs to be brought into line for the good of the service. They see this as the legitimate military approach, while angry young blacks see it as racism.

Black anger and black separatism are correspondingly on the increase. A number of black military groups now segregate themselves in clubs and dining halls. In Vietnam it is reported that all major United States enclaves have Negro-only clubs on their fringes, "from combination whorehouse and truck-wash emporiums outside Danang, to bars on Saigon's waterfront,"[21] just as whites have their favorite off-post meeting places. Jack Moskowitz, then Deputy Assistant Secretary of Defense for Civil Rights, has predicted that Negro protests would increase in Vietnam as the fighting decreased. "The young Negro serviceman is expressing his black awareness and wants to be respected."[22]

Alfred B. Fitt, Assistant Secretary of Defense for Manpower under President Johnson, has pointed out that military integration has been mainly institutional: "In all significant respects and all ways that can yield to objective analysis, in all matters over which we have any control, integration works. I would not suggest that in social, nonofficial conduct there is absence of all prejudice. In off-duty associations there is not necessarily the same kind of companionship of the duty period."[23]

According to Charles Moskos, sanctions imposed by military authori-

21. "The Other War: Whites Against Blacks in Vietnam," the *New Republic,* January 18, 1968.
22. *Washington Post,* November 15, 1968.
23. Interview, August 19, 1968.

ties keep on-duty racial incidents at a minimum and most "confrontations" occurred off duty, and many, off base. He found—in 1966—greater integration in basic training and maneuvers than on garrison duty, in sea versus shore duty, in combat rather than in noncombat service.

If these suggestions are correct, a slowdown or ceasefire reducing combat and sea duty, increasing noncombat garrison duty, could seriously heighten racial tension in the years to come. The acknowledged progress of Negroes in the armed services could bear the same relationship to present racial unrest as the rising expectations in civilian life probably bear to the urban rebellions. As a deprived group breaks out of confinement and sees the possibility of hope, the more impatient and angry its members become.

Despite the rising and ominous signs of racial polarization in the services, there are certain indications of positive attitudinal changes among whites, reflecting a similar paradox in the civilian society. Also paradoxical is the tendency of whites to perceive Negro progress more affirmatively than blacks do, a gap in perspective that, in itself, tends toward further alienation.

Young whites who have served in integrated units have, usually for the first time in their lives, had prolonged contact with Negroes under conditions of relative equality. According to studies of the impact of service in integrated combat units at the close of World War II, such service reduced racial prejudice among white soldiers.[24] Social contact is not enough to change attitudes; but social contact under conditions of mutual interdependence, which combat is, may lead to unit cohesion, self-esteem, and reduced prejudice.

A 1963 survey[25] indicated white and Negro agreement that an integrated military system was more efficient and more effective than a segregated one. But while whites, generally, felt that Negroes were their equals in combat effectiveness and that Negroes were afforded equal opportunities, Negroes, on the other hand, were skeptical about promotional practices and believed white officers discriminated against them. White soldiers felt, almost unanimously (except for those interviewed in an "alien culture," e.g., Korea or Hawaii) that social activities between the races should be kept to a minimum; they attributed lack of interaction between the races to "self-segregation."

24. "Opinions About Negro Infantry Platoons in White Companies of Seven Divisions," in Guy E. Swanson et al., Readings in Social Psychology (New York: Henry Holt, 1952), pp. 502-506.
25. Based on interviews with seventy-eight Negro and white enlisted men and officers in four service branches and a range of ranks in Europe, the Philippines, and Korea, and interpreted by Robert F. Holz, Boston University sociology professor. Robert F. Holz, "Negro-White Relationships in the Armed Forces," unpublished paper.

Of fifty-five white GI's interviewed in the summer of 1968 while awaiting discharge at Fort Knox, Kentucky, almost one-third said they "learned something [presumably positive] about Negroes in the Army." More than one-fourth indicated that they engaged in nonmilitary "social" activities with Negroes—drinking (45 per cent), attending post dances (22 per cent), accompanying Negroes on leave in town (42 per cent). When closer social relationships are explored, however, the color line is sharply drawn. Only 3 per cent approved interracial sex and/or marriage. Of a small sample of eighteen Southern white veterans responding to a third survey,[26] one-third indicated that they had become *more* prejudiced as a result of military experience; another third reported that their racial views had not changed, and slightly less than one-third said the military experience had made them less prejudiced. Questioned about interracial sex and marriage, a surprising number manifested modifications of once-rigid views. In this regard, Whitney M. Young, Jr., exective director of the National Urban League, quotes other white soldiers from the South as saying:

. . . they would never again be the victims of the most stupefying myths on which they were brought up. . . . It was an unusual experience to hear white men criticize a society which permitted them to grow up with superstitious notions about the Negro. These men will represent a strong and positive force for the kind of legislation and local action that will be needed when they return to their communities.[27]

Nevertheless, the majority of the small sample cited said their contacts with Negroes in the military had come primarily through compliance with orders and did not necessarily reflect "free choices," and the group tended to react with fear or hard-line attitudes toward recent civil disturbances— both indications that positive attitudinal change may not be sustained in civilian life. When white veterans come home, they return to segregated institutions and most of them readily adapt to racially defined civilian patterns, especially in housing. The conditions for maintaining interracial adhesion—mutual interdependence is a common cause—are no longer in force.

Service in an integrated unit appears to have greater impact on Negro service members. The style of life of the armed forces between Korea and

26. The personal experiences were obtained through interviews with veterans, most of them in Georgia, who are members of the American Legion. They were conducted "with the hope of shedding some light on the effects of the military at changing the attitudes of whites toward Negroes among a sample of whites who had been discharged from the military and had experienced some interracial contact in the military." Robert F. Holz, "Negro-White Relationships in the Armed Forces," unpublished paper.

27. National Urban League news release, July 27, 1966.

Vietnam represented to the Negro a partial achievement of the demands of the civil rights movement. At first, hostility toward whites often decreased. However, military experience contributes to rising expectations and, therefore, to more clear-cut demands among Negro veterans. At least one study indicates that black veterans experience greater difficulty in transition to civilian employment than do white veterans.[28] The long-term consequences on the civilian social structure appear to be in the direction of increased militancy in the black community. But the impact of racial integration in the armed forces extends beyond the experiences of the whites and blacks who served in the armed forces. The accomplishments of the armed forces—in particular the achievement of racial integration without violence or undue social stress—have provided a social experiment that strengthened and validated the demands of both Negro and white civil rights leaders.

In the final months of the Johnson administration, Assistant Secretary of Defense Fitt appraised the impact of military integration. First, military integration has served as a model indicating to the civilian society that Negroes and whites can live and work together successfully; second, it has changed racial attitudes of white servicemen; third, Negro servicemen return to civilian life prouder, more self-reliant, better able to make their way in civilian society—and less willing to tolerate unfair treatment; and fourth, affirmative efforts to assure equal treatment for Negroes while off duty have altered attitudes in communities near military posts, even in the Deep South communities.

The military, which originally followed the lead of the civilian society on racial matters, has, in recent years, assumed the initiative, comparatively speaking, and has served as a powerful stimulus for change in civilian practices. This process has been under way for roughly twenty years. In the early 1950's, before the Supreme Court handed down its landmark school desegregation decision, desegregation of schools for dependent children on Southern military bases had already begun; it was completed long before any Southern state began even token compliance with the 1954 Brown decision. Justice Department attorneys arguing the school integration case cited a book tracing the early military experience with desegregation, and chapters of the book in manuscript form were submitted for Supreme Court review.[29] In 1953, Judge Charles Fahy of the U.S. Court of Appeals for the District of Columbia cited the armed forces movement

28. James M. Fendrich and Michael Pearson, "Are Black Veterans Making It? A Study of Veterans' Readjustment to Civil Life in a Southern Metropolis," unpublished manuscript, Florida State University, 1969.

29. Lee Nichols, *Breakthrough on the Color Front* (New York: Random House, 1954). This is an account of the development of policies of military integration.

toward equal treatment in his minority opinion arguing for integration of Washington, D.C., restaurants. The armed forces' efforts to secure equal treatment in restaurants, in airports, and in bus and train stations for troops in transit undoubtedly affected segregation nationally in a visible way. An order banning segregation was signed by the Interstate Commerce Commission in 1961.

Until the 1960's, however, post commanders generally maintained *laissez-faire* policies toward the communities near or surrounding military bases. But in 1963, the U.S. Commission on Civil Rights reported that off-base discrimination had a detrimental effect on the morale and efficiency of "significant numbers of military personnel."[30] Similar findings were reported by the committee appointed by President Kennedy to investigate racial conditions in the armed forces.[31] Those reports were followed by a directive of July 26, 1963, from Secretary Robert McNamara, stating that every commander "has the responsibility to oppose discriminatory practices affecting his men and their dependents and to foster equal opportunity for them, not only in areas under his immediate control, but also in nearby communities where they may live or gather in off-duty hours." The Pentagon followed up the new order by requiring commanders of bases with 500 or more personnel to submit quarterly "Off-Base Equal Opportunity Inventories" (now reduced to annual reports), and a new office of Deputy Assistant Secretary of Defense for Civil Rights and Industrial Relations sent survey teams to check on progress and single out problem areas for further attention. Restaurants, bars, taxi services, even bathing beaches near military bases were desegregated after military intervention, usually brought about by complaints of Negro servicemen.

After sporadic attacks on the problem of equal access to off-base housing, the Defense Department in 1963, spurred by the Civil Rights Commission and the Gesell Committee, also ordered all leases for family housing to include a nondiscrimination clause. Base housing offices were directed to refuse any listings not available to all servicemen, but this policy proved difficult to enforce—a 1967 survey indicated that only 31 per cent of housing near bases was certified in writing by owners or base commanders as open to occupants of all races. In April of that year, the Defense Department ordered commanders to take a census of multiple dwelling units in their areas and to submit monthly reports on their

30. U.S. Commission on Civil Rights, *Overall Evaluation and Comments on the Department of Defense Study: The Services and Their Relations with the Community*, June 17, 1963.

31. The Gesell Committee, appointed by President Kennedy in 1962 and headed by Washington lawyer Gerhard Gesell, found that while within the formal framework of the military, "substantial progress . . . [has been made] toward equality of treatment and opportunity," there was a serious pattern of off-base discrimination that needed urgent attention.

efforts to end discriminatory practices. Metropolitan Washington was designated a "model area" for intensified efforts, and meetings were arranged between the service secretaries, civil leaders, and real estate agents.

On February 28, 1967, the Maryland General Assembly passed a resolution calling on the Secretary of Defense to end housing discrimination for all military personnel in Maryland. On June 22 the Defense Department declared multiple family rental facilities (apartments and trailer courts) within a prescribed radius of four main Maryland bases off limits to military personnel unless equally available to *all* military personnel. By September 1, the number of "open" facilities in Maryland increased by 270 per cent (175 facilities) and the number of units by 195 per cent (13,603), prompting the Department to step up a nationwide campaign for voluntary compliance. In 1968, after Congress passed a new civil rights act containing a fair housing provision, the Supreme Court in *Jones v. Mayer,* in effect, held housing discrimination unconstitutional; Defense Secretary Clark Clifford extended military housing sanctions to all United States bases. In June 1969, Secretary Clifford reported that 96 per cent of rental units nationwide were "open" to all servicemen.[32] Still, dwellings housing fewer than four families are excluded from the statistics and there are indications that areas designated to be covered by the sanctions have excluded sections near some bases in which prospects for compliance seemed limited. A member of the American Veterans Committee, surveying the area near a South Dakota base, for example, found only about half as many nondiscriminatory units as a Defense Department inventory. By August 31, however, the Defense Department reported that 91 per cent of facilities surveyed in forty-seven states were listed as open compared with 31 per cent a year earlier, a gain of 727,400 units to a total of 1,107,100.[33]

Several military programs designed to transform former rejects into effective soldiers, including Project Transition discussed in Chapter 20, also have long-range implications for civilian institutions, primarily in education and employment patterns. The original Project Transition was much expanded in 1968 by order of President Johnson. About the same time, the

32. Defense Department figures include two categories: "Open" and "Listed." The former are apartments or trailer courts declared open by management upon personal inquiry by a base commander or his senior representative. To be "listed" in the base housing referral listing, a facility must have either a signed assurance of open policy by management or a signed certificate by the base commander that adequate assurances have been received.

33. The figures for housing "open" but not "listed" were 92 per cent as of August 31, 1968, compared with 62 per cent a year earlier. By this calculation the gain in "open" units was about half that shown on Pentagon records—from 747,900 to 1,117,-200, an increase of 369,300 units.

Veterans Administration established Veterans Assistance Centers to give special aid to the "disadvantaged" in job placement and other benefits in cooperation with eight federal agencies. Names of all discharged servicemen are forwarded to the U.S. Employment Service of the Department of Labor, assuring postservice contact. Moreover, the National Urban League operates an ambitious program of postservice counseling, financed by grants from the Rockefeller Brothers Fund and a number of private firms. The Urban League job counselors, who have access to the names of discharged Negroes (apparently the first nongovernmental group accorded this privilege), report that most Negro veterans are highly employable and actively recruited by government and industry, although some are disappointed at their opportunities. Joseph Cannon, assistant director of the League's veterans' program, said industry is interested in the returned black veteran "because we have a salable product; besides skills, the Negro has obtained responsibility, developed leadership skills—he has been a squad leader, has done his share of decision-making under tension." A tank unit commander, for example, who has handled $40 to $60 million worth of equipment commented: "It's big business; these people are managers."

Clarence Mitchell, head of the Washington Bureau of the National Association for the Advancement of Colored People, has said he found that large numbers of Negroes had obtained a further impetus from military service—to enter public life, particularly politics. Their experience in the military had taught them not to be afraid of their environment.

Racial integration of military life has not served to increase the general prestige of the military. In fact, the reverse may be the case. Those in the white society who are liberals in racial matters are already the least sympathetic to the problems of the military. The military, instead, has traditionally drawn prestige and respect from Southern and rural civilians, who are the least sympathetic to racial integration. But the military establishment, whatever the remaining unsolved problems within or without its boundaries, has undoubtedly gone too far along the road to full integration and total equality of opportunity for all, regardless of class or race, to turn back. The establishment has assumed a certain responsibility for stimulating social change and has ceased to be contented solely with maintaining the status quo of the society it serves.

In his book, *The Essence of Security,* published shortly after he resigned as Defense Secretary, Robert McNamara made clear that social change was his conscious goal.

During my seven years in the Department it seemed to me that those vast resources could contribute to the attack on our tormenting social problems, both supporting our basic mission and adding to the quality of our national life.

For, in the end, poverty and social injustice may endanger our national security so much as any military threat.[34]

A continuing tension between that goal and the bureaucratic reality is characteristic of the role of the military establishment in the contemporary crisis of race relations.

34. Robert S. McNamara, *The Essence of Security* (New York: Harper & Row, 1968).

22

Military Justice and Individual Liberty

Military justice falls on rich and poor alike but it falls with special emphasis upon the adolescent, the maladjusted, the poorly educated, the black, and the dissenter, all groups strongly represented in the modern military. Its role, like that of any criminal law system, is one of deterrence and retribution, but it has a special function within the military as the coercive mechanism for maintaining the larger system of discipline. Military law has an impact on veterans and on civilians as well.

Justice in the military is administered by a complex system of courts and boards, with a civilian Court of Military Appeals at the top, intermediate Courts of Military Review, countless *ad hoc* courts-martial, and a network of quasi-judicial bodies including boards of inquiry and discharge review boards. More than 4,000 full-time military lawyers serve in the Judge Advocate General's corps of the services; many more civilian lawyers and nonlawyer personnel are actively engaged in administering the system. In 1968, the armed services conducted 85,000 courts-martial on charges ranging from routine military offenses like AWOL to civil-law felonies like murder and rape. About 20,000 prisoners are now confined in stockades, guardhouses, disciplinary barracks, and federal penitentiaries, serving sentences from a few months to life imprisonment.[1]

1. There were 1,700,000 courts-martial and 100 executions during World War II. When the war ended 45,000 servicemen were still imprisoned. After a clemency board was appointed in response to public demands for reform, sentences were remitted or reduced in 85 per cent of 27,000 cases reviewed. White, "The Background and the Problem," in *The Uniform Code of Military Justice—Its Promise and Performance (The First Decade: 1951–1961): A Symposium*, 35 St. John's Law Rev. 197, 200 (1961); Farmer and Wels, "Command Control—Or Military Justice?," 24 N.Y.U. Law Rev. 263, 265 (1949) citing Rep. War Dep't Advisory Bd. Clemency (1946).

"Military" crimes are predominantly AWOL's and desertions (70 per cent) and various types of disobedience (20 per cent). "Civilian" crimes are similar in distribution to national crime statistics, although the military percentages for drug use and sodomy are higher. The military, with its broad powers of search and seizure[2] through search warrants issued by commanders rather than by impartial magistrates, and through routine inspections and shakedowns, can detect drug usage more easily (usage, particularly of marijuana, appears to be widespread),[3] and the investigation and detection of homosexual conduct has a high priority in military law enforcement.

About half the military courts-martial are convened to deal with AWOL cases. One case, that of Mike O'Connor, indicates the web of trouble a soldier can find himself enmeshed in. O'Connor, the product of a broken home and a high school dropout, had enlisted in the Army in late 1969, but shortly after his first assignment, he went AWOL, apparently because he was denied leave. After being away fifty days, he was arrested by the Military Police, convicted in a special court-martial, and sentenced to six months' confinement in the Fort Bragg stockade, drawing forfeiture of pay and demotion as well. The stockade, like most stockades, was over-crowded, filled mostly with young AWOL's, and apparently lacked adequate programs for exercise, education, training, and psychiatric care. A month later, in a prisoner riot, O'Connor reported that a black prisoner, who had been in "the hole" was beaten in the face with a pistol belt after he attempted to break away from the guards. The other prisoners expelled the guards and held the compound for two days. O'Connor, suspected of being one of the leaders in the riot, was beaten by the guards and put in the hole for eleven days. He was released from the stockade a month later and promptly went AWOL again, this time for fifty-nine days. In Boston, he met members of "the Resistance," an antiwar organization, and found sanctuary at the Massachusetts Institute of Technology, where he took part in teach-ins. Two weeks later he was arrested and court-martialed. The court sentenced him to four months' confinement plus forfeiture of pay.

A month after the sentence, O'Connor slashed his eyelid with a razor blade in the stockade. He was promptly ordered into the hole, a standard punishment for breaking rules, though when he refused to go and threatened to resist, the order was revoked. O'Connor next sub-

2. Captain Richard P. Van Remortal has filed suit against the Army in protest after his driving privileges were revoked because he would not permit a search of his car in Fort Gordon. New York Times, April 26, 1970, p. 35.

3. Dr. John A. Talbott, an ex-Army psychiatrist, observed in a January 1969 American Psychiatric Association publication that the war in Vietnam is the first war in which the Army has been more concerned with marijuana than venereal disease; 30 to 50 per cent of the troops had smoked pot in Vietnam. New York Times, January 5, 1969, p. 78.

mitted an application for discharge as a conscientious objector, and several ministers testified to the sincerity of his beliefs. Like most such applications in recent years, however, his was refused. His lawyer then filed an unsuccessful suit in the Court of Military Appeals seeking further review of his case,[4] but on May 5, 1969, the Army abandoned interest in the struggle to compel Private O'Connor to adjust to the military, and he left the Fort Devens stockade with an undesirable administrative discharge. His thirteen-month experience with military justice was ended, but a new phase had begun, for an AWOL conviction of six months and an undesirable discharge carries with it a lifetime sentence of possible restriction on certain employment, and denial of most veterans' benefits.

Private O'Connor's tragic tale is not typical, nor is it without parallel in the current annals of civilian justice. But it is indicative of the permanent impact that the military justice system can have on a citizen-soldier who is ill-equipped to cope with situations of stress, and whose personal difficulties can make him a pawn in the worsening climate of political conflict.

The emergence of an organized antiwar dissent in the military in recent years has created a new class of political and conscientious dissenters. Most major military installations now have organized GI antiwar movements. A radical antiwar and antimilitary underground press has sprung up on military posts with papers called *The Ultimate Weapon* (Fort Dix), *Fun, Travel and Adventure* (Fort Knox), *Fatigue Press* (Fort Hood), and *Last Harass* (Fort Gordon),[5] plus a number of "antiwar servicemen's newspapers" published by veterans—*The Vietnam GI, The Ally, The Bond, Task Force,* and *Veteran's Stars and Stripes for Peace.*

The most ambitious attempt among GI's to organize for bargaining purposes was begun by ex-Private Andrew D. Stapp, who formed the American Servicemen's Union in December 1967. Now claiming membership in the thousands, the union seeks recognition as "bargaining agent" for servicemen, with eight demands ranging from racial equality and the right of free political association to election of officers by the men, "an end to saluting and sir-ring of officers," and "the right to disobey illegal orders—like orders

---

4. The suit claimed that O'Connor's constitutional rights had been abridged by, *inter alia*, the refusal of the convening authority to use "some random method" for selection for the one-third enlisted men for the court, to have a verbatim transcript made of the court-martial as requested by accused, and to assign a military defense counsel after the court-martial and pending review by the staff judge advocate's office.

5. Private Bruce Peterson, editor of *Fatigue Press*, was sentenced by court-martial to eight years in Leavenworth for possession of marijuana. (The civilian sentence for the crime is, typically, one to two years on a first offense and is often suspended.) Private First Class Dennis Davis, editor of *Last Harass*, was given a dishonorable discharge for fomenting "unrest and disloyalty among the troops," and Seaman Roger Lee Priest, publisher of *OM*, was found guilty by a Navy court of promoting disloyalty and disaffection among servicemen. *New York Times*, April 24, 1970.

to go and fight in an illegal war in Vietnam."[6] A second union, GI Association, formed by San Francisco Bay servicemen early in 1969, reflected a slightly less antimilitary stance. It sought collective bargaining rights and reforms affecting allegedly dishonest recruiting campaigns, enlistment contracts, arbitary discipline procedures, and less than honorable discharge policies.

Perhaps the most publicized program of the GI antiwar organizing movement has been the coffeehouse experiment. Antiwar coffeehouses were established in a number of towns adjoining military posts in the late 1960's, and several more have been opened since. They have drawn small, but enthusiastic, numbers of GI's, but due to difficulties with local law enforcement officials[7] and surveillance and threats of declaring them "off-limits" by the military, the antiwar movement has begun to lose interest in coffeehouses as a vehicle for reaching GI's.

The military brass reacted to the union movement with understandable hostility. Shortly after the ASU was formed, several commands took the position that membership in or association with members of a servicemen's union would subject a serviceman to court-martial under the article forbidding unlawful conspiracy. Commanders have gradually shifted to the position that membership in unions is not prohibited, but that positive programs should be adopted to counter the drive for union members. As the First Army Commander stated in a directive dated March 24, 1969: "The key is to remove the motivation to join a collective bargaining unit by convincing the soldier that those in positions of authority have a direct interest in his welfare and morale. Commanders should make themselves available to soldiers to hear their complaints and should take immediate and positive actions within the limits of their authority to remedy reasonable complaints."[8] Programs suggested were use of NCO councils "to ferret out problems" and "to publicize the commander's interest in the morale, welfare and spirit of his command," review of local regulations to insure "they contain nothing repugnant to a man's dignity," and emphasis upon positive leadership.

Some commanders have employed repressive tactics, MP raids,

6. Stapp, who had been a dishonorable discharge in 1968 for allegedly subversive associations, received an honorable discharge in May 1970, after successfully bringing suit in federal court against the Secretary of the Army. New York Times, May 17, 1970. The right to disobey illegal orders, derived from the Geneva Convention, is recognized by the Field Manual 27-10 (The Law of Land Warfare). The controversy centers on the nature and determination of an illegal order.

7. In April 1970 three civilian operators of a coffeehouse in Columbia, S.C., were found guilty and sentenced to six years each on charges of operating and maintaining a public nuisance. The ACLU is appealing to the State Supreme Court. New York Times, April 28-29, 1970.

8. Letter, AHABB-SI, Subject: American Servicemen's Union—Introduction of Subversive Literature at Army Installations, Dept. of Army, HQ, First U.S. Army, 24 March 1969, printed in The Bond, "Help Us to Organize for Justice."

harassment, transfers of leaders, and courts-martial to break up the organizing. Local civilian officials, as in Columbia, South Carolina, have harassed the coffeehouses. Soldiers have been convicted and dishonorably discharged for distributing antiwar literature on base.[9] But these tactics have drawn adverse publicity, and a policy of restraint has gradually come into favor at the higher commands. The first noticeable change came in 1969 when the Army, under pressure from a number of pending lawsuits and appeals, issued a new regulation providing that distribution of printed material could be permitted on posts with the prior approval of the commander.[10] The first test came when Private Joseph D. Miles, a twenty-year-old black who headed the Fort Bragg chapter of GI's United Against the War in Vietnam, requested permission to distribute a reprint of the Bill of Rights and the enlisted man's oath of induction. The commanding general granted permission and although the terms were restrictive—he could hand out only a limited number from 5:00 to 6:00 P.M. on two days from a single intersection on the post—this marked the first time an Army base commander had officially sanctioned on-base distribution of literature by a member of an antiwar group.[11] Since that time, similar permission has been granted on other posts, but distribution of critical literature is more often forbidden under the broad discretion given a commander to determine that it poses a "clear danger to the loyalty, discipline, or morale."

On May 27, 1969, the Department of the Army issued a directive entitled "Guidance on Dissent," which counseled restraint in dealing with dissenters:

It is important to remember that freedom of expression is a fundamental right secured by the Constitution. . . . Severe disciplinary action in response to a relatively insignificant manifestation of dissent can have a counterproductive effect on other members of the Command, because the reaction appears out of proportion to the threat which the dissent represents. Thus, rather than serving as a deterrent, such disproportionate actions may stimulate further breaches of discipline.[12]

The directive cautioned that a commander should not prevent distribution of a publication "simply because he does not like its contents"; could not prohibit mere possession of "an unauthorized publication"; could not discipline soldiers who work, off post, on their own time and with their own money, on underground newspapers; could not deny access to areas of the post to civilians where the public is generally granted access; could not prevent men from going to coffeehouses "unless it can be shown, for

9. *United States* v. *Amick and Stolte*, C.M. 418868 (ACM 1969).
10. AR 210-10, para. 515, ch. 1, 10 March 1969.
11. *New York Times*, May 14, 1969, p. 11; May 12, 1969, p. 4.
12. Dept. of Army, Office of the Adjutant General, AGAM-P (M) (27 May 1969) DSCPER-SARD, Subject: Guidance on Dissent, 28 May 1969.

example, that activities taking place in the coffeehouse include counseling soldiers to refuse to perform duty or to desert or otherwise involve illegal acts with a significant adverse effect on soldier health, morale or welfare"; and could not prevent membership in servicemen's unions although commanders "are not authorized to recognize or to bargain with such a union." It did, however, note that on-post demonstrations by members of the Army were still prohibited, pending the results of litigation. Off-post demonstrations while in uniform were also forbidden if "a breach of law and order" or "violence" was a likely consequence. This Army directive has now been followed by a less liberal Department of Defense directive on dissent which emphasized commander authority rather than servicemen's rights but which also somewhat broadened the permissible scope of servicemen's First Amendment activities.[13]

It is too early to determine whether the new directives will lead to a broad definition of the rights of free speech in the military. They do not advocate lessening of disciplinary and court-martial restrictions where the commander believes there is a threat to the good order and discipline of his unit, and the definition of good order and discipline is susceptible to inclusive interpretation.

The attempts of servicemen to express their opposition on the war, the draft system, and other issues have raised fundamental questions about disciplinary restrictions in a democracy. The traditional legal approach is to balance out the interests, setting the servicemen's right to free speech (and the fundamental interest of society in having a free exchange of ideas) against the military's need to maintain order and discipline (and the interest of society in having an effective fighting force). The military courts have tended to grant considerable leeway to the commander's discretion in deciding where that balance should be struck. A Naval Board of Review declared, in 1969:

The point at which the exercise of religious practices or freedom of speech must yield to regulation constitutes a responsible judgment made by those charged with keeping the peace, or in the service of maintaining discipline and morale. These are the spot judgments made by responsible individual members of the armed services and may be disturbed, if at all, only on a plain showing of unlawful abuse of discretion.[14]

This standard provides little limitation on a commander's power to suppress dissent if he views it as a threat to discipline and morale. As a result, dissenters have turned increasingly to the civilian courts and the public to intervene in behalf of civil liberties.

The case of two New York blacks, who were opposed to the Vietnam war, is instructive as a demonstration of the problem. William L. Harvey, a

13. DOD Directive No. 1325.6, Sept. 12, 1969.
14. *United States* v. *Daniels, NCM* 68-1733 (Navy Bd. of Rev., May 1969) at 3.

Marine volunteer and lance corporal, and Private George W. Daniels told a group of other Marines in an informal bull session that Vietnam was a white man's war, and that blacks should refuse to fight in it. It was the week of the Detroit ghetto riot in July 1967, and fourteen black Marines requested mast (a grievance procedure) the following day. When the commander refused to see them, a sergeant took signed statements which were turned over to the Office of Naval Intelligence. Harvey and Daniels and several others repeated that they were opposed to going to Vietnam (although this could not be disobedience of orders since they had no orders to Vietnam). A few weeks later Harvey and Daniels were arrested. Both were persuaded not to obtain civilian attorneys on the grounds that a Marine Corps court would be hostile to a civilian lawyer, and were assigned young Marine Corps lawyers. They were tried by separate courts-martial of Marine Corps officers.

On November 27, 1967, Harvey was convicted of making "disloyal statements . . . with design to promote disloyality among the troops," and was sentenced to six years' confinement at hard labor, total forfeiture of pay, and a dishonorable discharge. Ten days later, Daniels was convicted of a slightly different charge based on a provision of the 1950 Smith Act of advising, counseling, urging, causing, and attempting to cause insubordination, disloyalty, and refusal of duty. The prosecutor's summation had noted that since Daniels was reported to have said that he would go to jail before he went to Vietnam, "the government respectfully urges that you grant George Daniels' request."[15] The verdict was ten years at hard labor, total forfeiture, and a dishonorable discharge.

Since, at the time of the courts-martial, military practice did not recognize bail pending appeal in the military, Harvey and Daniels were jailed from the time of their arrest on August 27, 1967. After six months, they wrote to the American Civil Liberties Union, and civilian lawyers were provided for their appeals. A year and a half after their courts-martial, a Navy Board of Review affirmed the convictions, but reduced the sentences to four and three years, respectively.[16] Both were released in September 1969 pursuant to the new Military Justice Act[17] permitting release pending appeal at the discretion of the commander, but thereafter Daniels' release was revoked on the grounds that he was continuing to make antiwar statements, and Harvey went AWOL.

Finally, on July 10, 1970, the Court of Military Appeals unanimously reversed the convictions, but found both men guilty of the lesser offenses of

15. *Record of Trial of Pfc. George Daniels by General Court-Martial*, Camp Pendleton, Cal., 30 Nov. 1967, 1, 5, 6, & 7 Dec. 1967, at 124.
16. *United States* v. *Daniels*, NCM 68-1733 (Navy Bd. of Rev., May 1969); *United States* v. *Harvey*, NCM 68-1734 (Navy Bd. of Rev., 10 July 1969).
17. Public Law 90-632 (Oct. 24, 1968), 82 Stat. 1335, 10 U.S.C. Para. 871 (art. 71).

solicitation to insubordination and refusal of duty (which carried a maximum sentence of four months).[18] Even so, they spent over two years in jail. Their case has important implications as a precedent on the power of the military to punish what it regards as disloyal statements not associated with acts of disobedience. However, its decision on relatively narrow legal grounds of deficient instruction to members of the court on what constitutes disloyalty under the law leaves the central issue of dissent still unclear.

The court-martial, in February 1968 of Private First Class Daniel Amick and Private Kenneth Stolte is an even more troubling case for the civil libertarian. While waiting for a friend to complete his night shift at the post library at Fort Ord, California, one of the defendants, on the spur of the moment, typed out a statement which expressed opposition to the Vietnam war and informed its readers that, as citizens, they could do something to end it. The statement closed with a request to those who shared these views to join a union with Amick and Stolte for the purpose of expressing dissent and the grievances of soldiers. Both men were subsequently court-martialed and convicted of "uttering disloyal statements" and "conspiring to utter disloyal statements." They were sentenced to dishonorable discharge, forfeiture of all pay and allowances, and confinement at hard labor for four years (later reduced to three years).[19]

It is clearer here than in the case of Daniels and Harvey that no acts of disobedience were urged or advocated since nothing was said about refusal of service in Vietnam. In expressing their views, Amick and Stolte testified that they thought they were acting in accordance with the First Amendment protection of free speech. Soldiers have heard similar expressions of opposition to the war from far more influential persons. In fact, Amick and Stolte themselves said they were motivated by the remarks of retired Generals David M. Shoup and James M. Gavin.

Perhaps the most troublesome case thus far is presented by the court-martial of Lieutenant Henry Howe (in 1965) at Fort Bliss, Texas. Howe took part in an antiwar demonstration in downtown El Paso, organized by students and professors from a nearby college. Dressed in civilian clothes, he carried a sign reading "Let's have more than a choice between petty ignorant facists [sic] in 1968" on one side and "End Johnson's facist [sic] aggression" on the other. The Army convicted him of violating Article 88 (contemptuous words against the President") and Article 133 ("conduct unbecoming an officer"). The Board of Review and the Court of Military Appeals affirmed.

Lieutenant Howe's remarks were not specifically directed toward soldiers. He was playing the same role of civilian as the others in the demon-

18. *United States* v. *Daniels,* 19 U.S.C.M.A. 529, 42 C.M.R. 131 (1970); *United States* v. *Harvey,* 19 U.S.C.M.A. 539, 42 141 (1970).
19. See note 9 above.

stration. The government counsel even conceded that, had Howe actually been a civilian, his conduct could not have been deemed criminal. The reason for applying a more restrictive standard of free speech to Howe is unclear. Judge Kilday, speaking for the Court of Military Appeals, simply declared: "That in the present times and circumstances [i.e. the Vietnam war] such conduct *by an officer* constitutes a clear and present danger to discipline within our armed services, under the precedents established by the Supreme Court, seems to require no argument."[20]

The court-martial of Captain Howard Levy in 1967 for refusing to teach medicine to Green Beret troops and for criticizing the war to other servicemen raised issues relating to servicemen's obligations to obey alleged unlawful orders and to their exercise of free-speech rights. Captain Levy's principal defense on the charge of disobedience was based on medical ethics; he claimed that nonphysician Green Berets were to be trained to use drugs and medical techniques indiscriminately among the Vietnamese for tactical purposes. In the middle of the trial, however, the law officer ruled that if the defendant could prove the Green Berets were committing war crimes, he could raise the Nuremburg Defense: i.e., that an order to participate in war crimes was an unlawful order, and therefore that he was bound not to obey it. Levy presented some evidence of war crimes (such as unnecessary destruction of homes, multilation of the dead by encouraging cutting off ears of Vietcong, assassination assignments, and torturing of prisoners to obtain information), but the law officer found that the evidence was not sufficient to raise the Nuremburg Defense. Levy was given three years by the court-martial, and his conviction was affirmed by the military court.[21] An action is now pending in the federal courts attacking the conviction on the grounds that the order was illegal and that his criticism of the war was permitted by the First Amendment. Like the federal court suits also pending in the Howe, Daniels, and Amick-Stolte cases, it provides further legal challenge to the military handling of the Vietnam war dissent.

Most crimes in the articles of the Uniform Code of Military Justice (UCMJ),[22] which define court-martial offenses, are defined clearly and

---

20. *United States* v. *Howe*, 17 U.S.C.M.A. 165, 174, 37 C.M.R. 429, 438 (1967).

21. Levy, CM 416463 (Aug. 19, 1968).

22. The UCMJ took effect on May 31, 1951. The only major change in procedures occurred with the Military Justice Act of 1968, 10 U.S.C. para. 826, which replaced the "law officer," who was not a member of the court, with a "military judge," who has powers comparable to civilian judges. Rulings of the military judge on all questions of law and all interlocutory questions are final. Furthermore, since he is now appointed from a "field judiciary" not under the control of the commander, his independence is reinforced. The Act also extended to special courts-martial the right of the accused to a legally trained counsel (unless a lawyer cannot be obtained "on account of physical conditions or military exigencies"), and gave the commander discretion to grant bail pending the appeal (prior to the Act, such bail could not be granted).

specifically. But two general crimes differ considerably from standards of civilian law codes. One, Article 133, forbids "conduct unbecoming an officer and a gentleman," and the other, Article 134, "disorders and neglects to the prejudice of good order and discipline in the armed forces, all conduct of a nature to bring discredit upon the armed forces." The *Manual for Courts-Martial* lists fifty-eight acts (from abusing an animal to wearing unauthorized insignia) under Article 134, but this is only a suggested list. "Conduct unbecoming an officer and a gentleman" is also unspecific. The *Manual*'s statement that "there are certain moral attributes common to the ideal officer and the perfect gentleman"[22] provides little assistance in earmarking in advance what will be found to be criminal. The *Manual* mentions such things as "using insulting or defamatory language to another officer in his presence or about him to other military persons" and "being grossly drunk and conspicuously disorderly in a public place,"[23] but an objective and sober observer at some Saturday night parties at an officers' club would conclude justifiably that prosecutions under this article are selective. Servicemen call Article 134 the "Devil's Article" because the terms are so broad that virtually any conduct can come under it.[24] Both the "Devil's Article" and Article 133 represent a point of conflict between military and civilian justice. Both would probably be held unconstitutionally vague and overbroad in a civilian court, and both have been a principal device for court-martialing servicemen who have dissented against the Vietnam conflict.

The UCMJ also contains several traditionally military crimes dating back to the eighteenth-century British code, which have increasingly come into conflict with traditional attitudes toward free speech. For example, Article 88 forbids officers to use "contemptuous words" against the President, Vice President, Congress, Secretaries, Governors, and state legislatures, while Article 117 forbids "provoking or reproachful words or gestures toward any person subject to this code." Like many of the specifications under Article 134 (such as being "conspicuously disorderly in a public place"), these so-called crimes are committed daily, and are more honored in the breach than the observance. They provide a means of selective enforcement, and like the overbroad "breach of the peace" statutes once used to curb demonstrations but now ruled unconstitutional, they can be used by a commander to enforce conformity with his own views of right conduct.

Like foreign military establishments, the American military has never felt that broad free speech rights available to civilians could—or should—be

22. *Manual for Courts-Martial United States* (1969), para. 212 (hereinafter referred to as MCM).
23. *Ibid.*
24. See D. B. Nicholas, *"The Devil's Article,"* 22 Mil. Law Rev. 111 (October 1963).

granted to servicemen. Their view is that efficiency is the paramount consideration, that it can only be obtained by order and discipline, and that order and discipline cannot be maintained without broad powers of enforcement. The value placed on free speech and the free exchange of ideas in civilian life is overshadowed by the military priorities—uniformity of conduct, maintenance of "honor" by the officer class, loyalty to government, and adherence to a high standard of discipline.

Military justice differs from its civilian counterpart in procedure as well as in substance. Civilian law places great importance upon separation of various court functions among different and independent administrators. In theory, and usually in practice, the district attorney decides whether to prosecute; indictment is frequently required from a grand jury; the defense counsel is an independent lawyer hired by or appointed for the defendant; the jury is picked from the defendant's peers in the community by random selection; the trial is administered by independent judicial officials not connected with the district attorney's office; and the appeals courts are independent tribunals. But, under military law, the military commander plays a significant role in all of these functions. He decides whether to prosecute and can bring a man to court-martial even over the contrary recommendation of the investigating officer; he has the authority to handpick the jury from his command and the prosecutor and defense counsel from his legal officers (although the defendant may hire civilian counsel at his own expense); he has a wide variety of supervisory powers over the administration of the court-martial;[25] and when the trial is over, he has the power to review (although not to increase) the sentence.

When the UCMJ was in draft stage, reformers urged that the commander's role be restricted to that of appointing and directing the district attorney, without power to appoint the court personnel or supervise the administration of the court-martial, but the military argued that discipline and efficiency could not be maintained otherwise, and Congress agreed.

In practice, many of the commander's supervisory and administrative powers over a court-martial are carried out by his legal officer, the staff judge advocate (SJA).

Unlike a civilian law firm, a district attorney's office, or a public defender's officer, the SJA office works both sides of court-martial cases. The Judge Advocate General's lawyers who work together in the same office

25. E.g., the commander determines whether defense counsel may subpoena witnesses or evidence before trial, MCM, para. 115, can excuse court members both before and, in limited situations, during the trial, *United States* v. *Allen*, 5 U.S.C.M.A. 626, 18 C.M.R. 250 (1955); *United States* v. *Geraghty*, CM 419200 (Army Bd. of Rev., 1969), and can reverse a military judge's dismissal of charges on such grounds as denial of a speedy trial and order him tried anyway, *Priest* v. *Koch*, 19 U.S.C.M.A. 293, 41 C.M.R. (1970); *United States* v. *Boehm*, 17 U.S.C.M.A. 530, 38 C.M.R. 328 (1968).

serve as prosecutor and defense counsel in almost every case. Most civilian lawyers would find this an intolerable conflict of interest, and there is no precedent for it in the administration of civilian criminal law, where the independence of district attorney and defense counsel is considered sacrosanct.

The military's justification for the commander's role in the administration of the court-martial and the command-oriented structure of the legal corps is that a commander is charged with insuring discipline and order within his unit. The military has always contended that division of command functions would be disastrous to discipline and order. "Singleness of command" is regarded as essential to efficient military administration. There is no problem in serving both the interests of the command and the accused, the military maintains, because they are the same. It is also argued that, in recent years, the commander's undivided command control over courts-martial has been diminished in various ways. The expanded requirements for lawyers and due process rights have led to greater professionalism and independence in the legal corps. In the 1960's, the Army and Navy established field judiciaries so that law officers (now called military judges) would be appointed from an independent manpower pool not under the command of the convening authority.[26] And the Military Justice Act of 1968 formalized and extended the field judiciary concept to all the services, completing the removal of military judges from command control.[27] The court-martial itself now follows a judicial pattern with most of the trappings of a civilian trial, so that there has been a definite de-emphasis on the commander's role in the proceedings.

The selection and composition of the court is one of the most important differences between military and civilian justice. Trial by one's peers chosen at random, enshrined in the common law, has never been part of the court-martial tradition. On the contrary, service on courts-martial has been and still is considered a prerogative of officers. In 1919, General Samuel T. Ansell, acting Judge Advocate General of the Army, who led the first substantial military justice reform movement, proposed that three members of the court out of eight should have the same rank as the accused,[28] and that a three-fourths vote of the court be required for conviction (rather than two-thirds as at present) so that the individuals of the same rank as the accused would hold the determining vote. But Ansell's proposal was defeated, as was a similar proposal when the UCMJ was passed in 1950, on the grounds that enlisted men were not qualified to sit on courts, and

26. *Joint Hearings on S. 745-62, S. 2906-7, Part 3 Before the Subcomm. on Constl. Rts. of the Sen. Comm. on the Judiciary and a Spec. Subcomm. of the Comm. on Armed Service U.S. Senate,* 89th Congress, 2d Session, at 908-11; 935-36.
27. 10 U.S.C. para. 826 (art. 26(c)).
28. Article 5, S. 64, 66th Congress, 1st Session (1919).

might be improperly motivated by class antagonisms. The UCMJ permits a serviceman to request that one-third of the court be made up of enlisted men, but commanders then invariably appoint high-ranking noncommissioned officers, who tend to be more disciplinarian than officers. As a result, the right is rarely exercised.[29] Under the circumstances, with the jury made up of officers who are part of the command establishment, and who are likely to be sympathetic to command needs and attitudes, trial by such a court-martial is generally a more disciplinarian process than a civilian trial.

The military appeals system prescribed in the UCMJ, which borrows from civilian law concepts, still retains a number of distinctive military aspects. It provides for a three-tiered structure: administrative reviews, review by the Courts of Military Review, and appeal to the civilian Court of Military Appeals.[30] All court-martial convictions are reviewed by the commander who convened the court and by a Judge Advocate General's officer (usually under the commander). If a court-martial sentence as approved affects a general or a flag officer, or extends to death, dismissal of an officer, bad conduct discharge, or confinement for one year or more, the serviceman is entitled to review by a Court of Military Review. If the conviction involves a general or flag officer or a death sentence, there is automatic review by the civilian Court of Military Appeals. In all other cases, review by the Court of Military Appeals lies within the court's discretion.

Administrative reviews are a holdover from a time when the decision of a court-martial was not considered final until the commander had approved it. It has not been uncommon for commanders to let it be known that they prefer courts-martial to give the maximum sentence so that they have the power to cut it down.[31] This practice permits a certain paternalism which can work in the favor of the accused, but it can also result in a disciplinarianism which considerably increases the commander's role in court-martial proceedings.

Commanders sometimes become deeply involved in cases they consider to pose a particular threat to their disciplinary policies—cases involving homosexuals, barracks thieves, and political dissenters often fall in this category. The court-martial in March 1969 of the first three of twenty-seven servicemen who participated in the brief sitdown at San Francisco's Presidio stockade protesting a prisoner's death and conditions of alleged brutality is an example. They were given unusually severe sentences of fifteen, fourteen, and sixteen years, respectively, and the commanding gen-

---

29. See Edmund M. Morgan, "The Background of the Uniform Code of Military Justice," 28 Mil. Law Rev. 17, 25 (April 1965).

30. See UCMJ, arts, 64-67.

31. See Rep. of the War Dep't Advisory Comm. on Military Justice to the Sec. of War 61 (1946).

eral, who had been intensely involved in the case (having gone ahead with the courts-martial over the contrary recommendation of the investigating officer), approved the sentences with only slight reductions. Only after intense public criticism did the Judge Advocate General, who came under pressure from the Secretary of the Army and Army Chief of Staff, take the unprecedented step of cutting the sentences to two years before formal appeals had even begun.[32] When the cases were finally reviewed by a Court of Military Review, almost a year later, the mutiny convictions were reversed on the same grounds as the investigating officer had originally given for not trying them: that there was no evidence that the acts were mutinous.

Civilian appellate courts are independent of other government agencies and are made up of judges with a fixed term of office. But the members of the Courts of Military Review come from the staff of the Judge Advocate General, who assigns them as judges, and they have no tenure, thus reducing their independence. It has been alleged that in some cases members who tended to be sympathetic to defendants have been assigned to other duties.

The highest level of appeal is the Court of Military Appeals, established by the UCMJ as an entity independent of the military with its own building in Washington, D.C. Its members have had relative independence since they are appointed by the President for fifteen-year terms. However, its availability is severely limited, since only cases involving generals, flag officers, and a death penalty are entitled to automatic review. The court has reviewed fewer than 20 per cent of the cases which have petitioned it,[33] including the quite controversial Levy case, discussed above. Nevertheless, the court has produced a body of military common law through its interpretations and applications of the Constitution to military justice, and it has been the principal force, in recent years, for keeping the military abreast of the Supreme Court decisions on criminal due process.

Although the Court of Military Appeals has applied many constitutional due process requirements to the military (some of which were incorporated in the UCMJ even before the United States Supreme Court made them generally available to civilian defendants), it has refused to extend to servicemen a number of due process and other rights guaranteed to civilians. In the area of trial due process rights, for example, the court has held that a serviceman is not entitled to a court chosen at random or to trial by his peers, to a lawyer in a special court-martial, to review on the same basis as a general or flag officer, or to have a verbatim transcript made of special court-martial proceedings. These rulings are in sharp contrast to the court's extension of broad constitutional rights to servicemen in

32. *New York Times,* March 19, 1969, p. 7.
33. *Hearings Before the Comm. on Armed Services, U.S. Senate, 89th Cong., 2d Sess., on the Nomination of Judge Robert E. Quinn for Reappointment as Justice of the U.S. Court of Military Appeals,* May 12, 1969, 3.

such areas as police interrogation, search and seizure, and speedy and public trial, self-incrimination, and double jeopardy.[34]

The fact is that during most of its history the court has preferred its own concept of "military due process." But recently it has been willing to apply the constitutional guarantees more directly to servicemen. On substantive law it has been generally unwilling to challenge the UCMJ or to interfere with military practices. It has upheld most of the general articles and vague crimes against constitutional attack, and has adopted a narrow interpretation of the "clear and present danger" test in shaping free speech rights in the military.[35]

As a result of these limitations there has been a strong movement for expanded review of military determinations by federal courts. Traditionally it had been held that the federal courts could not review court-martial decisions except on habeas corpus, and had no jurisdiction to review military administrative determinations. However, in 1953, in *Burns* v. *Wilson*,[36] the Supreme Court expanded the scope of federal habeas corpus to permit review, after all military appeals have been completed, of denials of servicemen's constitutional rights in courts-martial, and in 1958, in *Harmon* v. *Brucker*,[37] it rejected the absolute rule nonreviewability in military administrative determinations, permitting review of a military discharge. The Vietnam war has brought a host of suits in federal courts seeking to obtain remedies for denials of constitutional rights of servicemen. A modest expansion of federal court jurisdiction to review military determinations, particularly in conscientious objector discharge cases, has resulted. This movement rests largely on the claim that the military justice system in its substantive law, its procedure, and its appellate review, is inadequate to assert and to protect the constitutional rights of servicemen; the Supreme Court's decision in *O'Callahan* v. *Parker*[38] that courts-martial lack jurisdiction over nonservice-connected civilian crimes is a product of this reasoning.

---

34. *United States* v. *Crawford,* 15 U.S.C.M.A. 31, 35 C.M.R. 3 (1963).

United States v. *Culp,* 14 U.S.C.M.A. 199, 33 C.M.R. 411 (1963) (however, the Military Justice Act of 1968 provides for a lawyer in most special courts-martial).

United States v. *Gallagher,* 15 U.S.C.M.A. 391, 35 C.M.R. 363 (1963). See also *Gallagher* v. *Quinn,* 363 F. 2d 301 (D.C. Cir.), *cert. denied,* 385 U.S. 881 (1966).

United States v. *Whitman,* 3 U.S.C.M.A. 179, 11 C.M.R. 179 (1953). See also *O'Connor* v. *Cushman, supra,* note 8; *United States* v. *Wade,* 34 C.M.R. 769 (1963).

United States v. *Tempia,* 16 U.S.C.M.A. 629, 37 C.M.R. 249 (1967); *United States* v. *Vierra,* 14 U.S.C.M.A. 48, 33 C.M.R. 260 (1963); *United States* v. *Schlack,* 14 U.S.C.M.A. 371, 34 C.M.R. 151 (1964); *United States* v. *Brown,* 7 U.S.C.M.A. 251, 22 C.M.R. 41 (1956); *United States* v. *Kemp,* 13 U.S.C.M.A. 89, 32 C.M.R. 89 (1962); *United States* v. *Ivory,* 9 U.S.C.M.A. 516, 26 C.M.R. 296 (1958). See also UCMJ, art. 44(a).

35. *United States* v. *Howe, op. cit. United States* v. *Daniels, op. cit.*

36. 346 U.S. 137 (1953).

37. 355 U.S. 579 (1958) (per curiam).

38. 395 U.S. 258 (1969).

The Court of Military Appeals is now under pressure to demonstrate that servicemen's rights can be protected as a curb against the growing judicial trend to limit court-martial jurisdiction and to expand federal court review of military decision.

The court-martial provides the formal legal mechanism for assessment of punishment under the military criminal law, but it is only one phase of the military justice system. An informal and nonjudicial system of rules and sanctions—the military system of discipline—operates independently of the formal code of crimes and court-martial procedures. The interaction of this disciplinary structure with the court-martial system leads to more coercive enforcement than civilian criminal law. Civilian criminal law is primarily a negative set of rules which, in spite of some restrictive laws such as those on sexual morality, does not generally attempt to regulate the private and personal lives of citizens. The military justice system, on the other hand, controls specific acts as well as prohibiting unlawful conduct. It claims the right, indeed the necessity, to influence the morale and attitudes as well as the conduct of servicemen, and to play a positive role in inculcating military values. Discipline is its principal vehicle.[39]

The impact of military justice extends beyond the boundaries of the system itself. Experiences with it appear to influence, to some extent at least, a veteran's attitudes toward civilian criminal justice and law and order. Lawyer Melvin Belli states that as a rule of thumb, he challenges active and retired members of the military as potential jurors when representing a plaintiff in a personal injury case or a defendant in a criminal case because "anyone who has sat on military courts-martial will believe that the civil criminal law is much too lenient to a defendant," and may be "inclined to refuse consideration for even the slightest dereliction."[40]

Even traditional veterans' groups such as the American Legion and Veterans of Foreign Wars, which can be counted on to support the military establishment, have often been critical of military justice. In 1959, the American Legion sponsored a sweeping bill for reform of the UCMJ, proposing removal of court-martial jurisdiction to try servicemen for civilian-type crimes, further limiting commanders' control of courts-martial, requiring lawyers in special courts-martial, and placing civilians on courts-martial and boards of review.[41] The Legion's position appears to have been based on a belief that substantial numbers of servicemen were not getting fair trials in courts-martial, and that the enlisted man, in particular, was getting the short end of the stick. Whenever hearings have been held

39. The Army is reportedly experimenting with behavior modification techniques using merit awards such as overnight and weekend passes for duties accomplished, in place of rigid disciplinary procedures. *New York Times,* June 23, 1970, p. 15.

40. Mr. Belli, 1 Modern Trails 823 (1954).

41. H.R. 3455, 86th Congress, 1st Session (1959).

on a new military justice bill, the veterans organizations have usually provided timely and relevant testimony on abuses in the system.

Understandably, veterans with the strongest feelings about military justice include those millions with military records of court-martial convictions and undesirable, bad conduct, or dishonorable discharges. The impact of military justice on their lives is direct and continuing. Most veterans' benefits are not available to veterans whose discharges were rated undesirable, bad conduct, or dishonorable, depriving them of the funds or opportunities provided by the GI Bill, VA housing, and other benefits. Such a discharge considerably restricts job opportunity, since they are virtually foreclosed from a security clearance for defense work, and are unlikely to be considered for government employment at all levels but especially for federal jobs. Many civilian employers, particularly large corporate and institutional employers, ask the type of military discharge granted, on their employment applications. Testimony before a Senate subcommittee in 1966 indicated that an unfavorable answer frequently prevented placement[42] (by contrast, the U.S. Civil Service Commission has now eliminated the question about civilian arrests from the standard employment application). In testifying before the subcommittee, the counsel for the Catholic War Veterans reported that: "Practically every petitioner who seeks our service as counsel, speaks of the hardship brought by the curse of the undesirable, bad conduct, and discharges under other than honorable conditions. . . . The stigma is designed to last throughout the life of the former serviceman. . . ."[43] Thousands of veterans attempt to have their discharges upgraded each year through Discharge Review Boards and Boards for Correction of Records, which were established after World War II, but they must prove that an injustice was done. The boards deny roughly 90 per cent of the requests.

Veterans with court-martial convictions also find that the record haunts them forever. If a veteran was convicted of a court-martial offense which is equivalent to a felony in a civilian law, as mentioned earlier, he will have a felony conviction on his record affecting his eligibility for a security clearance, government employment, some types of civilian employment, and, frequently, licensing in professions like law and medicine. Since a felony is defined as a crime punishable by more than a year in the penitentiary, a number of strictly military crimes (such as AWOL, disobedience of orders, or conduct punishable under the general articles) that do not involve the moral opprobrium ordinarily associated with a felony still carry the disabilities of a felony conviction, including the loss of the right to vote and to serve on juries.

Most civilians have no overt contact with the system of military justice,

42. *Joint Hearings, supra* note 41, at 835.
43. *Ibid.,* at 834.

but it has an indirect impact upon millions of draft-age potential service-men who are enrolled in reserve or ROTC programs or are likely to be drafted, upon communities situated near military installations, and upon certain state and local law enforcement and judicial institutions which have been influenced by military-trained personnel. It also has an impact on some 1,000,000 civil service employees of the Department of Defense, and upon the several million public and private employees who require security clearances for work on military contracts.

Young men who are contemplating the possibility of substituting some form of voluntary military service—whether as active duty officers, enlisted men, or reservists—for the luck of the draft lottery, may feel some hesita-tion at exercising their First Amendment rights as civilians, for fear that they will somehow be prejudiced in seeking a commission or a place in a reserve unit, or that they will be ruled out of consideration for the more interesting, and often at the same time more sensitive, assignments. The fact that, during the McCarthy era of the mid-1950's, some enlisted men were given less-than-honorable discharges on the basis of alleged pre-induction political associations may, to the extent that it is known and remembered, have an additional chilling effect.

The jurisdiction of the UCMJ over reservists is still unclear, but it appears that they are subject to court-martial only while on active duty or training (most national guard commanders, on the other hand, are given jurisdiction over their members at monthly meetings by state statutes).[44] Still, most are uncertain about the risks involved in taking a stand opposing official military positions. A number of cases have arisen during the Vietnam war of allegedly discriminatory actions by reserve commanders, involving denial of credit for attendance at meetings and punitive activation of reservists who have participated in antiwar activities. Some ROTC cadets who had participated in campus antiwar movements have been denied commissions and their draft boards notified for their immediate induction. The disciplinary powers of a reserve or ROTC com-mander are derived from the traditional military system and, despite the fact that the ultimate sanction of court-martial cannot be applied, discipline can be used to control or punish individual actions.

Civilian employees in the military establishment are subject to the same kinds of checks to which all federal government employees are subject: the Federal Bureau of Investigation "name check" for all posi-tions and, if any information turns up in the name check that might be regarded as derogatory, a so-called "full field investigation" covering everyone from neighbors to former employers. Where the employee's job is

44. See Robert Gerwig, "Court-Martial Jurisdiction Over Weekend Reservists," 44 Mil. Law Rev. 123 (1969).

designated as "sensitive" (a category that includes, for example, all positions in the two-thousand-man office of the Secretary of Defense) a full field investigation is prescribed in any event. Security checks, including full field investigations, are also prescribed for military personnel holding sensitive positions. Access to classified information (Confidential, Secret, and Top Secret) requires security clearances, and the bulk of classified paper originates in and circulates within the military establishment. Clearance through Secret can be had on the basis of a name check, while Top Secret clearances require a full investigation.[45]

A separate program, the industrial security program, established in 1955 by congressional action,[46] provides clearances for facilities and individuals working on defense contracts. After a considerable history of controversy and legislation, this program now provides probably the most effective procedural safeguards for individual rights of any personnel security program, and tends, also, to approach substantive issues in a more realistic and non-ideological atmosphere than other programs. There is no guarantee, however, given the subjective quality of the determination that clearance for a particular individual is "clearly consistent with national security," that past excesses[47] may not be repeated if the political climate in the country worsens. In the meantime, the fact that personnel security programs within the military establishment do deal with the protection of some real secrets tends to keep them more in touch with reality than, say, the program to clear scientists for National Institutes of Health research review panels.

Servicemen are subject to interrogation by intelligence officers and agents concerning past and present conduct and attitudes, with the possibility of loss of clearance or court-martial (the principal evidence of "disloyal statements" used against Corporal Harvey came from interrogation by a Naval Intelligence agent). Since early in the Vietnam war, Army non-commissioned officers cannot be promoted to the higher NCO grades without a security clearance; many military jobs, most of them desirable, require a clearance. The relative lack of objective standards for awarding or denying security clearances puts any individual with an unorthodox record in an unfavorable position. Membership in Students for a Democratic Society and other radical student organizations, or participation in "extreme" or violent antiwar or peace activities probably result, as of now, in refusal of a security

45. Some kinds of information, particularly in the intelligence field, are subject to special classification and clearance procedures, even to the extent of limiting the number of persons holding a particular clearance at any one time. There have been occasional (and perhaps inevitable) charges that access to some of these special clearances have been manipulated for political purposes, but by and large this does not appear to be the case.

46. 64 Stat. 992, 50 U.S.C. & 781 et. seq.

47. Documented in Case Studies in Personnel Security, Adam Yarmolinsky, ed. (Washington, D.C.: Bureau of National Affairs, 1955).

clearance. Thus, security clearance can serve as a deterrent against the exercise of First Amendment rights for servicemen, potential servicemen, and civilian employees of both the government and private defense contractors.[48]

The military impact upon civilians has recently been extended in ways that suggest dangerous implications for the freedom of citizens generally. In April 1970 the American Civil Liberties Union lost a round in a federal district court when it challenged an Army surveillance of civilian activities. It was contended that a special intelligence branch of the Army with offices across the country had, since 1965, secretly compiled dossiers on thousands of organizations and political dissenters. The Pentagon responded to congressional inquiries by announcing elimination of a computerized data bank of millions of names and associations but admitted that it has retained microfilm files of similar information on civilian political activity through the Counter-Intelligence Analysis Division. Senator Sam J. Ervin of North Carolina, chairman of the Subcommittee on Constitutional Rights of the Senate Judiciary Committee, observed that "regardless of the imaginary military objective, the chief casualty of this overkill is the Constitution of the United States."[49] A Justice Department lawyer, Kevin Maroney, defended the surveillance as necessary to prepare for emergencies such as the 1967 riots in Newark and Detroit.

There is growing pressure for reform of the system of military justice, spurred by the Vietnam dissenter cases and the repressive possibilities inherent in the court-martial structure. The board of inquiry that recommended court-martial for Commander Lloyd M. Bucher and other *Pueblo* personnel (overruled by the Secretary of the Navy) left a lingering public impression of fundamental unfairness and scapegoat-seeking hidden behind the elaborate formalities of the Navy hearings. The handling of the Green Beret murder case encouraged further doubts about the fairness of a trial system in which the commander is deeply interested and over which he exercises considerable control. And now the My Lai courts-martial, in which most of the defendants have sought federal court relief on the ground that they cannot receive a fair trial in a court-martial, continue to challenge the adequacy and impartiality of military justice.

If major changes in the military justice system do not occur, the process already begun—judicial limitation of court-martial jurisdiction and expanded federal court review of military determinations—will probably

48. See Adam Yarmolinsky, *Case Studies;* W. Gellhorn, *Security, Loyalty, and Science*, 203-234 (1950).

49. Christopher H. Pyle, "Conus Intelligence: The Army Watches Civilian Politics," *The Washington Monthly*, February 1970. Pyle is a former captain in Army Intelligence.

continue, with the likelihood that court-martial jurisdiction will be further limited and the independence of the military courts constricted. Some have argued for the abolition of the court-martial system. The West German military, for example, has no court-martial system; servicemen charged with crimes are tried in civilian courts. However, this procedure would create logistical problems for the United States, particularly, since crimes are often committed on foreign or isolated installations. A more plausible solution is reform of the UCMJ to insure at least the same quality of trial and related proceedings as that available in civilian courts.

A number of proposals for military justice reform are now pending before Congress, the four major proposals having been introduced by Senators Ervin, Tydings, Bayh, and Hatfield.[50] Senator Ervin's bill contains the remainder of the reforms of administrative discharge procedures which were not included in the Military Justice Act of 1968, providing for expanded due process rights to servicemen in such proceedings. The Tydings bill, as also the Bayh and Hatfield bills, would remove command control over court-martial machinery and appointments and establish a separate court-martial command independent of the commander to carry out such functions as appointment of counsel, supervision of the trial, and review of sentence. The Bayh and Hatfield bills would also make major structural changes in the military justice system, many of their proposals deriving from criticisms and suggestions madè in recent legal studies[51] and the 1970 Report of the Special Civilian Committee on the Army Confinement System, which proposed a major overhaul of army confinement and military justice procedures.[52] These bills would require random selection of court members from a broader-based group than the commander's officers; expand the powers of military judges and the extraordinary writs powers and review availability of military appellate courts; expand the availability of federal district court and direct Supreme Court review of courts-martial and military determinations; redraft a number of the military offenses and remove court-martial jurisdiction over others; and require increased civilianization of various aspects of court-martial trials.

The military's new directives on dissent and on racial matters are an encouraging display of concern and willingness to change. But the "long, hot summer" of 1969 with dozens of post racial disorders, stockade riots, and resort to sanctuaries attests to the complexity of the problems, and the need for continued reform. The military needs to formulate its disciplinary

50. S. 1266, 91st Cong., 1st Sess. (1969); S. 3117, 91st Cong., 1st Sess. (1969); S. 4191, 91st Cong., 2d Sess. (1970); S. 4168-78, 91st Cong., 2d Sess. (1970).

51. Sherman, *The Civilization of Military Law,* 2 Maine L. Rev. 3, 66-103. (1970).

52. *Report of the Special Civilian Committee for the Study of the United States Army Confinement System,* Department of the Army (1970).

policies around the fundamental fact that the soldier is also a citizen and, hence, is presumed to enjoy the same guarantees of individual liberty as a civilian. The courts, in each case, should compel the military to bear the burden of proving that it is essential to the effective functioning of the military that the soldier be subject to a more restrictive standard of freedom than his civilian counterpart.

For the first time, the military thus would be forced to articulate its needs—to compare and analyze the manifold "effects" which civilian and soldier speech can have on discipline and morale. A soldier's speech, for instance, may have the effect of persuading his fellows that the goals for which they fight are immoral, yet common sense suggests that similar words spoken by a retired general officer or a United States Senator can and have had that same effect, and some studies indicate that belief in such goals is, at best, of minor motivational importance.[53] Some have feared that a dissenting soldier's speech may alienate him from his fellows and thereby weaken morale, yet another study shows that "buddies" will tolerate from each other the most unacceptable behavior, e.g., desertion from the field of battle.[54] A searching analysis of the effect of dissent and symbolic speech—such as Afro haircuts and black-power salutes—on discipline would require the military to ask itself how much discipline is really necessary to maintain military effectiveness. Conventional wisdom on this point within the military has undergone radical change over the past half-century. Similarly, the sometimes alleged threat to civilian authority over the military posed by political speech of junior grade officers and soldiers must be recognized as unrealistic. Perhaps a more sensible criterion might be the rule that any officer invited to deliver a formal speech can be required to submit the text for clearance to higher authority; mere conversation must be immune from prior restraint as from subsequent punishment. Up to now, courts have allowed the military to meet this burden with the vaguest generalizations and clichés.

As the great divisive issues in American society—and particularly the issues of war in Southeast Asia and of race conflict at home—penetrate more and more deeply into the fabric of the military establishment, they challenge the system of military discipline in general and of military justice in particular to moderate between the requirements of military discipline and the rising demand for freedom of expression. There are already indications that the system is being modified in the direction of greater freedom of expression, without damage to discipline. But progress is uneven, and many military tribunals continue to apply outmoded and even mutually

53. See Edward Shils and Morris Janowitz, "Cohesion and Disintegration in the Wehrmacht in World War II," *Public Opinion Quarterly*, Summer 1948, pp. 280-315.

54. Roger W. Little, "Buddy Relations and Combat Performance," in *The New Military*, Morris Janowitz, ed. (New York: Russell Sage Foundation, 1964).

inconsistent standards to expression by soldiers and officers. If military commanders and military judges alike give greater scope to freedom of dissent as distinguished from refusal to accept discipline, or specific counsel to others to do so, tensions within the military are likely to be erased rather than exacerbated.

23

Military Management
in a Technological Society

The development of the federal government as a large-scale human enterprise in the United States is a phenomenon of recent decades. In 1932, when Franklin Roosevelt was elected President the federal budget was $4.2 billion, in monetary terms less than 2 per cent of its current scale of operation. The New Deal initiated the expansion in federal activity, but even so the budget had reached only $10 billion, or 11 per cent of GNP, on the eve of World War II. It was that war, and the world political struggle that followed, which drove the federal government into business on an unprecedented scale.

The management problems that accompanied this explosion of activity were also new. Defense, as much or more than any other area of activity, is a matter of public purpose, and hence market mechanisms for coordinating the myriad and diverse activities of individuals were unavailable. The procurement and operation of aircraft carriers, strategic bombers, and infantry divisions would not adjust automatically through the operations of the market. Over-all coherence and direction could only be given to the activities put into motion by the Defense budgets through conscious allocation of tax dollars. Techniques of rational planning for large-scale public spending were desperately needed, and military operations, which gave prime impetus to the problem, also brought forth the first approaches to its solution.

In World War II British scientists and engineers took the lead in applying simple mathematical techniques to management problems, seeking to bring greater discipline and greater effectiveness to planning operations by quantitative methods. British analysts were asked, for example, to allocate a certain number of aircraft to antisubmarine warfare missions in the Bay of

Biscay. They considered using the aircraft to escort convoys, to conduct search operations, and to launch attacks on submarine bases on the continent. With data from prior months of war, they calculated what each possible mission would mean in terms of numbers of allied ships saved from sinking by enemy submarines. Such calculations, which came to be known as operations research, in essence took the place of the mechanisms of the market (profit, and consumer demand) as a means of evaluating the efficiency and worth of military activity which could not otherwise be evaluated.

After the war, the techniques and perspectives of operations research were expanded in the United States to deal with broader questions of policy and more general issues of organizational management. In both dimensions —policy and management—incipient crisis was the stimulant. Defense policy was now based on deterrence—the ability to threaten destruction of any enemy who attacked. The highly complex and extremely expensive technology employed to implement this policy required, for intelligent direction of this effort, an ability to assess the relative value of diverse weapons systems in a rapidly changing technical environment. This task was not only intellectually difficult but politically difficult as well. The weapons involved— bombers, land- and sea-based missiles, and missile defense systems—were core programs of separate service organizations. The Army, the Marine Corps, the Navy, and the Air Force, proud of their traditions and jealous of their prerogatives, were not destined to embrace an abstract analysis whose logic might drive one or more of them out of business. Nor could one any longer rely upon chastening experience. The death of an entire society could now be a potential result of a serious mistake. Successful planning became a requisite for survival, and improvement of the existing planning process a matter of highest priority.

The most prominent of the external research centers—the RAND Corporation, organized in 1946, as a division of Douglas Aircraft, and later established as an independent, nonprofit corporation—became the focus for innovations both in policy analysis of defense issues and in the closely related organizational management techniques. Researchers at RAND began to develop models of possible procedures for strategic forces operations in case of war. These models served to focus available knowledge, to make planning assumptions explicit, and, wherever possible, to apply quantitative data. In a complicated world with spotty data and many unknowns, the emphasis was on explicitness more than quantification, and on critical examination of assumptions more than on elaborate computation. As this work developed in the 1950's, the policy analysts began to produce carefully reasoned arguments on the appropriate size and configuration of American strategic weapons. These arguments gradually began to connect to specific issues of decision; whether the United States should buy missiles or bombers or how many of each; what characteristics these forces really required and what they could do without. Often the arguments contradicted the conventional wisdom. They indicated in one case, for example, that the Air Force emphasis on the speed and range of advanced bombers was misplaced, since the utility of bombers for strategic missions was more related to their ability to carry special devices for confusing enemy radar. In economic terms, billions of dollars turned on an issue of this sort; in human terms, in the (hopefully unlikely) case of war, it was not hard to see millions of lives at stake.

As their conclusions diverged from the natural line of development the military services often sought to take, the policy analysts began to argue for institutionalizing their techniques as a means of instilling analytic discipline in military decisions. They were reaching for influence over much more fundamental questions of policy than those dealt with by operations researchers in World War II. They sought to include within the purview of their analysis not only the relatively low-level allocation issues of operations research, but basic questions of high policy as well—not only how planes are to be used but also what sort of planes to buy, how many, and whether antisubmarine missions, for example, were the critical ones. To catch that distinction, their analytic approach was labeled systems analysis.[1]

Concomitant with this policy-related research at RAND, a group of people (David Novick at RAND, Arthur Smithies at Harvard) began after the war to study the routine decision-making processes in the enlarged defense establishment, and to ask how well these processes were geared to the principles of systems analysis. They found that in the critical area of the budgetary process, for example, information was presented in a way that caused tremendous difficulty in attempts to make the cost calculations that systems analysis required. This deficiency alone made it reasonably clear that the explicit comparisons of weapons systems performing the same missions were not being done on a systematic basis. Picking up ideas that went back to the first decade of the century, RAND researchers developed the concepts of program budgeting and other ways to structure the operating practices of government agencies so that the principles of analytic planning could be more broadly applied.

The work done at RAND filtered gradually into the government during the 1950's, and then was introduced explicitly and systematically in 1961. Secretary McNamara brought key RAND personnel to his civilian staff— Charles Hitch, Alain Enthoven, Henry Rowen, Fred S. Hoffman, among others—and gave them a mandate to impose analytic discipline on the Pentagon's planning and budgeting process. Hitch became Comptroller; Entho-

1. The argument was first presented in C. J. Hitch and R. N. McKean, *The Economics of Defense in the Nuclear Age* (Cambridge: Harvard University Press, 1960).

ven later became Assistant Secretary for Systems Analysis. McNamara himself supplied the critical ingredients of political authority. He demanded analytic argument based on the RAND model, and authorized changes in the budgetary and planning process. A formal planning system—called planning, programming, budgeting (or PPB)—was established department-wide to pull together under the same budget heading separate programs in the several services, whose objectives were similar.[2] It sought to clarify the choices involved in weapons procurement and drive staff analysts to attempt to make costs and effectiveness comparisons across service lines and for weapons systems with the same defense mission.

Systems analysis is the systematic application of common sense to complex problems, and the essential logic of the analytic planning intended by the PPB system was quite simple. Any given program was required to justify itself in output terms—in terms of its contribution to the nation's defense. Thus, if a particular missile system was proposed, analysts had to consider whether it would be a better investment than other weapons doing the same job—that is, that for a given cost, it would provide more return in terms of some specific task or that it could do a given task more cheaply. The planning cycle involved the major weapons procurement choices to be made in a given year.

The Defense Budget formerly had been organized by service (Army, Navy, Air Force) and by classes of inputs (construction, pay of personnel, maintenance and operations, research and development) rather than outputs (although some individual services had maintained functional budgets for internal use). This over-all budget structure concealed the military *purposes* of the money to be spent. In 1961 this conventional budget (still used for congressional appropriation and many internal management purposes) was supplemented by a budget structure which revealed, cutting across service lines, how much was to be spent on strategic nuclear forces, continental defense, tactical air (land- and sea-based), antisubmarine warfare, reserve systems, research and development, and other major military missions and functions.

Several areas of policy were affected by these procedures. Major strategic programs proposed in the late 1950's and early 1960's failed to stand up to logical analysis. The B-70, an advanced bomber; Nike-Zeus, an early generation missile defense system; the Skybolt air-launched missile; and a nuclear powered aircraft carrier—all controversial weapons systems recommended strongly by the services that developed them—were rejected for procurement in significant part because of serious weaknesses which became apparent under analytic scrutiny. The nation was spared many billion dollars of expenditure, which would not have provided com-

2. David Novick, ed., *Program Budgeting: Program Analysis and the Federal Budget* (Cambridge: Harvard University Press, 1965).

mensurate returns. The threat to Europe from a conventional attack by Warsaw Pact forces was also assessed in the new analytic system, and the analysis strongly suggested that the threat had been grossly overestimated. The overestimate had driven NATO into a potentially dangerous reliance on early nuclear retaliation, and had discouraged productive investment in nonnuclear supply stockpiles for the NATO forces. It was one thing to achieve this insight and another thing to change direction in the complicated world of alliance politics, but the analysis did give greater coherence and purpose to American policy for NATO—a clear goal to move toward.

Other important benefits were achieved in management practices. A cost reduction program was implemented to eliminate unnecessary expenditures in ongoing programs. This program achieved more than $10 billion in audited savings during McNamara's tenure as Defense Secretary. Progress was also made for the first time toward achieving a rational grasp of manpower requirements. A control system (Program Evaluation and Review Technique, or PERT), first developed in the late 1950's by the Navy, was utilized to help work out optimal scheduling of the enormously complicated production cycles of major missile systems. A moribund, inefficient shipbuilding industry was encouraged to modernize its equipment, its production techniques, and its management practices.[3]

The techniques employed by the military establishment to determine future needs—systems analysis, functional budgeting, contingency planning, and the like—were not unanimously popular. Those whose pet projects were scuttled were displeased. Other critics raised basic questions of principle. Particular opprobrium was reserved for the process called war gaming, or simply gaming, on grounds of cold-bloodedness. The gaming process is worth exploring in this context.

War games are exercises that simulate the decision-making process in actual military conflict, at any level from full-fledged maneuvers of troops in the field to high level paper-and-pencil exercises in a subbasement of the Pentagon. The war game requires planners to put themselves, dramatically, in their antagonists' boots and, at the same time, requires them to take account of an antagonist's moves in a simulated real-life situation. Perhaps the greatest value of a war game is to the members of the enemy (Red) team since it gives more perspective on the other side's psychology, although the Blue team members can also gain significant insights into their own probable behavior, as well as the behavior of the other side. Many games involve a larger number of teams, simulating a typical multipolar system, with alliances and neutrals, and consequent exposure to a broader range of outlooks. In this sense a war game has some of the same psycho-

3. But see the critique of weapons-acquisition procedures in New period, in Chapter 17.

logical values as a psychodrama, in which people gain insight into their own roles by playing the role of their opposite numbers.

War games are conducted at many levels of the military establishment, and at the higher levels involve the State Department and the White House. The development of "scenarios" for war games is a recognized field of expertise, along with the management of games so that both teams have maximum exposure to problem situations. The games are regarded as important enough by the Pentagon that it has established a separate Joint War Games Directorate within the organization of the Joint Chiefs of Staff; they are regarded as important enough by cabinet-level officials and the White House staff that these officials make themselves available to join in the play.

A typical war game or "political-military exercise" totally absorbs the thought and emotion of the participants: to take a single example, the hypothetical game of SOPEX-4.

The object of SOPEX-4 is to test some of the consequences of the fourth version of a specific plan to counter a Soviet takeover of Egypt. The problem is obviously complex, involving both the political and military forces of several countries as well as the United Nations.

As the distinguished diplomats and military leaders who will participate arrive in the basement-gaming facility of the Pentagon, they are handed loose-leaf books with background data. A colonel asks for their attention so that he can brief them. He explains the object of the game, the basic rules, assigns player roles, and explains where players will sit. He explains that he will act as "control" or referee. There is a brief question-and-answer exchange, and then the players go to their assigned rooms. The players have been distributed among six "teams," each with its own private room: Soviets, U.S., Egyptian, Israeli, non-U.S. NATO, and U.N. Each "team" has several members, representing different government departments in the larger nation teams (State Department, Defense, CIA, Navy, etc., in the U.S. team) and several governments in the multination teams.

The teams are given a half-hour to formulate strategy. Then the game begins with a TWX bulletin from both "World Press" and national intelligence sources that Soviet airborne units have been airdropped into the Sinai Peninsula. This "input" is designed to force players into action. The options available in this game are both political and military.

The U.S. team immediately responds with both political and military actions. Diplomatic protests are sent to the Soviet team, and Mediterranean naval forces are ordered to stand by off Suez but to refrain from hostilities unless attacked. These responses take the form of written orders to various government departments, units, and commands. These orders are handed to couriers, who take them to control.

Control disposes of the orders of the various teams by allowing or disallowing them, and responding with information to those concerned. For example, the U.S. diplomatic protest was conveyed directly to the Soviet team, as was some limited intelligence about U.S. naval movements in the eastern Mediterranean. The Israeli and Egyptian teams were also informed, as if their intelligence services had observed their movements.

A series of moves and countermoves by all teams follows in compressed time (one hour of real time is taken to represent twelve hours of simulated game time, so that players can cover three entire days of simulated action in the six hours of elapsed play time). The game ends at the scheduled time six hours (three game days) later. In the course of the game the players will have been surprised, anxious, frustrated, enraged, jubilant, despondent, over the reported results of their moves and countermoves. All they know of their adversaries, allies, and neutrals is what they receive in intelligence and open bulletins delivered by the ubiquitous couriers. Now that the game is over, a debriefing is held in a conference room and all players once again face each other.

As the players reassemble there is some banter over who did what to whom. Control calls for silence and describes what happened. Occasionally there are gasps of surprise or interjections, as players learn how limited their view of reality had been. The leaders of the teams are asked to explain their respective strategies briefly. A general discussion ensues in which effective and ineffective strategies are identified. Control summarizes what seems to have been learned, what problems were identified that require further study, and what seemed realistic and unrealistic. The usual caveats are made that the game is not predictive, but only indicative. Following further animated discussion about the pros and cons of various moves, the players depart, and the games staff begins to write up the results.

To be able to speak or write, in cold blood, of "playing" a war game —a dangerous adult version of children playing with toy soldiers—is the crux of the popular criticism of war gaming. For most people who play war games, they are not games in any "fun and games" sense but an exercise in problem solving. The term has passed into the language as part of the civilian fallout from the military establishment; it is not uncommon now to hear people in the industrial or academic community speak of "war gaming" a particularly difficult problem. There is, however, the risk that war gaming may not take sufficient account of the irrationalities and the human intangibles injected into the decision-making process by the pressures of a real crisis, so that games may produce an unrealistically rational set of outcomes—that is, rational and consistent as means within the context of unchallenged assumptions about ends. Nor are the players often encouraged to question ultimate goals and purposes.

The popular criticism is not in fact addressed to the use of a particular analytical tool, which can be extremely valuable in sharpening and broadening the perceptions and insights of decision-makers. It is addressed rather to the tendency to treat war only as an abstract intellectual contest, as when a State Department official, referring to a proposed step-up in the bombing and strafing of Vietnam, proposed "that our orchestration should be mainly violins, but with periodic touches of brass."[4]

To the extent that no war game attempts to simulate the suffering and death that war produces, it may be argued that war gaming introduces a systematic bias, de-emphasizing the tragic aspects of war. Of course, the systematic and intensive application of rational methods to any problem, necessary as this is, tends to squeeze some of the living juices out of the problem itself. This is a difficulty that can arise as well in the examination of housing the poor as in the examination of scenarios for general nuclear war.

The analytic planning effort within the military establishment was controversial, as any strong initiative is likely to be. It is neither possible nor desirable, at this early date, to form a definitive judgment of the net benefit. Even the most unrestrained advocates would admit that much that the logic of systems analysis demanded was more than has yet been achieved. Blatant anomalies existed in the force structure throughout the 1960's. However, the success of the planning system in the Pentagon was apparent enough to stimulate a formal attempt to carry PPB procedures into the domestic agencies of government.

In August 1965 President Johnson directed that similar decision-making procedures be implemented within the nondefense sectors of the federal bureaucracy. The President's directive was the result of several factors. The first was the expectation by senior Budget Bureau officials and the Council of Economic Advisers that economic growth would yield major budget surpluses in the latter half of the 1960's. Members of the Executive Office were searching for a way to make these surpluses controllable—and thus more productively expendable—by the President and his cabinet. At this same time, it became increasingly apparent that the management reforms in the Department of Defense had given the civilian Secretary and the President unprecedented influence in the defense policy-making process.

President Johnson directed the establishment of programming-planning-budgeting systems at departmental and Budget Bureau levels in order to increase the government's ability to identify national goals with greater precision, to determine the relative urgency of those goals, to develop and

4. James C. Thomson, Jr., "How Could Vietnam Happen!," *The Atlantic,* April 1968, p. 51.

analyze alternative means of reaching those goals more effectively, and to ascertain directly the probable costs and impacts of these alternative programs.[5] The presidential message directed all domestic agencies to develop integrated PPB systems, and the Budget Bureau was assigned the central role of fostering, monitoring, and supervising the development of the intra-agency and agency-Bureau procedures.

A number of those who participated in PPB efforts had been employed by Defense and developed parallel systems based on a budget-oriented model. In addition, there was a concentration of economists on domestic PPB staffs. These factors plus the central role for the Budget Bureau led to an extensive, and in some cases excessive, concentration on the formal budget-making process in contrast with a focus on political or legislative considerations. Much of early criticism of domestic PPB efforts was a consequence of this priority. Critics argued that the major domestic policy decisions took place during the development and legislative enactment of new programs, and that a budgetary PPB system was not oriented toward bringing analytical judgment to bear on the really important decisions within the domestic (or nondefense) sector. Further, while the budget process might be the proper focus of decision-making in an agency in which procurement decisions had major policy impact, it was not necessarily appropriate in an area like education or welfare, in which agency procurement was largely limited to office supplies.

Analytic staffs were established throughout the domestic agencies[6] and efforts began to develop frameworks—program structures—within which the analytic process could be organized. A Program Evaluation Staff (later to become the Office of Program Evaluation) was set up in the Budget Bureau to manage the bureau's central PPB responsibilities. Analytical teams were established in the agencies and departments. In some instances the analysts were placed directly in the offices of the Secretary; in others they were put both in the Secretary's office and in the agency's budgeting offices. In a few departments former Pentagon analysts moved into leadership roles with the newly formed analytic offices, but for the most part staff was recruited among existing professional staffs of the departments; within the academic community (especially in graduate departments of economics and in business schools); and at managerial levels of the corporate sector, including management consulting firms.

Although defense analysts had concentrated extensively on the strategic sector of Defense Department policy, Secretary McNamara wanted the pro-

5. Statement by the President to Cabinet Members and Agency Heads on the New Government-Wide Planning and Budgeting System, August 25, 1965.

6. Although the presidential message directed all departments and agencies to establish PPB systems, the agencies were divided into several groupings which were to implement PPB at different times over a three-year period.

gram structure to cover the entire range of Defense activities, and turned to developing a series of studies of alternative force structures and policies for all Defense programs. The initial domestic PPB efforts were similarly directed toward developing program structures. But because of the limited experience and knowledge of policy and program impacts among the domestic staffs and the limited amount of domestic policy analysis attempted prior to 1965, the initial program budgeting efforts were of limited utility. Little analysis of policy alternatives was attempted, and the initial Program Memoranda, which paralleled similar documents in the Pentagon, were largely reformulations of traditional agency budget justifications.

These efforts did, however, have important impacts on the agencies' and departments' understanding of their objectives and the general orientation of their programs. In some departments, this understanding led to initiation of new program efforts when important objectives seemed to be weakly served. In others, the simple division of resources among the program budget categories led to serious attempts at reallocation. For example, when the division of departmental resources among various age groups was, later, presented to the Secretary of HEW, the Secretary found that though he had repeatedly stressed the importance of children to his department, children were, in reality, receiving little attention. The Department of Health, Education and Welfare, the Department of Housing and Urban Development, the Office of Economic Opportunity, and other agencies began to conduct research studies (summer studies, panels of experts, etc.) on existing programs, and to develop information systems through which performance and, wherever possible, data on impact would be routinely gathered to provide information for future analytic efforts.

At first nondefense policy-making was little affected. The early program structures were not well related to the appropriation categories in which the agencies' requests entered the congressional allocation process. Thus little of the PPB considerations were brought into this important area of the policy process. In addition, the financial constraints imposed on the domestic sector of federal operations by the Vietnam war and other military expenditures limited most decisions on domestic policy to minor incremental changes or reallocations of funds, and the quality of analysis was not yet sufficiently strong to influence politically difficult reallocation efforts. Nevertheless, important changes in the managerial processes of non-Defense agencies had been initiated, and important impacts on policy began to result.

Whereas early Program Memoranda (PMs) were simply wide-ranging discussions of agency objectives and activities, the memoranda have been reoriented as "decision documents" to discuss alternative strategies for reaching policy goals. The selective application of limited analytical manpower resources to areas of major policy concern has been made possible by limiting the number of PMs. Special Analytic Studies (SAS) provide back-up evidence to support PM recommendations. High-level Budget Bureau and agency personnel have taken an increasingly active role in defining issues of priority for analysis. In a cooperative process, the Budget Director instructs the agency head in "Issue Letters" to submit responses to a series of policy questions. Congress has also taken an active role by directing the Executive to conduct specific studies[7] and by questioning agency spokesmen on the results of studies. Other important changes in the PPB process were directed toward improving the quality of information available to the Executive on interagency and interprogram allocation issues. In Health, Education and Welfare, work began on a social report on domestic concerns, to parallel the annual Economic Report of the President. The PPB staff of the Budget Bureau also began to develop a series of "overview sheets" designed to provide an integrated view of the impacts in distribution and performance of the wide range of programs in a given area of domestic policy.

These efforts to integrate domestic policy programs or goals continued after the change in administrations in 1969. A project to develop "social indicators" against which to measure and compare domestic programs was begun within the White House Staff, and both the White House and Executive Office staffs were reorganized to provide a central Domestic Policy Council. Attempts to provide an integrated view of the multiplicity of federal domestic activities paralleled the use of the "Posture Statement," in which the Secretary of Defense combined an analysis of international problems with his recommendations for the appropriate force structure. The fact that RAND and other organizations had been heavily involved in defense analysis prior to 1961 had had important effects on the quality of subsequent Department of Defense analysis, but few domestic agencies, for their part, were able to call on such extensive prior research. Therefore, new research institutions (e.g., the Institute for Research on Poverty, largely funded by Office of Economic Opportunity support at the University of Wisconsin, and the Urban Institute, initially supported by Department of Housing and Urban Development and HEW funds) and existing research institutions (RAND, IDA, and CNA —to mention but a few of the military-oriented institutions that initiated domestic-sector research programs) began to provide information on do-

7. An example of this process can be found in the amendments to legislation on higher education, which directed the Executive to conduct a study and to present an integrated program for federal involvement in higher education. Studies were conducted by the PPB staff of HEW in conjunction with the Office of Education, the Budget Bureau, and other agencies involved in higher education. The response was a comprehensive and useful report, "Toward a Long-Range Plan for Federal Financial Support for Higher Education."

mestic problems. The growing domestic research programs of these institutions and the increasing interest in policy-related research among academic social scientists are likely in the future to yield extensive information which should considerably improve the policy process. It is expected, for example, that the National Science Foundation will begin to support several academic "policy institutes" in fiscal year 1971.

Unlike defense policy, however, domestic policy involves the interaction of all the levels of government within the federal system. Early in the process of installing PPB systems in the domestic sector of the federal bureaucracy, federal officials were brought up against the influence of state and local government on federal policy. Existing federal categorical grants were largely distributed to state and local governments, and the difficulty—in some cases the undesirability—of federal review and control of local decisions meant the quality of the programs was almost entirely out of federal hands. In many of the areas of increased federal concern—e.g., education —state and local governments provided the bulk of resources, and the support by federal programs was marginal in any case. The possibility that future federal aid would be in the form of tax- or revenue-sharing programs (e.g., the Heller-Pechman plan) meant that federal influence might decline even below its already low level. A natural parallel to the efforts to implement PPB in the federal domestic agencies was, therefore, an effort to improve the managerial and policy-forming capacities of state and local governments.

Several models of the PPB process were available to states and local communities. One model focused on analysis of specific policy alternatives, a "targets of opportunity" approach, which ignored the program budget and other formalizations of the policy process in order to commit scarce analytical resources as rapidly as possible to the decision-making process. The PPB system in New York City is using this approach. A small staff within the office of the Director of the Budget Bureau was formed to consider specific critical policy issues—both legislative and budgetary— which faced the mayor and the bureau director. As new executive agencies— the Housing and Development Administration, the Health Services Administration, etc.—were created, the mayor and the director sought to stimulate their administrators to form analytic units. The "targets of opportunity" approach has been criticized for its lack of permanence and its dependence on the interest of high-level decision-makers, but most observers of New York City feel that it has produced some useful and influential analysis. The city tried to formalize the process for a year, but quickly reversed its direction when it became apparent that formalization was producing less effective analytic work.

The second model available to state and local governments was the structured development process, which has been attempted by the federal domestic agencies. The Budget Bureau and the Department of Housing and Urban Development supported the initiation of the State-Local Finances Project at George Washington University to develop and stimulate PPB in state and local governments. The project organized five states, five counties, and five cities (hence titled the 5:5:5 Project) into a consortium to develop PPB systems. The limited ability of most of the state and local governments to recruit high-level analytic manpower, and the limited amount of applied research available on the issues faced by these governments led the 5:5:5 Project to follow the domestic PPB model of a formal program budget structure. A review of the project found important progress in the direction of establishing operational PPB systems[8] but little of usefulness in the policy-making process. The program budgets had been largely completed, but the executive budget submissions generally followed a pre-PPB format.

The federal government provided other stimuli for PPB in state and local governments. Nonfederal officials and employees were invited to attend federal training programs conducted by the Civil Service Commission. The Department of Housing and Urban Development 701 Planning grants were given to governments to support PPB development efforts, and the Budget Bureau assembled technical assistance teams of federal employees and consultants to aid in implementing PPB systems.

These efforts at the state and local levels have produced the same mixture of success and failure as in the federal domestic agencies. The reasons are essentially similar—lack of information and manpower and a pervasive absence of supportive and responsive decision makers. Collaborative efforts between the RAND Corporation and New York City, which resulted in the formation of the RAND-NYC Institute, and the developing cooperation between the Urban Institute and a number of cities and states will probably reduce the first of these barriers. Attempts to open the state and local civil service systems to professional manpower and to train existing employees will eventually ease the personnel problem. And as PPB becomes more clearly useful for the policy-making process, support and response from those responsible for decisions will doubtless increase.

It is difficult to assess the success and failure of the reforms at this point. All has not gone well, either inside or outside the Defense Department, and the general impact of PPB on substantive policy, as it has moved outward from the Pentagon, has been slight. In late 1966, President Johnson

8. The review found that more than twenty-five states and over fifty local governments were at least beginning to develop PPB systems in 1969. "Implementing P.P.B. in State, City, and County Government—a Report on the 555 Project," Selma Mushkin, Project Director, State & Local Finances Project of the George Washington University, Washington, D.C., June 1969.

commented that "Some agencies have put it [PPB] into effect even more rapidly than we anticipated. Too many agencies, however, have been slow in establishing effective Planning, Programming, Budgeting systems and when established they have often not been used in making top management decisions." But there are cases in which important decisions have come out differently as a result of analysis. There are also cases in which the nature of the policy debate has changed as a result of the analytic process, but not enough to alter decisions. Thus, a critical review of the PPB systems as they operated during the 1960's should not be taken as a justification for abandoning analysis or for not developing a conscious, rational policy-making process. Instead, it should provide insights into possible improvements to advance the difficult process of public policy-making.

Putting to one side its most tragic aspects, Vietnam is an example of all the complexities of the process. Despite a growing interest and development of American skills in counterinsurgency in the early 1960's, the available resources included an Army principally concerned with a major conventional conflict in Europe, an Air Force that had devoted most of its energies to nuclear operations, a Navy prepared mainly for deep-water operations and not for river patrols, a Department of State chiefly trained in the conduct of diplomacy, an Agency for International Development that specialized in economic development through capital and technical assistance and not in rural security, and an intelligence agency (CIA) whose primary energies had been devoted to classical intelligence. The resulting problems in a lengthening war did not reflect a rejection of the counterinsurgency approach by the "system." Rather, it reflected time lag in related decisions on budgets, forces, training, research and development, a process that took place imperfectly and, inevitably, slowly.

There are more important lessons to be drawn for this purpose from Vietnam. Organizations tend to have a life of their own. Different parts of the system can come to adopt different and incompatible objectives. There must be "cuts into" the system from different angles and at different levels of authority. In particular, there must be a systematic process of planning, of translating plans into programs and compatible financial decisions, force decisions and planning decisions. And one must take into account the degree of national commitment to the objectives to be implemented, its capacity to be sustained over time and in conflict with alternative commitments to other international and domestic objectives.

Further, critics of the process argue that an overemphasis on quantitative factors as contrasted to nonquantitative—as for example, political and social factors—has caused errors in decision-making. Those responsible for analytic work on defense problems have steadily maintained that they are conscious of the limitations of their own techniques, that they try to prepare analyses which allow for the importance of other factors, and that theirs is only one level of data among others in the decision-making process. The need for nonquantitative information at every stage of evaluation and review is clear, in both defense and domestic concerns. If the analytic process is too narrowly applied, as in Vietnam, where an adequate continuing examination of objectives and alternatives, costs and benefits, was not maintained, or in any domestic area, then the process becomes inadequate to provide decision-makers with a basis for rational action.

It is by no means clear to what degree the methods of system analysis can be transferred to civil problems such as housing, urban transportation, poverty, health, and communications.

There are a number of factors to consider. For example, many civil activities are less "public goods" than are defense activities. The defense establishment aims to defend everyone in the country, and more defense for one person presumably does not mean less defense for someone else. But this is not the case with many civil subsidy programs to such beneficiaries as farmers, residents of public housing projects, or businessmen. They do not, except indirectly, appear to benefit everyone. What some get, others do not. This fact leads to a diminished sense of the public interest and a greater sense of the private interest in many—though by no means all—civil activities. As a corollary, the problems of defense and space are technology-limited rather than people-limited. A relatively small number of people, in the present system, need to be convinced of the crucial decisions in Defense in order to proceed, in contrast with problems such as urban planning, in which the definition of objectives and the determination of the impact of alternative policies on various interest groups may be much more difficult than the technology itself.

Further, the greater role of the Congress and the relative weakness of the President on most domestic matters, compared with most foreign and defense matters, imposes more burden of fragmentation of support upon domestic programs. It is precisely this lack of sustained external review and countervailing influence that has reinforced concern about the unchecked power of the military. Fragmentation makes consistent decision difficult. Yet the absence of such checks and reviews may suggest a united national commitment to the decision that does not exist, or exists in insufficient depth to support a long-range military direction. This clearly was the case in the Vietnam war. The nation backed into war without a conscious commitment, via counterinsurgency and the Bay of Tonkin resolution. It has become clear that the national commitment to the "war on poverty" was also less than total.

In addition, many civil programs have a relatively small technological content compared with the defense programs (the space programs, supersonic transport program, the Post Office, and the highway program are important exceptions) and it is argued that areas where complex social objectives are dominant do not lend themselves as easily to systematic decision-making.

But, despite the difficulties, the diffusion of these methods in domestic affairs will continue at a pace that, however slow it may seem in the immediate perspective, will, in all probability, look rapid in the long run. Business firms as well as government agencies of all kinds by now, in varying degrees, sense the need for improved planning capability, and as the supply of well-trained people increases, the rate of adoption of these techniques will increase.

Further, while it is true that many functional relations are less well understood in race, poverty, and education than in certain other fields, this may well be an argument for more careful and systematic analysis, not less; in the easier areas we are perhaps simply less likely to make mistakes. One can make a rational assessment of causes and consequences even in the presence of what seem, on the surface, to be wholly irrational factors, such as racial prejudice (or, at least, there is not in theory any reason why this would not be possible if the commitment of resources and will to this end were clear).

However, there is an important caveat here: Many of these techniques are not—in themselves—appropriate to projects that cannot, by their nature, be closely controlled. There is, in fact, some danger that projects aimed at radical social innovation, with major political implications, may be misconceived as analogous to the Manhattan Project or the Polaris program, when the analogy is more misleading than it is useful. The military metaphor in the war against poverty probably did more harm than good, and the design of an integrated urban transit system is not really to be compared to the moon shot. The systems approach can be understood too narrowly, by its proponents as well as its opponents, as limiting consideration to quantifiable data. This would be a serious and dangerous error.

It is apparent, in any case, that in the future the cold calculating computer will not take over the making of significant decisions. Human beings, often confused, will still be in charge. Bargaining, adversary processes, and incremental decision-making will not go out of style. Decisions will continue to be a function of attitude and feeling as well as thought. Qualitative data will be weighed as part of the decision-making process itself—in fact, the rational process itself demands this.

Either the American public will lose faith completely in scientific rationality as a mode of dealing with present problems (as the leaders of the groups that perceive themselves as oppressed by modern society already have), or we shall gradually succeed in developing and deploying our intellectual resources for dealing with our problems. If this rational tendency wins out in the end, credit will be owing to the social capabilities for applying rational analysis to problem-solving.

The pattern of large-scale problem-solving through the application of enormous resources focused on a specific object has been set by the military establishment and its space-age offspring, and although the phenomenon is not an entirely new one in American history, earlier accomplishments like the first transcontinental railroads, the Brooklyn Bridge, and the Panama Canal were to a considerable extent victories for heroic individuals. Only in the last thirty years has the process been institutionalized. The levels of detail are now so many, and the interrelationships so complex that no one person can comprehend them; only a disciplined group effort can produce the desired result. At the same time, the process has been speeded up so that, while medieval cathedrals were centuries abuilding and the great canals of the nineteenth and early twentieth centuries took decades, more impressive tasks are accomplished in a few years—with the time of completion predicted, perhaps with something less than complete accuracy, at the outset.

Without the example of these military and quasi-military accomplishments the proponents of major programs would lack an important argument to support the feasibility of bold, large-scale project designs in housing, in education, in pollution control. It is also argued that big military projects have helped to develop management techniques without which big civilian projects could not be planned, much less accomplished.

The greatest contribution of the military to the solution of major social problems is the fact that military accomplishments in the ordering of great and disparate resources to specific ends gives heart to civilians confronted with tasks of even greater magnitude—and often of even greater importance.

24

The Military Establishment and Social Values

The impact of the military establishment—as of any other institution—on the nation's value system is not easily measured. Easy stereotypes of authoritarianism, conformity, aggression, and brutality are common. The evidence to support or refute them is less readily come by. What is clear is that the effort to sort out reality from myth is a crucial one. It is useful to survey so far as possible the character and range of military influence, tangible and intangible, on the quality of American life.

The history of the United States can be measured as it can for most nations from war to war, as many textbooks and children's book series bluntly indicate. It took one war to create the Union and another to preserve it. For most Americans, the military continues to be the most obvious manifestation of the federal presence, apart from the Post Office. Its influence extends nationwide more than almost any other institution. Soldiers are trained and serve far from home with comrades from every class, race, and region. Only at the executive level of large corporations—and perhaps not even there—does the pattern of movement begin to match the mobility of the military. During the lifetime of those now in their seventies the nation has engaged in five wars in which the United States was a major participant; those now over thirty have lived through three wars that have covered more than a third of their lives.

Until the time comes, if it ever does, when regional differences within the United States are significantly reduced by national television and the spread of other communications, broadly based educational influences and the architectural uniformity of shopping centers, housing developments, and office buildings—and until wars diminish or cease—the separate influence of the military will continue to serve as a unique and potent common national experience.

The military establishment has come a long way from the eighteenth-century mercenary armies, in which close order drill was instituted so that the men would be within the pistol range of their officers. Cadets at the Military Academy at West Point no longer even march to class. But the uniformed military, nevertheless, is still an island of authority and conformity in an increasingly permissive society. In no profession or calling in American society is tradition so clearly manifest. The military officer rises in the morning and puts on a uniform traditional in cut and color, decorated with badges of valor and insignia of rank. When he goes outdoors he is greeted by his juniors and greets his seniors with the traditional salute. In any headquarters, he encounters the flags of his country, his service, and his unit, often decorated with streamers commemorating past campaigns, and, flanking his own desk, if he is an officer of flag rank, his personal colors. He is frequently a participant in traditional ceremonies, more or less elaborate; if he wishes to avoid them, he must take special pains to do so. The civilian employee in the Defense Department finds himself surrounded by tradition and ceremony, and even the defense contractor feels the weight of the military tradition.

The visible forms of tradition reflect the continuity of the military establishment which adds to its impact on government policy. Among the cabinet departments, only State and Treasury are senior, and these are now tiny, and far weaker, principalities. Few institutions in the United States, governmental or private, excepting church, synagogue and the university, approach the military in established and continuous tradition. The recording that sounds retreat at the Air University at Maxwell Field, Alabama, echoes the notes that sounded over the forts in Indian territory more than a century ago. The music does not change. Small wonder that old words—and old ideas—persist.

"The military mind is no idle phrase," a persistent if sometimes captious critic of the military, C. Wright Mills, wrote. "It points to the results of a system of formal selection and common experiences and friendships and activities—all enclosed within similar routines."[1] The career officer, and to a lesser extent the career noncommissioned officer, is the custodian of the values of the military mind, but the career profession itself is of relatively recent origin in the United States. Samuel P. Huntington, in *The Soldier and the State,* observed that "the Constitution does not envisage a separate class of persons exclusively devoted to military leadership"[2] and traces the development of modern military professionalism in the United States to the post-Civil War period. The importance of the military professional

1. C. Wright Mills, *The Power Elite* (New York: Oxford University Press, 1959), p. 195.
2. Samuel P. Huntington, *The Soldier and the State* (Cambridge: Harvard University Press, Belknap Press, 1957), p. 135.

increased through the two world wars and especially during the post-World War II technological revolution.

The initial basic training period is the recruit's introduction to the rigid discipline of the military. The World War II Army humor best seller, *See Here, Private Hargrove,* explained the purposes of basic training to recruits:

All your persecution is deliberate, calculated, systematic. It is the collegiate practice of hazing, applied to the grim and highly important task of transforming a civilian into a soldier, a boy into a man. It is the Hardening Process. You won't get depressed; you won't feel sorry for yourself. You'll just get mad as hell. You'll be breathing fire before it's over. Believe me or not, at the end of that minor ordeal, you'll be feeling good. You'll be full of spirit and energy and you will have found yourself.[3]

Intentional disruption of civilian patterns of adjustment, replacement of individual gratifications with group goals, inculcation of unquestioning acceptance of authority, development of conformity to official attitudes and conduct—all have been cited by military administrators as goals of basic training.

The function of discipline, according to the military, is that of promoting organized living. All too frequently, however, military discipline in practice involves an arbitrary display of power by those in positions of authority.

Commander Ralph Earle wrote in 1917 of the function of discipline in the military:

The discipline of the Naval Academy well illustrates the principle that in every community discipline means simply organized living. It is the condition of living right because without right living, civilization cannot exist. Persons who will not live right must be compelled to do so, and upon such misguided individuals there must be placed restraints. To these alone is discipline ever harsh or a form of punishment.[4]

But military discipline is not always a model for organized living. It often seems erratic and arbitrary. Some commanders are particularly concerned with the appearance of their men; for example, one man was court-martialed for failing to get a "white sidewall" haircut (the head shaved bare from ears to crown) because the commander felt "members of the honor guard should look alike."[5] Some commanders emphasize inspection: disciplinary proceedings have resulted from a man's failure to have his towel exactly three fingers' distance from the corner of the bed and from

3. Marion Hargrove, *See Here, Private Hargrove* (New York: Henry Holt, 1942), p. 3.
4. Ralph Earle, *Life at the United States Naval Academy* (New York: G. P. Putnam's, 1917), p. 165.
5. *New York Times,* July 29, 1956, p. 5.

failure to clean inside his toothpaste cap. Some commanders stress military courtesy: the recent order of a general that men who failed to salute properly would be sent to the front in Vietnam was only withdrawn after adverse criticism in the press.[6] These demands of discipline centering on appearance, cleanliness, exactitude of detail, and respect for tradition and rank are viewed by important elements within the military as essential to the maintenance of an effective military force.

When those requirements conflict with other values, conflict arises. Disciplinary rules, for example, may be applied so as to deny First Amendment rights (forbidding the reading of certain newspapers, attendance at a peaceful off-post political meeting, or the expression of opinions which conflict with official policies); or so as to deny individual freedoms involving little discernible military interest (such as ordering a serviceman to refrain from drinking, to attend church, or to pay a disputed bill); or so as to be clearly arbitrary and discriminatory (such as calculated harassment of an individual or a group). Because of the clash between the values of many young recruits and those of the career military in the Vietnam war, the permissible boundaries for regulation of conduct through discipline have become a subject of fervent dispute and a number of courts-martial. (See Chapter 22.)

Military training and discipline clash with the democratic and egalitarian values of civilian society at many points. The military's group-oriented value system based on rank consciousness, unit loyalty, desire for combat, unquestioning patriotism, and instant response to command runs counter to the egalitarian, individualistic, inquiring humanistic ideals of American civil society.

There is inevitably a penumbra of restraint surrounding the military establishment that reaches beyond the military. The prospect of military service, or of the need for a security clearance in the civilian sector of the military establishment can and does have a "chilling" effect on dissent in American society. And, despite the fact that dissent is endemic in the civilian sector, dissent in the military often arouses civilian resentment. The harassment by local authorities of coffeehouses established by antiwar groups seems to have at least the tacit approval of the local military. Self-interest may also dampen dissent—workers in California defense plants wear buttons reading "Don't knock the war that feeds you." And as we have seen, the revelation of the extensive files maintained by Army intelligence on citizens who might, in its view, constitute a threat to internal security suggests an ominous potential for restraint of legitimate dissent.

Nevertheless, the basic training of the recruit and sustained military disci-

6. *New York Times,* October 17, 1968, p. 13.

pline fail to achieve subordination to authority for increasing numbers of young men. Desertions and AWOL's have climbed continuously since 1961, and as Table 24.1 indicates, have spurted in the last years in response to an increasingly unpopular war.

Table 24.1 Number of Desertions and AWOL's
Fiscal Years 1967-69

Year	Desertions (Absent without leave more than 30 days)	AWOL (Absent without leave less than 30 days)
1967	40,227	134,668
1968	53,357	155,536
1969	(c. 75,000)	NA

NA-not available

The monthly averages of desertions and AWOL's in 1970 are running even higher, with a projection of almost 100,000 desertions and 250,000 AWOL's for the year.

The military's explanation for this state of affairs has often been simplistic. A House subcommittee in June 1969 asked the Deputy Chief of Staff for Army Personnel, Lieutenant General Albert O. Connor, why desertion rates had increased. Connor replied, "We are getting more young men who are coming in undisciplined, the product of a society that trains them to resist authority."[7]

Endurance of physical hardships, ability to accept enforced obedience, toleration of stress and group indoctrination are obviously essential to military effectiveness. The military must have sufficient authority to maintain order and discipline among its personnel. Nevertheless, the military itself needs to make further adjustments to the realities of the socialization process for young people today, and perhaps to assess its human resources more shrewdly, in particular different periods of national life. Understaffed psychiatric services should be reinforced to cope with adjustment and identity crises. The principles of adolescent psychology need to be better understood by those in command. Experiments in motivational stimulus, such as the rewarding of recruits for achievement with movie or weekend pass privileges, and in less harsh and more rational uses of authority, seem to be promising efforts in the direction of constructive institutional adaptation.

A logical extension of these developments might be an all-volunteer Army, as has been proposed by the Gates Commission and others. On the

7. *New York Times,* June 21, 1969, p. 5.

other hand, tempting as the concept is to the millions of young men who would thereby be protected from service, except in time of general war, an all-volunteer "professional" Army would deprive the military of the salutary consquences that derive from the presence in its ranks of a large proportion of men who think of themselves as citizens first and soldiers a poor second. Draftees, while somewhat inhibited from complaining to their congressmen for fear of a sergeant's wrath, might be far more inhibited if they had long-term careers to protect. By the same token, the Congress would probably show greater concern about what happens to drafted men, and especially about their being sent overseas into unstable areas, than it would be about what happens to volunteers. In addition to the risk to the man involved, the possibility of military movements triggering greater American involvement abroad might, therefore, be increased with a volunteer Army.[8]

If military service led to heightened authoritarian responses or rigid absolutist military perspectives, this impact should be most effective among long-term career noncommissioned officers. These men must accommodate to the internal pressures of a role that stands between the rank and file of enlisted personnel and the officer corps. The commissioned officer's educational background and skill requirements are linked to the larger society and its values; rank-and-file enlisted men are generally reluctant to leave civilian life for the military term, and their basic ties are nonmilitary.

The impact of prolonged exposure to combat, especially intense combat, has observable and immediately disruptive consequences on recruits.[9] Data on long-term consequences, for example, in aggressiveness, are less adequate. The ideological impact seems relatively weak—the formation of a veteran's ideology depends on his joining other ex-combat soldiers in intimate social and fraternal groups, and most peacetime recruits do not join veterans' groups at all.

The impact of military service on personal social values can be observed from one perspective by examining the success or failure of delinquents, who are often encouraged to join or are informally "paroled" into the armed forces. Since the armed forces are prepared to disregard a young man's previous record once he is admitted into service, he can earn an honorable discharge, which will supersede his past police record. Recruitment policies encourage the induction of personnel with minor criminal records during wartime, though less so at other periods. Hans Mattick has produced evi-

8. But rapid increases in the size of the armed forces can be accomplished with less domestic political friction by increasing draft calls than by calling up Reserves— the only practicable alternative available with an all-volunteer force.

9. Roy R. Grinker and John P. Spiegel, *Men Under Stress* (Philadelphia: Blakiston, 1945).

dence that felons paroled into the armed forces during World War II had a much lower recidivism rate than those paroled into civilian life.[10]

The most profound changes, of course, take place in basic training, where the intensity of experience, the sharp contrast with civilian life, and the high sense of social solidarity combine to make an often traumatic impact on the recruit. In his study of forty-eight squads in the basic infantry training cycle at Fort Dix during the summer of 1952,[11] Richard Christie found an improvement in self-esteem and personal adjustment—as measured by the recruit's perception of his own physical and psychological condition—and improvement in positive relations with his peers. The study, interestingly enough, revealed that recruits who remained in contact with their homes and family made the poorest adjustment to military training. In addition, the practice of involving the trainees in the leadership hierarchy on a rotation basis produced a strikingly more positive adjustment than the experience of those who had no such opportunity. Christie found a slight and statistically insignificant increase in authoritarianism during the basic six-week training cycle.[12] At the same time, basic training produced in those studied more negative opinions about officers and noncommissioned officers than before training. In effect, basic training apparently served as a form of prophylaxis against authoritarianism.

According to other research, authoritarianism actually decreases as training becomes more complex and more advanced. Two researchers who set out to prove that air cadet training would increase authoritarian predispositions among the officer candidates found instead a decrease in authoritarian traits among cadets after one year of training.[13] Since a characteristic of the military organizaton is its authoritarian procedures, and since authoritarian personality tendencies imply the predisposition both to dominate arbitrarily others of lower status and simultaneously to submit to arbitrary higher authority, participation in the military training program, they had reasoned, would heighten authoritarian personality tenden-

10. Hans W. Mattick, "Parolees in the Army During World War II," *Federal Probation*, September 1960; see also Peter B. Legins, U.S. Senate Report No. 130, 85th Congress, 1st Session, *Juvenile Deliquency*, "Juvenile Delinquency and the Armed Forces," 1957.

11. The study of the impact of military service on personal values and self-esteem requires panel data on a group of recruits as they pass through basic training and military service, but although millions of men have passed through basic training, only one detailed study has been made on selective aspects of the impact of basic training. Richard Christie, *Transition from Civilian to Army Life* (Washington, D.C.: HumRRO Technical Report No. 13, October 1954).

12. Richard Christie, "Changes in Authoritarianism as Related Situational Factors," *American Psychologist*, Vol. 7, 1962, pp. 307-308.

13. Donald T. Campbell and Thelma H. McCormack, "Military Experiences and Attitudes Toward Authority," *American Journal of Sociology*, Vol. 62, March 1957, pp. 482-490. The California scale was used.

cies among those who pass such training successfully. The authors were tempted to conclude that their research tools might have been inadequate. But direct examination of combat flight training indicated an emphasis on group interdependence and a concept of team coordination necessary for survival which should have been cautionary. The military environment has the features of any large-scale bureaucracy, including exercise of authority and the special characteristics of preparation for combat, but a modern managerialism and a pragmatic sense of the limits of authority have come to pervade wide sectors of the military structure. (See Chapter 6 for detailed discussion.)

Military attitudes toward disciplinary rules and their enforcement have undergone some changes in recent years. The military has been affected by the inevitable bureaucratization of its personnel functions, and has discovered that absolute demands for conformity are not always the best method for obtaining high achievement. Morris Janowitz, in his study *The Professional Soldier*, concluded that there has been a gradual change in the twentieth century, and particularly in the post-World War II era, "from authoritarian domination toward a greater reliance on manipulation, persuasion, and group consensus."[14] "Leadership" has become a byword for "command," and some of the rigid authoritarianism of the old military has given way to a consciousness, particularly at high command levels, of public relations, group dynamics, and psychology. As Janowitz observes:

It is common to point out that military organization is rigidly stratified and authoritarian in character because of the necessities of command. . . . It is not generally recognized, however, that a great deal of the military establishment resembles a civilian bureaucracy, as it deals with problems of research, development, supply, and logistics. Even in those areas of the military establishment which are dedicated primarily to combat or to the maintenance of combat readiness, a central concern of top commanders is not the enforcement of rigid discipline but rather the maintenance of high levels of initiative and morale.[15]

The increasing proportion of lateral organizational relationships within the military is discussed in Chapter 6 above.

The military establishment has also made attempts to ameliorate some of the harmful effects of military discipline. In 1963, General Westmoreland, then Superintendent of the U.S. Military Academy, proposed to the Association of Military Surgeons that mental hygiene staffs should be brought to commanders' headquarters in order to be more available to the troops.[16]

14. Morris Janowitz, *The Professional Soldier: A Social and Political Portrait* (Glencoe, Ill.: The Free Press, 1960), p. 8.
15. Morris Janowitz, *The Military in the Political Development of New Nations* (Chicago: University of Chicago Press, 1964), pp. 119-120.
16. William C. Westmoreland, "Military Medicine," 128 *American Journal of Psychiatry*, 209, 1963.

Efforts like the Navy's moral leadership program have attempted to use the chaplains' corps to induce a more sympathetic response within the service hierarchy to servicemen's problems. According to then Secretary of the Navy Thomas Gates:

"Instead of preaching to the men, the chaplains talked to them and drew them out, and the men preached to them."[17]

These programs indicate an increased awareness in the military that certain qualities in servicemen which are desirable in the modern bureaucracy, such as initiative, high morale, and self-satisfaction, are often difficult to develop in a rigid disciplinary system.

Studies of motivation and morale indicate that the military, even in combat situations, respond to the dynamics of social cohesion as civilian groups do. A study by Roger Little of the Office of Military Psychology and Leadership at West Point[18] has described the "network of interpersonal relationships formed by buddies" which has an impact on morale, efficiency, and operational effectiveness in combat greater than compliance with the formal standards of discipline with which it is often at odds.[19] Janowitz indicates that research has reaffirmed the findings that "group cohesion rather than ideological motivation is the basis for understanding contemporary military 'morale.' "[20]

Technology has transformed the military into a bureaucracy in many ways more like civilian society than the traditional military. Most servicemen work an eight-hour day in jobs that resemble a civil servant's or a corporation employee's, and substantial numbers live off post. In the 1950's the Army created a new category of enlisted men, called specialists, who carry the grade and pay of noncommissioned officers but perform primarily technical tasks and are not in the chain of command. Fifty-four per cent of soldiers have technical specialties (electronics, mechanics, crafts, etc.), 36 per cent have service specialties (administration, clerical, food, etc.),[21] and only 10 per cent specialize in combat skills. The majority never receive specialized combat training. On the contrary about twenty men are now required in support for every combat soldier. The convergence of styles be-

17. Message to Commanding Officers from Chief, Naval Personnel, NAVPERS 15913, July 1968, "Effective Naval Leadership."

18. The West Point Office of Military Psychology and Leadership was established in 1946. Its principal duties are the teaching of the behavioral sciences, some research in the behavioral sciences, and guidance counseling for the undergraduates.

19. Roger W. Little, "Buddy Relations and Combat Performance," in *The New Military*, Morris Janowitz, ed. (New York: Russell Sage Foundation, 1964), p. 195.

20. Productivity levels and job satisfaction are adversely affected by overly authoritarian administration. See Kerner, "Rational and Legal Authority Within Hierarchical and Autonomous Bureaucratic Structures," Ph.D. dissertation, Indiana University, August 1969.

21. J. Shelburne and K. Groves, *Education in the Armed Forces* (1965), p. 37.

tween the civilian and the military, noted in Chapter 6, is reflected in the pattern of occupational distribution.

Combat is still, however, a fundamental ingredient of basic training—bayonet drill, and rifle and grenade practice. Janowitz, among others, has questioned the validity of the pervasiveness of this "combat standard,"[22] particularly in view of the changes in functions in the military itself. And Albert D. Biderman, senior research associate of the Bureau of Social Science Research, has described the "many disabling neuroticisms" which afflict the military in a society and in a world that does not regard combat as one of the most honorable and exalted of human activities; he questions whether civilian society should "sustain an institution for which systematic violence is a central and sacred goal."[23] As discussed in Chapter 1, Biderman suggests redefining the central function of the military to involve basically noncombat objectives.

The coincidence between the cycle of military popularity and the cycle of military expansion is not peculiarly American. Other nations have experienced the same phenomenon. When the military has been strong it has, by and large, been popular and accepted as necessary to national defense. Yet, for the first time in American history, a phase of increased popularity and expansion occurred in a time when there was no declared war. Then, at the end of the sixties and the beginning of the seventies, when the United States military establishment was at the height of its strength and power, after an era of unprecedented popularity, in the eyes of a significant element of opinion leadership in the United States (as well as abroad) and particularly in the expressed views of some of the nation's most articulate young people, the American military became an object of fear and hate.

The war in Vietnam is not the single nor even the dominant issue that divides our society today. The issue of race is clearly primary; it has imposed strains on the structure of the country greater than those of all the other issues put together. But the military establishment is a major divisive issue as well. Several thousand young Americans have chosen to put their citizenship at risk by fleeing the country rather than accept service in the armed forces. Tens of thousands of others, young and old, have joined in demonstrations designed to obstruct recruiting and the movement of troops within the United States.

Violent protest against the military establishment seems to be confined to issues directly related to the Vietnam war—and, at least at this writing,

22. Janowitz, *The Professional Soldier,* pp. 38-51.
23. Albert D. Biderman, "What Is Military?," in *The Draft: A Handbook of Facts and Alternatives,* Sol Tax, ed. (Chicago: University of Chicago Press, 1967), p. 135.

to a small segment of the population. But the violence of this protest tends to exacerbate the violence of protests on other issues, and it has been accompanied by the general alienation of a much larger minority from the military establishment. During the march on the Pentagon in the summer of 1967 large-scale violence was avoided only by the deep concern and extraordinary ingenuity of the federal officials directly responsible for handling the demonstrations. The leaders of the November 1969 peace demonstrations in Washington made heroic—and generally successful— efforts to prevent those who sought to provoke violence with violence from involving the mass of the demonstrators. At the same time, administration spokesmen retreated, under popular pressure, from potentially self-fulfilling prophecies about the likelihood of serious violence attending the demonstrations.[24]

The severe alienation of many youths from the military or other governmental service is relatively new. In the early 1960's, the Alianza para el Progreso and the Peace Corps—and, originally, the Green Berets—were expressions of a concern for social justice that transcended national interests and captured the attention of youth. The increasing disaffection of young people from government in the late 1960's has focused particularly on the uses of violence, which took some of the most promising young leaders of the country by assassination, and involved many thousands of others in urban riots or foreign combat. The military establishment and the police, as symbols of officially condoned force, became primary objects of this alienation. The confidence of youth in their country had been eroded by the growing awareness of the problems of race and poverty, and of the poisoning of the environment, by the growing recognition of the deterioration in the general quality of life, and by the resentment of the personal sacrifice which is demanded from them for service in a war many think immoral in ends as well as means. They believe—and their elders find it hard to deny—that the massive misuse of military power in Southeast Asia threatens the careers and the lives of succeeding generations, and siphons off resources desperately needed to resolve domestic problems. In the face of such profound antipathy, the traditional function of the military is grudgingly accepted at best or at worst rejected outright by those few, but articulate, young people—among them many potential leaders—who feel that a society so

24. In other cities, antiwar and prowar demonstrations have resulted in serious violence, both by demonstrators and by police, and in at least two instances, in Los Angeles and Chicago, police violence, amounting to what has been characterized as a "police riot," erupted against nonviolent demonstrators. Whether these partial breakdowns of police discipline were attributable to the depth of division within the country over the use of the military, or whether they resulted more from accumulated resentments on other issues, or from lack of adequate training in crowd control, remains an unanswered question. The shooting of students at Kent State and at Jackson State in May of 1970 was an even more tragic confrontation.

defective is not worth protecting. Many have opted out, as a consequence, through drugs or other escapist devices.

The prototype of the young political activist, as a result, is no longer the whiz kid or the political candidate challenging the bureaucracy from within the system in order to make it more effective, but the lawyer or the community organizer confronting the system in order to change its fundamental goals and purposes. And the prototype of the young radical is no longer a disciplined, institutionally oriented cell member, but an anti-institutional individual capable, at one extreme, of naïve and childlike concern for simplicity and purity and, at the other, of random amoral violence.

The military is not only the nation's largest bureaucracy, but it is probably the most entrenched, and the least amenable to confrontation or to change. All established American institutions have felt the shock of alienation of the young, but none more than the military.[25] Perhaps even more seriously, there seems to be growing cynicism among the more moderate youth about the validity of American institutions and their capacity for constructive change. If the military establishment is not to be a continuing source of bitterness and divisiveness within the country, and if it is to be effective even in limited ways, it must assume a lower and more flexible posture, not only in the demands it makes on national resources, but in the justification that it offers for those demands.

The symptoms of student alienation—ostracizing or banishment of college ROTC units and violence directed against ROTC buildings, opposition to defense-supported research, and, for a small but articulate and committed minority, the choice of prison or exile rather than military service—are growing in number and in scope. Even apart from the destructive consequences for individuals, alienation between the military establishment and the minority endangers the political cohesion of the country. Whether the primary target is the war in Vietnam, in which they may be called to serve, the size of the military budget, or the pervasiveness of military influence in American life, the disaffection of young people tends to overflow the limits of the military establishment and to poison the attitudes of these youths toward American government in general and American society at large. The military is regarded not as a passive beneficiary of a skewed system of national priorities but as a wicked, greedy aggressor conspiring with other vested interests to subvert the American dream.

25. The resistance to conformity has touched the military elite as well. At one of the service academies the students could be divided, according to an informed observer, into three categories: "engineers," who accept the system as necessary, "Eagle Scouts," who accept the system enthusiastically, and "mods" and rebels. See *Administration of the Service Academies, Report and Hearings of the Special Subcommittee on Service Academies of the House Armed Services Committee*, 90th Congress, 1st and 2nd Sessions, 1967–1968, pp. 10912-10913.

Alienation, in a way, begets alienation, for polarization in the nation increases as vehement minority reaction evokes a response from the "silent majority," young and old, which takes criticism of the military and demands for institutional change as an affront and a danger.

A disturbing related question goes to the core of contemporary American values. Many middle Americans have tended to embrace the concepts of authority and conformity that are associated with military life, and have increasingly opposed traditional American liberties. How far this civilian rigidity is a reaction to the disconcerting styles of radical youth, how far a response to the unrest in society generally, and how far an effect of the extensive influence of the military itself is unclear. The evidence suggests that all are relevant. Moreover, the most articulate antimilitary spokesmen are under thirty, and the most articulate defenders are over forty. which only accentuates the gap and hardens the polarization. And since so many of the alienated minority are among the brightest of the young, their disaffection makes more difficult the development of a rational philosophy of public policy, including a rational strategy for the uses of military power at home and overseas.

As citizens of the only nation to employ nuclear weapons to attack human targets, many in the United States have suffered a recurrent sense of guilt, a guilt that may have been prolonged and accentuated by the Dulles doctrine of massive nuclear retaliation.

Many American scientists, particularly, have been greatly troubled at the uses to which their knowledge has been put in the service of war. As recently as February 1970, Dr. Charles Schwartz of the University of California at Berkeley circulated a pledge of conscience among his colleagues of the American Physical Society. It carried a drawing of a mushroom cloud and read: "I pledge that I will not participate in war research or weapons production; I further pledge to counsel my students and urge my colleagues to do the same."[26]

But this burden of conscience probably has escaped the majority of the American people. For those who had guilt feelings, the Kennedy administration's substitution of the doctrine of flexible response, designed to deploy military force at the low end of the spectrum, was a matter of considerable moral relief. The sense of reprieve was soon broken by American action at the Bay of Pigs, and later intervention in the Dominican Republic, producing a moral as well as a political division on the propriety of offensive military action. With the extension of the war in Vietnam, and the gradual revelation of the despoliation of land and villages and the extent of civilian casualties, the moral liability for the use of United States military power

26. *New York Times,* February 1, 1970.

impacted on the consciousness of American society with splintering force.

An articulate minority, made up primarily of young students and old liberals, reacted with shock and horror to the delayed revelations of My Lai and other military atrocities. Others either refused to believe the stories, or chose to regard the alleged atrocities as justified by the exigencies of war. The division on the moral issue heightened the political tension between hawks and doves, and polarized the civilian society even further. When a fund-raising campaign to pay for civilian counsel was launched on behalf of one of the military defendants, many responded in defense of the conduct itself, although others perhaps did so in protest against what they regarded as unfair exploitation of a scapegoat for the military establishment as a whole. West Point cadets cheered their commandant, Major General Samuel Koster, when he announced his resignation from the academy, citing the charges against him as the commander of the division involved at My Lai. Many doubtless cheered in affirmation of their loyalty to the Point, at a time when it seemed under attack, but those who read or heard of the event could legitimately raise serious questions about the moral discrimination of young men chosen for military leadership, and the choice they might later make as officers, if called upon to do so, between their loyalty to the military institution and their obligation to hold the institution accountable to the country.

The popular reactions to My Lai stimulated grave reflections about national dedication to fundamental principles of human conduct. One began to hear troubled references to possible parallels, in kind, although certainly not in degree, to the national guilt and the moral indifference of "the good Germans." The apparent cover up of earlier investigations of My Lai at all levels of military command has implicated the system as a whole in the minds of many. Only when a former soldier brought the events to the public, did the military respond and consider indictments. But there was no overwhelming public outcry. Whether the acceptance by a sizable portion of the population of conduct previously considered contrary to the laws of war is a consequence, in part, of the growing public reliance on the military, or a contributing cause, it may well produce a brutalizing effect on the moral sensibilities of the country, extending beyond the immediate precipitating events. Insensitivity to unwarranted police violence and insensitivity to brutality in military actions—abroad and at home—may be unrelated phenomena, but they cannot escape mutual reinforcement.

V

CONCLUSIONS

25

"How Much Is Enough?"

The United States military establishment is the largest institutional complex within the United States government. It is so much larger than all the other institutions of government that its operations, and its impacts—on the economy, on class and racial minorities, on science and research, on higher education, on the legal system of justice, on the national scheme of values—are literally of another order of magnitude. Not only is it larger but it is more pervasive than any other governmental institution except the Post Office and the Internal Revenue Service, extending its impacts into almost every community in the United States.

The military establishment is not growing. In fact, it is shrinking, both as a percentage of our rapidly increasing gross national product, and in absolute terms, measured in constant—and even in inflating—dollars. But it is shrinking slowly. It remains the single most powerful and pervasive establishment in our society.

The magnitude of the impact of the military establishment derives from two primary factors: its absolute size, and extensive ramifications; and its size relative to other important public enterprises, international and domestic: health, education, foreign aid, family planning and community organization at home and abroad, environmental controls, and the war against poverty.

The absolute size of the establishment makes it uniquely difficult to control (although it is by no means monolithic) and encourages expansionary tendencies for which internal or even external checks and balances are, as we have seen, often inadequate. But it is difficult to imagine early changes in the international climate that would permit the reduction of the United States military budget by more than, say, 50 per cent, and a military budget of $40 billion—or even of $20 billion—presents the same kind of problems of management and control as a budget of $80 billion, although such a reduction might well make a qualitative difference in the society.

The problem of relative size, which was implicit in the smaller military budgets of the mid-1950's, did not then become explicit because other critical national problems had not surfaced, and the costs of dealing with them had not been generally realized. It will continue to be a major issue even as the military budget continues to decline as a percentage of the gross national product and of the federal budget.

The size and impact of the military establishment is likely, therefore, to remain a special problem in America for the foreseeable future. Whether it becomes a manageable problem, or whether it turns out to be the rock on which the country is split depends first on general understanding of and control over the uses of military power in the nuclear age; and second on the achievement of a general agreement that no automatic priority attaches to the stated requirements of the military establishment as against the stated requirements of other contenders for a share of national resources.

Any general understanding of the uses of military power, however, is obscured by the traditional ambivalence in American attitudes toward the military establishment—an ambivalence that is exacerbated by the threat of thermonuclear destruction and by the continuing drain of the war in Southeast Asia on the nation's human, material, and moral resources. It is difficult to be rational about a military establishment consisting of a nuclear component that can destroy us all if it is ever unleashed, and a nonnuclear component of which a large part has been engaged for the last five years in a tragic demonstration of the ineffectiveness of military force in controlling violence in the Third World. But a rational perspective remains essential if the proper uses of a military establishment in the United States are to be settled, so that the elements not required for those uses can be eliminated without cutting out vital functions, and a foundation can be laid to answer the perplexing question, "How much is enough?"

The underlying rationale for the nuclear establishment is less difficult to state than for the nonnuclear forces, although still full of uncertainties. It begins with the prevailing situation of nuclear parity between the two nuclear superpowers, and recognizes that neither side can profit from disturbing the balance, because the other side can and must respond by restoring it at a higher level of expenditure—and possibly with new weapons that are themselves destabilizing (because, for example, they are, like MIRV, harder to count). Since there are so many uncertainties in the balance, neither side can afford to take a "worst case" approach. As was pointed out by the American Assembly:

We must recognize that it is at least as dangerous to focus on "worst cases" as it is to overlook significant threats to our deterrent. If one proceeds from the most pessimistic view of U.S. capabilities, and the most generous view of the Soviet capabilities, one arrives at a U.S. second-strike posture that may look to the Soviets so much like a first-strike posture that they will be inclined to increase their own forces, thereby continuing the arms race and increasing the danger of nuclear war. In fact the proper test for the adequacy of U.S. nuclear retaliatory power is not the U.S. worst estimate of its effectiveness, but the Soviet estimate of the damage it would suffer in a nuclear exchange. That estimate will not be based on assumptions that take the Soviet performance at its best possible level and the U.S. performance at its worst. If we arm against a "parade of imaginary horribles" on the part of an adversary, the adversary will do the same, and we will have devised a sure prescription for a dangerous and wasteful arms race.[1]

In order to avoid endless rounds of escalation, stable nuclear parity depends on continuing negotiations like the Strategic Arms Limitation Talks (SALT), on mutual restraints through formal agreement, or through informal, even tacit, understanding (as in the American and Soviet parallel cutbacks in the production of fissionable materials in 1963), and sometimes on unilateral decisions to hold back on exploiting new technological developments, in order to give the Soviets an opportunity to respond (as in the United States nuclear test moratorium of 1959). There can be and there are sharp differences of opinion on the necessary size and shape of the nuclear arsenal; the danger of a runaway nuclear arms race is always present; and the actual size and shape of the arsenal is probably still determined as much by political exploitation of irrational fears, and by pressures from within the military establishment, as it is by rational analysis. But at least there is a framework for discussion, more and more generally accepted, of the question, "How much nuclear armament is enough?"

On the nonnuclear side, the question is even more difficult to spell out, let alone to answer. It is obscured by the distortion of history and the perpetuation of cold war ideology that have issued from the official apologists for the Vietnam war. So long as this or similar processes of justification continue, it is difficult for Americans to recognize the limits of the national interest that would call for the use of nonnuclear military force, or the options for impact on other societies that do not include military force at all. The country tends to be polarized, one group regarding the United States as a global policeman, ready to intervene in internal revolutions or to counter blatant or insidious aggression, and the other group—growing in numbers— willing to withdraw into a fortress America or hoping to substitute policies embodying a narrow interpretation of national interest.

An important lesson of Vietnam that is gradually emerging in the American consciousness is how little military force can accomplish in the Third World where the writ of United States sovereignty does not run. The tempta-

1. *Final Report of the American Assembly on Arms Limitation,* Arden House, Harriman, New York, March 31-April 2, 1970, p. 8.

tion to intervene with military force in order to help preserve, or try to preserve, regimes thought to be friendly to the United States is likely to be a good deal less attractive in the post-Vietnam world. Yet, the possibility of military adventures in the Third World is not a significant determinant of the size and shape of the permanent military establishment. There were 900 American military "advisers" in Vietnam in 1960. It took less than 15,000 men for the United States to become enmeshed in Vietnam in 1963. To deal with the consequences of our involvement it finally took several times more men than the permanent establishment as a whole could supply—that is, 550,000 over the decade of deepening commitment.

The primary determinant of the size and shape of the nonnuclear forces is the deterrence of aggression against our allies—in Europe, in North Asia, and perhaps in the Middle East—just below the threshold of nuclear deterrence. Calculations in these matters are necessarily imprecise, and involve political as much as military judgments. They do not necessarily contemplate a Soviet or even a Chinese attack, but rather turn on considerations of possible deterioration in political stability in a climate of weakened military security, inviting dangerous international misunderstandings. How many troops must America maintain in Europe in order to prevent NATO from unraveling, with consequent destabilizing developments, including new initiatives for national nuclear forces, frictions between the two Germanys, and, perhaps as West Germany bulks larger on the European military scene, between West Germany and her western neighbors? How important also is the United States troop commitment to maintaining a favorable attitude in Western Europe toward the Strategic Arms Limitation Talks, and toward continuing direct negotiations between Bonn and Moscow? What is the political impact of deployed naval forces, as compared to ground forces? On the other side of the world, can the United States troop commitment in Korea be reduced, on the ground that it is more than the South Koreans need to help them repel an attack by North Korea alone, but less than would be needed to hold off an attack in which Communist China joined North Korea? Again, it may not be possible to raise the issue effectively until Korean units are withdrawn from Vietnam.

The complex issue of nonnuclear force levels is even more difficult to resolve than issues of nuclear force levels. Nor can those nonnuclear issues be resolved by opting always for the higher force level or the more sophisticated weapons system, even if there were no budgetary constraints. Too many American troops in Europe might be as destabilizing as too few, and ultrasophisticated weapons are not as ready or as flexible as less sophisticated ones. These difficulties point up the impossibility of making any absolute determination of the amount of military spending necessary for national security. There are too many unknowns, too many variables, and too many elements of judgment, including nonmilitary judgment, and even if every doubtful issue were decided in favor of more spending, the net effect, both on the nuclear and on the nonnuclear side, conceivably might be to decrease our security. In any event there is the ubiquitous facts of diminishing returns and opportunity costs.

In the face of these uncertainties, the automatic priority for military spending that has prevailed over the last decade demands reconsideration. The argument that the military establishment should have first claim on the public purse finds support from a number of sources, as has been indicated above, but when the military claim is met first, other national needs, some of them vital needs, are neglected. So long as the civil-military budgetary relationship assumes the primacy of the military, even temporary subordination of military demands indicates to the public that the demands have been unreasonable, and to the military that not only their drafts on the public treasury but they themselves are being dishonored. Such a division can become a national political issue, and a dangerous one for the country. In other societies, and in other ages, it has been a fatal division.

If, however, the military is recognized as one of a number of valid claimants, the necessary periodic adjustment of priorities can be accomplished. Of course, the transition from primacy to competition among equals is never easy; it will be as difficult for this generation of the American military as for the first-born who has to learn that while his parents still care for him, he is not an only child any more. But the transition has to be made; one way —among others—to encourage it would be to make the opportunity to draw on a national service pool available to other priority claimants on public spending, or to make voluntary service with such other claimants grounds for exemption from military service.

No other institution, private or public, is now authorized to use compulsory processes to make up its manpower deficit—and even in periods of peace, or undeclared war. The United States has experienced and is experiencing critical shortages of health services personnel, teachers and teachers' aides, and police officers—to name only a few areas of scarcity. But the nation has never assumed a responsibility for ensuring that these shortages are met. If, for example, the principle of mandatory service were not only accepted but also applied beyond the military to other forms of national service, equally urgent and important for the country, the military would have the benefits of a public policy declaration in favor of a priority allocation of manpower as befits a critical public function, but it would not be identified as the sole repository of the responsibility for safeguarding the nation's security and its most sacred values. Other activities—the education of disadvantaged children, the delivery of health services to groups whose health needs are badly neglected, the organization of communities to achieve genuine participation in American society, the preservation of domestic public order with justice—all these and more could then be recognized, as they are not now, as essential in the same sense that the military function is regarded as essential.

How a national service pool should be organized raises a host of questions as to scale, timing, coverage, supervision, the selection of functions to be performed, and institutions to be included. The fundamental issue is the extent (if any) to which compulsion can or should be substituted for incentives and voluntary action. These are all issues to be debated before decisions can be made. Initially, the selective service principle might be employed for essential civilian as well as military service (i.e., by requiring service of a limited portion of the age group), perhaps with a more inclusive lottery. General acceptance of the national service principle, on the other hand, might permit abandonment of compulsory military service, without giving way to a wholly professional military, made up of career volunteers. It is doubtful, too, whether a program of this kind could be begun during wartime. As a first step, however, a major national program of voluntary service, administered by state and local government and private organizations with federal financial help, could be launched immediately.

A program of national service would serve another broader purpose as well, softening the impact of other establishments in addition to the military establishment on the society. American society is increasingly professionalized, and at the same time, the dominant role of the professional is increasingly challenged from outside the organizations that he dominates. In schools, in hospitals and clinics, in social service agencies, professional qualifications are multiplied, and extended into lower ranks, while consumers of services become increasingly restive. The injection of young nonprofessional, noncareer people into increasingly professional organizations, even at the bottom of the organizational pyramid, tends to restore useful communication between the institution and its clientele, and to remind the career bureaucrats of the needs and demands of the world beyond organizational horizons. It may also reduce the impact of professionals on nonprofessionals, by putting some of the nonprofessionals on the professional side of the encounter.

The issue will be resolved only when the partisans of a better quality of life can persuade the American public to invest national resources in implementing their goals on an equal—or superior—basis to the investment of natural resources in the goals of the military establishment.

An enormous organization, growing less recognizable as distinctively military with the convergence of military and civilian styles, more bureaucratized, and more and more expensive, and without effective countervailing power to balance its own power, cannot be permitted to regulate itself without comprehensive and workable external controls. The internal controls within the military establishment, both on the governmental and on the industrial side, must also be further refined and developed. On the government side, the primary need is to reduce some of the expansionary forces generated within the organization by loosening up the bureaucratic structure. More nonbureaucratic influence must be brought to bear, particularly on issues of strategy and force structure. A larger role for short-term or non-career people not only loosens up the system, but makes it more responsive to enlightened public opinion. Persons who come into the Department of Defense from outside the military establishment, and who expect to return to careers outside the establishment, are better able to see the claims of the establishment in perspective, against other high-priority claims on the increasingly beleaguered resources of the United States; and they are better able to communicate this perspective to the general public, always provided the civilian impact on the military is at least as great as the impact of the military on the civilian.

Systems analysis has established an important role for itself in the choice of weapons systems; it does not yet occupy a central role in working out the relationships between forces and strategy. The commander in the field must necessarily have great freedom of action to deal with the crises that confront him daily. But planning for the kinds of campaigns the commander may undertake, and the forces with which he should be supplied to undertake them, can give a larger role to analysts who are outside the chain of command, and whose professional background includes work in nonmilitary organizations—from universities to private research groups.

There should also be a larger role for these analysts in postauditing military operations,[2] and a significant, perhaps primary, role for civilian policy leaders in leading an open, as well as an internal, debate on the implications of military choices and the decisions most appropriate to the nation's larger goals.

At the same time, a more effective flow of information to the top civilian authorities in the Pentagon on the execution of their policy directives is also needed. The military departments have their inspectors general at every level down to small units, but no inspector general function, broadly conceived, exists within the Office of the Secretary of Defense. Although an inspector general cannot solve the problem of carrying out the intentions of the chief policy-maker down through all the layers of bureaucracy, he can flag those points where the process is breaking down.

Within the military bureaucracy itself, various measures—variable terms of service, lateral entry, more civilianized education, etc.—are useful

2. There is an analogy here to the growing practice of teaching hospitals to review operations done by all members of the hospital staff, including physicians with private patients, in periodic sessions of the so-called Tissue Committee.

elements in the loosening-up process. Thought might be given to further strengthening and institutionalizing analytic processes, by creating a separate promotion system or systems for staff officers—recognizing that the person who excels at staff work may not be best suited to large commands.[3] The problems of innovative organization within an essentially hierarchical structure are more fully discussed in Chapter 17.

The key instrument of presidential authority in control of the military is the budgetary instrument. The President controls the over-all size and shape of the military budget as it is transmitted to the Congress, and unlike, for example, the rivers and harbors appropriation, it is unusual for the Congress to make major additions to (or subtractions from) the budget as the President submits it. One can argue that the military budget is essentially the product of pressures exerted by generals, defense contractors, labor leaders, and their allies and supporters; but in fact the President has a good deal more freedom of choice than he ordinarily uses in controlling the military expenditures. Base closures are a sore subject for Congressmen, but Presidents Kennedy and Johnson, working with a strong Secretary of Defense, managed in less than four years to close or reduce activity at 547 United States bases and installations, with payrolls covering 85,800 men and annual savings of $577 million.[4] A single press release in November 1964 announced plans to close or reduce activity at 95 installations, for an annual saving of $477 million.[5] During the same period, a number of major weapons systems, in various stages of development, were terminated, including the Dyna-Soar, Skybolt, the B-70 bomber, the atomic-powered airplane, a separate Navy interdiction fighter, Nike-Zeus ABM, and railway-mounted Minutemen ICBM, all of which had involved development expenditures of more than $5 billion. And President Nixon succeeded in cutting his first Defense budget by $3 billion. As Commander-in-Chief, the President is the ultimate authority over all military actions and responsible, therefore, for all excesses, however difficult they are in practice to control.

The Congress, for its part, needs to apply more effective countervailing power to the military establishment and its industrial and scientific components than it has done to date. It must overcome self-interest in major contracts for districts, states, and regions; and in wasteful development and procurement procedures. It must break through unnecessary secrecy, which impedes full public debate and constituent response, and ensures self-

3. This issue must be distinguished from the perennial suggestion that the Joint Staff be replaced by a single general staff—a suggestion not to be rejected simply because it has been so often advanced.

4. Department of Defense, *Productive Civilian Uses of Former Defense Department Installations*, November 1964.

5. DOD Press Release No. 822-64, *Department of Defense Announces Actions to Discontinue, Reduce, or Consolidate Activities*, 19 November 1964.

perpetuation and expansion of the establishment without public decision. It must avoid timidity in the face of technical expertise, complex data, and projected images of alarm and danger based on the "worst" view of potential enemies. It must overcome a sense of ambivalence, one part awe and one part hostility, toward military power, which reflects the public's own ambivalence and inhibits rational decision-making on military methods and goals. With the Executive, it must assume the responsibility necessary for a civilian-controlled society in critical review of the military-industrial establishment, in setting the goals which the military is required to carry out, and in evaluating how consistently the military holds to these goals. The goals must not be set, by default or momentum, by the military itself. Indeed, there are signs that this role, to a considerable extent abdicated since World War II, is now being reassumed by the legislative branch.

The Judiciary, with assistance from the other governmental branches, is also involved in the process of checking excesses of the system of military justice. Certainly this appears true for those military requirements which run counter to constitutional prescriptions in matters of individual liberty. While men in service will never have access to freedoms equal to their civilian counterparts, so long as service is compulsory and discipline is required for military effectiveness, greater fairness in the application of due process could be achieved without endangering military effectiveness. If due process is not observed, individual protests, even group insurrections, will likely show a rapid increase, particularly if the nation continues to engage in undeclared wars; there is a prospect that more and more youths will be convicted and punished severely for acts that are not punishable in the civilian society.

In the last analysis, the key to defense policy in a democratic society is still the attitude of the general public. As de Tocqueville observed: "The remedy for the vices of the Army is not to be found in the Army itself, but in the country."[6] By and large, the American people get the kind of military establishment they deserve.

Public attitudes depend on public information, and the military establishment is a powerful and effective advocate on its own behalf. Critical comment and evaluations of the establishment must be made publicly available for genuine debate. At present much is kept back from the American public that is readily available to espionage agents of our allies and of our actual and potential enemies.

The public, through its representatives in government and through strengthened countervailing institutions, must keep a wary eye on where the military is heading and why and at how much cost. The demands of the

6. Alexis de Tocqueville, *Democracy in America* (New York: New American Library, Mentor Edition), Book III, Chapter 49, p. 279.

military, moreover, must be compared to the demands and the cost of competing national needs.

The public must watch and check the reach of the military as it appears to threaten the effectiveness of countervailing groups—whether through overclassification of research data, through surveillance of civilian dissent, by encouraging industrial monopolies dependent on its support, or by reinforcing general decision-making in terms of rational quantifiable options without testing the primary assumptions or the qualitative nature of consequences. It must refrain from undermining civilian control of domestic order by calling on the military to intervene increasingly—and preventively—to put down civic unrest; it must go beyond containment of violence to get at the root causes of violence. If the United States is to avoid becoming a militarized society, the public and its civilian representatives must retain the ultimate right of decision on such central political issues as counter-revolution and insurgency, war and peace.

Index

71 72 73 10 9 8 7 6 5 4 3 2